If Rock Bottom Had a Basement

A. Marc von Wellsheim

Copyright © 2020 A. Marc von Wellsheim

All rights reserved.

ISBN: **9798690565732**

DEDICATION

My beautiful offspring Madison, Mac, and Hayden, and my mod brothers; Nojo, Anthony, Rob, Rocky, Jacob, Sean, Cory, Greg, Karl. I thank the Lord for the men that I have found.

ACKNOWLEDGMENTS

Thank you, God. In the words of Rich Mullins, "If I stand, I hope I stand in some way for you. When I fall, I hope it is always back to you."

For my beautiful offspring Madison, Mac, and Hayden. In the words of Melvin Udall from the motion picture *As Good as it Gets*, "You make me want to be a better man." My parents and their unconditional love. Mom and Dad, you both taught me being an asshole isn't all bad. Ed, my stepfather, you grounded me. All three stood by this vagabond writer. To most of the men that touched my life at Saint Matthew's House. Even the douche bags taught me a thing or two. To the Giles Family, thank you for allowing me to invade your home, even when your friends warned against me. Paul, you have taught me that there is a loyalty deeper than mere sentiments. A special thanks to Steven English, Melissa Julian, and Stacey Lee Knuston for believing in my writing when I did not. Thank you to Mikaila Adams for paving the way and keeping me from having a nervous breakdown. Brianna Torres! Optimism can do wonders, but you are brilliant, and this project needed you. You made me a better wordsmith. NES your cover design is beyond words. You stepped up and you hardly knew me. Annette Ortega you never allowed me to take the easy way out. To all the other beautiful losers, vagabonds, and spiritually unfit: let's not acclaim each other for our strength or shame each other over our weaknesses. "The pain that you've been feeling can't compare to the joy that is coming," Romans 8:18.

Me

I am scared. I Just really want this to be technically perfect and perfectly told.

Brandie Welch

A story about an imperfect man. Nobody is going to care about grammar mistakes.

Cue the Fun song, "Carry on."

CHAPTER 1

"It's not easy being drunk all the time, if it were easy everyone would be doing it." ~ Tyrion Lannister, from Game of Thrones

"Addiction begins with the hope that something out there can instantly fill up the emptiness inside." ~ Dan B Allender

"I have never met anyone with an ego the size of yours." ~ Svetlana Kuznetsova speaking to me.

I don't have the constitution to commit suicide.

Cue the Disturbed song, "The Light."

It is a feeling of being a million miles away, and yet I had never left my bed. I was simply at the end of myself. Disengaged from living and seeking relief from disconnection. Living in the garden of loneliness, selfishness, and shame. I don't dare look inside my thoughts because that is why I need this escape in the first place. I'm like Tom Hanks, but not the heroic Hanks from motion pictures such as *Saving Private Ryan* or *Captain Phillips*. No. I am Tom Hanks from *Cast Away*, alone and homeless. Still just a frightened angry boy masquerading as a man. A restless mind that I could not tame. The blinds were closed, and I was living in desperate isolation. Just making friends with my walls (remember Wilson from *Cast Away*?) and the bottles of Bourbon that I could afford. I had loving friends, but their words always fell away. In some ways I am tougher than most people. I can take one hell of a beating from a bottle of dirty water. I can rise the following day knowing full well that I will get my ass beat if I step back into the ring. I have a longing to learn, but I am so slow to be taught. So, I climb right back in.

Always looking for a way to take the hard edges of this world away. God should take away our memories when He takes things away from us. Exercising my erroneous efforts for temporary self-salvation. My drunken escape has a strange intention and order to it. The aim is just to drink for the night or maybe even a day. This is when I buy the expensive stuff, like Wild Turkey 101, Maker's Mark, or maybe even Jameson. However, a few days into drunken debauchery and I am buying the cheapest of the brown liquors. No more being impressive with name brands. Now I have absurdity to maintain and only more dignity to lose. Yet, the victory is the silencing of the voices inside my head. Those are the bullies I am trying to break free from. Their grip resembles supervillain Bane's from the Batman comics, strong and held with vengeance.

Outside my doors is a world waiting to gnaw at

my wounds. I didn't need a place to hide or a getaway destination. I had been concealed in my oversized studio apartment for over a month. Most of that was spent on my back. In any corner of this obscurity, I could pass out anywhere and at any time. My home was more than hard times, it had become death's waiting room. For weeks I had been embalming myself with dark liquor. I was tired that the fire of Bourbon was all the breath that I knew or had left. A night is supposed to belong to lovers, but my lover was a bottle. I was ready to go through a portal into the next life. A call needed to be made. The woman who had promised me until death do us part, but later decided I wasn't worth dying for. Today she lives in a huge house of broken promises built by her new and improved architect husband. Still, being the first husband should give me certain squatters rights to that ass. With this logic it was fair to suspect she deserved a phone call. Alcohol gives me strange ideas, but this seemed valid.

I had an outlandish, powerful realization. The house was cold. I was naked and breathing in snowflakes. Outside it was January, but I still had the air conditioner blasting. I was living this same sad story. A man who had derailed his life and desire to live. A mind full of emotional traffic. Still in shock that I am only human. Even if I had a victory, it was accompanied in some version of failure. Life served with a few side dishes of smiles right alongside an entrée of loss. My same old act of returning to this life was over. I grabbed my phone. Baby Mama answered. This was unusual, because she usually ignored me like a staph infection.

She had been my muse, my love, and the mother

of my beautiful offspring. My years with her turned every black evening sky into something beautiful. My pride wants to say I never loved her, but it would be years later before I would dislike the woman she has become. In her youth, she was a beautiful and supportive ally. It wasn't until she grew older that she changed to a shell of the person I once loved. The similar miserable story is I was another broken man from a war called marriage. All those battles of who is wrong and who is right left us so far lost we never found our way again. With her gone, I had been steady learning lonely and my home became my graveyard jail.

    I was no longer the man I wanted to be. I would have those snot nosed cries alone frequently. You know the cry I am talking about; it leaves you gasping for breath. Shame really became the only garment I was wearing on the daily. I survived drunk between selfish rage and forgiveness. Like most nights I washed any convictions away and passed out until 3 AM. Waking up is an unwanted intrusion. The spirits of the late-night hours are mean and unrelenting. Their job is to torment, and they excel at their work. Yet, this morning the demons had arrived in a different form - maggots.

    My face glowed from the light on my phone. Drinking doesn't diminish my addiction for social media. My cellphone could give me glimpses of feeling relevant. I didn't realize at the time that a need for connection was still driving me. How many likes did I have on Facebook? The sad reality was that my life was minimized, my dreams had died, and possibly I was more addicted to conflict than bourbon. In fact, I can be very stoic and shy when I am sober, but a few drinks into the night and I am trolling people I haven't thought of in years. I had not eaten in weeks. Even when I bought food, it died waiting for my interest. Sustenance absorbs alcohol, and I wanted nothing to do with that. So how could I explain these few crumbs that had fallen in the middle of my chest? I flicked them off. One of these intruding morsels somehow landed on my phone. In the darkness I studied it. It appeared to be moving. This consciousness was disturbing. I had been saying for years that sobriety in all its forms was overrated. Being aware meant I needed to be proactive and that did not appeal to my senses. Drinking is never the problem, reality is, and drinking is the cure!

Forgive me Roger Waters (co-founder of Pink Floyd), I was hardly Comfortably Numb. I made it to my feet to find my glasses. Everything was such a blur because I was wasted, hammered, inebriated to the fourth power. I studied the specimen. This was one time that I would turn on my light. I spent most of my days hiding from the break of dawn. Turning on a light was a huge departure from my normal. Invitation of illumination was a commitment. Now I realized some fly had vomited on me during my drunken stupor. What kind of low is it when maggots are growing on you? I was dying too slow to be living in this hell.

Addiction is when we take our basic needs and prioritize them to a place of extremist destruction. I dabbled in masturbation and pornography, but that created a bigger void. I beat my dick like it owed me money, but the stimulus and response bored me. There was no enlightenment or fulfillment in solo sex. Paddling the pink canoe, playing the five to one, shucking the corn, shaking hands with the milkman, the five-knuckle shuffle, cuffing the carrot, polishing the banister, or whatever you wish to call it was not fulfilling, but possibly a good investment. I did not have time for another broken heart. I had lost my first wife, Mary, and Heather (Heather was the most broken, but also head and shoulders above in sincerity.)

Earlier, I called Baby Mama and with my final resolve and matter of fact attitude. I read her my obituary. I was not emotional; I wasn't even shopping for sympathy. I simply explained that I was going to drink myself to death. In some peculiar way I felt she should be told by me. After all we did say, "Until death do us part." Yet sometimes what we say and what we mean are hardly the same thing. This time, even the stranger that lives inside myself knew I was ready for my expiration.

"If you do this, I will never forgive you," she demanded.

"You fucked the neighbor; we can call it even," I reasoned. Some things in life we forget, some things take ahold and never let go.

What she said next floored, freaked, and flooded me with a realization I had failed to consider. Maybe it was this voice of reason that I longed for so much. I had long ago lost my attraction to her. Stealing another woman's husband and life was a cruelty that I never expected from my wife. The price she was willing to pay surprised me, but the price she would make other's pay surpassed all sane reasoning. This reduced her in my eyes. Of course, my years of being an arrogant asshole had reduced me in her eyes. I suppose we were on a level playing field of mutual disdain.

I can't really blame my beautiful offspring's mother for falling out of love with me. I am an artist at heart. A man tormented by his insecurities that crash into so-called brilliance. These days I simply see me as different, but back in the day I was sure I was superior to humankind. Imagine my shock and dismay to realize I was just a mere mortal. I treated Baby Mama poorly at times. I was a fool. It wasn't so much an issue of fidelity (though we had both been challenged in this area), but of neglect. With Baby Mama my head was not on straight and I was a big stupid fool. I was hardly abusive physically or verbally. Yet, I took her for granted. Men should know that once we win a woman's heart over, it is not permission to stop trying. Pursue that woman for the rest of your life regardless how solid the relationship is. My marriage was built on a fault line. Our union had a fracture from day one. We spent years trying to speak each other's love language, and it just left us both lonely. We both chocked on the fumes of anger and hurt, but she was always better at pretending. She grew up in an environment that valued image and pretty exteriors. I just can't live fake. I can live a lie, I can live broken, but not fake. I even had a little affair while she was pregnant. Being an alcoholic, among all my brokenness and hurt, my prevailing trait was self-centeredness.

"And I doubt your children will forgive you either." She spoke clearly and in my mind's eye, I could see her expression perfectly. Her face somehow always looks longer in disappointment. Her eyes droop and her head tilts down looking up at a person (or at least me). She acts hesitant to confrontation but is poised for it. She is a calculating woman. The only thing more disturbing than her image in my mind's eyes, was her words.

Cue the Bill Conti instrumental "Going the Distance" from *Rocky*. Just like that she delivered the jab, uppercut, right hook, and southpaw stance! Rocky Balboa had nothing on her. She met Ali and he told her she was the greatest. You know you are in a bad place when Whiskey cannot kill the reasoning in your head. A foundation of convictions was trying to be laid and I wanted no part of it.

I had always dreamed of teaching my beautiful offspring something that they would otherwise not know. I think of the greatest lessons I learned from my father. I think of people that have taught, mentored, and molded me over the years. The lessons were rarely if ever passed down. No, I caught what I learned from being in their presence. Improbable and fortunate my education always came through the hand of providence. I could not even comprehend how far I had gone that I wanted to deny my children all they I am. Even if there is nothing really that special about me, God could surely use this man to teach redemption, grace, and disrespect of all religious manipulation.

Suddenly, I was up against the ropes in the final round. She put me at an impasse. Disagreements are one thing, but to disagree with yourself is a real bitch! It was already a sin not wanting to live or be grateful about being alive. I had never once considered how this all might affect my children, otherwise known as my beautiful offspring. I was worse off than even I realized. The silence kept getting louder and my thoughts another form of torture. Regrets were outlasting and outperforming the alcohol. Again, allow me to state that this is a real bitch!

The sun would be up again soon, and I would resent the invasion once more. There is nothing more harassing than the reality daylight brings with it. I had been laying around waiting for my life to end. I wanted the credits of my life to roll with a big fuck you to all who didn't comply to my arrogance. Now the mention of my children had me reconsidering my strategy. Being a fool who felt sorry for myself was all I thought I knew. Sitting around thinking of what might have been, remembering how things once were in our lives. Now I hated living. However, occasionally, there is a gross phenomenon that overthrows me. I find there is something I actually care about.

I laid my head back down into the early AM solitude. I knew if I stopped drinking now, I was headed for the most violent detoxing soon. The maggots were a new low and my children were a new motivation. I was so quiet. I could easily focus on every sound of the apartment and night. Small sounds felt so profound. Bourbon had been my best friend. The barrel-aged distilled spirit made from corn was always faithful. I knew what to expect from Whiskey. It would kick my ass. It would make sure there was no wish in my well. Then I whispered the most profound prayer I have ever said.

IF ROCK BOTTOM HAD A BASEMENT

"God Help!"

CHAPTER 2

"As an alcoholic, you will violate your standards quicker than you can lower them." ~ **Robin Williams**

"You can't embrace God's strength until you own your own weakness." ~ **Matt Wilson**

"You don't have to say a prayer for me, I just said one for myself." ~ **Toby Keith**

Breathing just isn't fun

anymore.

Cue the Meatloaf song, "The Future Ain't What It Used to Be."

"God help!" I must have said those same words

over and over at least a dozen times. I spoke the words aloud; I spoke them in a whisper and recited them in my mind. God Help was my battle cry. I was afraid to allow this heart of stone to feel again, but I prayed my two words with more conviction, sincerity, and desperation than any other prayer I had prayed in my entire life. Maybe it was time to stop living in the lost and not found.

I want to make something clear here. Maybe you as my reader are reading this book from some remote place in your soul. Maybe your life is more than a little upside down. This is where I want to say that I am familiar with your sorrow and hurt. Maybe you are losing bad in your life because of your own hand and ego. This is where I remind you that no matter how many steps you take away from God, no matter the days or the distance, it is always only one step back to God. All those showboat prayers you have heard in church do not move God like the prayer of the desperate. Psalm 10:18 reads, "You will hear the cries of the oppressed and the orphans; you will judge in their favor, so that mortal men may cause terror no more." This includes even if the man that tormented you was your own doing. I know you have been thinking that there has got to be more. Going back and forth and we think there is worth in what we do, but I promise you God is listening. I am not masquerading as a wise man, only a fool, but I am so certain God heard me because I wrote the book you are holding. I curse a lot because I want you to know God could love a filthy rag like me and you too.

With the end game being death, I always left my front door unlocked. I had extraordinarily little interest in my life, and yet my corpse demanded some vanity. I had a few friends that would come and check on me from time to time. Annette would send the police when she could not get across town. In a daytime drunken state, I could always explain to the cops that I worked the graveyard shift and slept during the day. This explained my appearance and gave reason for my absence. Paul was fond of coming over with the paramedics and the fire department. Still, even inebriated I knew exactly the words to say to keep me free of a hospital or institution. God only knows what the neighbors must have thought seeing siren lights at my front door so often. Really, what did I care.

Rumor had it that I was fond of pissing naked in my front yard when blackout drunk. I can neither confirm nor deny, but I do have a faint memory that demands a verdict. Yeah, I urinated in my front yard a few times. Paul and Annette were both champions in their efforts, but I was a professional alcoholic. Much like a criminal, I learned the system. I had been Baker-Acted twice and this proved to be a valuable education.

Annette is a friend of mine from our marriages. Assets are not all that are divided in divorce, so are people. She was married to a short man from Puerto Rico who we will not name. They were one of our first married couple friends. As two couples, we had truly little in common outside of motion pictures, but the relationships worked. Once they moved to the other side of town, we drifted apart. Life is funny that way sometimes. Years later after the detonation of my marriage, Annette found me on social media, and we reconnected.

I hate to be mothered by the women I date. In fact, I have broken up with women because they kept cleaning my apartment. They were being sweet and kind, but I felt the implication to be that I was too much of a mess to care for myself. Annette on the other hand was not only a friend, but a mother figure in some ways. She is remarkably good at reasoning, planning, and executing. Her only flaw was her inability to understand that I cannot multitask as well as her. Universally most men cannot multitask as well as women. She can function at full speed and be doing several things a minute. My mind starts to resemble a nuclear war zone just trying to follow her. For addicts, our motto is one day at a time or maybe even hour by hour or minute by minute. Annette could never slow down with her pace or demands. Some people are very well meaning but dangerous to the addict. Annette fell into this category.

Addiction is a complex brain disease. The primary symptom is compulsive and harmful behaviors that cater to desire. People without addiction have a variety of common misconceptions. I knew my addiction was emotionally draining on Annette probably more than any other person in my life. If the disease is tricky and manipulative for the addict, imagine the impact on the non-addict. That would definitively define my relationship with Annette in later years. Her only flaw is that she places expectations on people. I just don't think that is in the heart of God and I know that is detrimental to an addict.

My memories of her ex-husband were always good until I met his new woman. He is a small man and was ridiculously small minded in his early days. I once tried to talk to him about books I enjoyed or wanted to read. He looked at me with the most bored expression and asked if I was serious. Annette was his strength, wisdom, and anchor while they were married. On his own, he became a slave to his ignorance and vices. Then I met his new woman, and she is the definitive version of every Disney villain (Ursula from *The Little Mermaid* comes to mind). Come to think of it Scuttle describes Annette's ex-husband perfectly from the same motion picture. Now with a new woman he became a complete jerk. The new girlfriend is this ogre of a woman who somehow managed to control her Scuttle man. She was also fiercely jealous of Annette. Let's keep it real, that woman was extra, as the kids say today. She made sure at every turn to make things difficult for Annette. Scuttle man was simply following the lead of his penis. A crime every man is guilty of.

Cue the Zac Brown Band's song, "Cold Hearted." Her ex-husband is a sex addict who enjoyed porn and fellow nurses that he worked with from time to time. Annette was fiercely loyal, and over time she simply could not stomach her husband's infidelities any longer. She grew tired of being unsure of his sexuality as well. I think Annette was a lot like me when she began her divorce and separation proceedings. We both thought the severity of our actions would be a wake-up call to our happily ever after. Nothing could have been further from the truth. I know in Baby Mama's case; I had just got out of her way. Now she was free to be with Doughboy Draftsman and his wife. Baby Mama had discovered swinging and took to it like a fish in water. I tried to get into swinging as well under pressure from my wife. What man does not find a sexually bold and confident woman attractive and maybe intimidating? I loved the idea of my wife being this adventurous in theory. Fantasies were fun and exciting, and I encouraged it. The actual execution I found gross. Annette was the second person to Baker-Act me.

In Florida, a Baker Act is the misfortune of an addict. It is the unwelcome interruption of our high or drunk that keeps us in our anesthetic state. Involuntarily, you are detained for mental health evaluation. Usually they hold you for 72 hours, but I was held for five days the second time I was Baker-Acted. My first Baker-Act was a vacation gift from my sister Beth. With Annette, apparently in a drunken state of mind, I claimed I had taken some pills or something. Who knows what we say when we are inebriated or why we say it? I always say drunks don't lie; they believe the bullshit that comes from their mouths. This is the deal when a person is out of their right mind; who knows what is real? After all, alcohol is known as spirits and I am sure those spirits are tormenting. Certainly not the one black out drunk. I wasn't kept in a padded room, but I was forced to be there. The experience was entirely unwanted. I suppose some people maybe get the straitjacket accommodations, but I never did. In the hospital, I was under observation and not permitted to be alone. I look around the place and *One Flew Over the Cuckoo's Nest* had become my reality.

The first time this happened the police showed up at my door, courtesy of a sister's invitation. Like a fool, I answered the knock. For 72 hours I denied I had a problem, because to me, my drinking was a choice and a privilege! I had no intention of stopping! Every minute held against my will; my rage grew at my sister for trying to save my life. Jack Daniels and Jim Beam may have been kicking my ass, but no one should come between those battles. Not being the kind of guy to back down, when I got out, I drank extra hard. The Baker-Act didn't play fair, and I wouldn't drink fair. I had the stupidity of a Superman complex that drinks kryptonite willingly. Oh, the irony of fighting for things we don't really want while letting what matters go so easily.

My second vacation with a Baker-Act was in New Port Richie, Florida, and this was Annette's invitation. I was also on suicide watch, which I found very insulting. This was my five-day stay. Apparently drunk, I made some suicidal type statements. Living in a trailer with a friend, I had the front room. Apparently, the neighbor across the street saw me fighting in my room with myself. I take shadowboxing very seriously when blacked out. This of course alarmed everyone, and the paramedics were called. In the hospital, a nurse had to sit with me 24 hours because I was on suicide watch. The nurse was cute enough but sucked at her job. I knew this because she was able to resist laughing at some of my best jokes. Somehow, I always managed to take humiliation to a new low. Maybe I should say I took the humiliation to new heights. Because when you are that degraded, it feels like everyone is looking down at you.

In the hospital I did not initially realize I was under suicide watch. The nurse sitting with me felt odd at first until the realization hit me. As I said, I tried to make conversation with my potluck guardian, but she was bored and uninterested in me. From the hospital they sent me to a treatment facility. It was late in the evening and the sun was setting as the police escorted me. I kept thinking that if only my children knew half of the stuff I have done. In fact, what do my beautiful offspring even think of their old man?

Checking in took hours. I sat locked in a room waiting until well past midnight. What was taking so long? I have no idea, but the women behind the desk had no sense of urgency. Alone in a holding room I was clearly the only one with a reservation. When you have nothing to do, you just stare at the workers behind the counter. Clearly these women could never work a customer service job. They had no skills whatsoever, no personality, and were seemingly lazy. The experience made an afternoon in the DMV feel like a real holiday. Efficiency never matters to those paid by the hour or working for Uncle Sam.

Once I signed a few papers. I was walked back to yet another front desk of my facility. I kept wondering why these two women at a Pasco County mental health facility were hired. I thought people in these types of fields had a calling, passion, and even compassion, but not these slugs. Two ladies that reminded me of Roz from the 2001 animated film, *Monsters Inc.* I felt as though (and correctly so) that they were more worthless than my existence.

My room was empty and white. The windows were high enough you couldn't see out. Streetlights hung even higher outside and glowed into the room with intrusive light. It had three beds and the other two guys were fast asleep. I laid down well aware that I was going to remain wide awake. I made a few trips to the bathroom just to look at my blood shot red eyes. Eventually, I would ask for a sedative to sleep, but even that wasn't strong enough. I just laid in bed with my consuming thoughts and embarrassment. I suppose I have always been one to die by my own hand. How many times can one heart break?

The man who was at the wall horizontal to me was pissing and puking all over himself. Could there really be a man in this facility worse off than me? I listened and thanked God that I wasn't downwind from the smells. The staff removed him and cleaned everything up splendidly. I suspect they sent him to a real hospital. Was he sick or had he planned an escape from the mental facility? Once he was gone, I never saw him again. I halfheartedly pretended to be asleep. I wanted nothing to do with the chaos of my mental health mate. May I be so bold as to suggest, mine was an Academy Award worthy performance. No one acknowledged me or asked for any such help.

The next morning, I would shower early and before breakfast meet with a medical doctor. We were not allowed anything other than a toothbrush. Without gel, my thick hair was standing straight up. I looked like Henry from the David Lynch motion picture, *Eraserhead*. I waited in a hallway for my turn to visit with the overrated nurse practitioner. Everything was feeling like a circus ride that just would not end. A young man that resembled Pugsley Adams from The Adams Family sat next to me. He perched himself there, occasionally looking my way, but he rarely said anything. There were chairs everywhere, but he needed to be right next to Marc. This was awkward, but I was in his crazy house. His mannerisms were odd, and I found him uncomfortable. Was there no value of personal space in this arena of the wild ones? I wondered if he was trying to make a boyfriend or maybe wanting to impress dominance over me. He remained silent and shortly I became sure he was harmless. Then a young woman with long dark hair walked past us. Her head was bowed, and arms folded. She was thin and cute. I reasoned she must be Italian or maybe Hispanic. She paced back and forth never making eye contact, smiling, or uttering a word. This young broken woman had captured my attention and imagination. What had broken her heart? Damaged her soul? Defeated her resistance? What caused her to disconnect with this world? What was her heart feeling and mind thinking? Pugsley spoke.

"She has been here longer than anyone, and all she does is walk around in circles. She never says anything to any of us. She is weird." Pugsley was weird too, so for him to think she is strange struck me as comical and odd. Oh, how unaware we all are of ourselves and our own fallacy. His eyes now following her. He spoke as if we had been friends for years and he was confiding in me. Suddenly, this strange little biscuit fed man started to feel like my sidekick, Robin to my Batman, Tonto to my Lone Ranger, Spock to my Captain Kirk. I must admit this young girl intrigued me. I felt compassion for this wandering stranger of our halls.

I watched her until I was called into see the nurse. I remained fixated on the girl. Something about her was breaking my heart. She was pretty and reminded me of my own beautiful offspring. What would I think, feel, or do if that was one of my beautiful offspring? Since she was a young lady, I thought of Madison and imagined my daughter in that state.

My nurse practitioner had the personality of a wet mop. Forgive me, but yes that is my optimism writing. I am not even sure what he really was in the medical community. Maybe he was some type of intern. He seldom looked up from his clip board. He asked questions and checked off boxes. It occurred to me to try and start saying some off the wall shit to see if the man was paying attention. However, I did not want to jeopardize my release. I wanted my vacation stay to be as limited as possible. This was the definitive *Patch Adams* moment (a 1998 comedy/drama directed by Tom Shadyac and starring Robin Williams); I could have told that doctor I wanted to use my dick as a pogo stick and I doubt he would have heard it. He sucked at his job!

At breakfast would be the first time I met all the residents in my wing. There were two sides of this crazy house, and I was never sure how we were separated. Maybe more fragile patients at one side. Most likely just an architectural design. I don't know. I have learned to be very leery of architects.

Cue the Duran Duran song, "Rio." "Moving on the floor now babe you are a bird of paradise", the song begins. I sat and listened to wild stories of how people ended up in the cuckoo house. Some accounts felt honest, and a few had amazing tale spins. It was always interesting to see who was able to just be real. Let me assure you, I was swimming in the river of denial, but I knew how I got there. My walking friend came in and sat for less than five minutes. I wondered if she had a fire beneath those far away eyes. I had named her Rio by now, in honor of the Duran Duran song, and the lyrics seemed very fitting. As a professional people watcher, I am accustomed to assigning meaning and back stories to strangers I would never meet. This girl needed a name. She sat alone keeping herself isolated even in a room full of people. She hardly ate, maintaining her heroin chick look. I always had a slight admiration for addictions that keep people thin. Unfortunately, I picked the craving for Bourbon. On the bright, side I wasn't in need of needles in my arm. A bottle of dirty water is far safer way to go of enslavement. Before long she was walking again. Her steps slow, but consistent. Mostly the other residents ignored her. Some judged her and whispered as she passed. I kept thinking, what if my own children were this lost? What would I say to them? Would I be able to try and reach out? I had no idea. What church of the poisoned mind had she worshiped? I thought of Heather, my second ex disaster. Once again, the lyrics of the song "And when she shines, she really shows you all she can." Both women lived lives removed from reality and sanity. Yet, both women possessed a purity that is ever so rare in this wasteland world we live in. I wondered if I could reach Rio in a way I wasn't able to with Heather. This motivated me a great deal. I did not have a need to be relevant or a savior, but it would be nice to be or do good for someone. Maybe my need for connection was flaring up. Certainly, I was not on some ethical high ground. I did want to help people and maybe even offer the simplicity of listening and caring.

Today I feel rescued from my first marriage. She has turned into a crochety piece of beef jerky. Time has erased any love we shared, but Heather is a completely different story. The other three women in my life that have been like catnip are Heather, Mary, and Giovanni. The latter being the only woman I still talk to often. Giovanni has a muse-type effect on me.

When I first spoke to Heather I was immediately smitten, aroused, and in love. That was just her voice. Ours was immediately a whimsical and whirlwind romance. She speaks in a way that no other woman has ever been gifted to do and it is all natural. Which was strange because she had a fake tan and fake hair. She was accustomed to primping. It was strange to me that she always had metal clamps holding hair in place that wasn't her own. She was innocent. Her beauty is astounding and indescribable. She may be the closest version my eyes have known of a cherub. Her voice had the power to control and transform me; it was a sweet childlike voice until it would turn into a snarl. We could talk on the phone for hours. She was also thrilling to be around. She was complex, original, authentic, bratty, and most of all, endearing. She had a northern charm and a very limited world view, but she was completely feminine, sexy, and bawdy. She was also crazy as a sack of cats, and I found that HOT. She was capably flirtatious, but only on her own terms. She was easily frustrated, agitated, and even fiercely focused when channeled in a direction. However, she often had trouble articulating thoughts and could feel threatened easily. She frequently took offense at imaginary or perceived slights. She would become dark, oppressive, and tense. When she didn't get her way, she became a black hole, sucking all the life out of everything in her path. She is a woman taken advantage of and used by many, and I came along just in time for the victim to turn into the predator. I could never please her or make her happy. My love language is words of affirmation. Heather was only ever to speak of my failures, missteps, or straight up what she didn't like. She didn't like a lot of things about me or the world. We would even argue during sex! I wanted to slay her dragons, but she would suck the life out of me faster than a handle of good whiskey could get me hammered. Even good bourbon was no match for her. Independently we are fine, but collectively we are too much crazy for one relationship. Many women can bring out the best in me. Many women can bring out the worst, but only a select few can do both. Heather was like a broken heart that you can't wait to have. Some things and people mix like whiskey and soda, and others don't mix like you hope, like Heather and me.

Unlike most human beings, Heather has always been incapable of lying. This is complicated by the reality that her perceptions are almost always wrong. A trait no doubt passed down from her father; he simply isn't a man capable of rational thought or understanding. He has no discernment. They both are only able to see above the surface and never into the depth of still waters. Sadly, Heather is so far up her father's anus she sees the world as one giant colon. The things they would suspect of me were almost never true. In fact, my reality was far less colorful than their consistent accusations, but I applaud their imagination. They found me to be an appalling narcissist, but I was too self-loathing for even that to be true.

With Heather I lied all the time. Lying was self-defense. I was not wanting to be dishonest, but to try and give answers that would chill her out. She thought every single woman in the world craved me. I wanted to enjoy the extravagance of her claims, but in truth I am not that desired (or am I?). In time, I started lying for amusement. For instance, I once claimed to her and her parents that I started worshipping forces of darkness. I was not surprised at all that they believed me without much question. Truth is so much stranger than fiction and often far less believable. The simpletons took everything at face value. I was mocking her father and mother and I do regret that, but I have never been one to back down from confrontations.

In the end it is simply stated. I wasn't a good enough man to win the fight for Heather, and I certainly could not slay her dragons. That still stings, and what is worse - she married a real ball sack of a man. Her sequel husband isn't exactly Gollum (whose given Hobbit name is Smeagol) from *The Lord of The Rings*, but there is a resemblance. Speaking as an enormously unliked person, it can be difficult for me to hold grudges against all who dislike me, but I make room for Gollum the sequel. His marriage has only worked because Heather did not want two failed relationships on her resume.

Heather was riddled with trauma and false accusations. Her life was a series of bad choices and bad men. Unlike Baby Mama she was authentic. That is a trait I find most rare in all of us. Now let us return to the Baker-Act I was serving.

In the facility I had a counselor. She was considerably younger than me, making her textbook smart and real world unpractical. I had to visit with her every morning. She was a kind and soft lady barely into her career and early twenties, or so she seemed to me. She was always sitting and appeared to be pregnant, but I was afraid to comment. I have had baby bump assumptions go wrong before. The only difference between the baby bump assumption going wrong and the Titanic is that the Titanic had a band! I understood she was my gate keeper. I also knew that I had a minimum 72 hour stay ahead of me. If I was hoping to get out on time, I needed to impress her, convince her that my bullshit was sincere. Keep in mind, I only lied about my will to live.

"You tried to kill yourself." Was she stating or asking? Was she judging or sincere?

"No, I would never kill myself; that would hurt." I offered.

"Alfred, you had a blood alcohol level that would kill most people. You were 0.33 percent." 0.35 to 0.40 percent is the standard lethal dose for most humans. She used my first name, and that was reassurance that I was lost among my demons. Only one friend calls me Alfred, and her name is Becky.

"See I didn't die! I always knew I had a superpower." Sadly, people who work in these kinds of facilities do not have a sense of humor. She didn't crack a smile, and I refused to waste anymore good material. God forbid we use humor in this so-called life.

"So, you were not trying to kill yourself," she continued with a grimace. Her words spoken slowly and methodical. As if I may not understand her question. This is when the truth gets tricky, because I did want to die, but that had been a well-guarded secret. People would accuse me of being lazy or not trying in life, but no one realized I was waiting out my liver. Now I was sitting across from a well-meaning woman who wanted to help. Yet, I wasn't about to share my secrets. I couldn't win, and now I couldn't even lose. I needed to say exactly what she needed to hear. Otherwise, I would be a diluted version of I Know Why the Caged Bird Sings. One thing was certain, the woman behind the desk seemed to be immune to my humor and charm. I have made a life out of using laughter to get my way. Now I was Luke Skywalker just arriving on the swam-covered planet Dagobah from *The Empire Strikes Back*. Unfamiliar with everything and wondering why I was there.

I quickly become friendly with the other prisoners of the crazy train. Eventually I come out of my shell, and the comedian of the wounded emerges. In the TV room, I did my version of recovery stand up, I imitated and made fun of the staff. I was quiet the first day, kept to myself, and mostly observed. Usually what I do in a new environment is try and get a feel for the climate. Who is weak, who is strong and more importantly who do I trust? Once I am settled in and comfortable, I begin to interact more intimately, but it is a slow process. In this environment, I warmed up quickly. We may have had different monkeys on our backs, but our common ground was enslavement. The residents thought I was the funniest man alive. With Robin Williams, Bob Hope, and Jack Benny all graduated from this life, maybe I am the funniest person alive after all? Oh wait, Billy Crystal has me beat, and a list starts to scroll my mind's eye of funnier people than me. Damn! Maybe that is my common ground with Baby Mama we were both attention starved whores.

In rehab and recovery centers, they have many workshops. All kinds of guest speakers and volunteers come to the program. I am not sure if they are trying to comfort us, distract us, or help us replace our substances, but they are keeping us busy and calm. This sobriety vacation introduced me to coloring sheets and markers on every table. I thought this was silly at first, but quickly enjoyed the exercise. I noticed that my stress and anxiety lessened greatly. It also helped me focus on the present and not worry about what was next. Tomorrow and the thought of it has always been a great source of anxiety for me. I was unplugged from my life and had no idea how this was going to affect my job and living situation. Coloring reminded me of Aunt Gussie.

When I was a little boy, (adorable as I am sure you suspect) she taught me to scribble on pages and then color in between the lines. I began doing this and the people at my table thought it was genius. Just call me patient Picasso. In life we collect lessons, ideas, and knowledge that makes us brilliant to some people over time. It was fun to participate and contribute to the group.

I always found it more natural to sit with women, and this program was coed. So, I sat with two younger girls and we talked and colored like old friends out to lunch. That is when I noticed Rio walking aimlessly again. I also observed several of the residents noticing her as well. I arose from the table. I didn't give myself time to reason why I should not bother her. I could not stand to see those sad eyes, and something had to stop her bad dreams, memories, and the effects of her trauma. Kindness can be exactly what we need to mend us at times. I just walked up to her and said the most natural thing that came to mind. "Hey!"

She stopped, and her arms were not folded for once. If there is any truth to these body language rumors, maybe she was open to being approached.
"Would you like to color some pictures with us?" I asked softly and gently.

"I can't; I need to burn off all this energy." She answered, and I was surprised she looked at me when she spoke. Her eyes were a beautiful chocolate brown and her tone so heartfelt. I could not help but think with her snail's pace walk, how much energy could she really be exerting? However, slow and steady does win the race taught to me by the tortoise and the hare. I didn't want to give up. Rio wasn't as resistant as I imagined she would be. She allowed me to stand with her in stillness briefly. All of a sudden, wisdom of biblical proportion fell on me and I spoke. The world wasn't revolving around just me. My population doubled from just me to us.

"I have an idea. Instead of burning energy with your legs, let's try using your arms. Use your arms instead of your legs."

Her eyebrows rose, reveling even more of her soul behind those chocolate browns. I had her attention and I suspect curiosity.

"Why don't you come over there and color with us? In fact, do you like Marvel movies? I think we have some Marvel coloring sheets over there as well."

She paused and then looked at me with a soft and subtle smile. I smiled right back. She likes Marvel motion pictures and that was a touchdown.

"Oh, come on, all of us are going through a little something, something."

I was still surprised that eye contact didn't seem to intimidate her. She thought a minute and then nodded yes with that faint smile still intact. We walked over to a table with two other girls and sat down. Her sitting with us was a miracle that was not lost on anyone.

She was very still and focused on her artwork at first. She would look up but didn't speak. I have always used motion pictures to break the ice with strangers. If I ask you what your favorite film of all time is, then I have taken an interest in you. I first posed the question to the other girls, and we went around the table. I didn't want Rio to feel she was targeted or singled out. The strategy worked. In no time she was talking about all kinds of things, including who were her favorite superheroes (incidentally Iron Man was high on her list). Soon there were four of us just sitting and talking and coloring. Just to see a twinkle in Rio made my stay in that facility worth it. For a brief time in my life, I wasn't thinking about the graveyard, and I liked how I felt. I felt a tingle of purpose. Touching a life pulled me in, and I liked not being only about first-person pronouns.

As I said, coloring for adults is supposed to relieve anxiety and stress. Seemingly, coloring brings people into the present and a state of mindfulness. It was successful for my wandering friend. She took to the colored pencils brilliantly and successfully.

Later, one of the few guardians of the crazies came up to me. I liked this guy; he was softer and calmer. One might even accuse him of being monotone. He spoke very directly to me.

"She has been here for over 30 days and nobody has been able to break through to her. You broke through within a day of being here. Maybe you should be on staff." He was as serious as a heart attack, and I wasn't sure if he had a hidden meaning or agenda. Was he trying to help me find some sort of purpose, my path, or passion? My hypocritical virtue may have inspired him, but it didn't impress me at all. I may have fooled you, but I knew better. I was more accustomed at being a disappointment and a disaster. Cue the Eric Church song, "Mr. Misunderstood.".

I simply smiled at the nice facilitator. I am not sure if that conversation or Rio inspired me, but a shift took place in my perspective. From that moment forward, every time a new person was admitted, I went and sat with them, told the newcomer what to expect and tried to bring some form of comfort. Remember that Baker-Acts are involuntary. I couldn't rescue anyone, but I could make the transition easier. Over the next few days, I got to share meals, more coloring pages, and time with Rio. She wouldn't share about her personal life too much. I never learned the names of her demons, but we talked about a lot of things like a shared love of a local pizza parlor.

When we talked about music, she compared my tastes to her dad's. So, this is what it feels like to slip out of leading man roles into a character actor. I wasn't looking for a romantic relationship with Rio, but I also wasn't ready to be a daddy figure. I still wonder about her from time to time. In a way that resembles the ending of *The Prince of Tides* (a 1991 film directed by Barbra Streisand) when Nick Nolte's character is driving over the long bridge and simply says "Lowenstein," signifying that though they no longer see each other, Lowenstein had an impact on his life. She changed him and helped heal him from his nighttime full of demons.

Baby Mama left me for a better life. Essentially saying that I wasn't good enough. I am sure she would argue that my long list of mistakes and disqualifications made me a horrible husband, a terrible provider, and a less than stellar human. In fact, her scoring of me would be just beneath pond scum. Maybe all this was true, but she knew that going into the marriage. Funny how two people marry each other knowing we are sinners. Then we are surprised that the other person sins. I have never been one to hide who I am. In losing her, I lost my children and my joy. Joy only comes from relationships and connections. Happiness comes from experiences and possibly things. I became depressed and isolated in my dark corners of weeping. I was internally imprisoned. I was in a place where I could not hide or find peace with a remote control, working, toys, food or any form of distractions. I sought comfort and peace under every rock I could turn over, but there was no such fix. Friends became judgmental and scarce. It was mostly me, God, and this reality that I had to face. My friend Polozola told me one day, "The blessing of your struggle is that you learn who your true friends are." I learned there are a lot of devils in my temple; however, I had a few gemstones in my life, and one was Paul.

CHAPTER 3

"There can be as much value in the blink of an eye as in months of rational analysis." ~ Malcom Gladwell

"I was spiritually bankrupt, and when that happens, it's like a spiritual cancer afflicts you." ~ Mel Gibson

"There are ways of killing yourself without killing yourself." ~ Tony Manero, *Saturday Night Fever*

Numb and empty Paul has

the best worst idea ever.

Love is never proven by words alone. Paul had the guts, insight, courage, candor, and availability to love me exactly where I am or where I was as opposed to holding expectations. He would come check on me day in and day out. I knew I would be dead soon. I wanted Paul to be able to find me and make sure my body didn't rot undiscovered for days or even weeks. My perverted perspective of vanity concerning death has always surprised me.

Baby Mama had direct blue eyes and light brown hair disguised as blonde. She is slim with fair skin and probably 5'6 (it has been years since I have seen her, and I like it that way). She is very Anglo-Saxon. She can be very warm and open, and I liked her at once when we first met. Her greatest gifts are reading people and becoming what you need her to be. She could be complex, precocious, endearing, but never original. I learned quickly that her tribe were Christian clones that lacked diversity and acceptance. She is flirtatious and charming when need be, but she is masterful at turning on a person like a switch. She read me like a label and became exactly what I wanted in a woman. She is a multi-talented woman, but her greatest skills are manipulation and deceit. She is a pastor's daughter and as a result, you never really know why a woman like that is on her knees.

Among friends she was always on stage and I found that to be exhausting and often in bad taste. However, she did manage to win my heart. I genuinely loved her at one point and for years. Even during her affair, I still loved her. One day we were speaking on the phone and I knew I did not love her anymore; I didn't even like or respect her. It happened in the blink of an eye. I had been visiting some mutual friends, and that experience conjured up some good memories. I tried to call my bride. She was out with her new tribe of friends having drinks and no doubt reducing and mocking her husband. My wife developed a need to vilify me. A practice that she engages in even a few weeks ago. She never had to reach high or search long to find faults. When she called me back, she absolutely took full advantage of cursing me down. She felt I was checking up on her which was odd because I already knew she was fervently fucking the neighbors. At this point she was in huge into threesomes. Was she shaming me for missing my wife? I felt stupid. She once celebrated me for my strength and now enjoyed breaking me spirit.

In Robert Fulghum's book, *All I Really Need to Know I Learned in Kindergarten,* he writes about loggers from the Solomon Islands in the South Pacific. Apparently, when the islanders come across a tree too big to cut down, they revert to a method of yelling at it. For thirty days, every morning they yell at the tree. The concept is that they are killing the spirit of the tree; it eventually dies and falls over on its own. In that conversation with Baby Mama, she clearly blew out my pilot light. I suppose I should have been smart enough to expect that from a woman that lacks substance and whose greatest goals are prestige and ambition.

I never wanted her again. I didn't love her, I didn't hate her, I just didn't care outside of our shared beautiful offspring. The opposite of love is not hate, it is indifference. I am far worse than a hopeless romantic, I am a hopeful one. In some way I still love every woman I have ever loved. Some of the women I have loved for years and some months, but all forever, except Baby Mama. The reasons I love them may differ, but I never completely stopped loving any of them except for one. What she thinks of me no longer mattered and never would again. I was free from her and it has been nothing less than wonderful, but I worried about her influence over my children. The great news is that my beautiful offspring grew up. They love their mother and I am glad, but they also see her for who she really is, and I like that even more. Her stepchildren see her as nothing more than the woman who destroyed families and stole their dad from their mom. To at least two people in this world, Baby Mama will always be Lady Tremaine (Cinderella). I know I am not supposed to like that, but I do grin this shit eating grin God gave me at the thought.

Most of Baby Mama's friends I found to be gross. Cue the song "Church of the Poison Mind" by Culture Club. Homo sapiens consumed by church that did not transform their private lives. People who like to think that God watches over them except in the privacy of their own bedrooms and lewd acts. This would only get worse with time. Baby Mama likes the superficial and wealthy kind of humans. She reeked with desperation to be elite. I guess we all desire to be relevant, for me it is in my authenticity and writing. She wanted to belong to the West Palm Beach socialite crowd. Yet, she hid behind a veiled Baptist persona. A trait no doubt learned in her religious upbringing. A childhood otherwise known as the colostomy bag of Christianity, taught and led by her old man.

Once in Christian college she fit in perfectly with a bunch of people who lived counterfeit lives. Junior Pharisees in their pompous pretentious training of superior sanctity. The faithful believers that are also Saturday night sinners. I was amazed to learn that these women who carried bibles, prudence, and discretion also burned the candle at both ends (or at least their vaginas did). I don't care about people's carnal knowledge, but I despise the hypocrisy. They were mostly as fake as their spray on tans. Considering how much smoke they blow up each other's ass,' I wonder how many will or have died from lung cancer.

The people I love are thieves, prostitutes, addicts, and outcasts. Even my heroes are leaders with a limp. They are burdened with shame and often straddled with regret. Come as you are because I relate to the broken-hearted. Those of us drowning in our own despair and yet speaking life to each other. My church of the transformed soul has been found in secret addict meetings. Our sanctuaries found hidden all over cities and at all times of the day. What a wonderful way to come alive, learn, love, and be accepted. I have never slept with a prostitute, but only because I can't afford it. Love is a costly pursuit no matter how we go about it. In truth it is a lot less expensive to pay for sex up front as opposed to after a divorce. However, I have spent a lot of time with some of the most beautifully abandoned people.

Am I judging Baby Mama's family and friends? No, much more of just going all Don Rickles on them. I realize we all park our morality when the occasion serves us. Rickles was an American comedian best known for his insult and observational comedy. For my younger readers, Rickles was Mr. Potato Head in *Toy Story*.

Furthermore, my wife had a way of not hearing me. I have always felt the cry of a man's soul is at a pitch most women can't hear. I don't think women refuse to hear, I just think the languages of men and women are confused. Genesis 11:7 says, "Come, let us go down and therefore cofound {mix-up, confuse} their language, that they may not understand one another's speech." I suspect we mostly think that applies to nations and tribes, but I believe it is true even within the words we know. Baby Mama would not hear me, but when she would read things I wrote, she responded. Maybe I hope she reads this and understands my insanity. Not to sound self-serving, but why else write a memoir if not to be a little self-serving?

I first met Paul and was unimpressed. I simply wasn't willing to give any of her friends a chance. Most of the guys she knew were just dudes dressed with polo players on their left chest, jacking off to the latest Victoria Secret's catalog. A few years later, I met Paul again. This time our chance encounter was on a super bowl Sunday. I am not a football fan, so I find this American ritual boring. Ask me what film won best picture in 1973 and I can tell you immediately (it was *The Godfather*). Ask a football fan who won the super bowl in 1973 and they are clueless without their smart internet phone.

We were at church. Paul had recently married his new bride and moved to the Orlando area. Baby Mama was on the worship team (Of course she was. After all that is where the stage is. I must give her credit - she had a singing voice that is inspiring. There is bliss when she sings.) and I was sitting next to a dirt bag friend (When life gives you a black eye, you learn who are your allies versus the critics. My struggle revealed the kind of judgmental ass wipe I was sitting next to that morning.) Paul was approaching us, and I turned to the ass wipe "Quick, who is in the Super Bowl?" I asked because I knew that would be Paul's prelude. My prediction was prophetic. In the years to come, Paul (a younger man) became my hero and his family accepted me as the sinner I am. A light that shined on me and never stopped. Despite some sensationally strong spoken opposition from their friends about the potential pedophile that I may be. They can lick my sack, but I digress.

One of my favorite stories about The Giles family involves their middle daughter Kylie. When Kylie was still noticeably young, I was visiting their home one evening. Sheryll was laughing at some stories I was sharing. The big blue-eyed little girl was sitting on the floor both observing and investigating me. Kylie looks up and asks if I wanted a wife. She suggested that I might want to pursue a young Egyptian woman from church. Move over! We have a new host for the now defunct game show "Love Connection," her little features displaying concern and calculation.

"But there is one thing about her," Kylie offered innocently, "she smells," spoken sternly and matter of fact.

This from an eight-year-old was hysterical.

"Not everyone has the same hygiene standards as we do here in America. Is she pretty?"

Kylie nodded yes, but it was not the strong assurance a man wants when being set up.

"When you see her on Sunday, please be sure to tell her you know a good-looking funny man she might be interested in."

Kylie looked at me harshly as if I had just stolen all her candy from an Easter basket. She walked over to her mother and whispered in Sheryll's ear. Sheryll looked at me and I immediately knew the inquisition concerned me. How had I fallen off this pedestal so rapidly? Sheryll started laughing.

"Kylie, Marc is one of the funniest people I know," Sheryll defended.

Kylie was less than convinced or impressed. She looked back at me and walked slowly and, methodically my way.

"You're funny? A stand-up comedian?" she asked in disgust.

What was this little girl saying or asking? Children had always been a great demographic for me.

"I am more of a sit-down comedian," I said in my defense.

Kylie looked me over. It was clear in her eyes that she didn't find me funny in the slightest. Furthermore, was she upset with her mother's dishonesty or just bad taste? Was she judging Sheryll for being easily amused? Yes, she certainly was. I went home that night a convicted man. My crime: impersonation of a funny person. The sit-down comedian had disgusted her and left her suspect of adult judgement. Years later we would learn she hates almost every motion picture she watches; the girl is just a tough critic.

It was several weeks later I was invited over for dinner. At this point, Paul and I had a history of stories. The three girls asked me to tell them about their dad. So, I shared several musings, and everyone kept laughing. Soon dinner was over, and the table was being cleared. Kylie walked over to me and leaned across the table. She was stoic once again. There we sat face-to-face like the seconds before the gunfight at the O.K. Corral on October 26, 1881. Only difference is that I did not have the confidence of Gary Cooper from *High Noon*. Her glare gave no indication of what had crossed her mind, and when she spoke it was both a judgement and a declaration.

"So, you really are the sit-down comedian," and just like that I was validated in a young girl's mind. If only I had that kind of favor with older women. Sheryll, washing dishes from the other side of the counter nodded her head disbelief as well. There would be more judgement in the future over my picks of ice cream flavors, but that night knew victory!

I have had friends reach out to me in my life. All too often they want praise, recognition, or even payback. One friend has a history of trying to dictate what social media posts I should make about him. Paul is one of the few friends that could bring peace to my segregated humanity. He and his wife Sheryll went to college with Baby Mama. Yet, somehow, I scored them in the divorce. This isn't surprising – my ex-wife survives on secrecy and a Teflon existence. She wears a different mask according to her surroundings. It is impressive that she can do such a quick personality change in the blink of an eye. Paul is the kind of friend to ask hard questions. Baby Mama did not want anyone in her life that might resemble accountability or even cause her conscience to itch. She spent a lifetime dulling her conviction, and authentic people like Paul are not allowed to dampen that effort.

I struggle with seeing men that are passive as worthless, but God is working on me. As humans, I think we primarily learn by example and direct experience. Intimacy is never found in superior relationships. It is found in common ground, and Paul is not afraid to be real and share his struggles, mistakes, and regrets. Paul has always been an example of the real thing. He was critical in helping me overcome the forgery of faith that my father-in-law taught (the colostomy bag of Christianity - I really like saying that). Most people claim that they believe in something, but never live in accordance with their own standards. This is not Paul! While my cries were inaudible to human ears, Paul saw my suffering. He would bring me comfort, camaraderie, relief, and often food. He isn't just a man of faith, (The bible says faith without works is dead. Faith is Paul's superpower.) but one of practice as well. He wore a lot of hats in my life, and I wanted to add undertaker to that list. Many of my friends reach out to me and I am grateful, but they want praise and glory, never Paul. He is flawed like the rest of us, but his pursuit of living a real Christian life is thus far unparalleled to anything I have ever seen in a man. This is why it should be no surprise that Paul walked into my home the next morning.

So, there I was in bed. The sun was up and trying to peek from around the window blinds. I had been praying only a few hours earlier "God help." The front door opens. The outside light violated every sense of my being. This lost soul preferred to be tucked away in shadows. I had not seen natural light in weeks. Paul walked in with Sheryll following. I shot up in humiliation when I saw his wife. I was naked, so I made sure all my beauty parts were covered. Funny how I had not showered in weeks and alone I could not have cared less about hygiene. Yet my vanity still found its way to the surface. Many moons later, Paul would confess my home smelled rotten. Sheryll never had to clarify her thoughts that day because I could see it in her eyes.

Sheryll is the kind of woman that is as close to celestial as you will ever meet. Just to look at her she has a glacial Nordic vibe going on; you would never expect her to be funny or fun, but that is exactly what she is. Her brown eyes are always wide and perfectly expressing her every thought and emotion. In one sense she is as easy to read as a drug store novel. Yet, she has never had an ounce of judgment in her gaze towards me or any of God's creations. She met Paul in college, they married, and she balances him almost perfectly. She has that perfect supermodel look without the pale skin and sunken in eyes of starvation and heroin. Now cue the Andrew Gold song, "Thank You for Being a Friend." Yeah, I just made them my Golden Girls (show from the eighties).

When they were early in their marriage, I had predicted that she would one day leave Paul. Her husband was more of an absentee landlord than a mate. He worked hard, a lot, and has always been an excellent provider. He also had his hobbies like, wake boarding and surfing, and would leave his wife home at the drop of a hat to pursue any interest. She mostly lived alone as a widowed woman. Somehow and someway between his bended knee towards God and the exceptional person Sheryll is, Paul changed his life. Moved his office into his home and became a truly functioning member of the family. I have always envied their family life. Although, I wonder if I would be good in a family. I have mostly only known being alone.

Together they had three beautiful daughters. When I say beautiful, I mean not a runt in the bunch! Girls that are not typical teenagers either. They care about character, family, and God. Paul turned out to be a pretty good old man to his daughters as well. I have lived with this family a few times, and I always felt like I belonged. Living with this family always provided a lot of laughs.

"Listen," he announced with the voice of a trumpet. Paul had way too much energy; a gift only awarded to the sober.

I was his captive audience. I pulled myself up. Paul and his wife were blurry. I tried to focus, but my body ached, and my head felt like it was smashed in. I had been on one hell of a ride. Paul spoke, and I stared at him. He had a proposition and he is a salesman. When he pitches an idea, he oozes enthusiasm.

"I have heard about this program in Naples. It is called Saint Matthew's House. They have a year program. My friend's son went, and he totally changed his life around," Paul shared. So, this was the pitch, a yearlong vacation from the world in rehab. Negative, never, and no were the first words screaming in my head. The voices were louder than my pain. How do I shut this shit down?

Lather, rinse, repeat! What was Paul thinking? I would want to become a self-imposed prisoner. I don't go to Paul's home and try and knock the drinks out of his hand. Had the lasting and devastating effects of the Florida humidity warped his brain? Cue the Eddie Money song, "Two Tickets to Paradise." However, my friend's inspirational idea of paradise was Naples, Florida.

I knew immediately that I would never make this trip. Now, I simply needed a way to get this chainsaw of an idea out of my ass. If only I could grow some wings and fly away from these ideas. He was being sweet, so I could not just shoot down his most wholehearted proposal. Yet, as I tried to be cordial, I also knew there was simply no chance I would ever commit a year of my life to a program of any kind. Maybe a few months, but sobriety is way overrated I reasoned. I looked back over at Sheryll. She stood quiet and still. I could feel her prayers and pity. She was still shocked to see such wreckage of a life. Years later, she would confess to me that it was the floor covered in liquor bottles that blew her mind. She never made mention of what the stench of me not showering for over a month must have been like. Then I studied Paul. His best efforts would never get me into this Saint Matthew's House, but there he stood between the funk and filth of my small world. He was offering his brilliant solution. It occurred to me... how dare I want to die so desperately when he was fighting for my life. My selfish nature was stronger than Paul's rationale. My narcissistic, emotionally unavailable, commitment phobia was drinking my own poison Kool-Aid. I wasn't yet fearful because I wouldn't even consider the proposal.

I ran my fingers through my grease matted hair. This had become that moment when I already knew my answer. Therefore, the objective had become to escort him and his idea out the front door. Briefly I worried about all the life I would miss out on. Let's keep it real, you are not missing out on anything while getting your shit together. The deal was made that I would pray and think about a yearlong rehab. They left. I felt like it was all going to end, and I knew it was my fault. I tried to dismiss their proposal. Maybe I had become too familiar with the failure, frustration, confusion, and detachment. I could no longer imagine a life with success, freedom, joy, and relationships. At the very least, I should consider sticking around to see if I was ever right about anything.

I had no problem believing in God. It was His people that I had a problem with. Baby Mama comes from a very Baptist background. Her father, Larry, is a minister. His hero is Billy Graham, and I admired Larry for a while. That was a mistake. They say never meet your heroes; I get it. I believed in his rhetoric even though I felt he was old fashioned and out of touch. I would soon learn that there were two versions of this man. A man determined to bring Christianity to heathens everywhere and another man who demonized people like me. Funny how so many people of God want you to be an upstanding member of their church. They love you when you are giving to their ministries and supporting their lifestyles'. They expect you to dress and carry yourself a certain way and submit.

Corrupt religion always demands we blindly fall in line. They claim to preach and live by the bible, but do they read it? The word of God is filled with stories of people like me - addicts, thieves, whores, and inmates. He was hardly the man I thought. He was weak and did nothing that I could discern to help save our marriage. Maybe that was an unfair expectation (A leopard cannot change his spots. Larry will always be weak. Maybe just destiny and not his fault?), but he helped her divorce me. In fact, Larry continued to repeatedly tell me that his daughter's affair was all in my head. It was like a person trying to convince me the sky was not blue. After a while he had started to make me question my own truth. Today Baby Mama has married the Doughboy Draftsman and his molten lava body that she left me for. She stole another woman's husband and life. She lives in a huge home and her exterior is perfect. I wonder if Larry still maintains she isn't fucking the guy. Years later he would tell my daughter he wanted to speak to me but doubted I would. Of course, I reject the offer, because there is nothing else to say.

Then there is the matter of God. I simply saw God as fucking with me. God had become a trickster that was in the habit of taking things I loved away from me. He started with my family, but his second act was my dreams. If I touched it, God snatched it. People would offer their cliché sayings of encouragement. I would be told that God was refining me so he could answer the prayers I prayed. The cost was too great for me. I wanted a refund. After all, read the Bible. God was always doing things that made no sense at all. I wanted control. Admitting that my life had become unmanageable was simple. I could even admit I needed a higher power, but I didn't trust that higher power. Furthermore, the idea of a life without bourbon meant losing more control and power of my own life. Drinking may be destructive, but it is faithful. It took me further than I wanted to go, and costs more than I wanted to pay, but to stop drinking was another hopeless feeling.

Job was considered a righteous man. God was pleased with Job, but then Job loses everything because God had a little wager with Satan. Then what about Joseph? God promises Joseph that he will rise to a place of power above his brothers and worldly father. Yet, Joseph ends up being rejected by his brothers and sold into slavery. The bible is full of this Holy trickery or pranks, and I wanted nothing to do with it. Did God come through in the end? Absolutely, but who wants that noise in their lives? Which brings me to looking at Paul and Sheryll with my mixed feelings and confusion.

My friends left my cave. I laid back down and before I could settle into my misery, two words presented themselves to my mind. "God Help!" I heard those words that I was pleading in the dead of darkness just a few hours earlier. "God help!" It was as if God was saying to me, "I heard you." God was offering me the single one answer that I did not want. Yet, when I prayed, I wasn't specific. Most drunken days do not stand out, and often my memory goes astray. Paul's offer made this one loud. The real world was harassing me, and I wanted to be left alone. When Paul was in my home the answer to rehab was completely, utterly, totally no! Seconds after their departure, in the blink of an eye, I knew! That rehab was my destiny. It was time to unfriend my bourbon-drenched life. My life, relationships and state of mind were all unacceptable. It was time to schedule some ups after all my downs. Cue the Bob Seger song, "Against the Wind." - Because I sure as hell wish I didn't know now what I didn't know just an hour earlier.

My choices had taken me to a place where my existence was beyond despair. Yet, I still wanted to think that my life had hardly become like the motion pictures *Trainspotting, Drugstore Cowboy, Rush* or *Requiem for a Dream*. I knew I needed help, but I wanted it on my terms. Unfortunately for me, all my best efforts were failing. My intelligent rationale was failing me. Change already proved more than just hard, it would require sacrifice, others, and a great deal of agonizing. It was time to stop just crossing my fingers, wanting the stars to align, or waiting on fate for me to end my addictive behavior. I had to admit the stumbling blocks and, hurdles (both inner and outer) were too big for me to tackle. I needed to submit to others, and that felt weak and unnatural.

I had no issue admitting that my life had become unmanageable, and I was powerless over alcohol. That is the first step of the famous 12. I had no problem with step 2, which demanded I believe a power greater than me could restore me to sanity. However, the idea that some of that power greater than me was people who paved the way before me. That was a different matter altogether. Church had preconditioned me to trust no one in leadership. I think this was my first step, thought, early stage of hope. Paul was right, and this resonated in my soul. Over the years my choices led me to this place of darkness. How could I expect to make better choices alone? This is the thing; my choices had buried me in addiction and misery.

My decisions could no longer be trusted. I needed a coach, discipleship, and mentor, whatever you want to call it.

The winds always stand still in the eye of a hurricane. There I was in the eye. My mind had clarity and I accepted that Saint Matthew's House was my calling, healing, and future. Even the ghosts of memories seemed to be silenced. I could have precision in making this choice. I said my silent prayers even though my faith had mostly been depleted. This is the beauty of God's currency. He tells us that faith the size of a mustard seed is all we need.

I was going to and committing to rehab. I called my job to resign only to discover they had resigned me. They had had enough of me being passed out and calling out of work. Honestly, I could hardly blame them, but it still sucks to realize I wasn't wanted. I did love my job, but more importantly I loved my friends.

Annette is a strong and capable friend and woman. She had convictions that were deep rooted. Life was black and white for her back in those days. Unlike Paul, she was never afraid of packing my bags for a guilt trip. She did not understand that guilt, shame, and disappointment are enemies of sobriety. The addict already feels remorse. They cannot explain or understand why they exhibit such irrational behavior. They are stuck in a maze of loss, pity, and turmoil. During one of Annette's fierce and unrelenting lectures, I made a promise to seek a program if I did not stop drinking. I never had any intention of fulfilling that promise because I honestly thought my efforts would win. I sat in that bed and I thought deep and hard about her value of a promise. Now was my time to try and thank her by taking things to another level. I did not like being vertical, but I sat up. I grabbed my computer and started researching the oasis of sobriety.

At this stage, I thought rehab was a lot like McDonalds. You just walk in and tell them what you want. Next thing you know you are off the grid and in life-transforming situations. I had no idea there was an admissions process. I was clueless that they could turn me away. That they do turn some applicants down. How could I not qualify? After all, I had been nursing a bottle of bourbon for about 10 or 11 years. I put a lot of distillery children from Tennessee and Kentucky through college. Not to mention or forget the kids from Ontario. I always bought Canadian Mist or some other well brand when my buzz was on a budget. I felt I paid my dues, made a mess of me, and should be a poster child for rehabilitation. In fact, I should be their great redemption story, and they must use me for promoting the program. I still did not want to go!

Back in these days Saint Matthew's did not have the most friendly or easy to navigate website. This combined with me not exactly being a real genius online proved problematic. Getting answers and information about this facility felt impossible. I called every number I could find. Most of the time there was simply no answers. Occasionally, I would get a human voice and all I knew was that these people were not admissions. I needed to speak with Joel or Joe. Did I hear that correctly? Joe or Joel? These two names were eerily similar, and I had been drunk for over a month. I started leaving these men messages daily.

The program takes no more than 15 men a month. The criteria are men who have hit their rock bottom. Going through a rough patch, a bender, or even downhill is not good enough. They are looking for the men who are dancing with the Grimm Reaper. This organization aspired to save lives. We needed to be desperate men. You cannot call on behalf of an addicted relative or friend. Each man must reach out on their own behalf. Everyone wants their lost loved one to seek help and change their lives, but that doesn't mean shit if a person doesn't want it for themselves.

I have heard it told that Florida is a hot bed for fake rehabs. The numbers are astounding of the places that will take your insurance money, but never actually help you. In some cases, they will even supply you with drugs and accommodate the addiction. All done in an effort to collect insurance money. It is a sad and evil reality that some people can't find help.

Once I had realized this so-called new way of living was truly to be my path, I kept reaching out, always to no avail, and this confused me. One minute I felt certain that this was God's answer to my prayer. A few minutes later, I wondered if God was playing a joke on me again. The world felt too heavy and I felt like hope was bluffing. Eventually, I reached out to other rehabs. Everyone had a glitch or rule that would turn me off. In one case I was too old for their program. I found it hard to imagine a facility would assign an expiration date to a person, but they did. And so the search continued. However, the voice inside my head was not still or quiet; it would scream to me, "No! You are supposed to be at Saint Matthew's House!"

Discouragement is a friend that stays perched on my shoulder. Maybe I was wrong, maybe God didn't want me in Naples. That is when my thoughts hopped onto a one-way street that was leading me towards giving up. It felt like all my ideas and plans were disjointed. As providence would have it, my friend from San Diego called.

His name is Michael, and we have been friends since college. We were roommates when I was a youth pastor. I have had a lot of jobs, wore a lot of different hats. Some of those hats I have shared with Michael. Our shoes walked a lot of the same miles. Just to throw it out there, I am the better looking of us (a long-standing joke).

I do not always respond well to what people tell me. I do receive correction well when I feel safe and cared for. Not to mention, that Michael had a voice much like Heather's. It had a comforting and calming effect on me. As he spoke, I could feel myself taking a rest from the fight. In our conversation I felt able to trust the process. I hate the process.

I told him about my dilemma, frustrations, and defeat with my California friend. These were the times Baby Mama would always have some insight that would make me need to hold on tight. My wife was like the stiff drink when I needed one, but tonight Michael would have to be her substitute, and he did amazing. My friend simply suggested he would fly out and drive me to Naples. Together we would learn how to execute my next steps. Just like that, a plan was in place. In the words of John Hannibal from the television series, "The A-team," "I love it when a plan comes together." I was already on a new journey and it began with a glorious unfolding.

CHAPTER 4

"Healing is a matter of time, but it is sometimes also a matter of opportunity." ~ Hippocrates

"There is a beautiful transparency to honest disciples who never wear a false face and do not pretend to be anything, but who they are." ~ Brennan Manning

"Just because you are a character doesn't mean that you have character." ~ The Wolf, *Pulp Fiction*

Did I graduate to purgatory?

I think the first step in healing is always going to be overcoming fear. No matter how great the program, how ideal the circumstances are, there is one prevailing must on the path of recovery. The addict must give their consent to change. In other words, if the person doesn't want to change, it is a waste of time and energy for everyone.

Most every American knows somebody with a

substance abuse problem. Often family members call me on behalf of the addict looking for answers. I enjoy talking with the wounded and broken-hearted person. It is inevitable that I will be asked this question, "What can we do to save blank?" Insert any number of relationships here mother, father, son, daughter, husband, friend, or co-worker.

The answer is always the same, and I try to share it with great enthusiasm.

"The bad news is there is nothing you can do if the person doesn't want healing. The good news is there is nothing you can do to save the person from dependency." I stress the point that we cannot be responsible for another person's actions. Therefore, it is not to our credit if they seek help, and it is not our fault if they die. This revelation is a harsh reality, but a simple truth. At this stage of my recovery I wore a crown of absolute fear. I was a complete mess of confusion and contradictions. I wanted to stop drinking, but I was so unsure of the cost. This is when a guiding hand can make a difference. Michael arrives from the West Coast.

Michael is the kind of person that teaches me constantly, although I am sure iron had sharpened iron in our relationship. As a writer, I am terrified to not be heard or relevant. Michael showed me that far more than speaking, listening might just be the ultimate gift of love in human form.

When we were roommates, Michael and I would play various versions of gin for hours. Pool rummy, deal rummy, point rummy, gin, knock gin, the ways to play this card game are endless. We would talk politics, music, and women for hours at a time. The CD player would play for hours as we shared our eclectic tastes in music and the validity of the artists we adored. He was a player back in those days and women flocked to the guy. I think they were attracted to his very laid-back demeanor. I know I admired how he never seemed to have a stressed-out fiber in his being; he never suffered uncertainty. Sometimes we would argue over official gin rules. Then one day he looked me dead in the eyes and said, "Marc, I will play by your rules and still win." He may be of Mexican decent, but that was some Steve McQueen spoken that day. Damn if he didn't live up to his calm declaration. I have stolen and used than line in every area of my life ever since. Now he was calling me from San Diego.

After our conversation, the dawning reality that Michael was willing to fly all the way across country to help me. It felt good to be believed in. Here my ego was trying to consume me, and yet I had three friends deeply involved and invested in my recovery, salvation, and deliverance. Paul, Annette, and Michael were reason enough for me to forget my rejections and know I am loved. Cue the Pete Townsend song, "Let My Love Open the Door." Yes, I had other friends, but at this moment in time, these were the ones closest to my derailment, next move, sorrow, and situation. I needed to find my desire to live, come what may (I don't talk much about Mary in this book, Come What May was the title of our love story. Our story is an entirely different tale worth telling). Still, I lay back down and realized that I had become the good reasons Baby Mama had left me. For every ounce of faith that she did not have in me, I proved her prophesies true.

Those demons were unforgiving and relentless. Hope was presenting itself, and my thoughts were working against me. The battle of life truly is in the mind! The shadows played on my fears. I really had no idea how to push this gloom away. In many ways, obscurity had become my companion.

I used to have these nightmares that I lost my marriage. I would wake up and see my wife lying next to me. The relief that I had just had a bad dream gave me little comfort. I would crawl right next to her and hold her while she slept. Now this wicked world was real. Freddy Krueger had found his way out of my dreams and into my real world. She was in love and married to another man. The Doughboy Draftsman she married never had any appreciation for another man's dignity. Therefore, he is the worst type of scoundrel, and his reputation in business reflects it. Worse yet, I had talked to the man several times. Every conversation I had with the man left me feeling like cockroaches were crawling all over my body much like the huge bug problem in the 1982 film, *Creepshow*. At the very least, I always felt that he got his Aqua Velva stank on me. He has the personality of a character from a commercial. Maybe that isn't fair to some great commercials and the amazing television series about advertising *Mad Men*.

Baby Mama and I had talked about swinging with him and his first wife a lot. An idea that in theory is thrilling, adventurous, fun, and hot. Only I did not find it desirable at all. Baby Mama had a history of dropping her standards as fast as her panties. I am not sure which was faster, but she was not averse to spreading those legs like butter.

She no longer was in love with me. How could I learn to live without my bride, my eve, and my truest love? I think a man loves and looks at the mother of his children in a way that no other woman will ever capture him. Now I wondered if I ever really knew her. I had discovered she was capable of gross misconduct and actions I never imagined. I knew growing up in window dressing Christianity had only taught her to keep secrets and protect her persona. Celebrities have press agents to do their lying, but in ministry you do your own lying. However, she was not who she portrayed herself to be. In fact, I think she has no idea who she is even now. Let me be clear that I no longer care enough about her to hate her. In fact, there are parts of my life that I still owe her gratitude. However, I do not count her as person I would ever want back or even a causal relationship with. Did she have secret ambitions all along? I don't know, but I do know she became the kind of person I would not want in my inner circle. It would be years after my divorce before my father confessed that at my wedding, he said to his then wife "Who is this bitch my son is marrying?" Note to dad: next time speak up sooner. As if that would have made a difference. All these years later, my father still holds it against me that I didn't marry my high school and college sweetheart Denise.

We tried marriage counseling. This is when you go and tell your deepest, most intimate details to a stranger on a couch. Akin to open heart surgery where they come up with a chainsaw through your ass. A total bloodbath of emotions and embarrassment. I quickly realized that the preacher's daughter was stacking the deck against me. She and the therapist named Bob demised a plan to reveal all my moral failures one day. She had come with a list. An ambush had ensued, and Bob was only another brick in the enemies' wall. Were her points and lists correct? Absolutely! Everything I had ever done wrong (and there were pages) I heard from her perspective. I was a vile human! I was relationally incompetent! I was unpredictable, unstable, and uncontrollable. I was often unresponsive and abandoned her emotionally. Basically, I had all the developmental issues that children from divorce often adhere to. Cue the Jim Croce song, "Lovers Cross." I had made her laugh more and harder than she ever will, but I also hurt her twice as much. I cried that day on that couch with Bob's blues eyes fixated on me. Pity from a pious preacher is the worst hurt and humiliation. Baby Mama left and I stayed paralyzed and sobbing. I literally cried for the next few days without any reprieve. Bob helped opened a wound, but he sent me out into a real world with that wound open. An open-heart surgeon that failed to sow me back up. On more than one occasion I would drive and weep on my way to work. It was an ugly worked up cry that could not be easily hidden. From the parking lot, I would explain to a manager my situation, position and pray for grace. I think they always allowed me the time I needed to compose myself.

Eventually Bob would ask his secretary wife to call me and say he could not see me anymore. He felt, I was a conflict of interest. In truth, Bob knew who really buttered his bread. My in-law's family were a steady stream of income. I really wanted to heal and move on from him. To this day, I wish Bob well but hope he has retired. Bob hush your fucking mouth and go sell insurance, but that is none of my business!

IF ROCK BOTTOM HAD A BASEMENT

As I said before, I was living with my floor a sea of empty bottles. Any trip to the bathroom would always require kicking debris out of my way as my feet shuffled across the room. Voices shouting in my head of a world crumbling that I didn't even like or understand. Where does one hide when he feels like the world is headed for hell? My only reality was that I might not wake up tomorrow and it be a better, brighter day. I would cry uncontrollably and not stop for hours. I never had any clue of the time and only a faint hint of the day. Sometimes just trying to walk to the bathroom I would collapse and pass out. Only to wake up back into the unbearable anguish and suffocating silence. The only sound I heard was the air conditioner. I acquired a lot of bruises and aches I was too blackout drunk to account for.

Often, I was too drunk to drive to a liquor store. As a result, I was depending on my local 7-11 to feed my addiction. I could walk a few blocks up the street. Although, I think I fell in almost every yard along the way during those benders. I vigorously cleared their wine section completely out. I would start with the reds, and once the merlots, cabernets, and pinot noir were depleted, in desperation, I turned to the whites. I hate Chardonnay, Sauvignon blanc, and Pinot Grigio, but they were what was available just before last call. Still, even in my most depraved desperation, I kept some form of dysfunctional dignity and never once turned to the blush, rose', or white zinfandels. One of the girls would no longer sell to me and the other simply proclaimed I needed help. Was she really saying these things out loud? Every new bottle felt like I was unsnapping the jeans of a woman for the first time. That thrilling feeling of finding a new lover and new adventure that awaits. I chased the feeling with more zeal than I had anything in my life for years. I could not get loose from the craving even when fighting like hell. The real madness of addiction is when what we want and what we do are polar opposites.

Toneka was her name, and she was a tall beautiful creature that worked at 7-11. A black woman that had captured my attention and I was infatuated with her. Her dark eyes and unknown back-story could keep me talking to her for hours. Every man that she served was immediately smitten with her, and I was no exception. She could talk to anyone, and you were never a stranger. My reasoning told me she had a history of fending off advances from potential suiters. I never have been one to watch a lot of TV, and on some boring evenings I would walk up and visit with her. Simply hanging around the convenience store talking and laughing with her between customers. Whenever our conversation got to the deep end, a patron would intrude.

Sometimes if she had not seen me for days, she would even stop by my place to check on me. I literally lived less that a quarter mile from her store. We had the ultimate game of cat and mouse going on. Every time I thought I had caught her she would disappear. Her defense mechanism was equal parts clever and maddening. I knew from her social media posts that she did not protect her inner peace well. I also knew from being near her that a simple glance could woo me. She had a temper and was not the type of woman to easily apologize. She was a mystery. In fact, I think we might have been lovers had my life not been nothing more than wreckage. My problematic drinking made me to much of a risk. As for me I was still seeking a woman to complete me and not complement me. I wasn't a healthy person spiritually.

She never bothered to stop selling me my wine, but her smiles diminished to looks of disapproval. Maybe she is just forbidden fruit and that was my fascination. However, I still think about her from time to time. A single kiss from her would have been magnificent. It bothers me she only ever saw me at my worst, but she sold me my wine. At the time that was all I would ask for. In truth, had we become more than friends that may have altered my real destiny in Naples.

Alone with just my memories, the torment was relentless and I on borrowed time. The painful silence, the ever-growing anxiety, desperate and rapidly I fill with fear. They say the mind is a battlefield. Memories are like missiles that cause huge explosions. Life may just be the accumulation of moments, but I had too many painful ones. The harsh reality of my war had worn me down. There was a time I liked the man I was, but these days life had called my bluff.

I crawled out of bed and stumbled to the bathroom once again. I had not eaten any food in days bordering on weeks. My stomach must have been trying to eat my backbone. Only bourbon and wine sustained me. The bathroom door had a full-length mirror hanging on it. I did not recognize my reflection. I turned to my side, and my stomach was flat. Cue the Bruce Springsteen song, "Streets of Philadelphia." A song from the motion picture, *Philadelphia*, but ever so fitting for my Orlando hell. My clothes hung on me. Could I have felt any sorrier for myself? Living in the bottle was taking a toll. I felt like I had been shot from a gun. I stumbled to my kitchen. The wine was gone! I braced myself for a humbling, stumbling, struggle of a walk for more fermented grape juice. I sat on the edge of my bed and wondered if I could make the short walk without falling in anyone's yard. The is answer is that I would fall several times. Each time hoping that only different eyes saw me tumbling down.

Michael arrived late one Saturday evening. Of course, I was drunk, and he was patient. He could see that killing time was killing me. Later, I learned that his wife was worried that I might hurt her husband. I suppose that is a reasonable concern, but I am much more of a happy or sad drunk. It would be years before I met Laura, a lovely Italian woman with valid questions about my character. It was my brother Patrick that told me I had a habit of pissing in the front yard. At least, that explains those dirty little glances the neighbors would give me. Oh, come on neighbors? I was probably the most interesting disaster in the neighborhood. Note to the reader, being humble is not a prerequisite to be a drunk.

We spent Sunday playing the "get Marc sober" game. Just like old times, we played a lot of gin. Surprisingly, I was winning. Then Monday we drove from Orlando to Naples. I was detoxing and felt spent. The trip is just under four hours. As we departed the highway, my heart started to race up the exit ramp. It was a one-year program or death. These were my limited choices, and death still felt like a viable option. My restless heart was rationalizing that I didn't need the program. In truth I was as scared as a jackrabbit. Every time I had doubts or became discouraged, Michael piped up with solutions. I also had some troubling thoughts about a friend of mine. Kristen.

CHAPTER 5

"The earth owes you nothing. It was here first." ~ Mark Twain

Hope is defective. Naples.

Kristen. Long before I knew her, I wanted to know her. She was tall, but not towering. She had blue eyes, light hair, and carried a disinterested resting face. She slouched just a little bit like taller girls tend to do. Yet, when you knew her, she was shyer and more unsure of herself than anything. She is one of the most beautiful people I had ever seen and before I knew her, I would often steal secret glances. One afternoon I sat quietly in the break room listening to her talk and giggle with friends. Could this be the woman to rescue me from my icy solitude? Cue the Bon Jovi song, "Mystery Train." Kristen wasn't like other women, she was magic, tragic, and soulful. It would take months of effort to learn who she was. The kind of woman that men would build and empire or go to war for.

Where we worked, I was surrounded by the most surreal, exotic, and beautiful women. Yet, only Kristen was intoxicating. I was lonely and lacked confidence. Still, living in the aftermath of broken relationships. Still, very much in love with Heather. I continued to secretly investigate Kristen and as fate would remain cruel, she was married. That would never stop me from melting at the sight of her. We would never be lovers or share any physical intimacy of any kind, but I would love her as much as any woman ever in my life.

At work, she was a whisper, but at night we would talk freely. I got to know much about her, and yet I knew nothing about her. She was like a Rubik's cube I never got tired of trying to solve. If I slept, I would wake up at 3 AM just because I knew that was when to expect her call or texts. Our conversations were wild and safe, and I always knew we were going to go to a place that I had never visited before. She would cry when she was happy, but never when she was sad. In Naples, Kristen was on my mind a lot. Something about our conversation earlier that morning was off. She had always been mysterious, but never aloof.

I always felt very lonely and isolated. My life was an absurd and amusing sideshow. I always felt it best to keep my mouth shut and not prove my idiosyncrasies and foolishness. Joseph in the bible had a coat of many colors, but I wore a cloak of doubt and depression. Even now when I wake up, I still try and take this coat off before I begin my day. Some days are harder than others. One afternoon, I was at work and Kristen looked at me, she tilted her head to the side and says:

"I read your posts on Facebook. One day some girl is going to be incredibly lucky to have you." She spoke casually almost as if it were nothing more than a greeting in passing. This exquisite woman just validated me. I have always dreamed that my writing would touch souls. She managed to soothe my greatest fear, touch my great wish, and even offered healing. For the next couple days there was no room for misery and angst. I carry those words with me to this very day. It feels nice to be believed in, even if I was not believing in myself.

She was married to a man named George whom I had never met. He wasn't a bad guy or so it seemed, but her assessment was he was lazy. He wasn't a leader, motivated, or held a job very well. She had a love for him, but not respect. She wanted out of the marriage, but two children made her feel stuck. The marriage was lifeless. The wheels were turning in her mind. She would talk often about her dilemma and I mostly listened. On occasion I would try and insert something of value.

"Do you still love him at all?"

"Yes."

"Then leave him sooner than later. Leave him while you still love the guy." This was my Socrates moment. I may not be in academia, but I had philosophies too.

"What kind of chance?"

"A chance to win you back. Trust me you have told him a thousand times in a thousand ways you aren't happy. I assure you from your description of George, he will be the last to know." I explained. I was speaking from the perspective of a man that lost his wife.

I told her that women usually don't physically leave a relationship until they have dipped out emotionally. Most often by the time she is gone, the husband was foolish enough to be the last to know. She broke ties before she ever walked out the door. I reasoned that if she left while she continued to love George, he had a chance.

We weren't lovers, in fact far from it. However, I fed off her like she was significant in a lover's kind of way. She always spoke life into me, and I imagine others as well. Words of affirmation are my thing. She was also praised my writing. She inspired me like my own queen of hearts. She talked a lot about her husband. She spoke lovingly of her children and their care. The youngest boy has special needs. I think this is how I fell so deeply in love with her. The attention and love she gave her children were captivating. One night we were messaging, and something was wrong. Our conversation was like a verse to a song that wasn't working. I carried this imbalance with me into Naples.

We had become each other's shoulder to lean on. We brought each other our hurts like burnt offerings. We shared dreams as if we were paying for the relationship with them. Now she was distant and different. She was asking me to come over to her house at 3 AM. I loved her, but I wasn't about to have an affair. What was wrong? Why was she changing? What was hurting her so deeply? I could not identify this new version of her. The path of tenderness that we shared was becoming unfamiliar, and I didn't like it. We were only texting and nonverbally communicating, but her voice changed! Her tone was unfamiliar. A change that was significant. There was a madness to her, and my words were not easing her mind.

That night in Naples, we would meet with one of Michael's friends. Her name is Monica. She is a sweet and pretty woman that resembles Amy Adams. However, if it were not for bad luck this lady would not have any luck at all. Every story in her life was a tragedy in some form or another. All her relationships (not just romantic) revolved around someone cheating her. Still, Monica was cute and endearing. She madly wanted children and would talk to her unborn frequently. We would walk on the pier and the beach. We took amazing pictures of the sunset and each other. I was almost having a perfect night. Monica was entertaining, and I enjoyed the witty banter Michael provided. But I kept thinking my friend Kristen is hurting. I would not post any pictures of that evening. I didn't want my good times to hurt Kristen. The heart catches things that the mind can't see.

At Saint Matthew's House earlier, Michael dropped me off and went to fill the rental car up with gas. I walked into the office. I was practically trembling. My anxiety needed a drink desperately. My first encounter was Miss Dee. She sat in a low chair behind a tall counter desk.

The set up did not make for the most welcoming office space. Later I would discover Miss Dee to be a fantastic person, but on this day, she just seemed detached and uninterested. My background is Disney and guest services, where people are so sweet, I can feel cavities coming on just in conversation. Miss Dee was a different kind of gatekeeper. She was alarmingly direct and to the point. I wanted to give up at that moment. I had no idea that I was really in the foyer of a homeless shelter. I explained why I was there, and she seemed more than willing to brush me off. This woman should have been working for an important CEO. She is a strong presence, and I didn't want to cross this lady. In desperation, I explained that we drove from Orlando, because I could not get anyone on the phone. I had been calling every day and some days multiple times. I had left voice messages on every machine I could reach all to no avail. To this day the intake process of Saint Matthew's confuses me and seems unorganized, but maybe there is a method to their madness. I know they have done amazing things to get people in the program. Miss Dee gave me directions that were simple enough. Leave the office and take a left and walk down to the old firehouse. However, no longer being a firehouse, how was I to know what structure to look for? I was looking for Justin's Place. This was just a branch of the Saint Matthew's House Tree. I hadn't felt so lost and confused since being a college freshman on a new campus.

The property is huge. They have a homeless shelter, car wash, thrift store, and even their own Starbucks. What kind of alternate reality was I walking in where homeless shelters have a Starbucks? Only in America! Incidentally where is the suggestion box? I would like to lobby for a Dunkin Donuts. The thrift store is huge, and the selection of furniture was not worn-down crap that housed bed bugs. Naples is a very wealthy area. This thrift store looked like an expensive department store. The denotations here were high class and expensive stuff that was well maintained. Tall aluminum buildings behind the store were used to refurbish certain items. If there is such a thing as a premium thrift store, this was it.

Walking across the spread out and long campus was puzzling. I simply could not comprehend the size and magnitude of this organization. People were blowing around everywhere like leaves. I was confused. It felt a lot like being in an amusement park.

Justin's Place is the rehab of Saint Matthew's House for men. It is named after Justin Holecek, a man who lost his battle with addiction. Justin died September 18th, 2009 at the tender age of 30 from alcoholism. His parents donate tons of money to helping other men become free from addiction. It is both a sad and inspiring tale of redemption.

When you come into Justin's Place you stay in a beautifully renovated fire department building. The bathroom has four showers. The bedroom houses about 16 bunks. The younger guys automatically get the top bunks. Lights are out between 9:30 and 10PM every night. Friday and Saturday nights, we can stay up 1 hour later. We are then forced to watch terrible mindless films that the younger guys think are way cool. It is often torment and gross stories that excel in special effects and little else, but I kept in mind why I am there. I was older than most and therefore a minority. However, none of this had begun yet. On my first day there I was lost. I was all mixed up trying to figure out the differences between the buildings. It felt like a scene from a *Doctor Strange* motion picture. One minute I was in the real world. Now because of the sling ring I was in some alternate recovery universe. Did I mention they have their own Starbucks?

I continued to walk along Airport Road. I was not even sure why I felt so disturbed. I suppose it was my job as an alcoholic to be a walking contradiction. I still had a hangover hanging on every step of the way. A loud drum banged in my head. The building that I was looking for is on the edge of the property. I walked up to the two big glass doors. I pull, but they are locked. Where are the people? I knock a few times and nobody ever answers. All I can see is my reflection in the glass doors looking back at me. That unrecognizable face of mine. There was no kindness from strangers coming from the other side. Airport Road South held no mercy or pity. What was the price I would have to pay to find someone? I was giving everything, but up. Still I felt as if I were on some sort of twisted merry go round, but merry could go straight to hell. God, stop toying with me, I thought.

I felt alone and very defeated I walked back to the main building. I figured sometimes you lose even if you really are trying. My head was down, and my tail tucked between my legs. Why is this proving to be so hard? I start praying, "God was I wrong? Do you not want me here or not?" I was becoming tired and bored with this process. It felt like hopelessness had me surrounded once again. Sometimes you just slip between the cracks of this world. I knew how to combat these feelings. I just needed a bottle and to not be afraid of pulling the trigger by drowning myself in dirty water.

Meeting with Michael's friend, Monica, was still a few hours away.

"Did you go around back?" He was piping up again. "Did you ask God where you were supposed to go? How you could find the men you need to see. What are their names?"

"Joel and Joe." I answered. Michael is famous or maybe infamous for saying, "did you ask God." Part of why I drink is because I did not trust God. He struggled to take my advice as He looked down from His throne. As far as I was concerned God was rude.

I know what you are thinking. Is Marc suggesting he was angry with God? Damn right I was mad at God. I certainly didn't trust Him. Evidenced in the fact that when pain would come my way and pain is always lurking around the corner. I turned to escape and alcohol not divine help. I was not sure if God even noticed me, but if He was helping it all seemed very disastrous. He stays on His throne and I am left kicking around the ashes of what He left behind.

I decided long ago that if I am going to be mad at God, that is fine. Of course, He is all knowing so why try and keep it a secret from Him? Bottom line is that if you have a chip on your shoulder with God, just say it. You are not the only person to be disappointed in the divinity.

If Michael's heart were ever in ruin, I would never know. He was buried in enthusiasm. He suggested we park and wait at the firehouse building. He spoke in that calming manner that he has perfected. Immediately, I thought this suggestion was stupid. Nevertheless, I agreed, and we headed over to the building. I was involuntarily detoxing and that is a very wicked transformation. My body demanded the comfort of bourbon. I was familiar with withdrawals and they are a horror.

Sure enough, we rode to the back and people were everywhere. His dumbass proposition had merit. I was floored, and panic rushed me again. People required action on my part. What I didn't realize was that the Justin's Place facility feeds homeless people a hot lunch and dinner every day. So many of the individuals I talked to were clueless about the program. A lot of blank stares came from the men circling the parking lot. I was terrified about my decision and confused by the hopeless faces. I walked among the folks asking if they knew where I could find Joel or Joe. I was oblivious to the fact that these men had no clue. What kind of Wonderland hole had I fallen into? This ministry had more branches to it than our government. There was a door with a big sign that read, "Do Not Enter." However, it was glass door and all I saw were people on the inside. I charged in with little thought. Never underestimate a man with nothing to lose.

I walked right in the door that read do not enter. I wasn't being rebellious, but the truth was my desperation didn't even see the sign. I was coming out from under my shame. I had a determination and conviction that would not give way to defeat. I had to act while I was strong willed. This is when I first met Dan. Wearing a metallic purple shirt I thought he looked like a skinny, Latino version of Barney the dinosaur. He was kind but alarmed that I had entered uninvited. He reeked of political correctness and self-righteous indignation. He is a fucking kid!

"I am looking for Joe or Joel." I spoke with fear and caution, but not towards Dan. I was still worried about this leap of faith I was about to ask for.

Dan acted as if my unpredictability was a threat, but he was never rude. When he paused, I reinforced my resolve. My pain and hunger were stronger than this man child.

"I just drove here from Orlando because I could not get anyone on the phone." If I had nautical flags for distress, I would have been waving them frantically.

Dan was hesitating. He studied me. I clearly was a mess of a man. I was shaking, my skin red and pale, my eyes sunken in. I had put myself on death row - of course I looked like hell. I took a seat to suggest I wasn't going to leave. My desperation and instincts dictated my posture. Cautiously Dan stepped away and disappeared in an office. Clearly Dan was unsure of protocol with the new stranger among them. From out of the office I heard a commanding voice shout, "I will be right with you!" Touchdown! That was the first time I would hear Joe K's voice. He sounded like he had the stature of Thanos (The supervillain from Marvel comics that first appeared in The Invincible Iron Man #55 in 1973 and later in The Avengers motion pictures Infinity War and Endgame.)

IF ROCK BOTTOM HAD A BASEMENT

A gentleman in the kitchen named Wes greeted me. He was preparing dinner to be served to the homeless gathering outside. A tall and slender man with dark skin from a tan. Evidently, he worked outside. His head was shaved, and he had tattoos. He is at least a solid decade younger than me, but he reminded me of an uncle. He was new to the program, and he had very sympathetic eyes. When you are down in your life you notice every gesture and appearance of kindness. He made some small talk. I could tell he felt sorry for me, but he didn't need to. I knew what I looked like, destroyed. I felt sorry enough for myself for both of us. I didn't know at the time, but men were afraid of Wes. Apparently, he had a temper that ignited easily. With me he was calm, welcoming and concerned. I still talk to him to this day. He is a wonderful man that I hold dearly. While Dan was distant, unsure, and scrawny. Wes made me feel he was glad I was there.

They say infants feel unconditional love from smiles. Smiles make them feel safe and loved. Well, I was in my infancy, and Wes' smile meant a lot. A breakthrough was finally happening. I looked around and there were men of every type. Body art and outrageous haircuts seemed to be the dominant attire. I had no idea I would be friends with these men in a few short weeks. I had no clue these men would understand me on a level much deeper than I have ever been understood. In fact, we would become brothers. In the meantime, their empathetic glances did not escape me. These strangers had struggles of their own, and yet I could sense their pity. They too had been exhausted from running in circles. Their circumstances may differ, but their core battle was mine too. This day there was no humor, but later we would laugh at how I initially came across to these men. We would all laugh a lot as we healed.

Joe K. walked out, and I rose to my feet. He was a much smaller man than his voice implied. Just like in *The Wizard of Oz*, behind the curtain the man was much smaller, softer, friendlier, and human than I expected. He didn't have a powerful wrath as I had feared. Joe didn't seem like a man full of pretense. Still, his humanity played tricks on me. I followed him into his small office. He took a seat behind his desk and looked at me with this overwhelming concern. I did not sit down. His grimace looked up at me. I was sure there had been many fools like me in front of him.

What I didn't know then was that most of Justin Place's staff have been through the program. They had victories, failures, and stories as well. These were not college educated people with no experience concerning drugs, drinking, or desperation. These men on staff knew the devil I had been dancing with. They knew of all the little nuances of distress that accompanied me in that office. I had no idea Joe K. understood me so well. I had no idea Joe had his own story.

"I don't know if you have ever had an addiction problem," I began.

Joe K. offered no sign or signal that he had had a past or story of his own. He just looked up at me from the desk. His eyes never wandered off. I knew I had his attention.

"But it takes a lot to get to a place where you

know you need a program. It is a scary reality, but I am going to die if I don't get help."

I had a certain momentum that carried me, because I have no idea how I pitched my need. This program takes only a handful of men a month. Mothers, fathers, friends all try to help get their loved ones accepted, but Justin's Place will not even consider a candidate unless they make the move on their own behalf. There I was standing in front of Joe K. explaining how my energized despair had me taking a leap of faith. I searched his eyes for some sign as tension crawled up my back. In all the times I talked to Joe, his eyes never gave away his inner thoughts. With me he remained a hard read.

Joe K. has a unique story of his own. He was living in Las Vegas. He was a junkie. If I understand correctly, he didn't really have a drug of choice. He just aspired to stay high. The affinity we all share to steer clear of reality.

One morning he was watching a house. He intended to rob it as soon as he was sure the residents were gone. He waited in some form of a dark corner for the home to vacate. Once he was satisfied with their departure, he broke in. It was a home invasion with a most unusual outcome. The determination of an addict to stay high or drunk is outstanding. His crime soon turned into an episode of Amazing Stories. In Christian circles, we like to claim the hand of providence.

He broke in on a bible study. A group of Christians saw his reckless ass and broken condition. Instead of calling the police, they pooled their money together and put Joe K. on a plane to get into the Justin's Place program. Apparently, he was beyond a wounded man, but he wasn't dead. They tell me he was filthy from living on the streets. I never was able to draw close to Joe.

Joe K. never shared this story with me. It was one of legend around Saint Matthew's House. It inspired and encouraged me. In fact, I always had a hard time getting Joe K. to shoot the shit with me. He is a quiet, guarded, and seemingly detached man. This always bothered me, but I accepted it. What I did not realize was that he was going through a divorce while I was just starting the program. Another fucking detonation of holy matrimony.

He married a woman who had also been a part of the program. However, she grew tired of Joe after about a year. I always resented this stranger of a woman. Who knows what their story is, but I felt protective of Joe K. I suppose I am just too intimate with abandonment. It is not my place to judge a stranger, but I never hear a kind word spoken about her.

I never really felt that Baby Mama had just cause to divorce me. She had fallen in love with the neighbor across the street. He is an architect and compared to me he is rich. All I own can fit in a duffle bag. He owns all kinds of goodies, and they travel the country and world all year long. The kind of thing that easily makes me feel like half a man. He has all these riches and now he has my wife too. He built her and my children a huge home. I have friends in real estate, and they have shared with me that the Doughboy Draftsman is a snake in business. In fact, I am told he always only looks out for himself and will fuck a client over in a heartbeat. I hope she is happy, but her relationship with wine suggests otherwise. His ex-wife (the one Baby Mama had kicked to the curb) once told me that he had lost several friends in business dealings. His standing as a scoundrel is secured. I don't really wish to be cruel or cold, but I do believe that my ex-wife and her husband deserve each other. On occasion, I still pray for my ex-wife, but the words I utter resemble more of a Judy Garland quote "Always be a first-rate version of yourself instead of a second-rate version of somebody else."

One day visiting my children at a French café that my daughter worked at, Michael from San Diego was visiting. Baby Mama was parked in the alley behind the restaurant. She was drinking wine in her Mercedes SUV. Michael looked at me.

"You know what is going on there right?" he said in his calm way.

Damn! How does he have this inner peace that I can't find? I am not sure I really cared about anything pertaining to her.

"What?" I was inquisitive.

"She is drinking behind there alone, but she is going to tell her husband she went out and had a few drinks with friends after work."

"You really think so?"

"Isn't it obvious?"

The truth is that nothing was obvious about Baby

Mama. Her integrity had been a mystery to me for years now.

Somewhere along the line, "till death do us part" turned into I wasn't worth dying for. As a result, I felt for Joe K. because I knew he didn't want the divorce. I hate that faithless kiss and the thought that my dreams don't fit me anymore. This was the pain that needed anesthesia. I started drinking anything that could simply dull the pain. Having peace of mind was a wonderful sensation. Help-me-sleep medicine. I suppose I always had it in me to drink, but this was what pushed me along. It would be a few months of drinking fruity mixed drinks and Gin before I discovered I really love Bourbon.

That was my introduction to being alone. Even with people all around at work or any other social situation, I was stuck in a vastness of despair. I had no idea where our love went, but I knew it was gone. I even felt like I was right about most things but being right didn't bring her back. They say if you die in your dreams, you really die in your bed. I was dying every night and I was alive every morning. I was alone and that required the river of 101 proof. Worst of all, Baby Mama had become cold. She was angry and spewed venom at every opportunity. I was astonished that I had married a woman like the person she was showing me. Even now, I wish I didn't know the woman she turned into. I thought a metamorphosis made things beautiful, beauty for ashes kind of thing, but not this time. Yes, this is me being optimistic about her. Just imagine if I had been grimmer.

Joe K. kept a distance and I never understood it. I

had no real idea what he was thinking. He was making no promises or guarantees. He explained the program thoroughly, but I understood vaguely, and I didn't care. The devil is in the details. I always pray that God hides the specifics from me. I only want the bigger picture and never the cost revealed, because it overwhelms me. He printed me out an application. There must have been 25 sheets of paper come out of that printer. He explained that once I finished the paperwork, I should fax it back quickly because space was limited, and people were trying to get in from all over the country. After this step I would need a telephone interview. That would be the first time I get to talk with Joel. A lot of staff in the program became clones of one another, but not Joel; he is and remained original.

I left the office with hope and a bunch of paper. I was not taking anything about this opportunity for granted. Maybe I needed rehab to help renew a faith in humanity and Christianity more so than I needed it to recue me from drowning in Bourbon. Life had been hard and Wild Turkey helped me give this world the bird. Michael had been waiting patiently outside. We had a victory. As we drove away to go to the beach, I had one persistent thought - Kristen. Where was Kristen and how is her heart? I would be devastated when I got answers to my questions.

CHAPTER 6

"I wish the real world would just stop hassling me." ~ Matchbox 20

"I tell myself lies all the time. But I never believe me." ~ S.E. Hinton, The Outsiders

"Dying is a really hard way to learn about life." ~ Bob Jones, from the motion picture, *My Life*

Discovering my gift

of desperation. A memory

that serves me far too well.

Cue, the Matchbox 20 song, "Real World."

The following morning, I was awake early. An application was waiting for me. I sat at a table while Michael was still asleep. I thought about what these papers meant. I pondered what life would be like. I questioned myself repeatedly. Did I really want to make this leap? All that was inside me was screaming for a rescue, but still I talked myself out of the program about a dozen times. I had been clear with Joe K. that I would not fax it until the following day. He understood I was traveling a good distance. Still, something was stirring in the atmosphere. There was something wrong that I could not identify. The worst darkness was yet to come.

On Facebook, friends were posting about grief and shock. Why were these posts all so unclear as to what had happened? What was going on? What great tragedy had befallen us? The posts were both devastated and vague. I sent some early morning messages to Kristen. I would be available to meet up and talk as she requested. Maybe she could shed some light as to what was stirring among our circle. She didn't reply. This was uncommon, but her behavior had been uncommon the past few days. The curiosity and concern were starting to eat at me.

I messaged my friend Mel. Mel is a friend from the same restaurant I was working at with Kristen. We bonded over a mutual love for writing. As a writer, she is much more talented than me. Yet, she would entertain some stories I was working on. She always was so encouraging, and my love language is words of affirmation.

Mel knew little more than I understood. Mel wondered if something was wrong with Kristen. This struck a terror in me, but I reasoned the suspicion away. No, something was going on with Kristen somewhere, but it would not provoke such tragic posts. I needed the hand of fate to still these waters in my soul. I prayed and prayed. I begged God and I had no idea what I was asking of Him.

I returned to my application. Answering every kind of question. I was asked if I am a sex offender, which I am not. I was asked about incarceration. I have been arrested a few times, but never spent much more than a single night in jail. I was asked about my religious preference, which I felt included religion making a mockery of my faith. Hadn't religion made the personality of Jesus pure nonsense? I had to confess I didn't have a home church. Then came the question of all questions.

Had I experienced any significant loss? Yeah, I have lost everything. I had started a movie production company, but the film we made was dreadful. I felt the story was strong, but my director was not equipped to make scenes interesting, everything inside the frame should have been interesting. Instead, there were scenes set against plain white walls. My acting was mediocre at best and I am being very kind. In fact, it would be fair to say my acting was worse than the directing. What can I say? It was our first outing as film makers. The production was simply bland and boring. Much of the film looked like a seventy's sitcom or even a blander daytime soap opera. My performance was supposed to be a sympathetic man in pain, but I played him to be more creepy more than hurting. My whole life was loss. I lost my bride, I lost my business, and I've lost almost all my friends. My scandalous divorce cost me more than I could have imagined.

I was the one who walked out the door, However, my wife had left me years ago. She could no longer stomach her discontent. She could not love me and maybe she was right? Baby Mama had been having an affair with her lover for a few years. I walked out thinking that my absence would cause her to end their relationship. I did not feel my friends and family really needed to brand her with a Scarlett letter. As a result, I never explained why I walked out, and it only looked like I was the villain. In many ways I suppose I was the villain, but doesn't the villain always become the victim eventually? All my friends could see was a man walking out on a woman with two children. I thought I was creating a void, a need, and maybe a desire to save us. What I really did was get out of her way! Her relationship with The Doughboy Draftsman only blossomed. His wife was seemingly naïve about their relationship. A roundabout love triangle ensued.

Baby Mama was a predator on the prowl to their relationship. She played her hand well and eventually would win. Doughboy's wife was aware of the affair because I had told her, but the three of them became close friends. As with every threesome, it got crowded. Eventually the wife was kicked out of the click. Funny how writing about these events so many years later make me relive everything. Stirs emotions that I thought had long ago been laid to rest.

Yeah, I knew significant loss and was about to know more.

A few more texts between Mel and I continued.

She was becoming more confident that the bad news concerned Kristen. I was holding out hope but feeling the panic seep into my bones. In many of our talks, Kristen was unsure if she wanted to leave her husband. I hate divorce. I encouraged her that she did not need consent to stay. She could walk away whenever she felt it was time, but for now, I encouraged her not to leave George if she was not ready. I tried to be love's ambassador. I tried to be the friend that helped her find peace of mind. Relationships are hard, but worth fighting for. This would prove to be one of my greatest regrets.

Kristen had started dating this guy Tim. She admitted to me that he was mostly a distraction and just an avenue for fun, but she was with him. This complicated matters because her friends were encouraging her to leave her husband. In the early morning I was hearing her heart and trying to offer support. I didn't realize she was sleeping with the enemy. I continued to be an advocate for the marriage. She was uncertain about her choices, and I didn't want her to think she needed to be rash. She didn't need to be at the end of the line until she was sure and ready if ever.

As I finished my application, the deathblow punch came from my friend Mel. Kristen was dead! It felt like a hole was blown into my chest. A new wound that I didn't want to talk about. The first stage of grief kicked in, denial. Something was wrong with the information. There was simply no way my friend was dead. Her husband had strangled her early Saturday morning. It was now Wednesday. I tried to wrap my head around this new truth. Kristen had been dead for five days? Her husband made a

Facebook post for her that read, "Stupid me, I dropped my phone in the toilet. I am such a klutz." I sunk into my chair. Another truth revealed itself, and it was ugly. George was pretending to be Kristen on social media.

(In writing this book, I have had to revisit this day many times. First, the initial night I wrote these words. A few more times as I corrected my sloppy grammar. When I was trying to tighten the story and make sure the pace never was boring. Passing the chapter back and forth to my editor, the amazing Brianna. Every single time I am here, I see myself in a fast running river. I am holding my heart high above my head as the current tries to wash me away. I imagine the vision, image, or whatever that is called is self-evident. Then I put the story away for a while and pretend I didn't live this part. My composure comes back, but it takes a hot minute.)

When I thought I was talking to a despondent version of my friend, it was really George. He hacked her Facebook and was impersonating her. Right away Kristen's family knew something was wrong. I was the clueless one. I was too drunk to understand or piece anything together. He was the one inviting me over at 3 AM. What was he planning? George murdered my friend, and her body lay in their room for fucking 5 days. Kristen had become an international headline. He posed as his wife on Facebook. At least her behavior now made sense. Worst of all, it was my advice that got her killed. I felt responsible for her death, and I was not about to tell anyone. Kristen was dead, and my advice helped get her this way! At least this was my feeling. Why didn't I tell her to get the fuck out of that marriage? I returned to the paperwork with a numbness (in writing, I always take another break).

A few years earlier, I was having one of those late night "What if" conversation with a friend named Jenna. I was in Fort Lauderdale spending the night with friends of hers. We were playfully questioning what our boundaries were. The subject of murder arose.

"Do you think I could kill a person?" I asked. I had about half a fifth of bourbon making me brave.

Jenna at this point was one of my best friends. She paused and looked at me. I returned the glance and our eyes locked. Her demeanor changed. She was more serious.

"I know you could," she said plainly.

Her answer surprised me. I like to think of myself as a loving person. I know as a drunk I am prone to unpredictability - but kill a person? The conversation haunted me for days. I don't think I could kill a human being. I don't hunt or fish. Killing just isn't in my rolodex.

Now, George was a killer. In that moment I sat still and became quiet. An eye for an eye, I think I could have killed George in that moment. I couldn't kill him today, but there was a window. I needed to return to the application.

The next phase after faxing the application is a phone interview. I was expecting a call on a certain day, and it never came. Saint Matthew's House has a saying that is a huge part of their culture, "Everything is subject to change." Translated it means, never really hold the leadership accountable. I kept my phone with me 24/7. I missed one call because I was in the motion picture show with my beautiful offspring. I missed another call because of a nap. I was able to talk to Joel on a Friday afternoon. I hadn't met Joel when I was in Naples. I had no idea what to expect from him. I suspected he would be a lot like Joe K., but he was very much the opposite.

I was lying in bed trying to calm my mind when the phone rang. Yes, I had been drinking, but I made sure I paced myself. I was skirmish when I said, "Hello." Joel's voice was jovial and uplifting. He immediately began speaking as if we had met a dozen or so times. I felt instantly comfortable with him. We made some small talk and even shared a few laughs. Things were going well, but the elephant on the call was my acceptance into the program. We kept talking, we kept laughing, and there was no talk of admission. I became a little antsy.

"So, what are you needing to ask me?" I asked very carefully. My slow parade of fear and anxiety felt like marching feet stomping on every nerve in my body.

He started laughing or maybe more of a giggle. Joel's reply was a simple relief, "You drove down here from Orlando. That is all I need from you. You start the program at the beginning of February." It was all that simple. Joel continued to crack up. It was as if he was all too aware of my stress. Then he delighted in easing my mind. We talked for several more minutes. I sat up in my bed after I placed my phone down, my skin on fire and sight blurry. Shit just got real! I was in!

Just like that, I was going to be a resident of Justin's Place. I was thrilled and scared. I asked all kinds of questions. I wasn't sure if we wore scrubs (some rehabs make that the attire) or uniforms of any type. It was liberating to learn I just bring my own clothes. Make sure I had an outfit for church is all he emphasized. I had all the concerns and Joel just laughed and assured me I was making everything way too complicated. Now and then there is a light in the darkness. I was lying in a bed of broken pieces of self, and Joel's demeanor shined on me. I had another glimpse of hope. All these years later, Joel and I share on social media often.

The night we all discovered that we lost Kristen, everyone met at Cheers (a local bar and hang out) to celebrate her. Cheers had always been the popular hangout for our group, and she had spent many nights there. The place was fitting. Michael drove me, and we took seats in the back. It was not and is not my custom to go out drinking. I am an isolated drinker. The shots provided by a local pub only piss me off. My shots at home were from a bottle. Normal people who drink with rationale and responsibly can get drunk easily. I needed a head start and often drank in my car before going out with friends. I always wore cargo shorts filling the pockets with quarter pints of bourbon.

I truly had no idea that people knew of my relationship with Kristen. Sure, we were friends, but we had a bond. A connection that I always thought was private. At work we would talk whenever we found a private place of solitude, but we were never flamboyant about our relationship. Yet, many of my co-workers, a group that truly reflected family came over to console me. Many of them acknowledging that they knew we were thick as thieves.

We took our seats. Breathing felt like screaming. Once Tiffany locked eyes on me, she walked over and sat in my lap and there she stayed for the remainder of the night. With her big blue eyes resembling a Margaret Keane portrait, Tiffany looked right into my soul. I have never loved a person the way I do Tiffany; she was in my arms and on my lap, and she was keeping me strong. Michael was comfortable and relaxed among all these strangers and the world he did not know. It was his final night before flying back to San Diego.

"I know how close you were with her," and with that declaration Tiffany whispered as if she was protecting a secret. She hasn't left my side since. She is a friend that I value and adore sharing my life with. Simply stated, she is a breath-taking beauty, and yet that is shadowed by her heart and devotion. She reminds me of a line from the motion picture *28 Days*, "Don't be someone's slogan because you are poetry." If Picasso, van Gogh, da Vinci and all the great painters would have paid tribute to Tiffany. She is just an inspiring person and that is just with a smile. I am a writer, so I try and honor her with words. She is feisty and very protective of her friends. Her love was real, raw, present, and most of all genuine. A few times I looked at her and wondered. What would she think had she known my advice may have contributed to Kristen's death? My guilt and shame had demoralized me.

I kept my truth a secret. The problem with secrets

is that we keep them with the devil. Demons torment us as they twist the truths and turn them into accusations. I cannot overstate my dreadful regret at my own advice.

I was one confession away from being the most hated man in that bar. Give me something to stop feeling is all I could think. Cue the Rob Thomas song, "This is How a Heart Breaks." I glanced over a few times to see Kristen's boyfriend Tim starring at his drink. He looked as if rigor mortis had set in. There was no doubt Tim had fallen in love with Kristen. I could not blame him for that. A penny for his thoughts while he looked like the weight of the world was on his shoulders. Tim was clearly drinking enough to drown. I could relate to that remedy. I never did speak to Tim. I did not offer him any comfort or condolences. I don't know why I refrained, but I did. I look back and I think maybe I was being territorial with my grief.

Everything with Saint Matthew's House was coming together. Yet, no miracle could save us from this loss. Clearly the river of hope was still mostly a drought, and our savior had left town. My mind's eye kept seeing her struggle. Wondering about the final hours of her life. Was it a fight that went wrong? Was this injustice the result of her husband snapping? Did he know about Tim? Maybe he had planned on killing her for a while. The questions were emotionally crippling. My only certainty is I encouraged her not to leave the monster. The weight that we carry is worse when we are older.

Now I was two weeks away from entering rehab. I had already stopped working, and I was broke. No money for booze, or food. Michael would leave the following day, reintroducing me to my isolation. At the time we didn't know it, but he would come back. In fact, it was Michael that would drive and drop me off at Saint Matthew's House.

Coupled with making this choice came lot of fear. Fear of the unknown really is a big thing. My prayer kept being, "God please hide the cost from me." This prayer has served me well over the years. I needed to back myself in a corner. I needed to shut the doors that would allow me to walk away. To hold myself accountable, I started announcing my destination and plans. I told the world of my problem (Not that people didn't know. Everyone knew.) I didn't want to be a loser at recovery. Facebook updates started going out daily. I can be a great fighter and a great escape artist. In counseling they call this "Fight or flight," and I was proficient at both. Meanwhile, there was the looming funeral of Kristin. I could never show my face there, not with my secret and its magnitude!

Every day I would say a silent prayer. I studied her family on Facebook. Visiting all the profiles related to her that were not private.

"Reading your posts, you are going to make a lady a very lucky woman on day," I replayed Kristen's words a lot. Those words replayed in my head over and over. Even now I can replay that conversation in my mind's eye perfectly.

One day, we were standing in the kitchen of our job. I looked over at her. She was looking spectacular in all her splendor. She was wearing khaki pants, a safari shirt and a fanny pack. Our uniform at our themed restaurant. Silently I lean into her, "You really are beautiful" I shared. She looked down, but her grin was huge. Mission accomplished; I wanted her to feel the adoration we all have for her.

"You should see my sisters," she countered modestly. "They are the real beauties of the family." Just the way she answered, it can't be done justice with words.

"I am sure they are, but to me it's you Kristen." I knew Kristen's heart, pain, and struggle. The intimacy from all our talks. I gently rebuked the notion that the sisters had anything on her.

At the bar Tom Petty was blaring and I couldn't tell you what song it was. The night was ending.

Yanet walked in. For such a striking woman, she has great humility, Real humility. She makes an entrance without being haughty. She has that rare confidence that never diminishes others or makes us feel inferior. I called her my Ethiopian princess. I walk over to her. She is upset with me for isolating and makes it known. Might I also mention she does not hide her thoughts or disappointments.

"Why do you never allow people to be there for you?" She demanded in her Ethiopian tone of disproval. Her English is not broken and her words very distinct. I point to Michael.

"See that guy. His name is Michael and he is being here for me. That is his job. He looks after me and helps chase the blues away," I counter. I really need my clever little remarks and smile to work right now.

She looks over at Michael and then back at me. Was she unimpressed with him or agitated with me? It was the latter by far.

She was not at all pleased with my explanation. Bingo! Michael is safe, and I draw the short straw. "So, the rest of us don't get to know you, be there for you? Who are you Marc"? Her tone was a little angrier. I needed a healthy dose of wit, humor, and charm to keep this conversation from going south.

"Well right now I just want to be the best damn poet you have ever known." She most likely thought I was just being cute, but it was the truth. I always had the biggest crush on Yanet. She always wanted to reach out to me at my worst, but I wanted to project a better image. As a result, I did keep her at arm's length. I truly hoped she would fall in love with my writing, but she isn't really a reader. And, that folks, will make great lyrics for an Alanis Morrissette (or whomever is the great angry lyricist of the time) song. You are welcome! I really don't know how to manage a woman I can't seduce with words.

I never cared too much for a reprimand. This was Yanet; I would stand for about 20 minutes. I always knew she cared, so it wasn't painful. In fact, her concern was rather inviting. She is the type of woman who shares her strength when she speaks. She naturally shares faith, love, and hope, and she can reach my soul. She is a perfect mother and I imagine a valiant companion.

"Marry me."

"Be serious," she demanded.

How could she think I was not serious; this was hardly the first time I proposed to her? At least twice a month I talked to her about being married.

"You need to just say yes."

She shot me her stoic eyes.

"You have ruined me for white women. You can't make me face this world alone."

She never broke her stare, but her face did soften. Was I making progress? Was her armor coming off or was she bored? I had no idea.

Michael pulled me away from the conversation. It was time to get him home. He had a flight back to San Diego the following day.

Outside of Cheers, everyone stood under the stars looking up and toasting to Kristen. We were all in some form of embrace; many were more than a little drunk. Surprisingly I was dry as a bone. I could feel her lingering in the air, or at least our love for her. One day I will search for her on the other side. However, tonight I know she knows what Paradise is like. In the meantime, I will hunt for some sort of peace. I will wonder how to carry my secret. Goodbye Kristen. I would never allow her to be a part of my past. She is a part of my future on that fateful day I graduate from this life.

We got into the car. Michael paused and looked at me. His were eyes full of understanding and compassion. That damn calm demeanor that he has perfected over the years. How does one acquire such inner peace and resolve?

"I got to hand it to you. If ever there was a reason to drink, tonight was it and you didn't. I'm proud of you." Ah proud of me, never a good thing.

"Don't be proud of me, because then you will have to be disappointed."

A guilty king wears a broken crown. I knew if I had one drink, I would sink like a stone. I would wait for Michael to leave before I drank again and that would be as soon as he left for San Diego.

Cue the Taylor Swift song featuring Bon Iver, "Exile." I felt dead inside. I felt remorse. I felt alone. Why was Kristen's husband pretending to be her and talking to me? Why was he inviting me over? Did he want to hurt me? Did he want to talk as he claimed? The questions were swirling in my head. Questions without answers feels a lot like chasing shadows. Since I am a creative type, I kept playing out the scenario of her murder. How did he do it? What went wrong? Was it premeditated? None of these answers would bring her back.

Do not think I wasn't thinking about my beautiful offspring. I thought of them every day. In fact, I was scared to death what they would think of me as a coward, a disappointment, a failed man. Just another self-inflicted worry to trouble me when the night falls dark, and I am by myself.

CHAPTER 7

"Surrender is deeply misunderstood as an act of weakness. Surrender is the bravest and most lucid thing a human ever does." ~ Andrew Harvey

"Cannabis, alcohol, Nicotine, caffeine isn't a gateway drug, trauma is." ~Russell Brand

"I got a couple winks between nightmares." ~ Harry Monroe (Richard Pryor) from *Stir Crazy*

Do they know I don't

like confinement?

A Jolly Orange Giant.

Michael was gone. I had about two weeks before I went into the Justin's Place program. It was a long and lonely process. I spent most of my time thinking about Kristen. I drank a lot, but now it was only the 7-11 wine.

The house wasn't haunted, but I sure as hell was. I had been through so many changes and limitless reflecting that it was no wonder my only desire was to fill an empty grave. I had adapted well to my misery and the sanctuary of my mind. The pain was just agonizing, cruel, relentless and never wanted to subdue. I have always been so very self-aware, or so the professionals tell me. I no longer had to visit my hurts, or wrestle with why I wasn't good enough. Just stay drunk and resist an awakening. Now I was about to eject myself from this mindless state and into a deeper awareness. The Gift of Desperation is what they call it. When you have reached your rock bottom. Your epiphany is that you have no choice, but to reach out and seek help. There is one vital key to making this step work.

Don't worry about the next twenty years. Don't concern yourself with tomorrow. When I was making my first feature film, the was just more wreckage without any help from natural disasters. Public service announcement, hey kids, skip film school and just start making films. When push comes to shove, you will learn the hard way, but the education is invaluable.

"Just focus on the next thing you have to get done," dad told me. Wisdom of biblical proportion. Now, I just needed to do the next right thing. One very small step at a time. Because seeking sobriety was going to call for a lot of uncomfortable confrontations with myself, my own selfish desire and rage. Now, I just had to live through the remainder of January before I moved to

Naples. Overwhelming feelings of, stress, guilt, trauma and resentment are major players in an addict's need to escape. Take everything one day at a time. In some cases, we should take the journey minute by minute.

At night, I would wait for Kristen to message me, although the glow of my phone wasn't lighting up. I would look for her likes on my posts, but they were not coming. When her funeral came, I didn't dare go. How dare I show my face knowing that my advice contributed to her death? I felt like a coward. That afternoon I was too ashamed to go yet ashamed I didn't go; it was the ultimate rock and a hard place. The definitive damned if I do or damned if I don't. I had high energy fear, angry emotions, and nobody to reason with. At the same time, I was experiencing depression and shame, which are low energy emotions. It was like having my foot on the gas and the brake of a car at the same time. I was shaking and falling apart.

I would drink and wait. I was waiting for posts of the funeral from my friends. I knew there would be pictures. In every photo, I studied every face. What was I hoping to find? I had no idea.

The day before I was to leave for Naples, I had court. My charge was driving with a suspended driver's license. I spent the night in jail over that one. I am not made for jail! The food was disgusting! The people didn't harass me, but I was scared and uncomfortable. I have found that keeping to myself in these situations serves me well.

I had left my son's Christmas play. Apparently, I changed lanes incorrectly and a cop pulled me over. The blue flashing lights overpowered all my senses. I guess it was a slow crime night. After he approached my window, two other police cars showed up. With three cop cars and lights flashing, I knew the jig was up, but I really didn't know what was to come.

A friend of mine named Chase was with me. I absolutely hated going to events concerning my beautiful offspring. It just so happens that my children are extremely talented. So you can imagine there were always plays or some other function to attend. I would sit by myself feeling like the discarded leper. Baby Mama and her crew would inevitably take up a whole row of chairs or a pew. There sat Larry like the patriarch of the family. I call bullshit! Good, bad, or indifferent Larry was an absentee father. Teresa was the real patriarch!

I think I have established that I would not piss on Larry if he was on fire. Teresa is a vastly different story. She was thoroughly fucked over by her missionary man. Cue the Eurythmics song, "Missionary Man". Larry was out saving the world or so he thought, trying to mimic Billy Graham. His wife had no support at home. She had to play both roles for 2 boys and a daughter. I do think Teresa is too self-righteous for her own good, but she at least stood by her convictions. Larry abandoned his wife when she needed him the most. There are a lot of resentments toward Teresa from her offspring and Larry is to blame. He left his wife with a mess and he would return to be the Disney dad.

Chase stood next to me at the back of the tiny auditorium during Mac's Christmas play. Not bragging, but my mini-me had the lead. Before I would allow Chase to accompany me, I warned him that he might get a few stares from the southern Baptist crowd. Those Baptists have always been overly concerned with everyone's sin more than their own. Chase being gay, I was concerned. He did not give a shit! He stood by me at the play and it was nice to have a friend. With him there I felt accepted for the first time at one of those events. If by chance that anyone thought we were lovers, that was fine with me. At least I had the best-looking man in the church standing next to me.

  I figured I had lost my driving privilege because of child support. I asked why, but the officer insisted I knew. I did not know! I just realized that the handcuffs were slapped on me and that shit hurt. Next, I was sitting in the back of a car on hard plastic seats. My hands behind me and the cuffs digging into my wrists. I was having a bad night. I tried to get answers from the officers, but it was clear that I was just another nothing man to them.

  The restraints were on well over an hour, but it seemed like a lifetime. I was a traffic offender, not a murderer or drug dealer. I wasn't even pulled over for a DUI, a fate that I avoided somehow over the years. This was not a violent crime. I did not resist my arrest or the unwelcome invitation to a steel barred vacation. Yet, I was being treated like Al Capone. If I thought that this was uncomfortable, the other side of the bars were even more so.

  "Book em' Dano," a saying made famous by jack Lord and the original television series Hawaii Five-O.

Processing and finger printing is by far more dehumanizing than drunken humiliation. They then take some beautiful portrait that will be uploaded to the World Wide Web within minutes. Showing the world all my degradation and misery. I turned over all my personal belongings, and I was glad that I didn't have any cash on me. The police station was known to just keep your money and refer to it as the cost of your stay. Who are the thieves here?

There was one man there who frightened me. His skin was the darkest black I had ever seen. He had dreadlocks, and it appeared that he had some reverse type of cross-eyed shit going on. I had to show a courage that I did not understand. He talked crazy and a lot. His demeanor was as violent as his stories. I simply kept to myself and prayed my silence would come across as some Clint Eastwood character. It must have worked because when he spoke to me, he was very polite. He was not polite when he spoke to other men, and this was not lost on me. You might think I was tough; I call it amazing grace. He was bragging of his conquest and crimes. He talked about being chased on a motorcycle and described the climax of being caught. He was proud. I had a front row seat to a criminal showboating.

After that, I was ushered into a holding cell. That only being allowed one phone call rule has went away if it ever really was real. Hell was brewing, and I was calling everyone I knew between the hours of 10PM and 12AM. Paul's phone was on silent and on the charger. I must have called him a dozen times. I tried my buddy Stuart who was already sound asleep. In true desperation, I reached out to

Baby mama, the most humiliating part of my night so far. It took me a few minutes to get up the nerve. I needed to tuck my tail between my legs and try. She never bothered to answer. Not that I expected her to come to my rescue. She was more accustomed to making sure I drowned as opposed to being a life preserver. You know shit is real when you lower your pride to call the ever-evasive ex-wife. I was not inclined to want to stay at these accommodations. There I was and no successful contact with the outside world. Nobody knew where I was, and I feared nobody would anytime soon.

Weeks later I would learn that Baby Mama and her husband drove past me that evening. Mac pointed out to them that something was wrong with dad. He was worried; she didn't give a shit. She didn't miss my calls; she avoided them. She would never allow an opportunity to make me feel small pass her by. Evidently, someone is keeping score.

Once inside the cell, I laid on the only available top bunk. For some reason, they left me in my street clothes, but most guys had to change into their jumpsuit. A dark blue jump suit with paper underwear. They take your shoelaces, which can be used as a weapon or to hang yourself. My street attire gave me a false hope that I would not be stuck in the big house long. Oh no, I got the jump suit early the next morning. I didn't understand the purpose of the paper underwear, but I didn't ask questions. Too many guys talked shit to the guards. This made absolutely no sense to me! I guess some men knew they weren't leaving regardless. Maybe they felt they had nothing to lose, or maybe they were still high. I had something to lose, and it was freedom!

Shit was real now that I was in my grey bar hotel, the joint, slammer! It felt so far from home. I might as well have been on the other side of the world. It is a powerless feeling. That clanking of doors being shut behind you is not promising.

The following morning, the guards had us up early, but I wasn't sleeping anyway. I was not even closing my eyes. They lined us up outside of the cell in a hallway. They push this tall food warmer into the hallway. One by one, they handed each of us a tray and we retreated to our bunks. Honestly, I have no idea what Orange County was serving us. The food was unrecognizable, and it smelled rotten. I drank the carton of milk, but everything was untouched. Farm animals were fed a higher quality of slop than I was seeing. I placed my tray at the foot of the bed. Across from me, another guy was eating like he was starving. I was grossed out. When he finished his tray, I offered him mine and once again he ate like a savage. I tried not to stare, but who would eat this and with such enthusiasm? Obviously, him.

Later, I was taken in front of a judge. Cue the Don Williams song, "Lord, I hope this day is good." A lifeless old prune-looking man walks out, he is tall, but almost lifeless. Is he my judge or father time? Where did they get this man? He looked like he had been dead for decades and they dug him up. This is supposed to be a moment of great hope for all of us locked up. We were hoping for favor, grace, mercy, and most importantly a get out of jail free card. I figured the honorable judge would release me on my own recognizance. I was not arrested for a violent crime or felony. Keeping me would be pointless and ridiculous. This is a no bond promise that I would appear in court. All I would need to do is sign a paper. But the judge didn't grant any such thing. What was this cob webbed geezer thinking? I was sent back to a cell and nobody knew where I was or so I thought.

Ok what is jail protocol? I know if someone puts a candy bar on my pillow not to eat it. Eating the offering makes me someone's bitch!

Both Paul and Stuart had seen the missed calls the following morning. They realized that at that late hour, something was wrong. Stuart did some investigating work and discovered I was locked up. Stuart is one of those people that knows how to navigate a computer and find things out. He began working on getting me out, but I had no idea. In the cell there was one pay phone. We could make a collect call. In the holding area, we could call directly, but now the rules had changed.

I waited for the phone, but the line was long. Some of the men just talked for what felt like was forever. My peers were hardly the courteous type. My chances of being able to get Paul on the phone was looking very grim. Then the guards came to get us and took us to another room. I can only assume this was the next step before we were assigned our more permanent vacation stay. In this room there was no phone, just a television showing reruns of Green Acres. I could see the show, but you couldn't hear it over the inmate chatter. I had no idea what to expect next, but I could not imagine it was good. Then unexpectedly, a guard called my name. I acknowledged I was Alfred, and he told me to come with him. I stepped out of the room and down the hall we walked.

"You weren't able to make a phone call," the guard said.

"How did you know?" I asked excitedly.

He never answered, but he was the first friendly face I had seen in almost 24 hours. I was taken back to the cell I had been in. Only now it was empty and waiting for the next bunch of men that would be coming up shortly. The hand of providence had given me the phone all to myself. I had no idea how long I had or what would happen next. I called Paul and frantically prayed he would answer. He did! It was about noon time.

After explaining my situation, Paul made sure I was able to make bail. Around 5PM I was still in the cell and staring at the clock. I could see out in the hallway that they were pushing the dinner cart towards us. Then another guard called for Alfred. I walked over, and he never really told me anything. He took me to a window where my belongings were given to me. The woman on the other side asked if I needed a bus pass. This is when I knew definitively, I was being set free. He pointed to a room with no door. "You can change in there," he said gruffly. These people were hardly skilled in courtesy, but they were giving me exactly what I wanted.

In that little room, my hands were trembling, and I was filled with emotions. I felt like William Wallace from the motion picture *Braveheart*, screaming "Freeeedoooom!"

I had been found! Paul came through. Although I knew he was in New Smyrna Beach. This meant that bus pass was going to be another saving grace. When I walked out of jail Stuart, was sitting in the waiting area. He may not believe in God, but that was the most angelic sight I had seen in a long time.

"You look like shit," he said with a laugh.

"You think?"

When Stuart dropped me off at home, I walked straight to the liquor store. I was sick of sitting around trying to figure out why my life was in ruins. I realized that some consequences were the result of being my own worst enemy. A realization that only makes things worse. I really had no fight left in me, and I didn't care anymore that my little world had fallen apart. Life sucked and was just getting deeper.

At home I nursed bourbon and thought about open wounds. I had a few calls with Michael. He asked me if it was a good idea for him to come back and spend a few days with me before rehab. I liked this idea a lot, but I also wanted to take Pink Floyd's advice and become comfortably numb. I still believed the lie that easing my pain would get me on my feet somehow.

Michael decided it would be best to fly back and take me to Naples. I suppose there was still a concern I might not go to the program. A reasonable set of worries because I was getting cold feet. I had no idea what to expect. I simply knew I was going into a blackout month. Each month is devoted to one of the 12 steps of recovery.

Justin's Place has three primary stages. The first is the Motivational track (also known as Blackout). This is when you are tucked away from the outside world. No mail, no TV, no phone calls, nothing. We have classes five days a week in the morning. Often in the afternoon, we have service projects. We might pick up garbage on property or go help a local church with their needs. These service projects are a good tool and exercise to help us get out of our own heads. An important step out of darkness is making our lives not all about us. Addicts are selfish. At lunch and dinner, we feed the homeless people. We do not eat until all the homeless have gone first. It is not uncommon to run out of food. The meals are prepared in a kitchen from a real chef and culinary staff. Vann is the CEO of Saint Matthew's House. His conviction demanded the ministry feed underprivileged people just as he would want Jesus served. I found that very honorable.

The second stage is Discovery. They move us about an hour North to LaBelle, Florida. This is an old country club across from a marina that thrived in the eighties, but the location had lost its clientele and charm. Saint Matthew's bought the place for a steal. It is still a working hotel on the second floor. Program residents live on the third floor. This facility has a gym, pool, canoeing, and other amenities. Discovery stage is five months long. After that, you are moved back to Naples for what is known as Transition.

The Transitional track is about helping you get on your feet and building an individual life with accountability. This is where you live in your own apartment with some roommates. You get a job. A lot of times those jobs are at their carwash or thrift store - both are ways the ministry raises money for the program. However, there is a hidden track that no one ever told me about called Stabilization. As I have said, my prayers about the program were, "God, hide the cost from me." I knew I would run from the program if I was overwhelmed. Had I known anything about Stabilization I would have run the other way.

Stabilization is when we first arrive. They have us sleeping on the kitchen floor of the homeless shelter. The idea is, "How bad do you want recovery?" They are looking for people who have the gift of desperation. You must keep in mind that some of the people who don't enter the program will die from their addiction. That is a harsh reality and it was a rude awakening over the next year. A lot of people who left early died. As a result, they want to save the few openings they have each month for the committed. If we are not willing to do anything for the recovery, we simply won't get better.

The bottom line is that homeless people are dirty, and they have bugs. No way I would have agreed to the homeless shelter! As it turned out, I was right where I was supposed to be.

Michael dropped me off at the office. I had three bags. One filled with a variety of books. Once again, it was Miss Dee and me. I was unfamiliar with everything and felt adrift. I wanted desperately to be anywhere but where I was. I didn't really like her manner, but I didn't like anything, and most of all I didn't like me. I watched the people come in and out of the office. Men mostly, but women and children too. Each person wearing a story on their face that I had yet to read. The smaller children really stuck out. They seemed too innocent to realize what they didn't have. I wondered what the children knew and how they felt. Of course, this made me think of my own beautiful offspring. If they could see this rock bottom their old man was living in.

I had mostly gone through my withdrawal at my apartment. Some drug withdrawals are mostly mental like cocaine, marijuana, and ecstasy. However, alcohol, opiates, and tranquilizers produce significant physical withdrawals. Most of these withdrawals are extremely uncomfortable. Alcohol is very dangerous, because you run the risk of seizures, heart attacks, strokes, and even hallucinations. I mostly experienced sweating, skin tingling, twitches, tremors, and the most violent shakes, nausea, insomnia, anxiety, and depression. All of this makes for a very irritable person. When I am detoxing, I always see things that are not there out of the corner of my eye. Do angels and demons really interact with us unseen? At times, I have wondered if by chance I am seeing into the spirit realm. After all, alcohol is called spirits.

The first stage of withdrawal lasts a few weeks on average. This is usually when I promise God and anyone that will listen that I will never drink again. All the symptoms are so violent. I can't even hold a cup to drink water. This is also called the post-acute stage. A war is going on inside your heart; the voices in your head demand a quick fix because that will cure the symptoms. Most cures take time, but a drink to an alcoholic stops all the withdrawal symptoms almost instantly. The entire nightmare is a rollercoaster ride. I have never known anything as intense as post-acute withdrawal. Death becomes a welcome escape. I understand why many addicts give up at this point.

Freedom only comes with time. I was paralyzed in my bed. When I got up and tried to walk, the dry heaving attacks would brutally throw me to the floor. I was alone during this horrible struggle, and it is full-time exhausting. My only comfort is binge-watching Netflix on my phone. I could lay still and not get sick. I needed water, but only tiny sips at a time. Too much at once and my body violently wants to vomit. I know it is cliché'- to say, but I was much too young to feel that damn old.

Once most of the withdrawal is over, weeks can pass before another symptom arises. For me, it is usually violent shakes like tremors after an earthquake. My body and motor skills are no longer my own. I am never sure when the whole ordeal will truly be over. An ambush predator that lives within my own body.

As I come out of a binge I am starving because I haven't eaten in weeks. No food tastes the same and I can only eat very small portions. After a few days of only water and Gatorade I can eat and keep the food down. Nothing tastes the same. I think of Hendrix, Joplin, Morrison and know greater people than me have succumb to this monster merry go round. Still, I vow to never drink again, but addiction is a sneaky beast.

The only real way I knew to break addiction's grip is to change every aspect of my life. This includes leaving old friends behind, but I was a lone closet drinker. I didn't have drinking buddies. I needed to change my mind and behavior more than my surroundings.

Addicts need to avoid high stress, where feelings, guilt, and shame are all triggers. If you know an addict be careful how you deal with them. It is easy to be the catalyst that drives them deeper into their abyss. I have always said that well intended friends and family often make the situation worse in their efforts to rescue. I understand the desperation of wanting to help because death is a reality. I know people who have died, and it is never easy. Wives become widows, and children become orphans. I have said a lot of heroin good-byes and seen more than a few alcohol-induced deaths.

Addiction is most often surrounded by lies. If an addict calls and asks for help, never say yes or no. Simply say let me think about it and get back to you. If they are open to that, then they are way more likely to be really wanting help. If they become cold and upset with you, then they are working some type of angle. Remember, maintaining a high and protecting yourself from withdrawals are powerful pulls for anyone. Never give them money! If you feel inclined to help, buy them groceries or pay their power bill, but cash is never a wise idea.

As I sat in the office of the homeless shelter I waited and waited. My mind thought of all the things I could do or ways I could escape. I was entering willingly. Some people were court ordered. I had no need to escape; I was still reluctant. My posts on Facebook directly made me feel stuck. I had set my sights on a new direction, but my mind was getting in the way. Facebook posts and declarations trapped me. Those posts gave me a sense of accountability. I had friends all over the country. I had many friends in North Carolina that I could spend a year with, in hiding. I thought and planned several scenarios, but I stayed. There would be no breaking out a bottle to forget again, or at least not soon.

Gabe walks in and gestures for me. He is a tall ginger man from Nebraska. This was during the height of Duck Dynasty's popularity, and everyone was growing beards. Gabe was no exception. All I know about his homeland is the album, Nebraska from Bruce Springsteen. It was his sixth studio record just before "Born in the USA" blew him up. Now I met the Jolly Orange Giant, I now know two things about Nebraska. I kept looking at this man in disbelief. He is so tall.

Gabe came from a good home and loving parents. His mother was a caretaker for his cousin who was sick from Leukemia. Gabe started experimenting with painkillers and slowly graduated to stronger substances. By his own admission, he would damage all his relationships and could not keep a job. He flew to Florida and turned his life around at Justin's Place. Now he was admitting me. He talks slow and deliberate. He thinks and pauses a lot. I was not initially sure if he was listening or just lost. He sat at the computer asking me questions. Then he would hunt and peck at the keyboard. Gabe was a fascinating character to me. I studied him, asked him questions in return, and wondered what kind of man he really was. More importantly was Gabe self-aware? One thing was certain - behind a desk and at a keyboard Gabe was out of his element. He looked as awkward as I felt uncomfortable.

I dragged my bags to a tiny office in the homeless shelter barracks. I was still absorbing my surroundings. I looked down the hall and saw the many rows of bunk beds. It appeared they could easily house about 60 men, but I wasn't sure. I wondered if they would assign me a bunk or if it was like riding a greyhound and I just pick one. I had no clue that this part of the building would never be my home. The homeless barracks were actually off limits to those of us in the program.

"What are you hoping to accomplish here? What are your goals?" Gabe asked me slowly. His eyes wandered and seldom locked on me. I wondered if he was having trouble threading his thoughts together. I made mental comparisons to the motion picture *The Absent-Minded Professor*.

"Easy up on the Whiskey. Get right with Jesus. I am not so much here to get sober as much as I need faith. I believe in God, but I don't trust Him. I think I have more faith in Heaven," I explained.

Gabe did appear to listen, and this impressed me. When Gabe spoke, his eyes were everywhere, but when I answered his questions, he looked mostly directly at me. He wasn't at all dismissive.

He is young. I guessed he was on drugs because he was too young to drink. Young men are the absolute stupidest of the human species. Their egos outweigh their brains. Common sense is usually just loose change in a pocket. I was as stupid in my twenties as these guys will surely be. I made up my mind. I am here for sobriety not a life coach. My journey was about to require a lot of patients and faith.

We got up to take my bags to a locker. I was confused that we headed to another building. Much to my surprise, there was a locker in the outside cafeteria dining area. A screened in enclosure that was Africa hot. There were about 6 overhead fans that moved slow and made little difference. There were several long economy A-frame picnic tables decorated with graffiti and carvings. Each table had its own coffee can ashtray. This was strange to me. I thought we weren't allowed to smoke. Again, I didn't realize this wasn't the Justin's Place program. I was at the homeless shelter. This area had a different set of rules and guidelines. I asked where I would be sleeping.

"The Justin's Place guys sleep on the kitchen floor until they are ready for you at the firehouse."

Did this dumb ass really just say I was sleeping on the homeless shelter's kitchen floor?

I had just stopped drinking, so I was sure I misheard the Jolly Orange Giant. I had heard rumors of alcohol causing wet brain. Maybe Gabe had some drug related brain damage. I don't even think he realized he said I would be sleeping on a homeless shelter's kitchen floor. I guess I was just going to have to wait and see where I was supposed to slumber. Maybe Gabe was stupid, maybe he was hard of hearing, maybe he thought I was hungry? After all he did just say the kitchen!

I called this screened in enclosure a patio, but

everyone else called it a veranda. Interesting I thought. Is there a difference between a patio and a veranda? Who says veranda? Well, apparently the homeless guys and Gabe, the monotone orange giant.

"Okay let's go take your drug test," Gabe says next. This confirmed all my suspicions that the Jolly Orange Giant is stupid. I thought I made it clear I am an alcoholic. A drug test? I emphasized once more my drug of choice is dirty water. You know the kind made from fifty-one percent corn. Not to mention this is rehab, wasn't everyone expected to fail their drug tests? Were they trying to make sure no sober people were sneaking in to enjoy the Kitchen floor accommodations? I say that jokingly, but sure enough when the weather would get cold, homeless men entered the program just to stay dry and warm.

It is amazing how people get trapped in a mindset and can't break free. On occasion I would witness men take a homey bath in a restroom. A homey bath is when they basically wash from the bathroom sink. They strip down to their undies and wash. In LaBelle, we had our own bathrooms in our room, but homie baths were still common.

As we walked to another office where I would take a drug test, we saw a young man. He was sitting at a picnic table. His mother was dropping him off and crying. The young man could not even hold his head up. His eyes looked lifeless and still, like the dark eyes of a great white shark. His behavior was alarming. I wasn't sure the man even knew where he was. I didn't mind staring; he had no idea where he was much less what was happening around him.

"What is wrong with him?" I asked the Jolly Orange Giant.

"I don't know man," Gabe replied in his mellow way. I was horrified, but to Gabe this had little effect.

It alarmed me that Gabe wasn't fazed at all about this young man's manners. His hair is a thick black, and he had Pokémon' tattoos all over his arms. Silently I prayed that this man would leave and not be a part of my program. I was unsettled. I knew and continue to know almost nothing about drugs. It is not that I am not a drug addict; it is just that I have never been exposed to them. I'm sure if I was from Nebraska, I would be a junkie too. My brother knows drugs and those demons, but I am clueless.

As fate would have it, in just a few weeks Gabe would refer to Anthony as my son. That deflated man became one of my best friends. Going through the program he would almost be kicked out a dozen times. He would preach rebellion almost every morning. Still, along the way he would become one hell of a man! But that day he was creepy and freaking me out!

I had stopped drinking days before entering the program because I was afraid, they might reject me. Anthony on the other hand was shooting up one last time in the parking lot before he entered. Anthony was committed.

CHAPTER 8

"We must live together as brothers or perish together as fools." ~ **Martin Luther King Jr.**

"He ain't heavy, he's my brother." ~ **The Hollies**

Meeting a cast of characters.

The men who helped push

back the dark.

Slowly I began to meet the men that would be known as my mod brothers. A new group begins every 28 days and is known as a mod. Mods have distinctive personalities. A group of men that will love, fight, and grow together. We become brothers and the bond becomes deep and, in many cases, lifelong.

IF ROCK BOTTOM HAD A BASEMENT

My first friend was Tim. Unbeknownst to me, Tim thought I was gay. He had a hard time believing I was a straight guy, but I get that a lot. I am not the kind of man that likes beer, sports or even has an affinity for cars. I like living my life on my own terms. My father was a Green Beret and most men just can't intimidate me. I have no need or desire to act tough, and I do like musicals. I suppose this common misconception makes sense.

Tim is primarily an alcoholic. He had been homeless and begging for change outside of a Dunkin Donuts. One of the women he approached had a son that had been a part of the Saint Matthew's program. She had a heart for Tim and introduced him to the ministry. Tim immediately moved into the homeless shelter awaiting an opening into Justin's Place. The wait for acceptance into the program can be long. A time or two Tim lost a battle with his common sense and headed into the woods, where he would reside with his affordable liquor. At the shelter, it is easy to find day labor jobs. For Tim this meant money to drink.

Tim is a tall and very attractive man. His shoulders are usually slumped over, and his whole head looks down on you. He has a beard that he wears as both a mask and a crowning achievement. He always wore a cap like the kids wear. The bill was never in front or behind his head, but awkwardly shooting from the side. To me this look is ridiculous, but the kids think it is groovy. Tim's Dunkin Donut encounter led him to the shelter. A random encounter and a sweet lady took a chance and invested in Tim's future and life. This program is very responsive to people who walk in looking for help. Humility and being teachable are highly regarded by leadership.

Nojo's real name is Michael, but he doesn't respond to that. This man knows everything about everything, and because of this, he was a leader from the start. His intelligence made it difficult for him to be a follower. He questioned authority constantly. His battle between brilliance and frustration could be very entertaining at times. He had a history of homelessness and relapses. He also had periods of great success. He is book smart and can work with his hands. I am not sure how he attained so much knowledge, but over a short period of time you learn to trust it.

"I have been in a lot of homeless shelters, and this is by far the nicest one. This is by far the Ritz Carlton of shelters. However, if you see little red splats on the floor, that means they have a bed bug infestation," Nojo explained to me. Up until this point, I thought bed bugs were just a silly saying from a child's bedtime prayer. Hell, to the no, these things are real! Little reddish-brown bugs that feed on human and animal blood. I have never seen one but am told they are the size of an apple seed. Nojo had a knack for explaining things. He acted as a sort of mismatched tour guide. I didn't know what to think of him at first, and he became one of my all-time best friends. Nojo is the man I go to when I can't make heads or tails out of life. When my stupidity clouds my mind Nojo can always calibrate my thoughts.

Saint Matthew's was born out of love, but not experience. This has proved to be both a challenge and a victory for the ministry. At one point, they had a problem with these little critters. Considering they house and rehabilitate people from the streets, and woods bugs are to be expected. They struggled for a long time to get rid of their infestation. After replacing furniture, and bedding and paying for different pest control services, they found their real solution on the internet. Apparently, cedar wood and cedar wood oil kill bed bugs and help drive them away. After initially losing their battle with an infestation, this was the miracle that the organization needed.

I knew I had maggots growing on me at one point, but really bed bugs. I am a sweet guy: these bugs would delight in feeding off me. Panic must have draped my face. Nojo laughed and then further explained more about the history. Nojo knew I was naive in this new culture and he enjoyed that.

"No, man these are homeless people. They get bed bugs. I must say they have done a good job here of keeping that epidemic under control." This stranger could be skeptical and even critical, but overall, he consistently praised Saint Matthew's House.

Nojo is an avid speed-reader. He can read a book in a matter of hours and be very articulate about it when finished. I am a slow reader, and sometimes my mind wonders and I need to re-read. Again, I was fascinated by this character. This man is great.

Nojo has dark eyes that had a lot of anger and compassion. Unlike most addicts, Nojo didn't have that wounded vulnerability of most. He seemed less ruled by emotion than most of us.

IF ROCK BOTTOM HAD A BASEMENT

There were a couple of Jackson county boys, Greg and Cory. Somewhere in Jackson county, Ohio, a judge had discovered Saint Matthew's House. Apparently, Jackson county is overthrown with boredom and drugs. This judge was sending people south by means of his gavel every opportunity he had. I would meet so many men from Jackson county that were court ordered to be in the program. The men that never returned to Jackson county had a great success rate with sobriety. The men who returned home returned to old surroundings, old friends, and old habits. All of them would have varying depths of relapses.

Greg and Cory didn't know each other in Ohio but formed a very tight bond in Naples. They talked about Jackson county with both affection and disdain, often romanticizing their drug use and relatable experiences. They fed off each other in every way. When one was having a hard day and wanted to leave, they both wanted to leave. When one was grateful for the program, they were both grateful. They became inseparable

Both men came from very broken homes. Cory's mother was in jail at the time. Greg wouldn't even talk to his mother or really talk about her.

Both had very thin frames, wore hats, and had great posture. Greg never seemed comfortable in his own skin. I suppose that was the case for all of us. We all shared our pain, and this was our bond.

Greg had been in a horrific accident and lost all his teeth. He carried himself in such a way that it was not easily discernable. I never would have known had Greg not told me. At times he couldn't chew the food we were served, and it was frustrating for him. Greg mostly kept to himself. He was social, but he was not someone who typically opened his soul. As a worker, he would give 100% and valued his performance. Also, like the rest of us, he sought out words of affirmation. I recognize this in Greg not as a criticism, but because words of affirmation make me feel loved and valued too.

Cory was angry! A true rebel without a cause. His story was hard for me to relate to. His entire family raised him to be an addict. His mother, sister, and brother all excelled in their drug use. He did not have a family tree; it was more like a family rap sheet. He learned from every adult in his childhood how to get high. I always wanted to meet his mother. Not because I thought she was a monster, but I felt it would help me know Cory deeper. Cory can be a lot of fun underneath all that rage, but it comes and goes quickly. One thing that was evident was that Cory idolized his older brother. I immediately knew this was not going to serve him well.

One of our first nights at the shelter, I walked outside. Cory was with some other guys; they were free styling rap beats. I was blown away at how gifted Cory is.

Please allow me to be clear that any manual labor I have done in my life has been done purely by mistake. I hate to work outdoors. The Florida heat is just crippling to me. You step outside and read the thermostat, and it just reads HELL. Even in the restaurant business, I get very grumpy when I must work outside. However, if you insist on eating outside, I don't mind dripping sweat on your food. There is not enough baby powder to make the heat tolerable. Summer months in Florida are miserable. Sadly, summer in Florida usually lasts eleven months.

Oppositely, Greg loved to be outside. When we got to LaBelle, he was a grounds keeper and loved his life. I never understood this about Greg, but it interested me. When he was working landscaping, I would watch him sometimes. He was always alone and so focused. His overseer was a douchebag named Adam. Adam is good for nothing other than maybe licking someone's nut sack. Adam never talked to us, he talked at us. Yet somehow, he had a way with Greg, and Greg adored his shit for brains boss!

I first noticed Jacob talking and laughing with Cory and Greg. They were sitting at one of the picnic tables on the veranda. I was mostly sitting alone writing letters to almost everyone I knew. I still had vision of walking away and hiding for a year. My anxiety about this new world program was through the roof. Every letter I wrote helped me make a deeper commitment to my decision. Just like my Facebook posts about rehab, I was trapping myself. I spent a lot of time people watching and wondering about their stories. The three were all around the same age. Pretty much everything they were talking about; I had never heard of. I felt like an old man when they shared interest in music and rap artists. Not one mention of Led Zeppelin, The Doors, Bob Seger, Michael Jackson, or music that mattered. I didn't judge them for doing drugs, but music was another matter.

Jacob was our frat boy. He came to us courtesy of

The University of Florida. Apparently, he partied too hard and was flunking out of college. Jacob craved being the center of attention. In the world of any addict, I suppose our egos are insane. He was just outgoing and needed connection and inclusion always. At times it was hard to trust him, because we weren't sure who he really was. He seemed to be a chameleon changing his colors consistently.

He is a savant when it comes to the guitar. He really knows how to make an instrument talk. When Jacob was relaxed, he was extremely easy going and likeable. When he was trying too hard to fit in, he became a pain in the ass. Jacob is good enough, but just like the rest of us feels lost too often. He has that handsome face that you would expect to see in a real estate agents ad.

The times I always enjoyed with Jacob were when it was just the two of us. He was calm then and not onstage.

Karl looks a lot like the actor Ryan Gosling. Those first days at the homeless shelter he would sit near the other guys, but never at the same table. He had an icy exterior but warmed up steadily. His drug of choice was heroin, and he never appeared to be suffering from rapid detox.

Karl became one of my dearest friends, but at first, I found him creepy. He reminded me of Boo Radley from To Kill a Mockingbird. He keeps to himself and pays attention to everything. A slow and gentle man with the sculpted body of a Greek God. He took particularly good care of himself and was always exercising. He was a truck driver that traveled the country. He may not be talking, but he participates in every conversation by listening intently. Karl also was an avid reader and he enjoyed talk radio. He wasn't one to talk just to hear his own voice. When he spoke, it was always profound.

Sadly, he was court-ordered to the program as was Cory. Karl was not done using, and he was very honest about it. He had a legal obligation, and then he wanted to return to his old life. In a lot of ways Karl was the most at peace of all of us. Since he wasn't really aiming at changing his behavior, he had nothing to prove. He always maintained a calm and reserved demeanor.

Cue the John Mellencamp song, "Rumbleseat." Karl died in early August of 2020. It was a Sunday morning when I received the message. I was at work. I became paralyzed in disbelief and simply walked up to the hostess. Gave her my open checks, asked her to give them to a co-worker in three minutes. She agreed and I walked out of the door. I went to a grocery store and bought some wine. I relapsed for six days. It was not about me that Karl was gone, but he is a part of my life. I mourned, got drunker than a monkey and felt sorry for everyone. Even now, I am not always the big boy I wish.

Brian was in his sixties and had been homeless most of his life. I think it was a role he had just settled into and accepted. He often had a tent in an area of the woods that was known as tent city. Yes, there is community among the homeless populaces. Never get it twisted - there is as much corruption among homeless people as there is in our government, including the existence of a hierarchical system. I suppose all of humanity has greed, prejudice, and a pecking order.

Brian's story was riveting too. One of his wives committed suicide right in front of him. When he talked about it, I could tell he carried that wound with him daily. He couldn't let it go. Because Brian was older, he resented taking orders from young guys. The older men always did struggle with this. It is true the young guys lacked a lot of good leadership skills. This is an area where Saint Matthew's needs improvement. The people placed in authority roles need training. After all, this is a ministry that literally has the fate of people's lives in their hands.

The remaining members of our mod would not arrive until Stabilization track was over. Rob, Rocky, and Sean all arrived shortly after we were in discovery track and were able to avoid the homeless shelter floor. Lucky bastards.

Justin's Place was wonderful in the fact that 98% (this is a pretty good guess) of the leadership had been through the program. The men that were asking you to obey rules once had to do the very same things. Even Vann, the CEO, had a problem with alcohol at one point in his life. Usually about 6 or 7 months into the program, you could go into transition or a peer mentor position. Unfortunately, there are some men who get placed in leadership roles that are cruel, uneducated, and simplistic bullies, as was the case with Adam.

All too often, once a resident became a peer mentor, they no longer focused on their own recovery. Often it was a means of privileges. Just because a lot of these men made rank rarely meant they should have. Andy was a man who used his peer mentor status to have sex with women in the Saint Matthew's vans. His head was always bowed, staring at the glow of his phone. How he managed to look up and even see a woman baffled me. The only things Andy modeled was dishonesty, indecisiveness, negativity, and a lot of messy bullshit. Oh, and he got laid in a van! How dare I forget his crowning achievement.

The moment leadership fails to be understood as serving others it becomes corrupted. The power would go straight to their heads. Even Anthony struggled with his leadership skills when he first became a peer mentor. The men hated him. Surprisingly, in time Anthony grew in his role.

Brian just couldn't submit to younger men. Gabe was 26 when he admitted me. I simply thought, if you are successful in sobriety then you are more experienced than I am in the way that matters. When I want financial advice, I seek out people who are good with money! When I want relationship advice, I seek out people who haven't been divorced more times than Elizabeth Taylor! When I needed direction in sobriety, I turned to kids younger than me! It wasn't my plan, but it worked.

You had a case manager during Blackout. This is the equivalent of one-on-one counseling and attention. A way of monitoring your progress. Every two months, you had a new case manager. This man asked you about your progress through the steps and, how you were feeling. Their role was one of guidance more so than emotion. It is a crazy dynamic, but it works.

The reason these case managers work is because they tended to be the sincerest of the staff with similar backgrounds. Dan was the only case manager I never fully trusted. He always said the right things, but he felt more rehearsed than anything to me. He talked like a used car salesman. I would hear a lot of rumors about him compromising the program, but I never saw anything firsthand. I was just careful with him. He talked a good game about God, and biblical principles and whatnot. According to Dan, God was first in everything. Everything except knocking his girlfriend up out of wedlock. To me this was just more compromised Christianity. Why did Dan's behavior bother me? I could care less that he was fucking this woman. What I hated was that this is the only man who chased people out of the food line for failing the breathalyzer. There were also stories about Dan smoking pot in the canoes of LaBelle.

Soon I would meet the debonair, Connor. This guy is a class act. I had seen him walking around LaBelle with his head down, avoiding eye contact mostly, but I knew nothing about him. My third month in, and Connor was my newest case manager. Connor wasn't even 25. The only thing we could discuss was puberty. Turns out that kid had a lot of wisdom when it came to recovery. He is also a beautiful man. He is witty, intelligent, well-read, and extremely talented. His major flaw is self-doubt, and this can provide him with a very short fuse. Youth and insecurity were Connor's big obstacles. He could be very socially awkward, and most guys feared or didn't trust him. I instantly fell in love with the guy.

Brian would leave the program in a fit of anger before the Blackout period was over. He was humble at times but carried a chip on his shoulder with every step he took. Brian taught me just how entitled we all are. He was a homeless man that felt the rules didn't or shouldn't apply to him. He was owed everything and grateful for nothing. I suppose we all are like that at times. Substances were more important to Brian than sanity.

We were in class on the day Sean walked in. The classroom we used was the second-floor open space about two blocks from the firehouse. Underneath us were some offices and a workshop where they refurbish furniture for the thrift store. We sat in roll-away chairs, usually in a circle. Sean entered in the middle of class. It was obvious he wanted nothing to do with the program or people. He wore his bitterness and anger loudly. He kept his gaze towards the ground and never looked at anyone. One arm was folded across his chest with his hand gripping a shoulder. His free hand was fidgety, but not in an annoying way. His obstinance was comical to me, but not in a mean-spirited way. We understood him and I knew he had no idea that we were already on his team.

Our Mod was very welcoming, but he remained closed off to us for a long while. The recovery that Sean was interested in was to save his marriage. He too had a love of heroin. He had been doing it almost his entire adult life. Now his wife and son were disgusted with him. He may have been the king at one point, but there was a break in his armor now. His crown had fallen off. He resented where he had ended up, but most of us felt that way. There was a lot of self-disdain and it wore off over time.

He is a chiropractor and became exceedingly popular throughout the program. Everyone in LaBelle would come to see him and this was a great way for us to meet residents after Discovery track.

What distinguished Sean from others was that he had been shot. There was a bullet hole scar below one of his shoulders. Of all the guys, Sean was the least likely to have a gunshot wound. His neighbor, a drug dealer owed Sean some money. Sean was on the man's property. In Florida there is a law known as Stand Your Ground. This law makes it legal to shoot a person if you have reason to believe your life or safety is in danger. The issue that arises is that a paranoid drug dealer always thinks their life is in jeopardy. Call it the nature of the business. Mild mannered Sean was gangsta; you gotta love it. Imagine if you will the father from "The Brady Bunch" being shot for a drug deal gone bad, this was Sean.

It took several days for Sean to come out of his shell. His great fear was losing his wife, and he felt time was not on his side. She was clearly all he was living for. They met in college, and they had been married his whole adult life. He was terrified to lose her. He was in a rush to leave the program to be with her. I think the problem was that he never allowed her the time she needed to heal. About a year after I left the program, Sean found me on social media. He is still with his wife. I have no idea what manner of dysfunction or success they are living, but that is the story of all our lives. Living as we do on the tightrope of sanity.

It was a Friday night and just starting to get dark

when Rocky arrived. He was coming straight from jail. He is from the small town of Everglades City. A 2013 census reported Everglades City's population to be 402. By 2016, the population had risen to 411. Unsurprisingly, everyone knew everyone's business including the police. They warned Rocky to get into a program or they would arrest him. Well, Rocky wasn't interested, and they locked him up in county jail for no real reason. The cop just had a heart for Rocky's wellbeing. Rocky is every bit your southern gentleman. He was clearly the toughest of us all and had a strong head on his shoulders. Rocky didn't get his strength from a gym, but from outdoor activities such as fishing and catching alligators. He was completely fearless outdoors, and I truly looked up to that part of him. I am not an outdoorsman. You won't see me walking around carrying a baby alligator, but Rocky would pick them up without a second thought.

What I love most about Rocky is that he has such a sweet nature. He even caught and cooked an alligator for the guys once. That kind of stuff thrills him. In fact, if I went to his Facebook page right now, there would be a new picture of him and some type of big fish. Although these days he is a father, so we just might see some proud daddy photos too. I know Rocky is great father because he always knew how and when to nurture us. He also wasn't a dude to take shit.

As for me, I hate the outdoors because I hate hot weather. Florida is nothing but hot weather. In month five they take the mod on a camping trip that is called Wild at Heart. It is an adventure inspired from the book by John Eldredge. I read the book the year my first beautiful offspring was born. Ultimately it helped inspire both Baby Mama and me to go to graduate school in Virginia Beach. Now the program used it to inspire a rendezvous in nature. I do not go camping. When nature calls, I ignore it. This was hard for the staff to understand - because the camping trip was mandatory. Everybody in the program had slept along the riverbank in the woods. I would be the first to decline the offer and this upset people. If I had wanted to sleep in the woods, I could easily have stayed drunk and become homeless eventually. I am sure I could find a vacancy in tent city. I was aiming for sobriety to protect me from losing everything, not to sleep outdoors amongst the snakes, alligators, and mosquitos. Who knows maybe even bed bugs enjoyed dining on campers?

The first time I heard about this camping trip I had been in the program three months. I walked over to Michael's room; he was our head intern. Head intern's hate to be bothered in their rooms. This is because they love to pretend to be exhausted from their acts of service. Nevertheless, I must call bullshit here. Mostly they prefer to hide from reality and responsibility there. In one head intern's case, he would just consume his every free time in pornography. When he could arrange it, he would have women meet him in the parking lot after the residents were put to bed. Our cravings will always find a way to manifest themselves.

I knew I was intruding on Michael's peace, and I would be unwelcome. I did not care. We needed to clear the air about this camping trip immediately. I explained to Michael that the program was hard enough. I simply do not go camping. Michael agreed that all would be fine. I was pleasantly surprised how quickly he dismissed my concerns and assured me all was right in the world. Michael moved on and there was a new sheriff in town, Zach.

I had been saying all along I would not go on the camping trip. Now I was assured that I would be going under the new leadership. Zach is Gabe's younger brother, and he too aspired to a leadership role. Zach was much more hands on and involved than Gabe. Gabe is lazier than his brother. At service projects it was not unlike Gabe to watch the progress from a seat or some other perch. Zach was the type to work and help alongside the residents. One day I asked for a private audience with Zach. He was the head intern at this point and someone I liked a lot. We sat at a table across from each other. I had a habit of joking around a lot. I needed him to hear me.

"So, here is the deal about the camping trip. Now please listen to me before you speak. I am not a person that sleeps outside with snakes and gators. I have every intention of finishing this program. I also don't want to be a little bitch. So here is the deal. It you continue to insist I go camping, that is fine. I will stay here until the day before we pack to leave, but on that day before camping my mother will come and get me. I am not going to make a fuss, but I am too old to run around in the woods. Please look around. There are cows and gators outside these windows, I am not camping!" I insisted.

I hated to pull the "I will leave card," but that was the fact of the matter. I think Zach finally saw just how serious I was, because he ultimately decided I could stay behind. My sister, Beth, has always called me a princess or Sheldon (from The Big Bang series), because I have my mother's eccentricities. I didn't earn the nickname princess by camping.

For few weeks before camping. I am sure everyone thought they would change my mind because they tried. My friend Rodney gave the most heartfelt effort. I felt bad assuring him that the wilderness was not my home. It just wasn't the way I wanted to spend a night or day. Oddly, if we were in northern states and it was winter, I would have gone, but I don't do hot weather, snakes, and gators. I consider the Hampton Inn and free continental breakfast to be perfect accommodations for my camping experiences. If you talk to me sweet, maybe you can convince me to stay in a motel of some sort.

Rob was the last to join our group. He was also the one who clung tightest to his denial. At first, he was simply an arrogant pain in the ass that tried everyone's patience. Rob has a will so strong it can almost defy gravity. That also happens to be his charm once you get to know him. He has an issue with Xanax but tried to convince us he only smoked weed. Also, since he came late it was harder for him to bond with the group. He was court ordered but was always threatening to leave. Being so abrasive, he struggled, but when he settled in, he became the most loving. He has a heart the size of California, but he also guards that heart like Fort Knox.

The best thing about Rob is that when he laughs it is electrifying. He grabs you and pulls you into whatever is funny just by his nature. As the group bonded, there were tons of inside jokes and personal traits that required teasing. Rob was immaculate and thoroughly organized with his stuff. A favorite prank was to move his belongings around. It never failed to ruffle his feathers.

Rob and Rocky would become best friends. They had the most unique bond. They also argued like an old married couple. Maybe it is more appropriate to say that these guys were our golden girls (a Sitcom in the late eighties for my younger readers.)

Every morning during breakfast, those two men would bicker about everything. I think they were only half joking. It was a restless banter that could last for hours before a resolve some days. The breakfast table almost always set the tone for the remainder of the day. If there was ever a quarrel, Anthony wanted to be in the center of it.

Antagonizing is life's foreplay for Anthony. Some days he would begin his menstrual cycle, and everyone was fair game for his wrath. He would want to pounce on someone's vulnerability and at times even try to physically fight. At this point, we knew that Anthony's wounds were simply flaring up. He became easy to dismiss when he was agitated. Not because he wasn't loved, but because we loved him. You learn that this too shall pass. People in rehab are on an emotional roller coaster from a world that was cracked. Their body chemistry is changing, and they are not fully physically free of some substances for three to four months.

One by one I fell in love with these men. A love I carry even now.

These days not all my times are good. I have a lot to celebrate, but I do get into that funk of desperation from time to time. When I need a little inspiration, I remember these men and the world in which we shared. They are cause for celebration and comfort, and I dream of our time together. These men have made a lot of empty hours possible to stand. At any given moment, we can be unsure if we are blessed or cursed. This is when it is best for me to call on my friends that are also my brothers.

CHAPTER 9

"To improve is to change, to be perfect is to change often." ~ Winston Churchill

"Love can change a person the way a parent can change a baby, awkwardly and often with a great deal of mess." ~ Lemony Snicket

These walls aren't because

of bulimia.

The Justin's Place men were not allowed in the men's shelter. We were kept separate from the homeless residents. This meant we had use of a very public restroom. It was the same restroom that the homeless people off the street would use. It was one single toilet, one urinal, one sink, and one shower. If you stayed at Saint

Matthew's House, you had to take a Breathalyzer every night. Sometimes you had to take a random drug test, but those rules didn't apply to the non-residents. As a result, when they paid their 3 dollars to use the restroom and shower, they often did their drugs. Sometimes they were reacting to the drugs they had already taken, but either way the result was a stench. There was always puke in the sink and often the floor or walls as well. Within a few hours, I made a vow to only pee behind the building and all other bodily functions would need to wait. Later I learned that Tim was sneaking off to The Home Depot across the street and using their restrooms. Why didn't I think of this? Better yet, why didn't he share this brilliant idea? We weren't permitted off property, but in the words of Saint Matthew's House, "everything is subject to change."

What I understand, it is the heroin that causes vomiting. The drug alters the body's functions, and before the euphoria can kick in, a person vomits. The ecstasy kicks in after they throw up. The body naturally tries to reject the poison. The smell in the bathrooms was an overpowering putrid odor. Welcome to this side of sober! The stench had me questioning this program. I still wasn't fully able to distinguish between the rehab and the homeless shelter.

During Stabilization we had chores. We would have chores or jobs throughout rehab, but these were particularly gruesome. Ed was this douche kind of guy that was working at the homeless shelter. He had a look of retired law enforcement. Close cut hair, narrowing eyes, closed mind, and broad shoulders that gave his shorter and puffy stature buoyancy. He repeatedly relapsed, and I have always said "You can't relapse if you are not trying." It was Ed's pride and attitude that disturbed me. He was just another down-and-out addict like the rest of us, but he acted superior. His behavior was exhausting. As of this writing he was kicked out of the program again for a relapse. I take no delight in that, but it does prove an observation of mine. Humility comes before healing. Anger, resentments, and pride are always the sure signs that a relapse has begun long before drugs or alcohol have come back into a person's life. Relapse is a process most of the time and rarely a knee jerk reaction. He enjoyed being rude to people as if he found joy in it. I did not agree with Ed's approach, but I was the new drunk in town.

Ed came in one evening on his high horse, cloaked in self-importance. He started barking orders from underneath his mix of chevron and walrus mustache. This disturbed me because he was speaking to broken people. I didn't think a little tenderness or kindness could hurt. Ed had the upper hand and the hairy upper lip. He knew he was king for the day. Ed was fond of replying to people with these words, "If you don't like it leave!" I do agree there are times you need to be tough with a strong-willed resident, but this was not the situation. I found his approach tacky. He walked up to me with his grimaced look.

"Clean the bathrooms," he barked, but it was softer. I suspected Ed knew I was uncomfortable, but not afraid.

"With the vomit?" I replied. I think I was equally stalling.

"Somebody has to do it." He said, and he had a point, but why did this fate fall on me? I wasn't even using these bathrooms. I wasn't brushing my teeth or showering, and I was relieving myself behind a building. I had to pause for a few minutes. I knew there would be days like these. I reminded myself one simple realization and a personal truth, God called me here. This was the answer to my prayer, "God help". My desire was to tell Ed to go eat a bag of dicks, but that would have to wait. I sucked it up and would clean the restroom. I found gloves and dressed myself as close to a hazmat suit as I could. I even had a version of my own surgical mask to protect me from the foul smell and bacteria. Honestly, every few minutes I would have to go outside to breathe. The vomit was overpowering.

I wasn't cleaning long before Gabe the Jolly Orange Giant called us to leave for church. Who knew that church would be my savior? I still had a strong hate of congregations after the lessons my ex father-in-law had taught me. Church is a place where we dress in Teflon. We wear our nonstick coating and put on our best version of false self. Then we are supposed to walk around smiling and calling strangers brother. My brothers come from my mama and daddy and some shared experiences. You are not my brother if we don't have much in common. Although created in 1938, the Teflon philosophy was adopted by the religious people who care little about being a better person and more about outward appearances. Country club Christianity sprinkled with good deed mission trips to decorate our ministry websites. None of this fakery was my idea of a relationship with God. And it sure as hell doesn't make you my brother.

IF ROCK BOTTOM HAD A BASEMENT

This is how Baby Mama grew up. Protection of appearances outweighed integrity. To get married in her church we had to take a premarital class. I agreed, because this was her church home and what choice did, I have? On the first day of the class, we were supposed to sign a contract that we would not have sex until after our marriage. There was one problem! Baby Mama and I were already doing the nasty bumpies, having coitus, relations, shagging, humping, and the bedroom rodeo wasn't going to stop soon. Even though, sexual intercourse was happening almost everywhere except a bedroom! We were reasoning that it was fine because we were getting married. I refused to sign the paper, but not Baby Mama. She not only signed the false contract, but insisted I do the same thing. She tried to pressure me, so I spoke up loudly in a room full of Baptists. I was fully prepared to announce our fucking to the whole class and call most other couples' liars. I surely wasn't the only one offering the hot beef injection.

"But we are already having sex," I spoke with a roar in the classroom. I am not hesitant to be obnoxious among the righteous. Who heard me? I don't know, but I was loud. Baby Mama's eyes almost rolled back into her head; she crouched quickly as if dodging bullets. It was hysterical to watch her, and I did laugh-out loud. She resented me, but she did shut up! For the rest of the class I fought laughing at her.

She married me knowing I would not deliberately be fake, but she also left me because I wouldn't conform. These days she has had two children and had two husbands, and I am sure she would sign that contract just as easily if it served her well. I don't know why she has to be fake all the time.

You might be tempted to judge me for judging. Just know we can judge actions. God only forbids us from judging a person. In other words, what we do does not define us, at least not in God's eyes. Remember I believe in God, but at this point in my life I just didn't trust him. Religion is certainly a poison. Dust off your bible, take it off the shelf on occasion. Wasn't Jesus always the rebel with a cause tied up in some sort of conflict? Every single clash was with the religious upright. In fact, Jesus never quarreled with us so called Pagans. Nope, the hostility was with the religious. Is religion the enemy? If not, it is at least under the leadership of the enemy. Now, I was going to church for the first time in years.

At church in Naples, we had to go to the bathroom in threes for accountability. We were forbidden from talking to any women and we all sat together in the middle back row. The church was New Life Community. It was a middle of the road kind of place. Not too conservative and not overly charismatic. There would be no speaking in tongues during the service. We were attending on a Wednesday night.

Anthony was coming down from his high but could still barely hold his head up. He was drowsy and in severe discomfort. I could see the clouded mental state and his eyes were either closed or wild wide open. I had no idea what a sensation of heroin is like or the ill effects of withdrawals, but he wore the example well. I felt bad for him, but still would have been more comfortable if he just took his crazy elsewhere. They wanted to send him to David Lawrence detox center, but he kept refusing. The center was a hospital facility that was more equipped to handle the severity of his withdrawals. He refused and they kept him.

I could not help but feel like we were on display on that back row. We sat there like brave soldiers or ambassadors for addiction recovery. Mostly elderly people came over to welcome us and say sweet words of encouragement. I had just enough Jesus to handle the humiliation. Still, the wrinkled people seemed so much more real and sincere than what I was accustomed to from church goers. It is always the older people who are most reluctant to throw stones.

The pastor was a towering man with towering convictions. He was courteous enough and spoke to each one of us. He had a death star grip with his handshake, and he looked you dead in the eye when speaking to you. Still he was in ministry, and I have been conditioned to not trust a man with a calling. Jesus had a job! Why do men in ministry think it is appropriate to beg for money? Should your church or ministry bless you in a pastoral role? Sure, but work somewhere else and be connected to the way the rest of us must live! Even our missionaries are lazy. If you want to be effective, go to another country with a skill. Learn a trade and help improve the quality of life for people. That is a ministry I can support. Now that is a good word and don't shout me down when I am preaching good!

Over on the left side of the church was the girl's

program. Unlike us, they got to sit up in the front rows. It was interesting to watch them interact. One young girl kept looking back at us; she was clearly putting herself on display. She would bend over chairs in front of her and then look back. Not that anyone was disappointed, she was attractive. She just tended to make some bad hair choices over her time in the program. One of those bad choices was fucking Andy in a Saint Matt's van.

When church was over, we were ushered back to the van and to the homeless shelter. First order of business was to stand in line for the Breathalyzer. For the next year, this would be the way I would end every day. I never drank at the homeless shelter, but without a blood sample, the method of testing our blood alcohol content from our breath seemed very unreliable to me. I didn't understand breathalyzers cannot be easily fooled. A popular television show called "MythBusters" tried several attempts to fool the machine, using mouthwash, onions and even pennies. None of these methods fooled the test. On occasion, I would see a few people kicked out of the program from some type of trickery to drink or do drugs. At first, these evictions were shocking, but they quickly became heartbreaking, because you get to know these men. Worse yet, they were more common than not.

It was about to be my first broken down night in this new environment. Everything felt so uncertain, and yet I was supposed to be better off. I felt like every face could read my insecure and unsettled thoughts. Maybe we all get a little worn down by life at times, but tonight I felt like I was the only one. I was alone, and I missed my best friend, whiskey! Worse yet, the women who discarded me were proved right, I had gone from hero to zero (maybe hero is over stating things a bit).

The hardest part was over. I entered the Saint Matthew's house. These crazy twists and turns of the night led me to some lockers. The guys were pulling out mats and picking their spots on the kitchen floor. Two men could lay next to each other between the tables. As I watched the guys place their mats on the floor, I thought, damn, the Jolly Orange Giant wasn't lying or delusional. I was about to sleep on the kitchen floor of a homeless shelter. Sometimes I pray, but that night the words had a new level of low and desperation. However, I wasn't drowning on my last sip from a bottle. I had been living in filth, so the kitchen floor should not have caused any concern.

The other dudes had sheets and pillows. While I just had a plastic bright blue mat. Nojo knew everything, so I asked him how I could find these same comforts. He was already tucked in and comfortable on the floor reading a novel by Lee Childs. The author's real name is James Grant, a British writer best known for his Jack Reacher novels. For some reason, my mod group loved Jack Reacher and resented Tom Cruise for playing the role in the motion pictures. I never read Lee Childs, so I never shared the resentments. As for Tom Cruise, he is as crazy as a sack of cats, but his films are often entertaining. I have heard rumors that Tom Cruise doesn't like John Travolta. In which case Tom can lick my ball sack! Is that crude enough? Should I take things further? Okay, we will get back to the floor.

IF ROCK BOTTOM HAD A BASEMENT

As I predicted, Nojo had all the answers- one thing about Nojo he was so comfortable and at ease about our circumstances. I was intrigued that the pain and struggle I felt Nojo didn't share. My friend had peace like legendary Jedi Master Obi-Wan Kenobi. He also had confidence that the rest of us just didn't share under the circumstances. Nojo was never afraid to confront the impotent leadership, and I loved that.

Nojo is also a speed reader. He can devour a book in a matter of days. It takes me weeks to read anything because I am such a slow reader. Just another fascinating fact about the guy.

I am a huge fan of Malcolm Gladwell and have studied all his books such as The Tipping Point and Outliers. He is a Canadian journalist and staff writer for The New Yorker. His writing is informative and fascinating. He is a non-fiction writer who specializes in social sciences. I took a few of his books with me to rehab.

One day we were sharing about books and authors we enjoyed. I offered Nojo Gladwell's Outliers to read. I was testing him and the claim he could speed read. True to form, Nojo finished the book in just two days. Now he had read something that took me a month to digest. I was familiar, and I began to talk with Nojo about some of the examples and stories shared in the book. Nojo never faltered in his understanding of the material. This man really did have a unique gift; he could read at the speed of sound and retain the information! How could I not envy that?

I walked back up to the front desk. I forget the

girl's name but, was something common like Christine. I gave her a background story. She was pretty, but never felt pretty enough. She didn't wear her wounds like most people. Her struggles must have had a history of being well hidden. She had bright blue eyes that were big and sensitive. Her hair cropped short, straight, and a shade of burgundy brown red from a box. She was appropriate enough for customer service I felt. It was unsettling that she was seeing me at my worst. Yet, if she was working at the program, she clearly had a past of bad days too. I asked for my bedding, and she handed me a bunched-up bundle of sheets, a blanket, and pillow. I took them and was rudely reminded I wasn't at The Hyatt. As I walked away, I smelled the bundle and reasoned (and madly hoped) the sheets were clean.

Cue the U2 song, "Kite." Lights were off by 11. I lay on the floor next to a big industrial size refrigerator that made a loud sound about every 45 minutes. It was hard to sleep that first night. I tried to forget I was on the floor, but I could not escape this reality. Once I was the life of the party, now I only felt insignificant. My whole body ached. What had my life become? It was February 1st. I thought of the Christmas present Baby Mama's husband had given her, a Mercedes SUV. I know I am not supposed to be comparing myself to anyone else. She and her husband were living the dream, and I was flat on my back living out my Hell. Yes, she fucked her way into a life stollen from another wife. Yes, I consider success without integrity to be failure, but I couldn't argue her results. I wasn't afraid to die, but I was afraid to live.

As I tried to think good thoughts, I heard some

peculiar noises. I got the feeling like I was in a horror film. What creature lurked in the shadows? I listened intently to some erratic patter sound that was traveling. I started to suspect that I was hearing rats or maybe even roaches. The sounds would grow louder and fainter as something was clearly among us and it was alive. Soon, the obscenities started as a few of the guys saw the rats. The claim was the rats were huge and comparable to cats in size, but I trusted that to be an exaggeration. Again, I laid there and just thought to myself, "I believe this is where God wants me." That was how I learned to handle crises like rats, bullshit, Ed, or just being uncomfortable. I looked around and I was already tired of the view. There were people around, but I felt lonely. I reminded myself that I was sick of sorrow and that is why I was sleeping on that floor.

The fluorescent lights started screaming just before 5 AM. I had thought sunlight was rude. As the kitchen crew came in to begin preparations for their day, they had little sympathy for the floor dwellers. I wondered if all the banging was deliberate. His name was Bobby, and he had one of those hard personalities. Sympathy did not shine through him and that amazed me, because he had worked the program. His addiction had led him into jail a few times. He hadn't had a driver's license for years. He knew the darkness of being lost, but now lacked compassion. Those were the men I expected to have a heart, but many times they just didn't. Men like Bobby are known as dry drunks. They stop working their recovery, and bitterness takes root. Maybe their style was too strange for me. I just felt like they took their grace for granted. Months later, I met one of Bobby's ex-wives. She made it clear that being an asshole just ran through his veins. Even sober, I learned a Tiger can't or won't change his stripes.

Maybe we become monsters as a way of self-preservation. About two years later, Bobby was fired. I suspect even in Christian circles, the cause of termination read asshole extraordinaire! We all excel in something. Sadly, Bobby died in 2019 from a heroin overdose. This is what is so disheartening. Bobby overcame his addiction and had many victories, but what people remember is his relapse.

I talk about this phenomenon a lot. For addicts, every sober day is nothing short of a miracle. We have countless victories over temptation several times a day. I can't tell you how often I walk down the wine isle just to see what I am missing. Most times we overcome that desire or pull. Nobody sees that victory. However, when we succumb to the temptation, everyone knows. This is incredibly sad to me. If there is an addict in your life that is sober today, encourage them.

The noise was all I could take. I rose to my feet and packed up my little crude makeshift bed. I then took a seat at a picnic table on the veranda. I still think it is a screened in patio, but I will fall in line. I started writing letters and watching the walking dead come to life. The day labor people would pick up homeless workers by the vanloads. I have always been a people watcher. I like to pay attention to them and assign meaning to their lives. I give them a back story like I was doing with the girl who gave me my bedding. I imagine their stories, both the joys and hardships. I am sure I am never right with my imagination, but it never stops me. I was surprised at how many homeless men lined up looking for coffee and donated pastries. Saint Matthew's house gets food donated from all over. Usually, it is day old stuff that didn't sell, but nobody cared. Many companies were very generous. The shock is when the homeless people start complaining about the variety of donuts. I have been to other countries, and I have seen extreme poverty. My younger years were spent growing up in Haiti. Back in those days, I could never imagine any one of those Haitians being ungrateful for anything. Only in America are our homeless stuck up.

In 1988, a group of elderly women had a small bible study. One day they saw a picture of an underprivileged person on the front page of the newspaper. What that photograph depicted, I have no idea, but I am aware of its impact. The women felt that they could not just stand by and do nothing. Soon Saint Matthew's House was born. A mission of feeding, housing, and helping the people who were down and out was born. People didn't have to live in a great unknown anymore; there was help. The ministry continued to grow over the years to what it is today. While I was there, they had their hands in all kinds of fires. The start of a woman's addiction program was developing rapidly.

In addition to all its fundraising ventures, such as hosting special dinners, managing the thrift store, car wash and even a catering company known as Sprout Catering, they have a campus in Naples, LaBelle for men, and an 11-acre property in Alva, Florida for the women and the Immokalee friendship house, also a homeless shelter. I suspect by the time this book sees print, they will have acquired more ways to help and love people.

On the veranda, Tim was the first to come up off the floor and sit outside with me. I was surprised that homeless people were so entitled. Where was the gratitude? They picked over the pastries and demanded their coffee. I suppose over time you become so familiar with bitterness that you don't recognize benevolence as kindness. Being angry is all these men knew. In a way it made sense to me. What had these men lost? The stories varied greatly, from the loss of wives and children to death. Some watched how cancer takes a life over years. Some had seen unimaginable things like war. Some were simply hiding underground for crimes they could not undo. There were a lot of men who walked a fine line between Hell and playing with its fire. In ways you try not to judge, and in other ways you are desensitized to all the pain.

The demand was that everyone had to be off the property by 8 AM, no exceptions. The idea was you were either working or looking for work, but you could not return until 4 in the afternoon. I knew of at least one man who worked at night, but even he was not given any special privileges. He would hop on a bike and spend the day at his sister's. Working at night also made no provision for coming to the shelter after 11. All the rules applied equally to all the men. You broke the rules and you were kicked out and could not return for 30 days. This troubled me, because I have made a life working in the restaurant business. If everything were subject to change, why couldn't a service industry man have exceptions made? Being new and unfamiliar meant I would just accept the rules I didn't understand.

Across the garden was where the women and children lived. I think their rules were more lenient. Men and women were forbidden to fraternize. Which I suppose I understand, but it was weird to see people and be required to ignore them. Even still, I still tried to be polite and say things like "good morning," but the women never responded. I suppose when your home is at risk, their silence makes sense. Still, I think everything needs to be within reason. As for me, if I was looking to get laid - afternoon delight, banana in the fruit salad, bam-bam in the ham, boinking - I just don't see a homeless shelter as my go-to place. I guess we all have different standards. I fear the bible verse Luke 17:2, "It would be better for them to be thrown into the sea with a millstone tied around their neck than to cause these little ones to stumble." Would I really want to cause any of these women to stumble? I don't think I serve an angry God, but I am not trying to test that either.

Over my year, I would occasionally be accused of breaking the rules. This is something that I did deliberately only once. Other than that, I am sure I never even broke any other order. I broke the rules when I started talking to one woman I had met at the firehouse. My ways weren't working outside of those walls. I was there to submit even when that meant dealing with the tyranny of Ed or the anger of Bobby or smugness of Adam.

"If I was going to break the rules. I would just leave. I am here to try something different because my way wasn't working." I said this on more than one occasion.

They eventually believed me. I had turned the page on a world that was breaking me down. This new way needed to work. I knew I would either submit 100% or there was no point. I was trying to hold onto my new sobriety; it was all I had!

I may have had some silly rules to abide by, but the air I breathed was no longer heavy. Something was working. Even more so, I was falling in love with my new group of friends. I had a great love growing for Anthony and deep admiration for Nojo. Karl was slowly coming out of his shell. Greg and Cory were like children and I loved them even when their temper tantrums would flare. Jacob was still the most difficult to know well. I understood he wore masks because we all do. At this stage Rob, Sean and Rocky had yet to arrive.

The whole process felt a lot like military training. Where they try to tear you down and rebuild you. Mostly our will was an issue. Men simply do not like to succumb to a bedtime as an adult. I was no different, but I was desperate. In recovery, you must submit and commit 100%. If you try and half-ass the twelve steps, you will fail. It is not merely stopping drinking; you must modify your behavior and transform your mind. In essence, everything about me was wrong. It really is an all or nothing commitment and responsibility.

I knew I missed myself. The person I was before the great heartbreak. The person I was before the betrayal of someone I trusted. I don't talk a lot about Mary, but she was the most difficult person I ever lost. She understood me. However, I have written a book completely devoted to our story. Because of that, I don't share much here. Returning to life itself is not for cowards.

Outside the veranda is a courtyard with a tall cross. Nailed to it were small plaques that bared people's names. Even before I knew the significance of this cross, I recognized it commanded silence and respect. Just being near it made people reflective and still. The symbolism had a story to tell. I would soon learn that those names were of Saint Matthew's residents that died. The fallen bunch terminated by their addiction. I read only a few names. Sons, fathers, daughter, mothers, and friends who left this world in a way that caused a void. Hardcore lives cut short. It felt so rude. You want equality in this world? Look no further than addiction, because it excludes nobody! Come one, come all, because addiction knows no prejudice.

The reality is that a lot of people die from the disease of substance abuse. Individuals who dig their own graves. People often think drugs and alcohol are merely a choice, and this is true for some folks, but hardly all. Some people are predisposed to addictive behavior. Not all addiction is chemical either. Some people are addicted to sex, food, the glow of their phones, social media, gambling, pornography or even co-dependency to name a few. Addiction has all kinds of manifestations. It can take years or a lifetime to become self-aware of our own behavior. In the same way that we don't fault people for the color of their eyes, in the same way we don't shame people battling cancer, we should treat people with addiction with humanity and respect. I am convinced men and women want to slay this dragon in their lives. Yet oftentimes, unless you have the gift of desperation, many people do not even recognize their own challenges. Nobody wants this monster living inside them. Have you ever asked a child, "What do you want to be when you grow up?" and the answer be "I want to be addicted to meth?" It is a cunning disease that lies to everyone.

During my time at the homeless shelter there was a tiny area with weight training equipment in the back. It was old stuff that appeared to not have been used in a long time. I would work out very lightly a few times. Mostly during the daylight hours, we were given odd jobs like helping unloading trucks or cleaning. I didn't mind anything that made the hours pass. In truth, the work comforted me. In the evening after dinner, there were groups from local churches that would come and lead bible studies or recovery groups.

Ed boasted often about how well we all had it sleeping on the kitchen floor. Apparently when he first entered the program, new people slept in a run-down house. He painted his experience grimly, but with Ed you never knew what was true and what was exaggeration. Rambo he wasn't, but he wanted you to think as much. I also heard stories of people having to sleep on the floor for months or weeks. I was one of the lucky ones because I only had to endure the homeless shelter for about 3 days before we were moved.

Friday came, and we were all up and packed early. This was the day that we would all walk down and move into the Firehouse. The homeless shelter was about to be a part of my past. I still felt slightly drunk, but I had not had a drink in over a week. There was so much I just didn't understand.

We all met outside at a flagpole. We loaded our bags into a van, but we walked to our new location. This felt like the chain gang off to perform some menial or physically challenging task. The Jolly Orange Giant emphasized the rules repeatedly. We were not allowed to stop and talk to anyone. I had been in the firehouse when I first met Joe K. Although, I didn't pay much attention at the time. I was thrilled to have a bed and a clean restroom just a few blocks away.

CHAPTER 10

"Fear arises when we imagine that everything depends on us." ~ Elisabeth Elliot

"From now on, what's waited for tomorrow starts tonight." ~ Hugh Jackman, "From now on" from *The Greatest Showman*

Out of the frying pan into the Firehouse.

  The circus was finally settling in. We arrived before our predecessors had vacated the premises. They were busy cleaning the property and building thoroughly. This is known as deep cleaning. At the firehouse, we deep clean the building every Friday. I appreciated cleanliness like I have never in my entire life. Even living in the swamp of a place that I turned my apartment into. I had never been as grossed out as I had when I entered the bathroom at the shelter. Frank came out first and greeted us. He was covered in tattoos and looked mean as a junkyard dog. He had a sweet manner about him. He explained that he scrubbed our bathroom down. Frank looked like a man with his skin barely hanging on. I was guessing he put on about 15 pounds since he entered the program. Then he welcomed us all to our new home for the next month. He was the welcoming committee for back sliders just like him. Eventually the entire mod came out and greeted us. A motley group cast of characters. They had only been in the program 4 weeks longer than us, but they had advice and encouragement. I wondered if they were simply full of shit. I was still thick in my misery and skepticism, but I tried to be accepting.

The men that would be our peer mentors were Gabe, James, and Dan. Gabe was the Jolly Orange Giant that met me in the office that very first day. Dan, I had met when I first walked into the firehouse to speak with Joe K. I always felt Dan had a used car salesman way about him. It appeared he had his shit together. The problem was that he appeared to be a lot of things. I got the feeling he was more attentive to appearances. He talked a good game, but did he value integrity? My weird feelings about Dan were not his fault. He simply represented everything I learned to distrust about Christianity. Much like my ex father-in-law, Larry, he seemed to worship at First Church of Teflon; nothing sticks to him. When Dan spoke, he presented himself as intelligent, but he was simply regurgitating things he heard. There is a difference between intelligent and educated; Dan personified this.

James immediately concerned me. James was angry! He had so much anger. I felt the program was failing him. In fact, I liked James and at times resented the program, because I felt they allowed him to slip through the cracks. Anger is an addict's trigger. James seemed to be loaded with triggers. He walked defensively all the time, and he was a ticking time bomb. I also think James had a lot of passion, and that contributed to his outbursts. One thing I will always applaud about James is that his convictions are iron clad.

James is not your traditionally educated man. His wisdom came from the streets and common sense from experience. This also made him jagged and untrusting. He almost always wore a baseball cap like a uniform. I don't think James had any real idea of who he was before he began drugs. This meant he had no life to return to, no normal, and that is scary. In one sense your life can become anything you desire. However, who do you emulate? Who is your role model, and what will your path be?

James gave us the grand tour. We walked in through the kitchen. A few guys would be assigned to prepare the meals each day, and they were the only ones allowed in that space. The living room was a spacious area with a big TV, but only for DVDs. We were not at all permitted to know what was going on in the real world. Apparently, some guys in the past left from seeing news stories that maybe took place near their family's homes. We could only use the living room area after dinner. Mostly the living room was used for some type of small group study or bonding.

The bathroom was my oasis. Everything was new and so clean. It still had that new construction smell from the remodeling of the old firehouse. There were 2 toilets, 2 urinals, 3 sinks and 4 showers. I was in hygienic heaven! The entrance into our barracks was through the bathroom. James explained that our bags belonged under the bed. The bed had to be made every morning. James also made it clear that naps are forbidden. He then assigned us lockers and provided locks.

I trusted my guys and never once used that lock. I was probably the only one of us who had never served quality time in county jail or prison, but these guys would never steal from each other. Once I got to LaBelle, it would be another story. I didn't know guys over there, and I didn't trust everyone. In fact, my first few weeks in LaBelle, I slept with a sharp kitchen object under my mattress. I was not afraid to stab first and ask questions later.

Stump was a mod ahead of us, and he had sticky fingers for sure. In LaBelle, Stump liked to walk around with a single dollar. He would offer you that dollar for whatever it was you had that he wanted. The gimmick was you would feel bad and tell him to keep his dollar. Stump was not only a thief, but a con artist in its truest form.

After we settled in that first day was mostly free time. I took a nice long hot shower. Towels weren't readily available, so I used a clean T-shirt to dry off. To this day, that was the most rewarding shower I have ever had. It was a good feeling to not only shower, but also not feel overwhelmed. Outside, the weather was a crisp February cool. The south Florida heat can be stifling. It was a bonus treat that I would not be dripping in sweat minutes after my shower. Alcohol withdrawal can cause a person to sweat excessively, and I was not an exception. This was my new world, and I was loving it.

Twice a day, we fed the local homeless or down-on-their-luck crowd. These were not the same homeless that lived in the Saint Matthew's shelter. I have been a million places and seen a million things, but this was new. Homelessness also knows no prejudice. Our patio turned into a used car lot of humanity. Every single make and model, size and color of a person. I enjoyed this a lot. Though it was hard on me when I served families with children, seeing families with innocent young humans also made me think of my own. I had very little contact with my beautiful offspring before I went into rehab. I had no contact with my youngest son Hayden. He was only four at the time. I had no idea what they were thinking about their old man's situation. Now I was looking into the small and dirty faces of some children that lived in a car. I can't describe that feeling. I am not sure the word helplessness is adequate.

A couple guys would go to the homeless shelter and pick up the hot food. Once it was brought back to us, other men started preparing the meal. This usually only required some reheating of entrées. Maybe putting some salad in a serving dish, but mostly everything was ready to go. The hommies (as we called them) began to arrive sometimes as early as three, but the traffic really picked up around four, and we served at five. Women and children were always served first. The men formed a long line along the wall and into the side yard.

Dan was the single only staff member that would breathalyze the homeless. He was also the only staff member that would make anyone leave for failing the breathalyzer. Gabe would have us pack a meal for them before we sent them away. I thought this was harsh treatment. However, the logic is that it kept confrontations down. In the land of the unruly, anything can happen at any time. As a result, Dan must have wanted to minimize the risks. Still, we couldn't detect who was high, so why single out the drunks? "Be careful Dan, these are the people that God uses." I thought ". Some of those people had faith like Daniel in the lion's den. Just a handful of unqualified people, broken and exactly the ones God has a heart for. I just shook my head at Dan's youth and inexperience.

If ever your past is making a playground of your head and won't allow you to move on. If you are struggling with the weight of who you have been. If failures have turned to four walls that surround you. Don't sit alone, crying and wrestling with your pride and pain. Go feed the homeless. There is something about that experience that makes you feel like a treasure when life is saying you don't measure up. When your wife or husband have left you because you have no value. Trust me there are people who benefit from you! Sometimes the devil doesn't need to beat us up-he has people to do the work. I have replayed too many days in the middle of the night. I have seen and felt the backstabbing from a father-in-law law repeatedly. Yet, when I fed the homeless, I felt like I fit in.

We ate after everyone else was fed. It was the program's way of emphasizing humility and service. This also meant we sometimes ran out of food! We never went hungry, but we would often run out of something I was salivating for. In the program I was no longer in control of my meal choices. When something looked wonderful, it was a real treat because I can be food motivated. Sometimes a local Pizza hut would bring us several pizzas late in the evening. We would be so excited!

The first week we were serving the homeless, it was Anthony, Tim and me standing on the platform. Two women were sitting together at the farthest of picnic tables. Anthony nudged me.

"See those girls over there?"

I nodded yes.

"Tim got with both of them," he said, laughing. Tim always acted very nonchalant and you were never sure if he was paying attention.

"Tim," I called, trying to get him to focus. "You slept with those women?"

"Yeah, in the parking lot by the thrift store," he answered.

"Whose car were you in?"

"We weren't in a car man. We had sex between two cars in the parking lot."

"Who does something like that," I said under my breath.

"Tim!" Anthony answered and busted out laughing.

One early afternoon, I was sitting on the patio reading and writing letters. They made us sit outside a lot. The peer mentors would be inside napping, watching television, or playing on their phones. Mostly it gave them a break from us. They would try and make up random reasons why sitting on the patio was important, but those were all lies. This was when and where I realized my first miracle. If I had entered the program during one of the Florida summer months, I never would have stayed. I love Florida and I love our winters, but in the summer the heat is brutal. From May to September I am miserable. As it was, I entered the program in February, and some of the days were just cold. It was just another sign that I was exactly where I belonged.

We were next to a church. It is an attractive Methodist building. As I sat on the patio, I watched a funeral take place. At least I saw the hearse and the people enter the church. My curiosity wondered who was taking their 6-foot dirt nap. My reasoning suggested that it was an older retiree, but I was dead wrong (pun completely intended). It was a young woman who died of an overdose. I am not so sure how I got my hands on one of the programs, but I read and studied it. That death was almost me. It was a sobering realization. I thought about her life. I wondered what broke her, what was her trauma? I wondered who she left behind. Were there tears in a mother's eyes, and did she have children of her own? The grim reaper had taken one of my own, a fellow addict. I missed a person I never met, but I knew her well.

Nojo listens well and is good at calling you out on your shit. We adopted a deck of cards. Then we got in the habit of playing gin several times a day. This was when we grew close. We would discuss our judgments, frustrations, and victories. Throughout my year there, he remained my voice of reason. Right now, as I type these words, I miss playing Gin with Nojo and all the bonding that took place. He usually stomped me, but I always walked away enriched from our conversations.

We were all going through major chemical changes as our bodies adapted to sobriety. As a result, tensions and emotions could run high. We were men whose emotions, anxiety, and fear were all on high alert. A simple task, such as cleaning up, could turn into a major ordeal. I suspect we are also gaining a greater brain activity as we are coming to terms with changes. This was a time when our heavens and hells were just seconds apart. Surviving addiction and alcoholism is a victory, but we are often not as strong as we think we are. I saw that in all of us.

Cory and Jacob began to bond over their love of music. They were both talented in quite different ways and this made their collaborations fun. They spent a lot of time writing songs.

The patio is where most of the action took place. I sat at the picnic tables a lot. She sat a few tables across from me. I noticed her hospital wristband. She was a younger, attractive, black woman with bad posture, but there was something adorable about her at the same time. We made eye contact repeatedly. She seemed aware that I was not allowed to speak with her. I kept watching her and made no attempt to be subtle. She kept looking back at me, and we communicated without ever saying a word. She was waiting for the serving line to start, and I would make sure I served the food this day. It would be my only chance to interact with her. This is when I broke the rules.

We stood on a small platform behind a counter. The food was set up for us buffet style, and we served the people who came through the line. This was the only time we were permitted to speak with anyone outside of the program. I saw it as my chance to say something to this captivating woman. I was not lonely and had stayed single for the most part since Heather left me. There had been a few good women that had come into my life since Heather, but I was married to Bourbon. That life was simple and predictable. Predictability was safer for this old heart of mine.

I did not know she was homeless, but it stood to reason she would be. Apparently, she was very promiscuous, and I didn't know that yet either. Still I didn't care. There was something friendly and gentle about her. I did wonder if she was a prostitute. It is so much harder for a woman to get clean I'm told, because she always has a job. She can easily sell herself and get money for drugs. Still I knew those dungeons of judgement and shame. I only saw value in those brown eyes. She was not at all a guilty pleasure.

When my mystery girl came through the line, I made a point to speak to her and serve her as slowly as I could. She was awfully familiar with the rules and whispered her name.

"My name is Shianne." She offered.

"Hey, my name is Marc." It was a complicated interaction. I kept looking for peer mentors to notice the communication. They sat perched on a bench with their butts on the chair backs and their feet in the seat. The leader's eyes were wandering around surveying everyone's moves. Dan was the one that was the primary enforcer of order. While outside the program his Christian mask was falling off. As he shamed us and warned us against the evils of women and their negative impact on sobriety, he got his girlfriend pregnant. A typical hypocrite and his message. Dan clearly struggled to lead by example. Can anything be more diabolical than a double-minded leader? He raises the standards for those of us beneath him and lowers them for himself. Then God created me to call bullshit on the whole affair.

"Please come back for more," I said when she simply had to move on. When she sat down, I realized she seemed to know everyone. She was not a stranger. She came alive as her social circle grew. In fact, she lived in tent city. An improvised neighborhood in the woods. Their community would move depending on the rainy season. In the winter they were safe from the elements. However, during the spring and summer of everyday rains, their tent city would often be flooded out. I wondered how they all avoided snakes and alligators. I hate snakes! Throughout my life, every woman I ever dated that had a pet snake got dumped! That is my self-righteous rule! I figure if God takes your legs away because you pissed him off that badly - I don't have any use for you Mr. Snake (No, I am talking about a reptile not my ex father-in-law).

It was easy to catch feelings for Shianne, because she was such a pretty and cool person. She wasn't fake and I value that in people. Was she playing me? On some level I am sure she was. I just looked the other way when I knew she was lying to me. Currently I am away and graduated from the program for over two years. Still, I talk to Shianne and am always interested in her adventures. Even now, I never can tell a difference between truth and tale spins, but she remains in my life. She had made a lot of boyfriends from the program. Something she denied, but I knew better. Many men over the year would brag about having been with her. This always hurt me because she deserved so much more. We were two broken people that could never build a relationship on shifting sand. In another time and place, maybe.

Shianne had been conditioned to like the way these men treated her. When no one really tried to give her anything that she needed. I suppose we all like to be lied to when we are being held in another's arms. Cue the Sheryl Crow song, "Strong Enough". She is a smart girl. She had a military background, so she is tougher than most. I wasn't looking to give myself away. I am sure we were more attracted to familiar trauma. We think we want a certain look, sway or even stature, but it is our mutual wounds that draw us to each other like a magnet to steal.

There are two bathrooms outside from the veranda that homeless people used. They are attached to the outside of the main firehouse building. There was no lock on the doors to help prevent drug use, and it seemed to work. We never had to clean up barf. Shianne would leave me notes in the toilet paper tube. I in turn would sometimes do the same. These notes made me insanely paranoid. I knew if I got caught, there would be repercussions. Try as I did, Anthony and Karl would always find a way of keeping the notes. Eventually her flirtation turned straight sexual. This was kind of exciting, and I genuinely loved the attention, but I also ran from it. She kept insisting I meet her in a bathroom or on the side of the building. As aware as she was, Shianne lost sight of the fact that there were cameras everywhere. Even if I wanted a restroom rendezvous, we would have been caught. Quickly I realized her boldness came from experience. Other men must have welcomed her offer. After all, she was pretty. When she was a little higher, she would be more aggressive, calling me a pussy for not wanting the pussy. Simply stated I was never one to fuck for sport.

We never crossed the threshold into a romantic relationship. Maybe there is a man for her that can love and not use her. He must walk among us somewhere, but will she ever hold out for him? In the meantime, Shianne roams this world with fire in her soul and grace in her heart. I like that about her. She is the definitive hot mess. If we had met while I was a drinking disaster, it would have been a love story for the ages.

It was one of our very first nights in the old firehouse. As a group we were bonding strongly and fast. Still we were strangers. We knew each other's DOC (drug of Choice). We knew a lot about our broken places, but we didn't know much more.

Sometimes I feel like I am at the age when the only time I don't have to pee is when I am peeing. There is rarely a night that I do not get up for the restroom. It is amazing I never pissed my bed when I was hammered. Sometimes two or three times a night I must hit that bathroom. (Note to young people: this is what you have to look forward to when you get older.) Being in Justin's Place, nothing changed. Like a Zombie, I crawled out of bed. Unlike most nights, I was still very tired. Typically, I wake up and am alert, not to fall back asleep for hours. I was still very exhausted from my restless nights in the homeless shelter. As I made it back to the bunks, I did not get back into my own bed. Nojo slept to my right. I tried to lay down right on top of him. One of his knees was up, and I couldn't figure out what was in my bed. In the dead of night, Nojo burst out laughing. It was then I realized I was trying to get into the wrong bunk. I was not just embarrassed, I was horrified! If the tables had been turned, I would have thought someone was trying to make sweet love to me. I would have thought this is rehab, not prison! I was not about being some dude's punk. Thankfully, I was blessed because Nojo didn't try and stab me. He knew exactly what happened and thought it was hysterical. This was a story we shared many times throughout our year together. Nojo always got the biggest laugh from telling it. It still made me squirm to think that if it was anyone else, I could have got my ass beat.

On Monday nights, they would have people come share testimonies with us. Most often it was just long-winded rambling. Once in a great while, a story would speak to me. Tuesday night was an inspirational film. In other words, the worst of Christian films. I suspect these films primarily acted as our babysitter while the peer mentors hide away on their phones. Wednesday nights were back to New Community church. Thursdays we had a 10-step meeting. This was when we confronted each other about our hang-ups. It sounds dreadful, but it was truly effective. The idea was if something was bugging us about another brother, we talked about it. We learned to share feelings even when we weren't right. I loved this because we learned how to listen.

A few years later, I had a roommate in North Carolina. Every time I tried to talk with him about something that troubled me, he went defensive and never listened. I learned to value the 10-step even more. We sit in a circle and figured each other out.

On the weekends, we could watch motion pictures. Saturdays we would deep clean the Firehouse and sometimes do service projects, but we were always back in time to feed the homeless. They had us on a strict routine. Sundays were a little more lenient, and at times we would go to a park or the beach. James hated the beach and I never really understood why. Our Sunday activities were really the result of whoever won the argument over the activity. The peer mentors had passionately different ideas about what was fun. The mentor that lost would sulk and we suffered feeling uncomfortable.

Five mornings a week, a van went to the gym. Monday, Wednesday, and Fridays were mandatory, but Tuesday and Thursday were optional. I went 5 days a week. James resented getting up in the morning and complained all the way to and from. He would also cut our hour down to about 40 minutes. I have always enjoyed the gym, but never took to team sports. It always bothered me that James was angry all the time. I didn't resent him, but I was worried.

CHAPTER 11

"In a second, you're gonna say something impossibly charming. It's gonna be great. And then you're going to sweep me off my feet and we all know where that is going. It's going to end badly, and I just don't have time for the pain." ~ Will Hayes from the motion picture *Definitely Maybe*

Mary! She was only killing time

and it killed right back.

Cue the Mat Kearney song, "Hey Mama."

During blackout I had begun to really learn that being human is a collaborative effort. Standing in front of Joe K. a few weeks earlier was simultaneous obscene confidence and vulnerability. I was certain more every day that I was at the right place. Then a DVD began to change all that.

For most of my adult life I believed that salvation included a romantic relationship. If you asked me about my problems, I would instantly blame some part of my struggle on the women of my life. I still hadn't realized that I was unreasonable, demanding, and had unconscious expectations.

There have been 4 major loves in my life; Denise, Baby Mama, Brandie, Mary, and Heather. My father never forgave me for not marrying Denise, she was his favorite. Denise was simply too intense for me. She would ask "How are you?" If I answered fine, she replied, "You know if you are not, you are lying."

It is hard to believe I loved Baby Mama because I don't have fond memories of her. I am sure we had great times. However, once milk goes bad it can never be good again. Baby Mama is just a nasty human.

Brandie was another hot mess! I started spending a lot of time with her while my divorce was finalizing. She was pure fun. We laughed all the time and for hours. She remains one of my all-time best friends.

With Mary the loss was due to my arrogance and insecurity. Was she flawed, yes! She also loved wholeheartedly and uncynically. Her multitude of sisters were the cynics.

I met Mary in a counseling class we were taking together. She instantly caught my eye, but she was married.

We always talked, and she would listen to me as if I was the only person in the room. She had dark features with deep brown eyes. She was American Indian and from Alaska.

She left Florida with her husband and moved to Hawaii. There they worked on the television show, "Lost." She was in the office and he was on location. According to her, their marriage was rocky. What was true about their matrimonial failures, I have no idea. I love what Maggie Smith's character, Violet Crawley, says on Downton Abbey, "I never take side in a divorce because the truth is never to be found" (I am paraphrasing).

Mary and I started talking regularly. It got to the point where I looked forward to her call every evening. Sometimes we would talk and text for hours. At this point in my life, I was only drinking about a half pint of Bourbon a night. I would walk around the neighborhood talking to her with 2 quarter pints of Wild Turkey 101 in my pockets. I would get a great buzz, but I wasn't yet passing out.

Before they moved to Hawaii, they worked on a Kirk Cameron Christian film called *Fireproof*. Mary had an extremely minor role in the film. After we broke up, I never wanted to see it. Plus, she always told me stories about how weird Cameron is, and I find him to be more selfish than Christian. Two Baptist men named the Kendrick brothers produced the film and relied heavily on free labor. Yet, these guys made millions. Her stories about those guys really turned me off.

One night during blackout they were planning on

showing us Fireproof. This freaked me out. I loved Mary more than anyone. She spoke my love language and spoke life into me unlike anyone ever. I could not stand the thought of reliving her in even the slightest way. When Mary left me, the bow broke and that is when the binge drinking began. Prior to that I was day drinking on days off, but not every day.

Cue the Gavin DeGraw song, "Not Over You."

Mary left me to work on a film with her ex-husband. This offended me greatly. The morning that I dropped her off at the airport, I would not even speak to her. I was hurt and being cruel. I lost her that day forever, and no matter how much begging I did it never brought her back. She is married now with a child. Her dreams of being an actress gave way to becoming a military wife. I am sorry that she didn't pursue her dream of acting and performing because she is super talented.

Mary and I did things together that nurtured my soul. One time we were looking at Paintings. I asked her to pick her favorite and told her I would write her a story. She picked one. We went home, and I wrote a short story that would lead to a story I wrote called, The Nothing Man. She often told me that I was her favorite writer. I doubt she will ever read these words, but if she does, I hope she is pleased.

Last night, I wrote about Baby Mama in this paragraph and I laid in bed afterward and realized I wasn't completely fair to her. Yes, the version of the person she became I find gross, but she was good once. Then this morning, Art VanZanten had posted a short devotional on

Facebook. Lamentations 3: 20-25, "I will never forget this awful time, as I grieve my loss." When I met my beautiful offspring's mother, I loved her fairly quickly. She is an extremely talented and creative person. In fact, I think one of my greatest failures as her husband was not celebrating her creative genius better.

Dear reader, I beg you to never lose sight that I was a very compromised husband. I suppose we all start breaking promises while we are still saying our vows; it is the human condition. I was a terrible husband in this way. I wasn't cruel to her, but I was so very stupid. I demanded she meet my needs, and I was selfish. I failed my wife as a husband. Maybe she should have left me, but I wish she left me for a morally upright man - not the Doughboy Draftsman. I wish her character grew to care about the things that made her shine. As it stands, her values are having the biggest home in a neighborhood, owning an expensive luxury vehicle and always needing to be first. I wish she knew that success without integrity is failure. She changed, and that stings. I hate my beautiful offspring will never know the version of her I knew. Cue the Billy Joel song, "The Stranger."

When I lost my family, I discovered just how much a man can cry. I never dreamed that I could cry so much. When the power of love gives way to death, it is crushing. Love becomes poison. Sleep became so restless, and that empty bed felt so cold. The nights were ruthless. This was how I started drinking. I would do anything to make the pain and void go away.

The issue with Mary was she was always hearing

from God. Hearing God's voice and direction should be a good thing. But, in her case, God was always changing His mind. If I truly trusted what she claimed God was saying, I would be forced to think the Lord had schizophrenia.

Now they wanted to show *Fireproof.* A stack of memories I hardly needed awakened. I still missed Mary every day. Even now, she is still in my thoughts at times. Thinking about her would always take me down a lonely stretch of grey highway. I could feel her, smell her, taste her, and she could still get to me even though she had been gone for years. It was a darkness I didn't want to stir inside me. I suppose when I die, she will still be in my heart and soul. Now we have our own roads to take, but I miss Mary. My heart breaks for her new husband. I am sure her sisters are grinding his nerves raw! I am sure if she reads that, she will laugh and then get angry with me.

This DVD put me in a state of panic. It was a Monday, and I couldn't sleep with the threat of this film being our inspirational motion picture on Tuesday. Honestly, these films felt mostly like a waste of time. Around 3 in the morning, I went into the bathroom. I sat on the floor, and I wrote a letter to Morgan. Morgan was head intern at the Firehouse. I pleaded my case, asking him to please refrain from making me/us watch that film. I explained that the film would take my pain into a direction I wasn't prepared to handle. I am not sure if it was my words, Morgan's convictions, or God's prompting. Maybe a combination of all three, but *Fireproof* was never mentioned again and I survived. Today as I write this, I tremble at the mere thought of the damage the viewing might have caused me while I was already in my rock bottom's basement.

When all my worry was set aside, I grabbed the DVD. I thought for a moment and decided it was just best if it went missing. I am sure that no one ever found the film again. I am proud of my public service.

A few days into our blackout period, they brought us Rob. He looked like a skateboarder street rat. It was a difficult transition for him. It was as if Rob walked into the middle of a motion picture and couldn't figure out the story line. He felt out of place and like no one cared. He wore his badass pants and was defiant about everything. Every day he threatened to leave, and he was angry. Unlike most of us, he was court - ordered and he was not with us voluntarily. Our group was not bonding with him, because he would not allow it. Among other things, he refused to acknowledge his issue was Xanax bars. Xanax (also called zanies or planks) are used to calm people with anxiety, panic disorders, and insomnia. It is one of the most popular drugs among college students. Apparently, it is very easy to become hooked on Xanax. From what I have been told and what I've seen, the drug's effect - is very similar to the effect alcohol had on me. I drank to relax and help me sleep. Also, like alcohol, Xanax has a different effect on everyone.

It had all come down to Rob shutting everyone out. He was unhappy, and his body chemistry was changing. Rob was detoxing and having withdrawals. He would only hear what he wanted to hear. The first step towards change is becoming aware of our own bullshit. I think every addict gets stuck at this stage for a hot minute.

The group kept asking me to talk to him, but he was still too angry. I needed to wait until the time was appropriate, and so I kept resisting. Anthony was worried I was waiting too long. I knew I couldn't approach him too soon. He needed to be tired of being angry.

A few days passed, and I saw Rob walking out to throw the football with the guys. He walked slow, and with his shoulders slumped. His head was down, and it appeared being angry all the time was exhausting him. I felt the timing was right, and he was ready to connect. This is when I called him over and asked to have a seat at the picnic table. It was just the two of us. I have always found it best to speak with people when they don't have an audience. Take away their need to save face among others.

As he walked to me, I was reassured his demeanor had softened. We sat, we talked, and he set aside his mask. Rob was no different from the rest of us. He just came to us with his defenses up. Having missed the earlier days of the program, such as the stabilization track (the homeless shelter), he missed a great deal of bonding. In truth, I am not sure Rob's Obsessive-Compulsive Disorder could have handled sleeping on the shelter's kitchen floor. Rob's things and his life needed to be in a certain order. He was also addicted to hand sanitizer, and I loved that about him. He reminded me a lot of my relationship with Heather. When we lived together, she was constantly cleaning and organizing the apartment. She drove me crazy, but I did love her OCD ass.

We were just two haunted hearts sharing about our lives. I explained to Rob that he was among men that had a history of abandonment. Baby Mama had left me as did Mary, and later Heather. Heather wouldn't just leave me, but she would shut me out of my youngest son, Hayden's, life. It got much worse when Heather married her second husband, who I call The Sequel. The other guys had their own stories. It would be hard for us to get close to him if he kept threatening to leave. We needed him to join the tribe. This was not a place for victims to just come and go. We could not pretend. If he wanted a sanctuary, he had to take the risk to love us, but it was his move because up until this point he kept pushing us away. It is a devastating fear to love. Now I was asking Rob to love a dozen drunks and drug addicts. Even as adults, we still need the discomfort of growing up. The investment of sincerity required by all of us was borderline obscene.

Soon his big blue eyes began to fill with tears. I became very emotional as well because Rob was walking out of his no man's land. This may have been the most beautiful day of my recovery. Rob was understanding and had a willingness to learn for the first time. I had called him over without a clue of what to say or what to share. God's hand was on us. I think we both grew up a little that day. I think I was able to convey that we were all really on his side. I think about Rob often, because he really has stolen all of our hearts. I love him. Later, Rob would be the one who first began calling me Dad. Funny how life works. Heather sees no value in me as a father to our son, but these guys called me Dad. Honestly, it helped me, but I can't articulate it.

Understand this, no matter how many mistakes we make or how slow our progress, we are still way ahead of everyone who isn't trying to get sober. It is a battle to get clearheaded. With Brian it was never more apparent that this battle is not always won. The lines in his face were hard and told a story of the road he had been on. One-on-one he was a very sweet man. In groups it was evident how much he resented structure. It was heartbreaking to see a man not merely broken but shattered.

Step three in the twelve steps requires us to relinquish our own strategies. In my case this was narcissism, self-loathing, and strange sincerity, which only led me into a deep despair of drinking. I could not trust my own brain. Our thoughts, feelings, and actions have not worked. We have been left unsatisfied, void, anxious, and a mess. We managed these accomplishments on our own. Now we must accept help to recover and change. Step three needs us to admit we need a higher power, a power greater than us, and in many ways that higher power involves other people. Addicts need compassion from one another to really change. I had lived a life of erratic emotions and carried deep wounds from human relationships. At Saint Matthew's House, I was able to feel differently about my life and relationships. People were kind to me; they were supportive and showed me a lot of love. Unfortunately, Brian wasn't interested in discovering a new depth to his own life, and the people surrounding him. Some people just get stuck in low frequency thinking. I had been trapped in my own lows as well for eleven years. How wonderful it can be to let go of our crazy-eyed thinking.

It was easy to get frustrated during the blackout period. Mostly they made us sit outside on the patio when we were not in class or on a service project. I never will utterly understand this part of the process. Honestly, as I said this was the peer mentors' time to escape. They would turn the Firehouse into an improvised teacher's lounge. We were never permitted to nap, but the peer mentors napped often. These mentors were not that far ahead in their own recovery. This was frustrating for all, because the ones detoxing needed the rest the most. The veterans always share their battle scares as a means of justifying their actions. We just listened to the bullshit and made do. We also knew that this was the way the peer mentors of our peer mentors modeled leadership. Explaining the reasons for rules almost never happened. This was hard on me because I comply well when I understand. It is a system that works but is held together with duct tape. It was not lost on me that most peer mentors relapsed quickly.

The problem with the firehouse was that it was too self-contained. The inmates truly ran the asylum. We needed more maturity around, and the peer mentors deserved more training. This meant that the blackout period was operating in evident insufficiency. As I said before, they made a guy named Andy a peer mentor who used his privileges for his own gain. Andy was having sex in a van with one of the girls from the women's program. Andy also got in trouble over a trip to Wal-Mart. Andy kept his head buried in his phone. I would love to say he paid little attention to the residents, but he paid no attention to any of his responsibilities. Due to his negligence, a resident was able to purchase some over-the-counter drugs that he was able to get high on. All Andy had to do was show up to prevent that from happening, but he was always in another world of his phone. He got caught, but he never should have had the opportunity. When I heard about Andy, I was disappointed and hardly surprised. He had always been terrible in leadership and thus a self-consumed peer mentor. Now he was compromising a young girl's sobriety. In the words from one of the greatest motion pictures of all time *Jerry Maguire*, "He shoplifted the pooty." One thing was certain, the peer mentors were usually found out, but the selection process didn't seem to change. I like to think there was a method to this madness, and maybe there was, but I never understood it.

A definitive rule in the program was no smoking! Primarily I think this was more about keeping us all uniform. Cigarettes distinguished the haves from the have nots. Not everyone had the money to smoke. They also had seminars and special speakers from the state come and teach about the hazards of smoking. For some reason, smoking education had no effect on any of our guys. In fact, our group would recruit some of the homeless people to buy cigarettes for them. Anthony turned to Shianne as a go-to person for trips to the store. She was a friend, and I think it gave her purpose. She always marched to the beat of her own drum anyway.

Since we feed the homeless with all disposable silverware and paper plates, there are many trash trips. The dumpster was behind the Methodist church next door. For some reason, sneaky people always think their behavior and ideas are original. The guys who smoked always wanted to take the trash out. Every day, at least one person was sharing a smoke. The peer mentors were aware, because they did the same thing when they started the program. There was mostly nothing we could try or do that hadn't been done, but in the words of John Lennon, "But, you can learn how to play the game, its easy."

The most popular substitute for cigarettes was dip. A lot of time if the men didn't get too aggressive, they could get away with this. The problem is you can't trick a trickster. Even if you manage to tuck the tobacco perfectly in between your check and gums the smell could give you away.

When we left property, it was mandatory that we stayed together. Never wander from the group, and certainly never go anywhere without accountability. Brian was always the lone wanderer. He would drag behind and sometimes disappear. No matter how blatant or subtle, passive or aggressive, Brain had to be rebelling. The Bible says do not conform to this world; I suppose Brian was taking it to the extreme.

One Sunday after church, everyone was loaded in the vans. We were headed back to feed the homeless, and the timing was perfect except no Brian. Remember we fed the homeless twice a day. Brian's disappearance was annoying to all of us, but it really pissed off James. James was hot-headed anyway, and things that set him off only exaggerated his agitation. Brian was one of James' major triggers. Nobody knew where Brian had gone. Hell, I am not even sure Brian knew where he had hidden himself. Finally, he comes rolling along. He had no sense of urgency or respect for any of us that had been waiting for him. According to Brian's actions, it was his world and we just lived in it. Nonchalantly Brian gets into the van. All eyes were aggravated and on him. James was cocked and ready to argue.

Their verbal battle of a dirty little war had begun and continued throughout most of the ride. Brian went off calling James all kinds of names and challenging him to a fight. Brian's great insult was that James was hiding behind Jesus. James somehow managed to keep his composure. I was proud of James that day. I think secretly we all wanted James to punch Brian and knock the old man out. When we got back to the Firehouse, Brian packed his bags and left. It had been his third and final time to try the program. I don't think he was ever-welcome back. We pretend it doesn't bother us, but it never felt good to see anyone fall away from the pack. But we know that, addicts are fond of hitting the self-destruct button. Our unbridled minds are quick to lose rational thought, find misery, and self-medicate. It is a common symptom of a vicious disease, and we all show signs from time to time. In Brian's case, he just took it to another level. Personally, I think Brian wanted to return to the streets. It was home to him and where he became most comfortable. Don't we all find comfort in the misery we know as opposed as to the change we can't yet comprehend?

Brian taught me that sobriety comes at a price. Addiction is an even more expensive price. One way or another, you will be paying with time, money, and relationships. Either way you are working hard. It all depends on where you direct your efforts because you simply can't have it all. Of course, in getting clean there will be relapses.

You will read these words several times in this book because it is good preaching! "You can't relapse if you are not trying to be sober." The people who do not relapse are the ones who just stay in their addiction. It is a cruel reality that on average, an addict overcomes temptation several times a day. Some days are worse than others. Somedays we daydream of feeding our addiction as if lusting for a beautiful woman. Yet, it only takes one fall, and that is what people on the outside see. All your championship victories are lost in one moment of failure.

Once I noticed Brian sleeping over at the Methodist church. He had made a little bed on the side of the building. Gabe wouldn't let us speak to Brian; I suppose there was wisdom in that. Once you left the program you were always trespassed for thirty days. I trust they don't want one bad apple spoiling the bunch. Nonetheless, Gabe made sure Brian was fed and I always appreciated that. Gabe was a man of reason. He had flaws like the rest of us; however, I think Gabe tried to always err on the side of grace much more than correction or consequences. That was very refreshing of him. As I mentioned before, on occasion some of the homeless people would be high or drunk. As a result, they weren't welcome on property, but Gabe would have us bring the wayward drunkard a plate. It was nice that it wasn't lost on Gabe where he came from. I understood that drunk people are unpredictable. The idea is that you want to keep as much order as possible. As if life is ever predictable, but we can try and minimize our complications.

Rocky arrived on a Friday night straight from jail. He had wild cat eyes. You know how a cat looks all around his new surroundings. He also had the easiest transition of any of the latecomers. Rocky may have met people he didn't like, but he never met a stranger. He is a country guy and loves to fish and be outdoors. Once we got to LaBelle, it wasn't uncommon to see Rocky catching a baby gator or walking around with a snake in his hands. I hate snakes and am not fond of alligators, but Rocky is one with nature. Rocky was cool with that I hated snakes near me. With each one of my mod brothers, there was always something about them that I really admired. With Rocky it was his Crocodile Dundee way outdoors and his protective nature. I always felt safe with Rocky.

One afternoon they surprised us and took us to the woods for a scavenger hunt. Who the hell thought this was a good or fun idea I have no idea, but I was beyond annoyed. Becoming a mosquito buffet is hardly my idea of a good time. Anthony thought it was hysterical how much I hated this excursion. He always claimed I was sassy. Incidentally, my sister Beth always says I am sassy. I guess that is what we call the Bobbi (my mother) in me. My mother is a sassy bad ass that carries weapons. My sassy is genetic. What I know for sure, is that I don't belong in the woods! Not Florida nature trails that is for sure! You know what they say, "A sass a day keeps the basics away," (maybe I made that up) but apparently, I wasn't sassy enough because we were dropped off at a state park. Despicable!

I was ruined! Then my group wanted me to go off path. I was refusing! Rocky came and guided me through the high grass and uncertainty for a group photograph. Between Nojo's ability to discern the clues and Rocky's skill at tracking, the scavenger hunt was over within minutes. My mod was smarter than any of the peer mentors who put this scavenger hunt together. We were left out there in the heat sitting at picnic tables. I was miserable.

Our final last-minute entry into our mod during blackout was a young man named Dylan. A tall, skinny skateboard kid that looked like he was only about ten minutes out of high school. When he entered, he was very much detoxing and tried to sleep all the time. He is a great guy, but really didn't have much of a chance to experience the full first month. Our group was a week away from moving to LaBelle. The leaders eventually decided to hold him back. Good news for Dylan was that he escaped the homeless shelter's floor. We were bummed out when we learned he wasn't moving forward with us. However, because he had to stay behind, he met a man named Jerry.

Jerry proved to be a great friend and mentor to Dylan. We all need those mentors to help keep us from stumbling and fumbling as often as we do. Jerry was in the mod behind us. At first, he was very offended that I called grown men Pumpkin. But I refused to treat the men in the program like hard men with dark pasts. That was evident in the fact we were all in the program. I sought out terms of endearment, and the sillier and more foolish I sounded, the more I liked saying them. Some men like Dustin called me "Cupcake" and Hatley called me "Puddin" and we bonded over those silly names.

On Jerry's last day in LaBelle before he left to go to Wolfe Apartments, he walked over to me and gave me the greatest compliment. "Marc, I see a lot of these guys let power go to their heads. A lot of them start to think they are better than the rest of us, but not you. You stayed the same!" I felt honored by Jerry that day, and it has stayed with me all these years. These days Jerry will send me a bible verse or inspirational quote almost every day.

Once in LaBelle, I had the opportunity to meet Dylan's family. His stepmother, Maggie, is a beautiful woman with an even more beautiful heart. We became friends, and it appeared for a minute there was a romantic interest. She decided that we should remain friends just as we began talking. I wasn't really thrilled with her choice, but I accepted it. She made a wise decision because even though I had several months of sobriety under my belt, I was still a complicated disaster.

Blackout was refreshing, but it was over too quick. I wanted to go home often. I was bonding with my mod brothers. Most of all, I learned I could not run away. The blackout time gave me a good head start. I learned there were not going to be any short cuts. I could not go over, under, or around; I had to go through this entire process one step at a time.

In Orlando when I prayed, "God help," I had an instantaneous healing in mind. I was beginning to understand why this was a process. It wasn't a matter of just setting a bottle down. I had to change my disruptive thinking.

Thank God I had great men alongside me - a band of brothers. My rehab program reminded me a lot of the bible story of Joshua. God tells Joshua that he and his army are to march around the city's high walls for six days and seven times on the seventh day (Joshua Chapter 6). Simplifying the story, the walls came down on the seventh day. I know somebody that can preach could probably do wonders with this story. What always has stood out to me is that everything begins with baby steps. Just one step at a time. This is exactly how Justin's Place and the 12-step recovery program worked, just a step at a time. Always only doing the next right thing.

The first three steps of the twelve-step process can be done very quickly. You start by admitting you have a problem and that your addiction is unmanageable. You essentially have no control, and you are upside-down in a right-side up world. In the second step is when we come to believe that a power greater than ourselves can restore us to sanity. This is admitting we cannot get our lives back together without help. In the third step, we decide to turn our will and our lives over to the care of God as we understood Him. I had no problem with these first three steps. In fact, I had been professing the first step for years. I just didn't really want help. Possibly it is fairer to say, I really didn't think I would ever overcome my need for alcohol. I had not reached my rock bottom's basement yet. Now, I was walking out the first three steps. I found the process relatively easy, but there are nine more steps ahead of me. Shit just keeps getting real.

CHAPTER 12

"Notice: Elevator to sobriety, out of order…use the steps." ~ Unknown

"The truth is, unless you let go, unless you forgive yourself, unless you forgive the situation, unless you realize the situation is over, you cannot move forward." ~ Steve Maraboli

"True life is lived when tiny changes occur." ~ Leo Tolstoy

The new walking wounded

and living dead.

Welcome to LaBelle! A move that removed us from the frying pan and placed us into the fire. The weekend before they graduate us from Blackout to Discovery track, we get a Saturday mosey to visit and become familiar with our home for the next 5 months. It is their version of a preview of upcoming attractions. In order to be fixed or rebuilt, you first must be broken down. For steal or glass to be molded, there needs to be a fire. Black out served as a means of breaking us down. Now in LaBelle, we would begin to rebuild and rediscover ourselves. We are not merely making lemonade out of lemons; we are starting over. Yes, there is a real world and real consequences that await us outside of LaBelle, but this is the beginning of the new us. In the words of The Six Million Dollar Man, "They can rebuild us; they can make us stronger." All we must do is trust in our higher power and set aside our will. The problems arise because we are all so full of pride.

The thing about pride is that it can hide for a long time. If you are a thief, eventually you will get caught. If you are a cheater, eventually you are going to make a mistake will be found out. (I discovered Baby Mama's infidelity through a cell phone bill one time. She was calling the Doughboy Draftsman twenty times a day and as early as 3 AM.) However, pride can hide a long time. Sometimes it's pious pride, and other times it's stubborn pride, but regardless, it is a true bitch to overcome. Justin's Place was set up to expose our pride and help us grow. After all, we are our own worst enemy in attaining sobriety.

LaBelle is a city with a population of less than

5000. It is about 45-minutes west of Fort Myers in the middle of Florida. Riding into town, the biggest attraction I saw was a super Wal-Mart. Lots of empty buildings with failed businesses. Even some of the active companies looked closed from poor upkeep. Going through town takes less than five minutes. I felt I was nowhere near civilization. I may not be a New York City sized man, but I certainly was not prepared to live in such a small town. I wasn't even sure LaBelle was a town; I felt it might well be just a borough. LaBelle does have some charming spots, like their downtown area, but driving from interstate 75 you don't see that part of town.

Cue The Doors song, "People are Strange."

When we got there, we walked to the volleyball and pool area. We watched the peer mentors talk to all their old pals at first. Then everyone that was outside formed a huge circle around the volleyball court and held hands (I have never been one to enjoy holding hands or hugging strangers). They prayed us in, and the residents were trying to be inviting. At least that was their mandate. I looked around and there was nothing but green grass and cows as far as the eye could see. Sure, there were random homes here and there, but this was no city, and I was uncomfortable.

James assured me I would love LaBelle, and this was true eventually, initially not so much. James and Gabe were already on the other side of the program. They knew what was to come, and they had good memories. All I saw was empty space in the middle of nowhere. For me, there was absolutely nothing to get excited about.

Sean and I looked at each other. He was equally unimpressed.

The Port LaBelle Inn is adjacent to a Marina sitting on the Caloosahatchee River. Approximately 67 miles long, the river begins at Lake Hicpochee and runs to the Gulf of Mexico. In the eighties, the property was a thriving country club with several golf courses. Wealthy boat owners would anchor at the Marina and stay at the resort enjoying all the amenities. When the economy began to struggle in the late eighties and early nineties, the Club suffered. Over time, the property (worth millions) mostly housed migrant workers. It had been for sale for a while before Saint Matthew's House discovered it.

After some prayer, consideration, and guidance from the board, The Saint Matthew's House CEO, Vann, decided to buy the property. There was one small issue. Both the city commissioners and the county did not want a rehab in their community. The towns people had a reasonable concern.

The county originally tried to refuse the sale. In fact, they were determined to prevent the ministry from taking over the conference center. Still this didn't prove to be the obstacle the city had hoped. A gentleman that was associated with Saint Matthew's House pledged 5 million dollars towards legal fees against Hendry County. With all the county's best efforts, they could not afford a legal battle of that magnitude. The fine people of Hendry had to back down. Although the city did refuse to rezone the property for residents, and the location was only legal for short-term guests. Local politics was at its peak.

Once acquired, Saint Matthew's legal team had solutions, and Vann had a new mission. Vann had no intention of stepping on anyone's toes despite the county's distaste for the rehab in their community. If anything, Vann understood their worries. This is the thing about Vann that always impressed me, he has an ability to see things from several points of view. What is Vann like behind closed doors? I have no idea. He carries himself with humility and grace. After the Teflon Christianity and fake sincerity awarded me from Larry, my ex father-in-law, Vann was needed. Vann gave me a leader to feel good about. Larry left me with more faith in The Three Stooges! Although after being gone from the program for a few years, I often struggle to understand some of Vann's choices. I think much of the leadership is in question. Upper management seems to be paying as much attention as one normally does to a preflight safety demonstration. This is a concern I will tackle later in my final chapters. Let me emphasize that I have never been on a deep level relationship with Vann. I hardly know the man intimately, but I do think he has a good heart. No leader can hit every ball out of the park.

Vann wanted to prove that men in recovery would not terrorize their community! Vann respected the town's concerns and had faith in abandoned men. He had a belief in God and God's calling that makes him humble, but hardly passive. He is impressive.

As a result, the tradition was born that Saint Matthew's residents would wear a shirt and tie to dinner every night. They wanted to present the men as recovering members of society, not the hoodlums everyone feared. It was a brilliant first step for the organization. The residents would also do service projects for the community, sometimes helping individuals, churches, and sometimes the city itself. Over time they gained the public's trust and appreciation. Saint Matthews' always does these ventures free of charge. However, if led people can always donate to the ministry and they often do. Many of the local churches have events including a huge cookout for the LaBelle residents. This is common practice in the town very appreciated.

Our residents would always help and participate whenever invited. I enjoyed these ventures because they almost always included good food. Let's keep it real, church women can cook.

In 2017, I was there during Hurricane Irma that destroyed so much of southwest Florida. September's weather proved to be violent, and some areas were catastrophic. At some points, Irma was a category 5 storm, with its highest wind speed at 185 miles per hour. Between the flooding and property damage, it killed hundreds in Puerto Rico and devastated parts of Florida. When Irma came though LaBelle, it sounded like the roof was going to come off The Port LaBelle Inn.

Our men did community service projects for months afterwards. We were so involved with our neighbors, some guys complained that their recovery was suffering. However, Saint Matthew's House is all about serving. I remember we allowed people to use our showers for free. I personally gave away some blankets and pillows to people in need. I was proud to be associated with the ministry.

Today, Saint Matthew's House and The Justin's Place program are celebrated as a success and supported by Hendry County. It really is a fantastic testimony of God bringing the community and ministry together.

The building is three stories tall. The bottom level is mostly open to everyone. The second level is a functioning hotel. The third floor is where the residents of the program live. No one in the Justin's Place program is ever allowed on the second floor with guests. If family comes and stays at the hotel, the residents are still not permitted on the second floor. I have been told that some of this format has changed since I graduated and left the program.

That first mosey, I wanted nothing to do with living in the middle of no man's land. I mostly sat at the pool talking to Sean and the others from our group that flowed in and out from our table. On the other side of the fence, many of our mod members were playing volleyball.

Eventually I toured the property with Nojo. They have a small library, a gym furnished with donated equipment, canoes, fishing, and lots of other activities. I wanted the gym but could not see myself working out in the Florida summer heat of an aluminum barn.

On top of that, I hardly felt like the current residents of LaBelle were very inviting. That was until we met Frank. I had met Frank briefly at New Community church in Naples, and the day he was leaving the Firehouse as we were arriving. Frank was the optimistic man that had cleaned the Firehouse restroom before he left for LaBelle. Let me be clear that our rehab had lots of characters from all walks of life. However, no one was livelier, more emotionally driven, or more colorful than Frank. Frank gave us a guided tour and even took us into some rooms on the third floor. Frank is very consistent. You always fall in love with him, but at first you don't know what to think. Frank has no filter and can share stories at the drop of a dime. Many of these tales include very dark places his addiction has taken him to. Some stories would certainly earn an X rating by the Motion Picture Association of America. No one under seventeen should be allowed to hear Frank's stories.

Each room had four beds with, two bunk beds on each side of the room. There were only three dressers for possibly up to four residents. The rooms had a small desk in a corner that I would eventually spend a lot of time at. Frank opened his room to us for exploration. He could not have been more kind or hospitable. Frank was just awesome, and he shared the dos and don'ts of LaBelle.

Frank is covered neck to toe in tattoos. Much of his body art is of a religious nature, suggesting to me he had been a double-minded man and had been unstable in all his ways for a long time. Frank also proclaimed himself to be gay, but I was never so sure. I suspected he fell into a lifestyle of selling his body as a means of funding his addiction. His more significant relationships he would speak of were always with women. Women he claimed he emotional tormented. Addicts tend to seek any form of comfort. Dozens of outlets (like sex, food, the glow of a cellphone) all designed for pleasure and distraction. I think

Frank would rather be with anyone than with his thoughts. A lot of us would rather be with anyone than be alone. Men will go to extreme lengths to never be alone and have a warm body in their bed.

I developed a fondness for Frank. Yeah, he was crude and outlandish, but he is vulnerable and has a good heart. Even though he had created a life that demanded a needle in a vein. A world where he rejected the establishment and did what he wanted as opposed to what was right, he is still good. Still, I could tell he was tired of his rebel revolution. He was looking for structure, answers, and a new way of living. Weren't we all there because our ways were not working? A few were there to avoid prison. Since rehab is confidential, it is a very safe place to hide from law enforcement. In the rainy months of spring and summer, homeless people would enter for shelter because of the consistent rain. I remain impressed with Frank's determination. I sure liked to drown my demons and feel no pain. Though our drug of choice and sexuality differed, I wasn't all that different from Frank. I too had been telling the world to go to hell. You must wonder what makes us so defiant and reckless. I imagine we all have our own selfish agenda, reasons, discontent, scares and self-pity.

Later that day, Chef Jason made BBQ chicken for us. Chef Jason is a man of God with an angelic way about him. I loved him immediately, and usually if you claim God as your Lord, Christianity as your lifestyle, I automatically assume you are just another full of shit person. His voice was calming and nature nurturing. I simply enjoyed the peace he brings to whatever situation he is in. Men who are calm have always fascinated me. I am a high-strung individual with a temper, and I am reckless with words. My calm most often comes about 8 to 10 shots later.

BBQ chicken is an incredibly special food because my Grandma Tew always made this for me. Sometimes she would BBQ some pork chops. Whatever my grandma cooked, she cooked it was with magic and love. She wasn't a chef, but no Chef in the world could out-do her! Whenever I eat BBQ chicken, I feel reconnected to her. She also used to cook black eyed peas in lard. Sweet Lord that country cooking was delicious. They were so good they were like a drug. When she died, I never ate black eyes peas again, and I never will. Compared to my Grandma's cooking, everyone else's are gross. There is just something about a grandmother's love that shines from a kitchen.

At this point in my life if I need to feel grounded, if I am overwhelmed, I call Chef Jason. He doesn't just bring peace. He has great wisdom and reasoning. Most of all, I trust the man. I don't easily trust people or institutions. I have known him now several years, and he is consistent. He helps me out of my black holes.

Grandma had been battling cancer when I met Baby Mama. She never got to meet my children. She never knew me to take a wrong turn on bourbon Street or me to be haunted by my divorce. She did make it to my wedding. She rode to Florida from North Carolina with My Aunt Sue and cousins, Heather and Amy. Grandma never was one to travel without her pistol. The day I got married, I am sure she was the only guest sitting in the pew with a gun in their purse. For some crazy reason I was proud of that.

I am proud of the people I come from. My father never resembled Howard Cunningham, Andy Taylor, or Mike Brady (all famous TV dad characters) My dad was more a mix of Tony Soprano and Red Forman. (Forman mostly because my dear father didn't really understand Star Wars either). My point is he is hardly the traditional old man. My mother was hardly June Cleaver, Wilma Flintstone, or Caroline Ingalls. No, in that tiny body, mom was much more a mix the of Sophia Petrillo's sarcasm (from The Golden Girls) and some Game of Thrones shit. Mom was no stranger to throwing golf clubs at me or chasing a friend out of her house with a vacuum cleaner. More than one girlfriend has shared that they were afraid of my mom. With my parent's propensity to have tempers and fly off the deep end, of course, I have followed suit and mastered the art of being opinionated and possibly how to verbally attack a person. When I meet men like Chef Jason I am fascinated with their cool, calm, and caring demeanor. Not to imply my family is not caring.

I have a Yankee daddy and a southern mother. It has made for some crazy genetics. I would like to think some of my obstinance came from Grandma Tew. Bottom line is that I like my heritage.

At every meal in Labelle, everyone says what they are grateful for. Most of the time people are simple and quick, but some guys just would not shut up! The grateful time could take up well over 20 or 30 minutes at every meal. Though at times it gave me some real insight into the men's hearts. Sometimes they were silly or stupid, but mostly when the guys shared, it was sincere. I enjoyed that first meal in LaBelle. My first step to being open about the transition was because of Chef Jason.

Six short days later, we were living in LaBelle. I had no desire to move to the sticks. My last week in blackout, I was miserable. I have never been huge on change, but this move just felt so epic. I would think about ways to get in trouble and be held back. Over and over that dreaded move played in my head. Round and round and up and down, my thoughts played with me. This is where the value of Nojo came in again. He talked me off the ledge of leaving. Of course, there was the sobering consideration that I felt this was something God called me to do. My pride was too hard to swallow, so I just chewed it. I was in the right place, and the next move was a part of a plan. I just never could understand that God and leadership didn't consult me on decisions. There was a time this heart and mind of mine felt this way. Who are we kidding? I was thinking these thoughts just this morning. Where did this inflated ego come from? (Mom, dad, you've got some explaining to do.) The road to recovery really begins with deflating my self-importance.

CHAPTER 13

"The world as we have created it is a process of our thinking. It cannot be changed without changing our thinking." ~ Albert Einstein

"Yesterday I was clever, so I wanted to change the world. Today I am wise, so I am changing myself." ~ Rumi

With everything to gain,

some still lose it all.

One week later, we left the Naples Firehouse. I was not happy.

We pulled up to the back of the hotel midmorning. All our belongings had to be inspected. Then, two at a time we walked into a bathroom, and we had to pat ourselves down, run our fingers along the waistband of our underwear, and cup our balls. (I am less happy about this transition.) All to prove we were free and clear of paraphernalia. Mostly the staff was looking for tobacco products. In truth, it was usually the peer mentors that were bringing in dip and cigarettes. This caused resentments because some men could buy cigarettes and others had no money. Peer mentors could smoke, and I always felt this was a huge mistake. Because it was almost always the peer mentors that were bringing the tobacco into the program. Greg used to boast that Adam would buy him Skoal and cigarettes when they worked together. Yet, Adam poised himself to be the head bounty hunter during room checks. Adam was gross to the program and he is certainly one of my concerns regarding Vann's leadership. Surely Vann cannot be so clueless as to Adam's perversion of the program.

After our initial inspection was over, we were finally able to get our mail. I had been sending out letters every day since I arrived at the homeless shelter. I would sit on the patio and just write. The letters helped me reflect and provided me with self-imposed accountability. The more that people knew I was in the program, the less I wanted to fail. Maybe it was my ego actually working for me? As a result of my sowing, I reaped a lot of letters. I was told on several occasions that no one in the history of Saint Mathew's House received as much mail as I did. Sometimes I would even have a care package waiting for me. It was just a matter of cause and effect, but I was blessed to have so many people rooting for me. Every single letter, phone call, and care package fed my resolve to finish the program. Support like that is so very meaningful from friends and family.

Next, we went into a big lounge room. Isaac was a case manager. He handled the orientation. We all were given packets of the rules. For instance, we were forbidden to circumvent. In other words, we were not allowed to work mom against dad so to speak. No trying to get around or past anyone's authority. Leaders had a final say on the rules, and we were expected to accept and never challenge their authority by going to the next leader in line. This was a huge mistake, I felt. Peer mentors needed as much accountability as possible.

The problem I had with this was that the peer mentors often could be narrow minded and short sighted. A lot of their choices, a lot of their decisions, and some of their guidance was irrational. We should have been allowed to climb the chain of command if we felt there was a discrepancy of any nature. In the judicial system, you can always appeal to a higher court. I think this would have been a great life skill for our men to practice. I also struggled with the peer mentors, because often they were breaking the rules they were enforcing. Notice I said often and not occasionally or seldom, but often. This pissed me off, and offended me, but what could I do? A few people ahead of me in the program shared my complete disdain. On more than one trip off the property did I witness the peer mentors buy the forbidden fruit of tobacco.

Of course, there is also the issue of friends. I saw one peer mentor during room checks overlook broken rules. Andy was one who would help hide tobacco to protect his buddies and own interests. Even worse, when dip or cigarettes were confiscated, the mentors kept the stuff for themselves. Leading by example lacked big time. You had to take most of their leadership with a grain of salt; a lime and tequila certainly would have helped.

This is not to say that they were all bad. I witnessed some mentors really trying to be fair and just, but if they were not a part of the leadership click, they were forced out. Just like with homeless people, peer mentors had a hierarchy and politics.

If memory serves me well, it was my first week at The LaBelle Inn and Conference Center. I remember a peer mentor and his name vividly. He will remain a secret because he turned out to be one of the good guys.

"What was your drug of choice?" I asked. "Because if you ever relapse, I want to be sure to fund it for you." Not one of my proudest moments.

Every 28 days we switched rooms and consequently roommates. This is because the city refused to rezone our property for residency. Switching rooms was the loophole to our stay. I hated changing rooms every 28 days, but the strategy for overcoming the zoning laws was brilliant. The bible does say we should be cunning.

Matthew 10:16 "Pay attention, now! I am sending you out like sheep among wolves. So be as cunning as serpents and innocent as doves."

My first month, my roommates were Greg, Rob, and Cory. Rob was a super considerate roommate. In our group Nojo was the father. He would correct you and be honest. Both Rob and Rocky took on more of the mothering role. They were gentle and compassionate. They both knew I was full of anxiety and bat-shit crazy. Their kindness helped mold me into the new person I wanted to be. Hardly perfect, but my life is progressive and growing. I maintain perfection is boring.

Greg was just a simple guy with traditional wants. He craved his dip and sought it out a few times every day. From what I observed, the most difficult addiction to overcome appears to be nicotine. Every day during gratefuls, Greg shared the same words, "I am grateful for the simple things in life." This became Greg's mantra. Might I add a mantra I love.

Cory was the most excited about LaBelle. He had family to accompany. This was exciting for all of us because Cory had such a horrible family situation. His brother, Cody, had been sent to Naples by a Jackson County judge. I quickly noticed (and heard) that Cody was a tool and not to be trusted. I hoped the rumors were not true. Once the two brothers were joined, I noticed a shift in Cory's behavior and attitude. I brushed it off thinking I was over exaggerating things, but I should have trusted my instincts. My young friend was becoming more defiant, and that made no sense. Cory was such a sweet and talented kid back in Naples at the Firehouse. He laughed a lot and exhibited a lot of boy-like qualities. Up until the transition, he was mostly a delight. I loved watching him transform. I loved being a part of his laughter. He would have temper tantrums from time to time, but they never lasted long. He would have bouts with complaining, but they always passed. This time was different, and I could not identify what was changing in him. I should have seen that the nemesis to Cory's development was his older brother.

The three of us also had the only adjacent room on the third floor. Next to us were Nojo, Sean, and Jacob. Sean turned their room into a chiropractor's office. People were always coming over for Sean's services and skills. To maintain some privacy, we used a mattress pad and placed it in the doorway. Yeah, you could still hear noises and talking, but it was a lot less intrusive. Most importantly, it blocked out the light. I prefer my room to be as dark as possible when sleeping.

It was a quick adjustment to LaBelle for everyone except Cory. Cory's anger was returning and growing. He had become combative, defiant, and rebellious. He had an inner battel raging, and it was evident. He was torn between doing what was right and being loyal to his brother. Cory began to build walls.

His brother Cody is as fake as Astroturf and sneaky person. He tried to play both sides of the fence. In the community he pretended to value the program, his sobriety, and growth. In groups he would speak proudly of his commitment and his growth. His prayers were eloquent and his gratefuls at meals were plenty. Every time he spoke, I cringed. I wasn't buying the act. Privately, he was breaking rules and manipulating anything he could get away with. Sadly, Cody was Cory's downfall. Eventually I learned this behavior would be commonplace with the peer mentors, but at this point it was still shocking to me.

I felt over the hill there. I was usually in bed as early as 9 o'clock. I enjoyed waking up early because I was alone and could reenergize, read, and pray. I act like I am an extrovert, but really, I am very introverted. Sometimes I even went to the gym. It was just a few days into our new life. At the homeless shelter, we went to the office for the Breathalyzer. In LaBelle it was different; two guys came to our rooms.

This was when I first met Matthew, a Zephyrhills native, and Stump, our resident con artist. Matthew is tall, subtle, and to himself and most importantly he is likable. Stump is basically the Tasmanian devil from the Warner Brothers cartoons. Stump was rarely calm. He was clever and dim-witted at the same time: his appetite for chaos could be maddening. He mumbled, sighed, and whimpered when speaking unless complaining. Stump can be fun and is likable, but not at all trustworthy. The two were clearly a misfit as a duo. Matthew is just a good guy. Stump would come in like a freight train. He never shut up and never really had anything to say. Stump was always more tolerated than enjoyed. He simply did not have boundaries. At times during the program I would try and bond with Stump, but I never felt he was sincere.

When they breathalyzed together, Matthew was

very much in the background. He would just kind of laugh at Stump. Sometimes, he looked annoyed. I got a kick out of watching the two interact.

One evening the breathalyzer men had come and gone. Soon I would be sound asleep. I had no idea that this night would be tragically different when I first laid down. We were just a few days into our new residence. I was tired, and I just wanted to close my eyes. Within the hour, the breathalyzer boys were back in my room. Something had happened to cause retesting of everyone. This was very unusual, and the weight of drama was felt by all. Greg, Rob, and I looked at each other, our faces cold and concerned. Then it occurred to me Cory was not in his bunk. My thought could not be verbalized before he walked in. A peer mentor who had the most grimaced look accompanied Cory.

"Well, boys I just got kicked out for something stupid," Cory announced. The words hit like a brick to the face. He was defeated.

All three of us fired quick questions to Cory who was only packing. He remained silent. The peer mentor offered no answers as well and mostly just watched Cory and looked down. The room quickly fell silent with only the jostling of bags being filled. The emotions, actions and our faces were intense. A brother was going down! If a moment could be darker than sin, this was it! I love Cory; none of us wanted this. What could have gone so horribly wrong? Rob, Greg, and me kept a respectful silence as we watched our brother walk out of that room.

Cory, Cody, and some other guy had taken bikes

from the barn. In the dark of night, they rode up to a convenience store and bought Four Lokos, a line of caffeinated alcoholic beverages. These drinks come in 23.5-ounce cans and in many flavors. Depending on state regulations, these drinks range from 6 to 14% alcohol content. Usually one can is the equivalent of four beers. I had never heard of Four Lokos, because it's a drink that appeals mostly to college kids. A funny fact about Four Lokos is that in China they are referred to as the "lose virginity liquor." Cody and Cory are the prime demographic. Apparently, this was a practice that had been going on before we arrived in LaBelle. Cody and his friend had been making trips up to the gas station for weeks prior to our arrival. What Cory didn't realize is that the staff were simply waiting for proof of Cody's misadventures.

The plan was to bring the alcohol back to the property. After they passed the Breathalyzer, they would enjoy their drinks. They failed to consider the most obvious give away, the smell. The leadership was already onto their scent! Alcohol gets into your lungs and the smell cannot be masked.

While common sense had checked out, the boys enjoyed their drinks and the victory they were getting away with. Now here is the issue with alcohol - it takes about an hour to metabolize a single drink. In the meantime, until it is metabolized, it is all over your body, most importantly your blood, brain, and lungs. It is difficult to mask the smell, because the smell is coming from your lungs, not just your mouth. Also, you often sweat alcohol when you are drinking, and the odor can show up that way too. In simple terms, the boys got busted because they smelled like a brewery. I suspect that their youthful ideology had no idea they could not hide the stink. Every guilty person in the world has one common bond; they think they won't get caught. The simple and probably horrible reality is that everyone gets caught eventually. Even Pat Garrett caught up with Billy the kid. He died at the tender age of 21 from a gunshot wound. Regardless if you're a professional criminal or amateur rule breaker, the jig is up sooner or later.

There was a third guy included in this capper, but I never knew him. From what I understood the three guys were dropped off at a motel in Fort Myers. Just like that, Cory was the second to leave our group after Brian. In my gut I knew I didn't care about Cody. However, how do you tell a man his brother is bad news? Cory idolized his older brother and would have jumped off a cliff with him.

Many of us feel lost in the darkness of this world. For Cory though, it was different. He has a good, but lost heart which primarily stems from a radically broken family and their destructive influence. The street and thug life are mostly all he has known. No guidance from any of the related adults in his life. He occasionally spoke kindly or positively of his grandparents, but I still have doubts about them too.

Losing Cory had a powerful impact on us all. First, we grew to love him and missed him. Second was the reality that we were all one bad decision away from making another mess of our own lives. Sobriety and recovery together make up a thin line we walk. The people who walk it well are the ones who never lose sight of their own frailty. We basically can never get lazy. Most times relapse is a process, but I think Cory's fall was basically a knee jerk reaction to his brother's glory plot. Maybe Cory really wasn't ready yet, but I struggled with that. Like any opportunity, you strike while the iron is hot. At that time in his life, I think if Cory had not crossed paths with his brother, he would have succeeded. Sadly, we will never be able to know for sure, but even now I keep the faith. He is a good guy. Cory would return to the program two more tries. Each time he didn't make it past the blackout phase. He always had an excuse or a person to blame, but in the end, he was the common denominator of all three exits. That damn pride wouldn't allow him to accept responsibility.

This first time I noticed Cory's return I was so excited. Months later, I would be at a Saint Matthew's graduation. Looking over my shoulder I see Cory sitting in a pew with the guys in blackout. Cory had come back into our fold, but it was short lived. He willingly walked away the next time. For some of us, getting clean is a long walk home. If you walk 30 miles into the woods, you must walk 30 miles out. In my case, it was an 11-year struggle of being caught between a desire to die and the will to live. We don't always do what we want. I feel confident that Cory will discover his reason to begin again someday. The lesson is that you cannot return to the same surroundings and the same friends and expect to continue to recover. Remember it is easier to pull a person down than it is to pull them up.

Nowadays, I follow Cory on Facebook and social media. I message him routinely about the progress of this book. He is always excited about the progress.

Many times, people get down on others who are failing in recovery. May I remind them of a few biblical characters? Moses killed a man. Noah is infamous for getting drunk. Rahab was a prostitute. Do we really have the time for a bible study about King David? He had an affair, had a man killed, just an excess of dirty Laundry. King David writes in Psalm 51: 16-17 "You do not delight in sacrifice, or I would bring it; you do not take pleasure in burnt offerings. The sacrifices of God are a broken spirit; a broken and contrite heart, O God, you will not despise." If you are ever down on yourself read of all Psalm 51, God loves you and is eager to forgive. In the New Testament Paul raised the bar even higher in Romans 5:20, "Where sin increased, grace increased all the more."

Sean would be the next to go in a few months, but he always maintained he wasn't doing the whole year. It was sad to see Sean leave, but leaving voluntarily made all the difference in terms of acceptance. Sean was radical about his marriage and wife; he needed her. She was his every motivation.

CHAPTER 14

"What's right is what's left when everything else is wrong." ~ Robin Williams

"Preaching grace produces fruit. Preaching law produces nuts." ~ Steve McVey

The Greek and the

Moody blues.

When we first arrived in LaBelle, they had a special Greek speaker from New York City visiting our facility. The teaching was all day long and nobody knew what the hell this man was talking about. In a nutshell he was purely dreadful. They also had some guys visiting from Moody Bible Institute in Chicago. Between these men and the Greek preacher, Labelle was feeling more like a colon cleanse with a chainsaw. Moving to LaBelle was uncomfortable, but now I had my first real doubts about the program.

It was mandatory to sit in the Greek's lectures, but none of us lost sight that not one leader stayed in the room longer than an hour. I wanted to be mad at the leadership for splitting, hitting the road, shoving off, and heading out, but who could really blame them. If I had any way or excuse for getting away from this man's rambling, I would have taken it in a heartbeat. He was a sweet man, but he was completely unaware where we were at that time of recovery. He was a speaker that simply did not know his audience. We simply wanted to get away from this man.

The Moody guys were just condescending. Again, men that thought common sense was merely nickels and dimes in a person's pocket. Every time they shared or spoke, I wanted to vomit. They were there to earn Jesus brownie points. It was a chance for them to clutter their spiritual resume' with good works. The beauty of rehab is that broken addicts see straight through pretentious bullshit. Sorry Moody men stay -- the fuck in Chicago! In fact, it would be ideal if the Moody men moved out of the country or found another line of work. However, this revelation and declaration gets worse I was once just like these dudes and maybe sometimes still am. I suppose we all drink the religious Kool-Aid from time to time. As Wayne Jacobsen says, "The sad truth is that most Christians spend their entire lives trying to score points with someone who isn't keeping score."

Small towns have their charms, but I find comfort in noise. I wasn't at all enthralled with LaBelle. I longed for city streets and sirens in the middle of the night. Now the Greek was trying and good-hearted man but was not connecting with any part of who I was. Furthermore, he wasn't connecting to many of the guys.

Two men rerouted my downward spiral of not enjoying LaBelle.

First was an older guy who wore designer jeans and had a long white ponytail. Tommy is a Rock-n-Roll cowboy who is also a chaplain and teaches classes three days a week. He is that guy who visits men in jail. Tommy is down to earth, real, relevant and everything I hope to be when I grow up!

Because we were living in an old resort, and that the city had refused to rezone the area, Saint Matthew's house had to have us off the property often. As a result, we would go to the Baptist church for classes Monday through Wednesday. Tommy was the first older Christian man I had looked up to in years. He introduced me to the freedom to be real and to struggle. Unlike Larry he was not a thorn without a rose. Today Tommy is not just a mentor, but also a man I want to be like. Tommy is both real and relatable. Most importantly, Tommy is the man we go over our step 5 work with. In step 5, we admit to God, to ourselves and to another human being, the exact nature of our wrongs. Really? Another human being has the time to hear that I am an articulate madman.

IF ROCK BOTTOM HAD A BASEMENT

In my life, I have found most leadership to be stupid. Middle management type people are most often nothing more than monkeys we could send to space. They deal from the bottom of the deck of manipulation. I suspect there is more mercy at a tribunal hearing or from a lynching mob. I seek my wisdom and lessons from the broken folks that I can relate to. When Tommy shares, he doesn't hide his wounds or scars and that got my attention. Our lives are unpolished and unrehearsed, often humiliated, afraid, paralyzed, defeated, and full of mistakes. What is it we most often enjoy about the films we see and the books we read? It refreshes our souls to learn that others are as complicated and flawed as we are.

Tommy never hid his faults. He taught about a God that had unrelenting love for us. He never distorted the gospel message with an agenda or legalistic games. Tommy played music videos, used motion picture clips, and shared about real life to relate to the struggle of sobriety. He spoke a language that I understood and could relate to. He told stories of victory and loss and was never afraid to pull back the curtain on his own life. His story too closely resembled my own and left me in awe. I could sit at Tommy's feet for hours. He is a friend in this life and a man I will seek out in Heaven.

We began most classes with a song from Tracy Chapman, called "Change". A simple guitar driven tune that asks what it would take to get us to change. How can love challenge change in us? The lyrics are about losses and regret and turning back around. When Tommy began his first class with this song, I tried frantically to write down every word as it played. I had no idea that this would be our rehab song or form of school spirit if you will.

At this point, you should be as familiar with my parents as any in the book. Allow me to remind you, I come from amazing parents, but they are both hot headed. I love this about them in the sense that it has given me a fighting spirit at times. My father likes to win by strategy, but he still has a volcanic temper at times. My mother is purely driven by emotion and feelings. Her compassion and passion are what lights her fuse. As for me, I am somewhat of a mixed drink of the two of them. I can be insane or reasonable in actions, but my spirit tends to stay in turmoil. Someone like Tommy who appears so levelheaded is extremely attractive to me. In the same way I loved Chef Jason. He came into my life at the perfect time.

When I was in blackout, James used to always say to me "Wait until you get to LaBelle and meet Tommy. You will love him." James was so right. The pot smoking parasite Dwayne Gordon had something to do with firing Tommy. Do I despise people who smoke marijuana? Absolutely not! I have a disdain for people who proclaim the evils of cannabis with a joint in their roach clip. Dwayne would also have a hand in ending a relationship between Saint Matthew's House and Bill Barnett and his Storytellers Creative Arts ministry.

A week after our arrival in LaBelle, I met a man who would awaken a sleeping giant inside me. William Barnett is his name. Barnett's vision is to empower people's creativity and allow them to experience God through the Arts. My creativity was not dead, but very much dying. Any desire I had to tell a meaningful story was on life support. When he brought his team to Justin's Place, I was not initially interested at all.

Ever since I was a child, all I wanted to do was tell stories. Before I could read or write I would dictate my masterpieces to my mother. I see in my mind's eye clearly me telling her my adventures as she wrote at the dining room table. I watched her intently and when her hand stopped, I asked her to read back to me what I just said. My mother was hardly my mother in those moments. She worked for me and had a job to do. However, in my stupid mind she was an utter failure. Mom was grammatically correcting my words. She was rearranging the things I said to make sense. To me this was a complete violation of my story and creativity. I would throw a fit and demand she write my words EXACTLY as I said them. I fired my mother on several occasions. Clearly this is evidence that I was a Prima Donna right out of the womb. But, wasn't it General George S. Patton who said, "All successful commanders are Prima Donnas and should be so treated!" I was ahead of my time before kindergarten or my introduction to Pop Rocks. I suppose having a big ego is sort of a rite of passage for the artistic people. After all, who dares to think they have something to say that is so profound it can change hearts and enlighten minds? Probably no one more than the artists. Participating in Barnett's workshops shifted my resolve about being in LaBelle.

What changed? Why did I suddenly take an interest in Barnett's workshops? The answer is simple, Barnett believed in the power of a story. His batch of leaders and speakers reminded me that our gifts are part of God's pleasure in us. This realization immediately bonded me to the gentleman stranger. In many regards I am nothing but an egotistical and childish fool. I have been told on several occasions that my ego is the largest people have ever known. I find this hard to believe since I live in a constant state of turmoil. My thoughts and the voices in my head rarely rest. That tape of failures can make the days long and the nights longer. Barnett's group taught me that even when we sing a broken "Hallelujah," God still wants our song.

Now I have read all kinds of books about storytelling from Peter Guber's *Tell to Win* (which was excellent) to the dribble bullshit by the self-appointed guru of screenwriting, Robert McKee. Just reading his book entitled *Story* is enough to make you want to puke. The man teaches about film writing and has basically never sold a screenplay his entire life. Joe Eszterhas, writer of *Jagged Edge; Basic Instinct* and *Flashdance* is a man who can teach screenwriting.

Barnett did something that was uniquely and profoundly different. He would play music and ask us to write what the music inspired. This is something I have been doing all my life, but I had never had this introduced in a workshop. Barnett wasn't a simple-minded teacher of lecture. He was illuminating steps in my journey as was his team.

They say it only takes a spark (or pyromaniac) to start a fire. Cue the Billy Joel son, "We Didn't Start the Fire." (Not that the song fits, but it is fun, and the title does.) Storytellers helped ignite in me a desire to tell stories, that ministry was my catalyst. At a round table, I felt myself come fully alive as I talked about writing and stories with a small group of men. Some of them felt they had no skill telling stories, but they did. Often a person just needs help priming their pump. Barnett's group was creating an environment where creativity thrived in freedom and love. I was smitten immediately.

When William Bennett and his group left that Saturday, I went to my room. I wrote him a thank you card. I thanked him for his ministry and the men that joined him, but what I was thankful for was the CPR I needed in recovery. The Greek and Moody men were a truly rough introduction to where I was about to spend my next year. For me to really change I needed to submit 100% to the program. In other words, swallow the good with the bad, not just chew it like a cow and his cud. Tommy and William helped balance what we were being fed. Those leaders did not speak from authority, but from a place of God's heart. They understood transformation comes from within and awakening our spirits as opposed to conformity from expectations, regulations, rules, and fear.

IF ROCK BOTTOM HAD A BASEMENT

CHAPTER 15

"If they do it often, it isn't a mistake; it's just their behavior." ~ Dr. Steve Maraboli

"Rebellion against tyrants is obedience to God." ~ Benjamin Franklin

I will prove the pen is mightier

than a sword.

Cue, the Prince song, "Thieves in the Temple."

Working is as much a part of rehab as the steps. The first month in LaBelle, we work in what is called

Echo. Basically, this is gardening and grounds maintenance in the Florida heat. I hated every minute of every second of this work. I even hate remembering it and writing about that misery, but for a month I submitted to the outdoor labor. Most days we worked a few hours in the afternoon, but Thursday was an all-day workday. You walk outside and read a Florida thermometer and it just reads "Hell!" A miserable heat! You drip sweat in places that baby powder just fails you!

A huge part of Echo was the ego of the man who ran it. Adam was a graduate of the program that became employed by the organization. He was considered a poster boy for success and recovery, and he was Saint Matthews' favored child. The truth is that he is nothing more than a dry drunk asshole. He had an unsatisfiable need to be demeaning to people. He was mean, cruel, insensitive, and worst of all the most narcissistic person I have ever met. I thought nothing less of his involvement with these scared and broken men as gross! Even now I am confused and bewildered at the ministry's blindness to this man's behavior. For a while, after I left, he was running LaBelle and I feel the ministry owes an apology to Satan! Vann, how does something like this happen? Are you listening? LaBelle needed you!

Let me be clear, Jesus loves Adam, but the rest of us just think he is a smellfungus asshole. (I have a friend, Markell Senter, he knows how to insult people far better than me. He would have the perfect words for Adam.) I have no respect for Adam and found him to be magnificently ignorant. He was always speaking out of turn and his authority was consistently overshadowed by stupidity. Yet, we had to figure out a way to deal with him or avoid him. He delighted in overstepping his boundaries. I loved the leadership but concerning Adam they mostly just stuck their heads in the sand. Most of us were trying to grow spiritually and develop areas of our lives that needed development. Adam was a thorn in all our efforts. He is the kind of man that will kick a wounded dog just because he can. The fact that I survived him is a miracle! Make no mistake that I would not piss on this man if he were on fire!

As I write these words of conviction about Adam. I have not lost sight of my own ludicrous and terrible behavior. God loves Adam and sees value in the man. Nonetheless, he was absolutely a cancer to the ministry.

My last few weeks in the program I sent letters to people in Naples concerning Adam's conduct and performance. I even sent a copy of my letter to the CEO, Vann. If I believed any person in Naples to have authority, they got my letter. Oh, and I did this very privately.

Once the letters were out of my hands, my anxiety rose. Adam is a vindictive type. If he learned of my efforts to have him terminated, he would be livid. I had to be prepared for dirty revenge. Unless that man reads this book, he may never know. If Adam does read this and I suspect, he will, maybe there is hope he will change. I rest assured that the ones who share with him these truths of mine will be men who delight in pissing him off. He is a man of rage and represents the opposite of everything I love about that program. To be silent would tear me apart.

Enough days had passed that I began to be certain

my letters were discarded. My anxiety eased, and it was back to regular living for me. I realized I was wrong when Art asked me to come into his office. Damn! My battleship was sunk.

Art came to LaBelle about 5 months into my stretch there. He wore two hats as the new program director and hotel manager (Please forgive me if I get titles wrong. I wasn't really interested in pedigree back in those days. For that matter, I am still not.) He said things that made me immediately like him, respect him, and desire to learn from him. My distrust for people and institutions made it uncommon that I was effortlessly impressed. However, Art spoke of the same convictions I shared. I had great men in my life, but Larry (my ex father-in-law) made me distrust any man who claimed to be in ministry. In fact, I find it profane when someone says they are in ministry. After Larry I felt surrounded by liars and imposters in church.

Larry taught me that the character of a Godly, holy man was compromised. Ministers and movie stars are two people living in one body. There is the persona and image versus the real person. Cary Grant once said of his stardom, "Everybody wants to be Cary Grant including me". (For my younger readers, Cary Grant was an English born man who became one of Hollywood's definitive leading men. He was most celebrated for his debonair approach to acting and his impeccable comic timing.) Larry gave me a scar that I could talk about. Art gave us parables, words, and proverbs that the community needed, and I respected. I also prayed that Art would be able to identify and slay the dragon known as Adam. Yet, Adam is a cunning man. He is a magician in hiding his true colors, but not everyone was fooled.

In retrospect, Larry's failures as a human and those wounds shaped me in ways that I am truly proud of. I am unsure if he helped take me to deeper places faster or slower. I have always been drawn to the outcasts, vagabonds, and unique. I have nothing against the status quo, but they simply are not my style. In school, the cool kids bored me to tears. I sought out the different and introspective kids. Now I wanted to help the sinners become saints and the lost find their way. Because of Larry, I actively and purposely wanted to help the meek inherit this world. While Larry protected his glory, he showed me the cross and the sweet love of Jesus. I stopped looking for heroes and began looking for the lost. I embraced my frailty. Sadly, the wounds of love did not make me a better Husband, boyfriend, or lover, but maybe I did learn to love better, just maybe. Give me the lonely, the ones in need, the people who are barely holding on. That's my tribe - paupers, simpletons and rogues!

Is Larry a hypocrite? Of course, he is, and that is at his best, but aren't we all our own worst enemy? Take me for example, I think alcohol is bad and yet I love bourbon. He is also a man with no skills. Why in the world do people who want to be missionaries not develop a skill? Help the third world countries and underprivileged people with a skill. Teach how to grow food and provide plumbing or clean water. Larry simply wanted salvation numbers to decorate his newsletter and thus beg you for money! It might serve our American missionaries and evangelists well to become familiar with Maslow's

Hierarchy of Needs. They should try to meet basic needs before they try and shape people's spiritual identity.

Years later, he tried to shake my hand at my daughter's high school graduation. I avoid snakes and Larry. He took my hand and I instinctively jerked it form him. He is an elderly man now, I can't punch the bitch. It is not that I don't forgive Larry, but I don't respect him, and I would never want him to think otherwise. I find Larry to be a lazy man that begs for money to avoid real work. He is a gross imitation of the gospel who truly believes in his own bullshit. Larry's ministry is mostly hidden in small and impoverished countries. Intelligent people see through him quickly. It took me years to see him for his true self; I am not among the smart ones. My dumb and obstinate ass still has a lot of growing up to do. I must admit, I waited for years for an apology that was never going to come from him. In fact, I have little doubt he still thinks his baby girl isn't fucking the neighbor. Even though she stole him from his wife and married the Doughboy Draftsman. He told me for a year that the affair was all in my head. Larry flatly refused to hear me, but he only proved he is a dumbass.

A funny story about Larry. Baby Mama and I were married with two small children when we graduated with Masters' degrees. All our parents came to the graduation. A celebration lunch one afternoon and Larry walked over to my stepfather, Ed, and whispered, "We will pay for Baby Mama and the babies. You pay for Marc." My family thought he was a piece of shit forever more. My family is right! I wish to God that Larry had said that to my father. Al would have said something epic like, "Go fuck yourself!"

CHAPTER 16

"If their name isn't God, their opinion doesn't matter, and their approval isn't needed." ~ Anonymous

"Be messy and complicated and afraid and show up anyways." ~ Glennon Doyle Melton

"You meet the Lord in the furnace a long time before you meet him the sky." ~ Rich Mullins

Art, mushrooms and "Can I speak

with you?"

Step 4 has us searching and taking a fearless moral inventory of ourselves. This is how we learn what has molded our behavior, prevailing tendencies, and how we conduct ourselves with others. As I have made a point of stressing, I have trouble trusting people, organizations, leaders, and religious institutions. In this step we are addressing our resentments and grudges. This is also the step that you learn to let go of the expectations we place on others. Our happiness and peace of mind cannot be governed by others' actions.

It is a time where we expose a lot of false perceptions and broken core beliefs. You learn a lot about your defective characteristics. The first three steps were effortless for me. However, the fourth I must revisit often. At this point of my recovery, I had yet to begin step four. Even my first few attempts at writing about the things that messed me up were half assed. An examined life requires uncomfortable self-appraisal and surrender. My resentments towards Larry and others had a grip on me. I also spent years worrying my children would respect their grandfather. I worried my beautiful offspring would learn to hate gays and believe every other doctrine that differs from the ideology of Southern Baptists. I thank God every night that my children love their grandfather, but he did not poison their minds.

I no longer believed blindly in church or religion. I began challenging the rules and traditions that I had been taught. This made me very unwelcome in many circles of the righteous gatherings. My experience with questioning authority was met with a lot of opposition. I felt God worked, but the church did not. I began to see that most of the church's objective was to manipulate us. Even the manipulating leaders were nothing more than people who drank the Kool-Aid. They were losing the light to a dim darkness, and nobody cared to confront this. When I questioned anything about church, I was inevitably told I was rebellious. Am I? A mighty important caution, question everything.

It is not uncommon for me to tell pastors that they suck at their job and needed to go sell insurance. Looking back, I always challenged the church and religion. Baby Mama thought I was just lashing out. One night she was sitting up in bed. She was aggravated, but I was willing to wait for her to share when ready. I was never the type of husband to beg her to talk to me (Maybe that is partly where I went wrong. I should have pursued my wife.) As I walked out of the room, she asked me a question that stopped me in the doorway.

"Do you have to say the word fuck to everyone you meet in church?" She was mad, but I was matter of fact.

"Absolutely, because if they can't handle my sin, then what good are they?" Possibly some of the sincerest words I ever shared with her, but I knew they fell to the floor. My dad was right, who was this woman I had married? We just looked at each other for a bit. My only thought was to curse her father for polluting her Christianity, character, and authenticity. On the other side of those accusations had me wondering if she ever lived out what her daddy taught her. Because what I can tell of Baby Mama is that she has spent a lifetime cherishing appearances and decorating sin. The bible says to boast in my weakness (2 Corinthians 12:9). So, in proclaiming my weakness, I say fuck from time to time.

I want to be loved for the fallen man I am and never an image I can't sustain. I realized that night I embarrassed her. Again, looking back, I am not sure I regret that. Yeah, I doubt my heart and even my eyes at times, but I do not doubt my intention to live out loud. Please just don't ask me what that kind of life is supposed to look like. I would rather eat a bullet than deliberately suck on darkness and pretend I am some saint. Baby Mama is Jewish among Jews, a gentile among gentiles and certainly a sinner with the sinners, but most of all a poser in every climate. I don't care to bury myself beneath other people's needs. Step 4 required me to spend a lot of time with my values.

Cue the Rich Mullins song, "Where You Are."

Now Art has come into my life and I was impressed. He was a spiritual leader, and he wasn't wearing a mask. Art also walked into a few challenges, most notably mushrooms.

The LaBelle Inn and conference center had several golf courses back in its country club heyday. Today that land is leased to farmers raising cattle. Cows tend to fertilize the land well. Decomposing cow dung in pastures grows fungi. These mushrooms are often edible, sometimes poisonous, and are most famous for their psychedelic effects. Most often referred to as 'shrooms (at least by dead heads). Florida is the ideal climate for these fungi to grow right on top of the cow patties.

Upon Art's arrival, it was discovered that some

men were eating the 'shrooms for their exotic hallucinogen. Apparently, this is an intense experience that affects everyone differently. A person can experience fits of laughter, profound insights, anxiety, or just be uncomfortable. The possibilities of this high are endless. I never would have considered a mushroom trip, because the possibilities are too unpredictable. If I take a wrong turn on Bourbon, I know exactly what is going to happen. My only endless possibility is where will I pass out when I blackout? As for mushrooms they are fine on pizza.

For many, the world of rehab is a place of unwelcome accountability. My brother Patrick would call it snitching. I think it was Benjamin Franklin that said, "The only way to keep a secret between three people is if two of them are dead." In our case, there were several more than three people who had participated in the mellow mushroom effect. Somehow this all went down, and I had no idea. Someone ratted the whole situation out. Unexpectedly, the entire community is brought into an impromptu gathering. We sat in a large circle. Whispers of speculation swept across the room as we waited. I was clueless.

Several minutes later, Art is pacing in the middle of our circle. His walk had a stoic purpose. His face was determined, but his words were kind. He shared his vision for the program and residents. This wasn't merely about being sober but being men of integrity. (Integrity? If I ever can stomach a conversation with Larry again, I might introduce him to the concept. I will have to speak slow and explain it as if I am speaking with a three-year-old, but just maybe. On second thought, I just threw up in my mouth thinking about speaking with Larry.) Art spoke about character, change, and doing the right thing. He talked about God and what God honors. For a second, I thought this might be a pep rally. I was interested, because he spoke in such a way that I never once felt he was trying to manipulate or bury anyone in shame. I was inspired and encouraged. Art was new to us and clearly the man for the job!

Finally, the ultimatum came. For the ones that came forward and admitted their participation with 'shrooms, there would be some consequences, but they would not be discharged. The men who failed to be forthright and failed their drug test would be told they needed to leave, no exceptions. I watched Art intensely, studying his every move, expressions and hearing his tone. I was so impressed. He did not present the situation as a tragedy, but as an opportunity for the men to grow from their mistakes.

We were asked to look down and all close our eyes. If you wanted to come forward and be honest silently raise your hand. These men knew a lot of defeat and shame. Now Art was presenting them a chance to walk in integrity. He was offering them a win! He was saying you are not defined, by your bad choice. You will be celebrated for your next right choice. I didn't dare violate anyone's privacy and confession, and I kept my head down and eyes shut. I think only two men came forward. After the drug tests came back from a lab a few days later, we lost a few guys.

Now I was being asked to have a private audience

(Cary Grant said "private audience" in a film I saw, and I embraced this expression.) with Art in his office.

As I listened to Art's invitation, I heard the words in my heart from Exodus 1:8, "Then a new king, to whom Joseph meant nothing, came to power in Egypt."

When I first arrived in LaBelle, Neil was the director. He was only with us for a few months before he resigned to pursue other passions. He now works for another nonprofit organization, Florida Rights Restoration Coalition. They are all about helping rebuild convicted people and rights that have been taken from them. Neil has a huge heart and his compassion is obscene. I love this guy, but I never knew him too well. Every chance I had I would try and talk to him. I knew he had a book of his own published. I wanted to sit at his feet, but he was gone before I really had the chance. Art came in to replace Neil. I liked Art, but I had no idea what he might think of me.

I have been told a time or 200 that I am not immediately likable. At times, I come across as a prima donna, bossy, short tempered, and the list continues. What can I say? I am my parent's son. Maybe the words of Paul in 1Timothy 1:15 might sum up my character best. "Christ Jesus came into the world to save sinners and I am the worst of them." Art's first impression of me might not be favorable. Now I was walking into his office.

"So, you wrote a letter," he exclaimed with a combination of excitement and disbelief. His smile confused me. He was focused, but not intense. This meeting could go in any number of ways. He could be difficult to read. It was only when he spoke that I could get a clear sense of his intentions and heart.

I just nodded in agreement. A nonverbal confession that I had indeed written a letter. His eyes widened and he took a deep breath with a long exhale. It was my turn to wait, be still and patient. I would answer questions, but only those that were asked. If I tried too hard to justify my actions, I ran the risk of being misunderstood. That was an uncomfortable worry.

"And you sent it to the executive vice president and the president and CEO! I must admit that was impressive. I am not sure if I was you, I could have done that."

Listening to Art, you might have got the impression I was Evil Knievel (For my younger readers, Evil Knievel was a stunt performer most famous in the seventies. His relevance is best explained as such; I had his action figure and cherished it. Now feel free to Google and YouTube him.)

"So, what are you hoping will happen with this?" Art continued.

My time with Saint Matthew's House and Justin's Place program was ending. The days were long, but the weeks were short. I would be leaving within a month. I explained that I had wanted to say something for months, but for whatever reason decided not to be proactive. Most likely I was afraid of Adam's retaliation. He had the power to make my life difficult.

Adam was always a part of the room checks. I

watched him enjoy raiding residents' rooms and belongings. He seemed to have some sick satisfaction in catching men with tobacco or porn. Adam felt superior when he was able to put others down. Anything Adam could do to add to another's misery was fulfilling to him. People outside of the program often shared with me their discomfort with Adam. He radiated fake, Pharisee, and a cruelty.

I know extraordinarily little for certain. I despise anything that treats lightly or diminishes the struggle of an addict. I would pray daily that God would instantly remove my desire for Bourbon. Yet, every morning it was my first thought. Throughout my day at work I lusted to be walking into a liquor store. It occurs to me in recovery that addicts must daily affirm spiritual truths and dependency that most people neglect or take for granted.

A popular saying that I have heard in recovery groups, "Religion is for people who believe in Hell. Spirituality is for people who have been there." The men in the program knew despair more intimately than love. We know loneliness, rejection, emptiness, affliction so well that we needed relief. What will dull these hurts and possibly provide some euphoric escape? Alcohol and drugs work initially filling a void, only to create a bigger void. This is how addiction keeps enlarging.

I have learned from church that there are acceptable sins versus sins of disdain. I think it is the respectable sins that cause more damage to grace. Moral superiority will always condemn people as sinners, in some cases even exile people from their church. Recovery groups do an amazing job of dismantling the grouping of sins.

Romans 7:15 says, "I do not understand what I do. For what I want to do I do not do, but what I hate I do." (Read all the way to verse 20 if you look this verse up.) Human behavior is complex. Our foolishness can rarely be narrowed down to a single explanation. Inside every addict are two dogs fighting. One dog wants sobriety and the other dog wants their drug of choice. It is often a daily battle. Some days we are hanging on. Other days we are stronger. No days do we need a roadblock to peace when you enter a recovery program.

When an addict is at the end of themselves, stuck in the valley, sinking. I know what it is like to feel like I am stuck in the valley of the shadow of death. I know what it is like to resent living. The last thing we need, is a man like Adam making the journey difficult. Adam was a dam to the flow of God's Grace. Men were often hurt.

Now that I was leaving, I hoped the leadership would realize I had nothing to gain on a personal level. I just felt that the men who come into rehab are broken, desperate, and scared. It remains my opinion that anyone working for the ministry needed to have prerequisite personal traits such as kindness, compassion, and being humble. Adam displayed none of these traits. I feel strongly that anyone who is fighting for sobriety should be celebrated on every level. Adam was a natural disaster to grace, the most important part of ministering to broken lives.

I often wondered if I misunderstood Adam. We

have all seen enough wrong and right to know that not everything is black and white. Often, we are stuck in the in-between grey area. Did Adam just have some sort of mismanaged handicap in communicating? I think of all the times I have been misunderstood. Sadly, his actions demanded a verdict. I don't dare judge the man, but I absolutely judge his conduct.

Adam has a spirit of falsehood. Usually a spirit of falsehood is deeply religious, as is often seen and felt inside church walls, televangelists, or even witch trials. I have said for years that religion dangerously complicates grace. Adam was also very adapted at constantly changing for his environment. I radically felt that Adam distorted the nature of our program. Not to mention, the rumors of how he treated his women.

"I am not saying he needs to be fired, (I was lying through my teeth.) but his behavior needs to be modified. More importantly, everyone seems to be afraid of Adam and I felt the higher ups needed to know." My words betrayed my heart's desire. Yes, I wanted Adam thrown out on his ass. This was not a vendetta. I just see the man in the wrong profession and position. He needed a profession such as a jeweler, janitor, or embalmer-- anything he could do and not involve other people.

We now live in a world where bullying is being confronted on many levels. People are being protected at school, at work and even on social media. This is one area where Saint Matthew's was getting it wrong.

Now I did not expect my single letter to make a huge difference. After all. I was only one person with the guts to go straight to the top. Most of the men being bullied by Adam were straight out of their addiction into rehab. That early into recovery, you are still very scared about everything. You are addressing unbearable pain; you often feel alone, even among people.

What I was banking on is that my letter would be the first of many attempts to correct his behavior. A mentor of mine once told me, "If one person calls you a horse, ignore it. If two people call you a horse, give it some thought. However, if three people call you a horse, you are a horse." Now Adam is no horse, but very much a jackass! He was a problem that needed to be solved.

I shared the rumors and stories that I could not prove with Art. I think I frustrated my adored leader. At Saint Matthew's House, they always wanted proof. This never set well with me, although I am sure they are right. I would counter that this wasn't a court of law, it was a rehab, and almost always where there is smoke, someone's getting high. I urged Art that he and leadership needed to pay closer attention. We can discern spirits. The problem is that ministries like the Elvis approach to running an organization. Surround yourself with "Yes" people.

Adam's brother, Bill, was in the program as well. For some reason, Bill absolutely hated me and was very vocal about it. My buddy Dave got the biggest kick out of Bill's back door, behind-my-back criticisms. I never confronted Bill because it was a game I couldn't win. My approach to criticism and judgement is simple, God made me this pretty, Get mad at Him!

Because Bill was Adam's brother, he was able to

get a job as the maintenance man. Furthermore, because Bill was under Adam's wing, he was protected and untouchable. Bill worked as head of maintenance. He would go into the second-floor hotel rooms and hide, watching TV. His passion was video games, and often they consumed his time. What did not consume his time was work. Everyone was constantly complaining about Bill's work ethic. If something was broken, Bill might get to it.

Bill had a truck and was freely able to come and go from the property. He consistently walked around with a 44-ounce fountain cup. Several people claimed Bill would spike his drink.

With all of Bill's judgment on me, he was eventually asked to leave LaBelle, because he came back from a pass drunk. Sadly only a few short months later, he was found dead. I felt bad for both Bill and Adam, but I never reached out. Adam struck me as the type that would resent empathy more than anything.

However, I did point out to Art that Adam's rule did his brother no favors. It was never mean spirited, but it was important to say. I think Art truly realized my heart was focused on the men and not vindictive to Adam. He thanked me for my courage and guts to go balls to the wall. I left his office with one realization. The first letter and effort were complete. I would now have to set any expectations aside.

Today both Art and I have moved on from the program. Yet, Adam remained for a long time afterwards. People both above and below him are afraid of Adam. He was very cunning in making sure he instilled fear as soon as new guys went to LaBelle. What vice grip did he really have the other leaders' balls in? I suppose I will never know and that is ok, disheartening, but ok.

> Cue, the Tom Petty song, "I won't back down."

CHAPTER 17

"Real is not who stands next to you during your victories and rise, real is who stands next to you during your rock bottom" ~ Anonymous

"What lies behind us and what lies before us are tiny matters compared to what lies within us." ~ Ralph Waldo Emerson

Some days don't come easy

and some don't come hard.

My first month was over. I wanted as little to do

with outdoor activities as possible. I had just finished working with Adam outside and hated every single minute of it. I was never sure if Adam was stupid or ignorant, but clearly the two paths of his mind were parallel. Surprisingly, it wasn't even Adam that made me hate Echo. I hated the heat and the work.

I love hiking, exploring, and all kinds of outdoor activities, but I prefer them all in the colder months. As much as I love Florida, I become grumpy In May and stay that way until after September. The heat and humidity there are just cruel.

Immediately I was dropping hints like a Hollywood wannabe dropping names at a dinner party. What was it going to take to get me in the kitchen?

On Fridays, we had outdoor recreation. Most of the guys played volleyball or horseshoes, some swam or went canoeing, and others went fishing. All that shit sucked to me! Those activities took place in the heat, and I wanted no part of it. I realized if I worked in the kitchen, I could manage these silly outdoor adventures so much better. My plan, to make sure I was peeling potatoes every single time the community was outside. I had an agenda. As I used to tell my sister, "I am always working an angle."

I was standing in the dining room. The big picture windows allowed me to see the small river behind the property. I would watch the men canoe back and forth. Many of them took their fishing very seriously. Other guys had no idea how to keep a canoe upright. This is a river in Florida, and there are tons of Alligators. We would watch them swim in the river daily. I kept my delicious ass away from those alligators and out of that tiny river. I have no desire to be a tasty treat! Let's keep it real, I would be delicious. Also, there was one gator back there that was grabbing calves (baby cows) and pulling them into the river. Ultimately, they had a gator trapper come remove the giant reptile.

One afternoon, I was looking out the windows. A canoe tipped over! Holy cow, I watched the guys struggle in the water. Like a bullet shot from a gun, this guy named Dustin jumps in the water and swims out to the men struggling. The water is muddy brown, and Dustin could have no idea where the gators were. He helped the guys pull their canoe to the riverbank. I was thoroughly impressed because he seemingly had no fear or concern about the gators. I am not sure I could have jumped in those muddy waters. Nonetheless, I sure cheered them on from the sidelines.

Dustin is a blonde-haired hulk of a man. To be honest, I feared him at first. He is a little unpredictable and had a history of bashing men's heads in. I am talking Edward Norton type shit from the motion picture, *American History X*. I am partial to keeping my head intact. I am just funny that way. Turns out, Dustin is a huge hot-tempered teddy bear. Most of all, our men are the sweetest people you will ever meet. They are fiercely loyal people. They love deeply. They just so happen to have drug and alcohol issues. Most of all these men are heroic! It takes a ton of courage for a person to expose, address, and change their personal misery and character defects. I have a deep admiration for anyone that tries to take personal inventory of themselves. Overcoming addiction is so multifaceted and can't be cured by simply setting the bottle or needle down. After dealing with the maddening sting of human relationships and the volatile ways we hurt each other, relationships with people like Dustin help the mental process of this change.

Dustin had left the program a few weeks after I arrived in LaBelle. I was glad to see the giant go. All head bashing had been diverted. His departure was short lived. He simply ended up getting high in a seedy hotel for a few weeks. It was when he came back that I got to know him and fall in love with the guy. Funny how we fear what and who we do not know. I called a lot of the men pumpkin. It was my way of being endearing and not treating them as ill-tempered drug addicts. Dustin called me cupcake. Another friend Hatley called me puddin'. These hardcore men provided some of the most sincerity I had ever known.

Hatley was another man from Ohio. He was also a gentle giant. Unlike Dustin, Hatley is much more laid back. He laughs and jokes easily. His size and strength afforded him a freedom to speak his mind. Once he became a peer mentor, I was proud of him. He had the right head on his shoulders for the job. His girlfriend Mandy came down from Ohio to visit a few times. After meeting Mandy, there were two things I instantly loved about her. First and foremost, she thought I was hysterical. Second, and an awfully close second is that she is good for Hatley. She grounds him.

When Hatley became a peer mentor, they moved him to the firehouse in Naples. This was ideal because he would be working with men brand new to the program. He was visiting one day in LaBelle. We were sitting in the hotel foyer. Our conversation was hysterical.

"When I get back to Naples I have to go to Wal-Mart," Hatley shared.

"The Firehouse is so close to Wal-Mart you can just walk there," I suggested innocently.

Hatley looked at me with disgust.

"Allow me to say this as you would. Honey, I am not walking in this heat!" His impression of me was spot on and we laughed hard.

This I know! If ever I needed Hatley or Dustin to protect me from anyone or anything - I am protected!

Working in the kitchen was more than a job but instead was a chance to learn a skill for the outside world. I had had many jobs in restaurants over the years, always in the front of house. I also knew that when I returned to the real world, I would never apply for a back of the house job. Back of the house people work hard! I don't think I would excel with that pace. My first conversation with Chef Jason went something like this:

"What can you do?" Chef Jason was refereeing to kitchen skills and restaurant experience.

"Nothing. At least nothing that you are looking for," I answered.

Jason's head would bounce when he was surprised

by an answer. "What would you like to be able to do?" he continued.

"Nothing. Maybe cook a nice meal for a lovely lady one day. However, to be honest with you, I have never used any oven in any of my homes. I don't suspect that will change."

Chef laughed. He bobbed his head a little more. Clearly, I was not an ideal candidate. I think he just liked how frank I was with him. I think I amused him.

"I want to do all the jobs that require no thought such as peel the potatoes. I prefer to work from the neck down," implying I didn't want to have to think too hard. After all I was beginning step 4, and that demanded too much thought. This fearless moral inventory of myself was challenging enough. I was about to investigate the many complicated and interconnecting values that together made up the foundation for my behavior. I would visit institutions and people that have come and gone from my life. My molded matrix of discontentment. What resentments lurked beneath my humor. I was about to rewire my personality and reconstruct my behavior. The last thing I desired was to learn to bake a casserole. Chef Jason seemed to understand!

It appeared he liked me but was also a little unsure. He was thinking and laughing. I made a few jokes that went over well. I have always felt that if I can make you laugh, I can make you like me.

"Most importantly I will bring song and dance into this kitchen," I promised.

Chef laughed out loud and that is when I knew I was in!

"Really!" He finally exclaimed. Why would he think I was kidding about song and dance, I wondered?

Chef was an alcoholic at one point in his life as well. He did not go through the Justin's Place program, but he knew the struggle and the victories. As I said, he also had a very calm nature that I found inspiring and attractive. I don't handle stress well. I have extreme performance anxiety. I rarely think I am good enough. I tend to be exceedingly high strung about every minor little thing. If you say you need to talk to me, I have an internal panic attack. The crushing psychological weight of being alive is exactly why I needed to drink.

Chef is the calm man that I always wish I could be. We shared the same beliefs, convictions, and concerns. Immediately, it was evident I could talk to him about anything, and I did. His little shoebox size office often served as my couch for counseling. He helped me understand myself and saw a fair number of my tears. Most importantly, Chef kept my dealings with Adam at a minimum. It was working in the kitchen where I saw firsthand that Adam's brother, Bill, rarely fixed anything.

What I did offer Chef was that with me in the kitchen there would be a lot of laughs and occasionally break outs in song. I did not let him down. Some aren't too proud to beg! I am not too proud to sing and dance.

One time I was singing "Starfish and Coffee" for him, a song written and performed by Prince, but that I took all credit for. Over the years, I have enjoyed leading people to think this was my song. I am unsure if I ever actually claimed I wrote the lyrics, but I sure as hell implied it. It may have been a Prince song, but I added my stolen Michael Jackson emphasis on it. I think this is known as lying by omission. Just for the record, unless you read this book, I will continue to pretend that "Starfish and Coffee" is my masterpiece. Why? Because "Raspberry Beret" is too popular to pretend I wrote that song. Besides the song makes great memories and people love to sing along. Who doesn't love great memories?

One afternoon, Justin, (a kitchen co-worker, who would later be my enemy, then roommate and a best friend) realized Chef had never heard "Starfish and Coffee." Clearly all was not balanced in the universe, and both he and Glenn insisted I sing it. I think it was Glenn that got Chef a chair. I sang, they all laughed, and in walked a relative stranger, Connor. I have already introduced you, my reader, to Connor, but this was my first meeting of the man. Eventually Connor would be my case manager and I would come to know him with respect. Yet, on this day I did not know the man.

Up until this point, Connor was a complete mystery to me. I had seen his face, I had heard his name, but I didn't yet know what face belonged with that name. Connor is your definitive loner and keeps to himself. He was an odd fit for his position in some ways, but he had knowledge that surpassed his 24 years of age. I was always impressed with Connor. I love this guy. I can't say I love this guy too many times.

He is not the kind of man that greets you with his hand extended. He is not the kind of man that initiates conversation. He is shy and overwhelmingly self-critical. When he speaks, every word is calculated and careful. He is gifted and good-looking with a fondness for the arts. He could talk films and music or praise the wonders of south-side Chicago graffiti art. Yet getting him to speak was a lot like prying open an oyster. A lot of work, completely worth it. He also has one of those laughs that are just rewarding and infectious on so many levels. He had my mod brother Rob have laughs that pull you in. Yet, I didn't know the guy and wasn't sure if I liked him initially.

One day I was sitting with Connor in the dining room. We were just talking about everything that didn't matter. You know that kind of conversation that's just fun. I looked at Conner, and with all seriousness I posed a rhetorical question.

"You know what I don't miss? I don't miss those times in the bathroom after binging bourbon for days, and nothing but pure fire was shooting out of my ass. My ass would be so one fire, I couldn't even really sit on the toilet. And God forbid you don't wipe, just pat your ass gently." Connor was laughing so hard that I was sure I heard a snort. This was well after he saw my production in the kitchen. Laughing at the horrifying old days is very healing.

Now Connor walked in on my performance. I suppose it was a fitting introduction, but as difficult as it is to embarrass me, that did it. I must have turned cherry tomato red. I wanted to hide, but I really had no choice. Another member of the audience arrived, and he deserved the whole number. I had nothing else to do and even less to lose. I did what any natural self-respecting artist would do, I took it from the top. Everyone was laughing to the point of tears, and I felt accomplished. Connor merely grinned. Months later, Connor would tell me that I was one of a kind. I have heard that enough in my life that maybe there is some truth to it. I never tried to be one of a kind. I really only wanted to fit in.

The kitchen was crazy fun! I loved working catering events. I loved when outside groups had meetings at our hotel. I would always jump right in and help whenever and wherever possible, at times even helping guests decorate the dining or conference rooms they were using. I am good with people, and Chef never seemed to mind. A man named Smitty, aka Matthew, had vastly different feelings.

Smitty had a hard life and was a hard man. He claimed to have killed people while in the military. I was never sure if this was true, because my father was in Vietnam, and he never liked to talk about the combat he saw. Maybe Smitty was just looking for an outlet to share or maybe he was exaggerating. It was often a means of manipulation. I had no idea why he always emphasized death, but I did know he was a hot head that would lose his shit frequently. This was not ok! I saw *American Sniper* and I know PTSD (Post Traumatic Stress Syndrome) is a very real thing.

Smitty had a love/hate relationship with me. I genuinely loved the guy. His story would move the hardest heart to tears. He has no idea who his parents are, and he was in and out of foster care all his childhood. Like all of us, he longs for love, but battles anger. I cannot imagine how much greater that struggle is after seeing combat or a real war.

Smitty did have a good heart and very real feelings. I think he was just afraid like the rest of us are. Fear often translates to anger.

When I first arrived at Labelle. we had to be up and out of our rooms at 6:45AM. We had no alarm clock, and I was certain I would never wake up. Turned out that I woke up just fine. Every week, you can ask to go on the Saturday Wal-Mart trip, but only a handful of guys are chosen each week. You put in a request to your case manager, they in turn approve it or don't. The key to consent was a detailed request. It seemed the longer and more convincing your needs were, the more likely you would go shopping. I was not chosen my first week there. It was Smitty that picked up an alarm clock radio and a 24 pack of Mountain Dew for me. I thought he was a hero that day. I rarely drink Mountain Dew these days, but for years I craved it every day, all day.

The issue was that Smitty is very territorial and at times jealous if he felt you were doing his job. This became most apparent when I would work with Amanda, the hotel's sales director. Amanda was the only female contact most of us had. As a result, she had a lot of admirers. She was also one of the most fun people I have ever been around. We suspected that Smitty had a not-so-secret crush on Amanda. Nojo claimed it stood to reason, because Amanda was in close contact with Smitty a lot. A man has his will, but women have their way. They can capture our affections very easily.

The number one reason men left the program was women! Naturally, this obstacle is a problem. The solution for Saint Matthew's House was to limit as much contact as possible with the opposite sex. I always understood the rationale behind this rule. Under no circumstances were we allowed to fraternize. We were expected to be polite if spoken to, but never initiate a conversation. This seemed a bit extreme to me. Most of us, including me, had a string of failed relationships behind us. I felt the men needed to learn how to interact with women and choose women that would elevate them, not bring them down.

I once approached Connor about relationship classes. Our educational system has a huge void. People simply do not know how to relate to one another. Now that we live in social media age, I fear loneliness and isolation is at an all-time high. Teach the men to make good choices in their romantic interests. Most of these guys were using drugs with their girlfriends. In many cases, it was the women who turned the guys onto drugs. I didn't really know how to execute my idea. God knows I had made some very bad starry-eyed and stupid choices in my own love life. Although, these women have moved on with their lives, I prefer to think that I am a deep regret they can't resolve. Of the women I have loved with in my lifetime, I have clearly sought out the "crazy as a sack of cats" variety of female. As of this writing, there is still no agenda for these classes, but I hope the idea is still flirted with. The men in the program often lacked education, but they almost never lacked intelligence.

Over time, I became close with Amanda. This concerned Connor because I began to ask to go on pass with her. After a few months in the program, you have visitors. As time goes by, you work up to earning day passes that usually last about 6 hours. Finally, you can have overnight passes, but only with family. These milestones are epic in recovery. They are great goals to work towards.

When I asked Connor about a pass with Amanda, he paused. I was never one to break the rules in rehab. Why would I want to rebel? I offered myself to their guidance and correction. I had in fact surrendered to the institution. I wanted Justin's Place to show me how to live in a loving and sober way. I always maintained, "If I want to break the rules. I will just leave!" This was my truth, and over time I think the staff came to understand it. I was older than most of the men in the program, and maybe that validated me.

My response to Connor's pause was simple.

"If I wanted to be fucking her Connor I would be, but she is just my friend."

I have spent a lifetime being defiant, challenging authority, and rebelling. Connor was half my age and I was always especially careful to never be aggressive with him. I believed in him and wanted Connor to know. I wanted to honor him and see him grow. Because he was younger, it was important to me that he trusted, I was submitting to his authority. I remain a huge fan of Connor. He thought quietly and hard before he answered. His eyes looked heavy as he starred at me. He was standing and I was sitting. I knew it wasn't just me he had to think about.

How would my request affect the other men in the program?

"Alright," is all he said. Then walked into his office.

Eventually, I took a few passes with Amanda. She was a lot of fun, and we always laughed like children. We both have a mutual love for the motion picture, *The Greatest Showman* and it was not uncommon for us to sing at the top of our lungs in her car. Sadly, Amanda did not share my enthusiasm for Steve Martin's music such as the song, "Caroline." I guess we all can't share every taste in good music. She currently lives in Colorado, and I miss her.

She would drive us into Fort Myers or as I liked to call it ~ civilization. Our trips almost always included a motion picture show and eating at a fun restaurant. These adventures filled me with gratitude, and that is the thing about rehab you do become grateful. When your whole life is filled with structure, and you have been ripped of so many freedoms, small things are hugely impressive.

I suppose you may be wondering why I call movies, the motion picture show. My son Mac is to blame. When he was little and after my divorce from his mother, I always took my beautiful offspring to see films. Often after I snapped my son into his car seat, he would look with those innocent blue eyes and ask, "Dad are we going to go to the popcorn movie?" Even as my fingers walk across this keyboard, my mind wanders to his perfect little boy face. I knew he would grow out of calling movies the popcorn movie. So, I adopted the expression The Motion

Picture Show. This is how I preserve my little gentleman that has grown up into one of the finest men I know.

As for why I like to say to people, "May I have a private audience with you?" I stole that from a Cary Grant motion picture. I do love my black and white film stars of the golden age (I told you this about Cary Grant already, but I am sure you forgot, and the same old story is worth repeating.)

CHAPTER 18

"Look at how a single candle can both defy and define the darkness." ~ Anne Frank

"You can have faith or control, but you can't have both." ~ Nicole Reid

"You can't change what you can't connect to." ~ John Amaral

I failed a drug test.

Randomly we're picked to have drug tests. The idea is that we would be tested every 30 days. The reality was that sometimes I would be tested more than once in a week, and at other times I felt the computer had forgotten all about me. This was probably a good practice because it meant we never knew when our name would come up. However, one day when my name was called, I failed my drug test. I tested positive for crystal meth. I thought then and still think now that this was hysterical. I have never even seen meth.

Rodney administrated the test and had no idea what to do. I sat at a long table as he frantically called Connor who was at the gym during our crisis. I had been learning about other drugs from the guys. and there were a few facts that made it evident I wasn't on meth (also known as speed, ice or chalk on the street). First, meth makes you lose your appetite, and I was just too fat for that to be true. Also, paranoia, tweaking, and picking at hair and skin are all symptoms. I didn't have any of these signs. I value my hair because I have an egg-shaped head. I need this hair to protect me from looking like Vincent Price in the sixty's television Batman series.

When Connor entered the room, he sat down and examined my test. We were at opposite ends of the table. I just sat quietly and watched him. He then looked at me in a moment of silence; I could tell he was perplexed. This was also before he became my case manager and I knew extraordinarily little about him.

"You are remarkably calm for someone who just failed for Crystal Meth." Whenever Connor is deeply serious his eyes look heavy, almost as if he is very tired.

The truth was that I was uncomfortable. As I stated before leadership scares me. I have had a lot of bad experience with people in power and their grip on stupidity. Was I about to be thrown out of the program? I felt I was on the edge and maybe about to be pushed over.

"I wouldn't know what crystal meth looks like if you handed it to me right now. I was always a Bourbon man. Wild Turkey 101 to be specific, you know, so I can give the world the bird."

I wasn't sure if he cracked a smile or grimaced. I was sure my magnificent pun was not getting the credit it deserved. He went back to studying my pee. I have never administered a drug test, so I had no inkling of what he was reading or looking for. He mumbled something to Rodney about a faint line, but it was there. Just like that he took a deep breath as if he were still unsure.

"You're fine man," he said. Just like that, everything was over, and I could return to lunch.

Later I was told that drug tests easily give false positives based on medications and food. I have no clue what makes this the case, but I experienced it. In fact, as I continued in the program it was par for the course that sometimes I failed a drug test. I had to get my doctor to write a note saying some of my medications might cause a false positive. I have had high blood pressure most of my adult life.

When I walked back upstairs, lunch was in full swing. Nojo rightly suspected that failing a drug test would stress me out. I wasn't worried about guilt, but it bothered me that I had no explanation whatsoever. As I entered the dining hall, I got a small round of applause from my mod for failing the test. The jokes were plentiful for the next couple of days, but they were funny.

IF ROCK BOTTOM HAD A BASEMENT

Saturday nights were movie nights unless we collectively lost our privileges as a community. On occasion, the nicotine addicted dip spitters would litter the property with their spit. This would lead to room searches and loss of fun stuff like Saturday night films.

The guys could steal almost any first run film off the internet. This absolutely amazed me. This is the piracy that almost every VHS and DVD has a commercial about before the feature. I was a little surprised that this was such an accepted practice at a Christian organization. On the other hand, I wasn't sure that any of the upper level leaders had any knowledge of our crimes. I did have conviction about stolen films. After all, I had obtained a master's degree in filmmaking. I wanted to financially support laborers like the Key Grip, set designers, and make-up artists. That is a first message they preach at film school is that piracy is evil. As a film student, I needed to stand my higher ground, but in rehab all bets are off. Besides most of the films those younger guys watched were awful. I should have been paid by the film makers for watching that shit.

Those Saturday night films, stolen or not, were all we had to escape our reality. I wasn't about to bite the hand that entertained me.

I watched or at least tried to watch the Saturday night choices, but I was an old man among young men. Our tastes in films differed greatly. The guys' choices were mostly garbage; they love films like as *The Mighty Morphine Power Rangers*, *Chips* (the feature not the show) and other trash that I usually walked out of. I craved a strong story, but I was always out voted in favor of films that had the potential for nudity. It is amazing what grown men will use for pornography when in a program. I mean People magazine, really?

In fact, I would ask for special screening of films like *The Founder*, starring Michael Keaton on an alternate night. I knew if I tried to introduce my choices to the masses, I was risking definite persecution. I used to love to tell some of my more vocal adversaries about good motion pictures I had approved such as *Casablanca*, or some other black and white film for Saturday viewing. Just the thought of an option that was more than a year old would cause a meltdown for some. Yeah, I was lying, and I would never risk the revolt of classic choices, but the rise they gave me was worth the lie.

Glenn, who worked with me in the kitchen, was most fun to lie to about film choices. He had no desire to see anything that might resemble a classic! He simply had no desire for anything engaging only entertaining. I got a huge kick out of tormenting him. Because God knows when the flow wasn't going Glenn's way, we all heard about it. I like Glenn, but his mandate of life is "My way or no way!"

On Thursday nights we went to Cowboy Church. My imagination ran wild because of the name alone. Sure enough, the pastor was a small-town rodeo, radical, politically incorrect preacher. He worked all-day and preached twice a week on Thursday nights and Sunday mornings. His name is pastor Mike. I didn't agree with all his ideas or politics, but I appreciated him. He was a man that stood by what he preached. My ex-father-out-law stood by what was convenient and less headache. Larry changed his convictions like he does his underwear. Pastor Mike was a refreshing change.

The services were held outside at the Hendry County Rodeo Arena. This also was the venue for Labelle's annual Swamp Cabbage Festival. I was intimately familiar with Florida Swamp ass, but cabbage? For over 50 years in February, LaBelle has hosted this celebration of rodeos, a dance, a parade, vendors, and so much more. I never was clear on what Swamp Cabbage was or how this name came about. It was clear that Hendry county took a lot of pride in this festival.

We sat in the bleachers and listened to Pastor Mike Preach. He wore a pair of Wranglers; a snap button long sleeve cowboy style shirt, and the brim of his cowboy hat was always drenched in sweat. This was a man who loved God and had a work ethic. I was so impressed that he didn't live off the tithes of church people. He didn't hold golf tournaments to raise money for his ministry. This man of God had a job! Every Thursday night he would drive up in his truck. Sometimes he was running a little late, but he was always dirty from a hard day's work. This man of God had real world skills. Pastor Mike could relate to the working people he preached to. Larry is simply a street beggar on a larger scale who won't work. However, Larry's value is that he modeled everything that I didn't want to be as a Christian man.

His messages were unapologetically evangelical. He had a desire to see the whole world saved. He shared and spoke with an uncanny confidence. This guy had faith. Sometimes he was hard to follow, because he didn't often captivate the audience with stories. He talked about the word of God and was always just a little shy of fire and brimstone. However, I knew he had that passion of salvation message always burning inside of him.

When Pastor Mike called people down from the bleachers for prayer, almost all our guys went down every service. He would lay hands on people and pray for them. He didn't prophesy much, but he always hinted at it. Keeping his words, a little vague (a little like a newspaper horoscope), but still with impact. He kept his messages simple, but they were meaningful because you knew his story. My only drawback was that the message was always geared towards evangelism. I had peace with salvation, but I did not have peace with myself.

On Friday night we were driven to Naples for Celebrate Recovery at East Naples United Method Church. This ministry is aimed at all hurts, habits, and hang-ups. What I enjoyed about this group is the evening is in three parts. First, there is usually a dinner or themed snacks for the first hour. The second hour is group worship. The Justin's Place men mostly sit together. However, some men make their way closer to the front of the sanctuary. Usually some announcements follow and then a speaker. Most often a testimony that involves an overcomers journey. The final hour we break up into small groups and discuss exactly what our addiction has done to us. Sometimes men would jump to different small groups on various nights.

The first two hours were coed, but the small groups separated the men from the women. Once again, I would look around and see all these beautiful people. I could not imagine what their hang-ups or habits could be. Sometimes I would sit there and imagine what addictions and stories people had. I won't lie, the hot women were clearly sex addicts, at least in my mind.

A few other times a week we went to local AA meetings. Once again hearing stories, failures, and victories of people from different backgrounds. I felt like this was a critical role in our recovery. The Justin's Place guys were learning that their struggles had no boundaries. I think this validated a lot of men. It was good for us to witness that there are many people stuck between wrong and right, dark and light, old and new, a lot of people in the middle. Sometimes people were walking into their first meeting, and of course there were the old-timers, people who stuck with their recovery. They had deep water faith in shallow waters.

One evening, an older woman sat across from me. She shared that she wasn't feeling the contentment of peace and so she drank. Her voice was raspy from years of smoking. She was ashamed. Her husband and children were mad at her. I sat quietly and listened to this woman share that she had gotten lost between good and bad choices. I felt her heart's cry when her hands shook, when her voice was between a whisper and a yell. She had lost her surrender. Normally in those meetings, I remain silent. When she stopped speaking, I watched her head hang. Hands on either side of her rubbed her back. She felt alone. I waited and nobody offered insight, so it was my turn.

"Hello, my name is Marc and I am an alcoholic." You can never say "I was an alcoholic." That would cause a verbal riot.

"Hello Marc," the group responded in chorus. This was the protocol of acceptance.

"Your husband is pissed; your children are angry. That is wonderful for you." I smiled at her. "I know it is hard for you to see their anger as a blessing. I know. You feel small, and I am certain everyone in this room knows that feeling all to intimately. I have had more than my fair share days of feeling insignificant. Now here is the thing and what you need to know; your family is only mad or hurt because they care. Once they stop being upset, that is when you worry. There would be no pain in your actions if they didn't love you. They still love you. Look around this room."

Her eyes were fixed on me. For a moment it was as if we were the only people in the room.

"Not all of us have what you have. Some of our families have given up on us. Some of our actions have made us outcasts. Maybe there will be family restoration and maybe not. But your family still cares and that is no joke - (I paused for a minute.) You can't relapse if you are not trying. As a matter of fact, if you are sober today, you have a lot more than many."

She smiled, and I felt she heard me. Not just heard my words but felt them. We call that touchdown

Jesus. That woman was at every group meeting that I attended. We always exchanged smiles from across the table.

Addicts don't need anything more than a connection to begin their transformation and healing. We don't need ear pleasing people afraid of our circumstances. The reason groups like Celebrate Recovery and Alcoholics Anonymous work so well is because brotherhood and sisterhood are developed. People that are burned out, numb, and hopeless reaching out to people who fully understand. When an addict speaks with a person unfamiliar with their struggle, they might as well be speaking a foreign language. It is like trying to explain red to a blind person.

There were risks when the program would take us to do outside activities. Of course, every new person thinks it is their original idea to run off and buy tobacco. This seemed pointless to me, because (as I mentioned before) the peer mentors all too often smuggled in contraband.

Also, when men see women, there are certain biological factors that come in to play. Attraction is a very mysterious thing. Smell, kindness, hormones, voice (What I love most about Heather will always be her voice.) and any number of other factors. Personally, I think we are spiritually attracted to people who have similar wounds to our own. Bottom line is that at outside meetings, men met women. This also occurred a lot at churches on Sunday mornings.

Often, men would get caught passing a note to a

lady. This was very common. One guy got away with starting a relationship with a woman from the Friday night group. Eventually, he asked to go on pass with his sister, but in truth his sister turned out to be his new girlfriend. When he got caught, he left the program and moved in with her. That relationship didn't last too long. I understand a woman standing by her man when he enters the program for help. I never understood women who sought out men from the program. I know of one lady from Orlando who dated more than one of our guys. What was she thinking?

When our young man Grayson, wanted to meet one of the girls, he wrote her a note, and I insisted he use some of my Batman stickers for extra flair. Apparently, Grayson's girl was being brought to Celebrate Recovery by an older woman. Who this caretaker was is anyone's guess, but she confiscated and turned it in to one of the peer mentors. Grayson was impounded for that action. Connor wasn't too hard on Grayson, and I was happy about that. We all want a love story. I always say I am Johnny Cash looking for my June Carter Cash.

Tragically, after I left and graduated the program, Justin's Place hired a man by the name of Dwayne Gordon as the Vice President of Recovery. 1 Corinthians 15:33 reads, "Do not be misled: dad company corrupts good character." Dwayne was an epic mistake. If only Saint Matthew's had closed the door on this man's closed mind. His motto is "My way or the highway". The man does not have a heart to set the captives free, but to glorify the name of Dwayne. He has no compassion for the men in the program. He values blind allegiance. Of course, I speak out against him because who else is not afraid? The lives he impacted were stuck under his rule. Men started leaving the program like rats jumping from a burning ship. Dwayne is a douchebag, and that is being extremely kind. Under his leadership relapses skyrocketed among graduates. He terminated outside recovery groups such as A.A. and Celebrate Recovery. He did away with William Barnett's group Storytellers. Slowly, Dwayne the douchebag has stripped away everything that made Justin's Place special and unique. Men in the program would write me letters sharing their brokenness over this man.

Because of Dwayne's incompetence. I am told that men in the program were being ushered through quickly and missing steps. The men are needed at the graduations for appearances. The more men on display the better the show on graduation day. Do I sound like a cynical man with the spirit of rebellion? People who question leadership are often referred to as having a spirit of accusation. That can be true at times, but not every time. George Carlin said it best, "Inside every cynical person. There is a disappointed idealist." Love has never known a lost cause, but that man had no place at Saint Matthew's House.

Vann! What took you so long to hear the ministry's cry, it needed your intervention! Yet, this ministry kept Adam on staff knowing his reputation of hitting the women he dated.

Dwayne would be fired for failing drug tests, for cheating oh his wife. He would bring his mistresses to the LaBelle Inn and fuck them on the second floor. Dwayne is a smoker and he often smoked around the residents. He was also the chief advocate of discharging men who were caught smoking. This would make Art mad, but Dwayne came straight from Hell!

Our first month in LaBelle, we went to a tiny Baptist church on Wednesday nights and Sunday mornings. This pissed me off and offended every cell in my body. At this point in my life, I could not distinguish between Hell and a Baptist church. My conviction was that Southern Baptists were more kin to Satan than Jesus. Baby Mama's family are southern republican Baptists. Their doctrine was simple, everyone was going straight to hell that did not share their world view. Sorry, but the perfect Christian life is not living on a street free from every minority group and gays. As I have maybe grown up a bit, I may be learning, maybe sometimes people are simply wrong and not bad. As you can see maybe is a big word here.

In step 4, I began to realize I needed to let go of my expectations of people, places, and even God. Not to forget that trying to govern other people's behavior and actions is more than a little narcissistic.

CHAPTER 19

"You can do anything. But never go against the family." ~ Vito Don Corleone, *The Godfather*

"You know how I always seem to be struggling, even when the situation doesn't call for it." ~ Carrie Fisher

"If you don't know history, you don't know anything." ~ Michael Crichton

Yankee daddy and

southern mama.

People will tell you that blood is thicker than a marriage certificate. In this sense, I never faulted my father-in-law for siding with his daughter while she was having an affair. Yet, Larry was able to take things to a new and very different level. First, he fanatically denied the affair. On numerous occasions he would claim that I was wrong. He would insist that my imagination had gotten the better of me. At times Larry had me doubting what I knew for sure.

Baby Mama started out in a radical threesome with the Doughboy Draftsman and his wife. An affair that she tried to drag me into. Let's be clear, I was very tempted, and I even tried to get into all the craziness, but I didn't like it. What my ex-wife would do is take a baby monitor, put it upstairs in her parents' house, and go across the street with the speaker. She could have her sexual escapades and be a responsible mother at the same time. I am telling you, Baby Mama had good ideas.

The Doughboy Draftsman has a brother and sister-in-law that are hugely into swinging. One night, they were all over in their hot tub. The doughboy draftsman's brother and sister in law gave Baby Mama a full education on swinging. Who knew there are such clearly established rules to swinging? Baby Mama is a leading authority if you need a tutor. The night my wife shared the rules and guidelines with me, she had never been more excited. I looked at her that night and knew she was a lost cause. She was ensnared into a new lifestyle, and she loved it. Yet, I am hardly judging. We all have a past; it is just that some of us don't need penicillin to get through it!

Larry is a passive man and passive men disgust me. As I already told you, I was born to a Yankee daddy and a southern mother. In other words, I walk my country mile in a New York minute. Both of my parents may not be the most reasonable people in the world, but they are hardly passive. Bobbi is fearless, and my father has a blunt and confrontational side. I know there is value to all of us and that God loves us all, but I struggle with a weak man. Of course, as an alcoholic, the same could be said about me. Yet, when you drink 101 proof brown liquor straight with no chaser, that is hardly for the weak. I may not ever find the meaning of my drunken days, but even then, I was fighting. I remember sitting at a desk puking violently. My face a tragic shade of red, eyes so drenched I could hardly focus. My body rejecting every drink, but as the booze came up, I fought like hell to keep it down. Sometimes holding the vomited bourbon in my mouth until I could swallow it back down. I look back on those times and I pity the man I was, but I was still fighting. When the morning came, I would do it all over again. Unsure why I couldn't just die! My damaged perceptions and broken core beliefs demanded I needed those drinks. Importantly though, more about the parents that created me.

When I was in high school, I had a burgundy Toyota Corolla. I lived in Raleigh, N.C. and worked at the Crabtree Valley Pizza Hut up on a hill overlooking the backside of the mall. At the bottom of the hill, in the mall parking lot was Sears Automotive Center. I was 17 years old.

One fine day before work, I dropped my car off for an oil change. Then I walked up the hill to work a long lunch shift. When I was off, I walked down to Sears, paid for my service, and went to my car. Only the left taillight was busted. How it got busted I have no idea, but where it happened was clearly at Sears.

I walk inside and up to the service counter. A potbelly service tech greets me. I suspect his life was as miserable as his demeanor. Maybe he felt he was denied a lot in life that provided a manicure as opposed to grease and oil under his fingernails.

Kindly and cautiously I explain my issue. My taillight was broken while in his care.

"We didn't do it," was all he managed to offer. Just like that, I was dismissed. Immediately I could tell Pond Scum Amoeba of humanity had a higher priority than my skinny young self. Did this man really think I was going to be passive? This was not a matter of foolish pride, but a matter of justice! And justice needs a sheriff!

"Excuse me," I continued with his back half to me. I was about to be an asshole but remained polite. I realized that to this man I was meaningless, but there is a woman with a fire in her soul. That woman is my mother. "If you don't fix my light, I will call my mom." Just like that, there it was, the warning shot across the bow of his vessel. The potbelly idiot had been warned, but his foolishness failed to heed the warning. Now if he were a bright man, he would have started praying to Jesus instead of being aloof. I may have been young, but this brute did not sideline me.

When I hung up the pay phone, my mother must

have driven like Speed Racer. I really have no recollection of her taking much more than 15 minutes to pull into the parking lot next to me. She got out of her car and walked to the back of my Corolla. She examined the damage and then asked what the brute inside said to me. I didn't have to exaggerate as I explained. She paused, and I waited for it. Wait for it! Wait for it! Bingo! Touchdown! Contact! The nostrils began to turn red and flare. Mom is never really at her best until the nose single handedly expresses her rage. The flame of her anger had hit her bloodstream.

She marched inside, and I followed. Suddenly, it was like a school fight. You know the ones with the threats and demands of "meet me at the park" or some other place that draws a crowd. All day long, the classmates are either filled with anxiety or anticipation. These are the kind of fights that are an adolescent's variety of a *High Noon* (A 1952 American Western starring Gary Cooper. 96% on Rotten Tomatoes.) showdown. Only difference is that our high noon is at three after the final school bell. On this day, my mother made John Wayne look small.

I gestured towards the jerk and mom rode in with both guns blazing. His deadpan expression of misery was replaced with a kind of grimace that words will not do justice. He became the human form of a deer caught in headlights. I was watching, and I smiled at the brute coward. My mother does not care and will make a scene anywhere and anytime. Bobbi doesn't seek an audience, but strangers' eyes don't deter her. This brute bullied her young. He was not in an okay place. Not to mention, this was before mom made a habit of carrying weapons in her purse or car or both. Quickly, mom was drawing the attention of spectators. The brute was visibly uncomfortable, and clearly his butthole was clenched and eyes wide. I delighted in his every fumble.

In the end, Dumbo the brute, knew it was in his best interest to just fix the taillight. Mom walked away, and he glanced at me.

"I told you I would call my mom," and I said it with a grin. "It sucks to feel like less than a man doesn't it?" Oddly, what did I know about being a man; I was just a teenager. Even today, what do I know about being a man?

My Yankee father's stories are much simpler. As a younger man dad would pick a fight with a tree if he didn't like the color of its leaves. As an older man he mellowed out just a pinch. My favorite dad story must be a conversation he had with a judge during a divorce hearing. The dissolution of the marriage and the process just wasn't favoring dear ole dad. As is the case, most often the courts tend to favor women and mothers over men and fathers. This is a huge injustice to everyone! I suspect a lot of judicial people will spend eternity in a special place in Hell, being raped anally with hot pitch forks. Since when did the role of a father becoming so diluted?

The Judge favored one of dad's soon to be ex-wives. This was their second divorce. Dad married this one woman twice, so it is fair to say she was his favorite. He had two sons with her (both younger than my daughter). What can I say? My old man has got some game. What he does not have is an unbridled tongue. Unlike my mother, dad's anger does not have a buildup or a tell. "A "tell in poker is an unconscious, but dependable change in a person's behavior or demeanor that gives you a clue as to their next move." Just so happens my father is an excellent poker player, and that has spilled over into his real life. Dad is quiet, keeps to himself, and cannot be easily read. Some might call him stoic, but he is capable of an unreasonable rant or fit as well.

I am not sure what this looked like, what caused dad's bow to break, but he opened his mouth. Please forgive me as I share another person's story where the specifics may be muddled and muddy. My father asked the judge a question.

"What are you, fucking her now?" Take a moment. Allow the audacity of that question to sink in. The judge fined dad 500 dollars for his outburst, and did that slow him down? My Yankee father was not done and hardly silenced.

"What can I get for a thousand?" May we take another moment of pause to allow this audacity to sink in? You see to me, judges have the power to change my wardrobe and send me on a vacation. In simpler terms, I am not at all about orange being my new black.

Maybe this helps explain why the head in the sand approach to life that Larry takes is so disgusting to me. I am accustomed to living in fear of what my parents will do or say, because I know they will do something. If I need anyone in my corner, I will take either of my unreasonable parents. I know Bobbi will shoot first and ask questions later.

In 2015, my dad had a triple heart attack. My mother called me around 6 AM to tell me of the news. I was on an elliptical at a gym, when the call came. A sucker punch in my gut left me dazed and confused. I sat down and watched people come and go. Thinking to myself, that at any moment they too could get a call that would change their lives. A truth that is insidious - we have no control over life. We think we are in control, but what an illusion.

I left the gym to just walk highway 19 in Pasco County at the time. About two hours later, I got a call dad had died. He was always such an invincible figure to me. He can be the voice of reason and insanity at the same time. I never knew him to be vulnerable or weak, and now I am told he is dead. It turned out that the message got lost in translation. Dad did die on the operating table, and apparently, he died more than once. However, dad was still alive, but I would not know that for another 10 hours. They were able to revive him.

My uncle Matthew and his wife flew my broke (emotionally and monetarily) ass to Reno. I remember dad was expected to pass away any second. There was urgency to get me to the hospital quickly from the airport. The reality of the situation was surreal. We know we are supposed to outlive our parents, but there is no 101 class to prepare you for their death.

As we drove to the hospital, my heartbeat kept getting faster and stronger. It felt like someone was banging a drum inside of my chest. The walk down the hospital's intensive care unit's hallway was second only to the walk I took with Baby Mama on our wedding day. I was riddled with self-doubt. Every step felt loud and intense. I was scared! Cue the Bruce Springsteen song, "Walk Like a Man."

It was intensive care. Sounds were loud at times. The smell of disinfectant was everywhere. My senses were alert and over-stimulated. My father was almost at the end of the hall. I passed a lot of rooms and looked in on a few strangers, each room representing despair and hope. Each room with different patients, different families, and different stories. Not all these stories were victories.

We walked into his room. He was alone with no roommate. I found some reassurance in that, because that is exactly the way my dad would want it to be. My father would only want to share his room with a woman he was sleeping with. My father has been overly reliant on women his whole life. As for me, I am terrified of the opposite sex. Women break your heart.

His room was larger than you would expect. His bed squarely in the middle. Expensive equipment on either side of him. Wires and tubes attached all over his body.

My Aunt Margie and Uncle Mark were in the room. They were sweet and kind, but nothing more than strangers to me. Eventually, my father's near-death experience would teach me that he has an amazing, loving, and gentle family. However, growing up I didn't know them, and I didn't seek them out. Dad never talked much about anything, and certainly his family was no exception. I figured he was born and bred into a family full of bat-shit crazy individuals. My quota for bat-shit crazy had been over-stocked years ago; there was no room for back stock.

Dad was lying there being kept alive by machines. No words came to mind. I am not sure I have ever been so completely in a moment. No thoughts of the past or future polluted my mind. This was the first time I ever saw my dad vulnerable. Surprisingly, I had a peace that surpassed all my understanding. I didn't even fear my father dying.

There are three tent pole times in my life that seeing or being with my father made a strong emotional impact on me. Keep in mind, these are my adult experiences and are not from my childhood. Childhood memories fall into another category.

The first stand out memory was when I visited my dad in Las Vegas. My parents were divorced, and that creates a void in a child's life. Divorce falsely teaches children that love is not unconditional. When our parents abandon each other, they unwillingly teach us that there is something we can do to make them leave us too. There is an invisible line that once crossed, I could be lost and left forever. I do not think there is an adult child from divorce on this earth who doesn't have abandonment issues. If you come from divorce, there is a wound that gets better, but never fully heals.

It had been years in between visits with my father. My brother and his then-wife, Michelle, also lived in Las Vegas. I was the first-born and was brought into this world when the philosophy was that a child should be seen and not heard was still in full play. Dad was busy chasing his girls, goals, and golf balls. I don't think we bonded in those early years. Patrick on the other hand was daddy's boy.

The two had 100% adoration for each other. My brother never recovered from dad being gone. Because of this, he has chased my father his whole life. He seeks some sort of approval that I am not sure dad is equipped to give. Not to imply my father is unwilling.

    My visit with dad was exceptional. He wasn't yet married to the woman he would eventually divorce a second time in Reno. We had fun, and I felt the full presence of my father. My father has always been an extremely ambitious person. When I was younger, I always felt his attention was very divided. It was on that trip that I felt like my father was meeting me. Learning my sense of humor and finding out about me. Our conversations were no longer merely father-to-son, but of adult content. It was thrilling and rewarding to see him laugh and know I just did that. I wasn't looking for my father's validation, but it was coming to me. It is funny how things come to you when you are not chasing them. I have had a bad habit of seeking validation in my life. Often, I have hoped to find it in the women I have been with. Even at the height of my love for Baby Mama, I was always disappointed in my search. It took me years to discover the freedom of not needing validation. Only God can approve us in the way our souls need.

    On my last day in Las Vegas, dad was driving me to the airport. Now if you have ever been to a motion picture with me, you know I can cry during the opening credits before the story has begun. My eyes are not ashamed of tears. All of a sudden, as if we had a car accident with an unexpected impact from a collision, I started crying. Not the cute watery eyes kind of cry either.

The ugly snot-nosed kind of cry that alters your breathing rhythm then leaves your face a blotchy red. I had no idea what was involuntarily happening to me. Today, I realized I was missing my dad before I even had a chance to board the plane.

My second stand-out moment with my father was my wedding day. My parents had been divorced for years at this point. Memories of them together were as faded as an old picture. Mom had remarried my wonderful stepfather; Ed. Dad was on his third wife. Lives had moved on, and the landscape of my childhood was gone if not lost. I stepped out of a room into a hallway of the church we were about to make our lying vows in. What was I doing? Where I was going? Where was I coming from? I have no clue. What burned into my soul that day was my parents walking next to each other. The two adults who made me and raised me until I was 11 together were side-by-side and walking civilly. This was an episode of The Twilight Zone. Seeing them like that transported me to my early days in Canajoharie, New York. I felt as if I had been throat-punched. My larynx smashed closed.

Canajoharie is more of a village than it is a town. This is when and where my memories of life began. I do recall their big industry being the Beech-Nut baby factory. That industry had a 118-year residence in the little Mohawk River village. A plant that has since closed years ago. Located in upstate New York, I recall it being a very cute little town. Most of downtown is made up of classic brick buildings with a lot of character in the architecture. My memories are fond of that time. I was four when my brother was born, and I have vivid recollections of that as well.

Being that this was my wedding day, all my secret fears and insecurities were already playing with my psyche. My sensitivities strong. My mind was dominated with feelings of inadequacy. I was captivated by my bride and excited to be her husband. In previous relationships, I may have talked about marriage, but I never burned to be anyone elses' husband. In fact, I met Baby Mama in May and we were married the following March. Once my mind was made up, waiting or a long engagement felt stupid. Back then, I had never acknowledged the fear and feelings of worthlessness that governed my life. With an unconsciously guarded heart, I was ill prepared to be a husband. I am not sure Baby Mama was prepared to be a wife either. Her mother, Teresa, played both parental roles while Larry was trying to convert sinners to saints. He was often gone four out of seven days of the week. Baby Mama didn't have any role models as a child. All she witnessed was an abandoned mother doing everything!

I remember dad wearing a blue blazer and Khaki pants. My mother looked beautiful in a flattering dress. Seeing my parents together, the emotions were like a Tsunami. Their relationship was volatile at best. At one point my mother even threatened to boycott my wedding if I invited my father. As I reflected later that evening, it felt nice that my wedding inspired them to play nice. They appeared as friends and that remains touching. My father always told me that funerals and weddings bring people together.

My third overwhelming moment as an adult with

my father was seeing him lifeless in that bed. My father's sister, Margie, and two brothers, Matthew and Mark, were very kind and compassionate. They were also very realistic. The prognosis was that my father would be dead soon. In all practical senses and with all the evidence surrounding me, I still had my doubts.

A doctor walked into the room and asked who was in charge. There was a slight pause, but I quickly spoke up. He pulled me to the side, but not out of earshot from the rest of the family. His bedside manner was caring, but never misleading. The facts were that dad would be gone soon. However, to me facts do not always equate to truth. He even suggested that if dad had another heart attack or died again that we don't try and revive him. Monitors were not showing any brain activity. I appreciated the good doctor's candor.

"Don't count him out just yet, he is one tough son of a bitch," I offered politely. My father was on his deathbed, but I kept feeling this certainty that he wasn't going to die. I never shared my feelings because I feared that they would be dismissed as merely the first stage of grief, which is denial.

Cue The Bleachers song, "Everybody Lost Somebody."

I remember vividly there was a brief time it was just the two of us in his hospital room. I placed my hand on my father's leg. I did not close my eyes. "God, I don't know how to pray right now. I pray you heal my father." Nobody knew I said that prayer. In fact, the first time I ever shared that prayer was just now.

The following day, his health continued to decline. The signs of emanate death were only becoming more profound. The doctor explained his kidneys were starting to fail, and that was a warning against hope. My dad taught me to always just do the next right thing. Do not get ahead of myself and never count my chickens before they hatch. Now I was applying this counsel to his situation. I told the doctor we would just take things one day at a time. Every next level of your life requires and demands a different you. I was about to see what I was made of. I had no idea how to process these overwhelming feelings and the weight of the situation.

Looking back, maybe my faith was stronger than I realized or maybe I was naïve. It never once occurred to me to investigate funeral arrangements. Matthew suggested his sisters could help with the logistics of dad's passing. I know all our days are numbered, but until dad flatlined, I just kept calm. I took it one step at a time, even though some of those steps felt backwards.

I had arrived in Reno early on a Thursday evening. On Saturday, they had scheduled to put dad on dialysis, but out of the blue dad's kidneys began to function again. Dialysis was called off. That stubborn son of a bitch was fighting. I knew he had it in him! Even as I type this, I get the same goosebumps I got the day we learned that dad's body was responding.

When Baby Mama was leaving me for her upgraded life, I was devastated. Looks can't kill, but she was certainly trying with scowls. If we ever spoke, I was desperate, and she was demeaning. Breaking me wasn't enough; she needed to belittle. Cue the Paul Simon song, "50 ways to leave your lover." She had given me a scar I could talk about and that would always serve as reminder that nothing is forever. During our separation, I told my mother that Baby Mama said I was an asshole. The mother of my children had such disdain in her voice. My own mother hesitated before she spoke. It was as if she had a secret from me kept locked away my entire life.

"Well son, between me and your father, you never stood a chance." Mom presented her truth and it resonated with me. Losing her and existing in a life without my beautiful offspring was lonely. Reality has a way of robbing you of faith. I became a wreck. Bring in the booze.

With my father's standards and resolve, he was the kind of man I respected. To no one's surprise, a man like my Larry was a huge disappointment. Nonetheless, I never struggled with hating him until a day in court. The day his index finger stabbed me in the back!

CHAPTER 20

"We may be through with the past, but the past isn't through with us." ~ Donnie Smith, *Magnolia*

"Temper's the one thing you can't get rid of, by losing it." ~ Dr. Buddy Rydell, *Anger Management*

"Everyone suffers at least one bad betrayal in their lifetime. It's what unites us." ~ Sherrilyn Kenyon

The index finger of

betrayal. I felt that shit.

It all began on a Thursday afternoon. The beautiful offspring were very young. Baby Mama had her own house, and I was living by myself in a small studio apartment. I was still holding out hope in big and small ways that our family would stay intact. Larry was assuring me that any idea I had about my wife's affair was simply wrong. He would tell me that my imagination had gotten the best of me. He was always helping me solve mysteries without any clues. Honestly, I started to doubt what I knew. It was like a motion picture where people are trying to suppress the truth from the protagonist's hidden evil agendas. After a while, I truly started to think that maybe I was crazy. This was the time that I had felt most alone and confused. I had no idea things were about to get darker.

I picked up my kids from school. We rushed off to see a motion picture. The motion picture that day was a Disney film, *Invincible*. Time was tight, but I knew there would be no crowd on a weekday. We made it to the theater and bought all our concessions just in time. We always had a mini buffet line of candy and popcorn being passed between us. When my children were young, we went to the bathroom a lot! Enjoying a film was no exception. They had amazing accuracy at needing to pee in the most crucial parts of a motion picture. They usually had to pee during all the great parts. This day would be no different.

Because of my beautiful offspring's age, they were never allowed out of my sight. My daughter needed to use the restroom so the three of us went into the men's room. Mac and I waited outside of the last stall. When my daughter was washing her hands, we were all having a casual conversation about the film were watching. Everything was relaxed and fun, but that was about to change.

Out from the darkened theater I noticed Madison had a bruise on her forehead. In the bright fluorescent lights of the bathroom I could see it was a few days old and healing.

"Honey, what happened to your head?"

"I fell off my bed from jumping," her brown eyes were so innocent and sweet looking up at me.

"Where was your mom?" I had no idea that my body chemistry was about to change. That bruise had a story!

"Mommy was in her room with Mr. Doughboy Draftsman." Of course, Madison used his real name.

It was the definitive moment that I knew our marriage was over. Baby Mama had been lying to me. She. just like her father and his gelatin spine, had led me all kinds of astray about her affair. He was still very much a part of her life. Just like Elvis, hope left the building! Truth became crystal clear! Baby Mama had gone to counseling with me. We had even gone on a marriage retreat. She was saying all the right things at the right time, but she was just playing us all. Slowly she was shutting the door on all efforts. She proved both her father and me a fool. At this point, I didn't really love Baby Mama, she had become gross to me. However, I wanted my family intact.

Hearing my daughter's words, I realized I was standing on a fault line, the focus of my own personal earthquake. She had been having her affair with the Doughboy Draftsman at this point for over two years. Her lies and secrets were as commonplace in our marriage as hours in a day. I didn't have much, but I still had hope, but that day hope and a whole bunch of shit died inside of me. Baby Mama didn't see any value in saving our marriage, and she sure didn't care that the Doughboy Draftsman was married as well. However, at this point she was lovers with the man and his wife. Eventually, as is the case with all threesomes, they become too crowded.

I now know how Bruce Banner (His name was David in the Bill Bixby television series.) feels when rage takes over and he turns into The Hulk. My catastrophic disaster cursed me to transform into a man I pray I never see again. I have heard it said the only difference between a murderer and the rest of us is that the murderer killed a person. I could have easily spent the rest of my natural days in prison after I realized Baby Mama was still lying. She was still fucking the married man and for all I knew other swinging friends as well.

There is a 2003 motion picture called *Matchstick Men* starring Nicholas Cage and directed by the great Ridley Scott. Allison Lohman play's Cage's daughter, Angela, in the film. The character's practice of deception is a brilliant example of Baby Mama. She had an agenda and was cleverly underhanded. Every little thing I understood about her as my wife was washed away in reality.

A few minutes later, I was feeling damned and like an engine of insults and destruction. I called Baby Mama in wrath and called her every kind of whore, liar, and fake I could think of (Sadly, I wasn't wrong.) I spoke a language of hate that I had no idea any human could know or experience. As I write this and relive the events, I loathe the woman who gave me my beautiful offspring. Every woman I have ever loved, I still love in some way. I appreciate the value they were to me at a time of my life. But do not get it twisted, there is no love for Baby Mama. I suppose we all have our own serpents that invade our Garden of Eden. When I see a person from my past love life, there is always a reminiscence of something good. With Baby Mama, I still just see evil. I suppose that is why all our good memories are hidden from me.

Up until this day Baby Mama had been careful, calculated, and cunning. Some people are good. Some people are fake, and Baby Mama is real good at being fake. In my brokenness, she had me not just thinking, but also believing that all the hardships and hurt in our relationship was my fault. I could never play the role of a victim, because she had convinced me I was the predator. Now, I knew better and would never see her the same way again. Sadly, over the years since, I have heard many stories and rumors about Baby Mama. Word from the grapevine is that she is as deep as a mud puddle. What was once a feeling of abandonment turned into gratitude. I feel saved from her! Being right means nothing. There is no trophy, reward, prize, or gratification. Life remains broken. I don't know if she was always phony, but I know I am free and never miss her.

I suppose our marriage had been dead longer than I accepted or realized. So much wasted time on this wasteland of a life. I became dangerous, defeated, and blinded by hurt and hate. As the sun was about to descend, I called my ex-father in law. All my wounds were open and burning.

That day I told Larry, "I will gladly burn in hell alongside of you to make sure that is where you spend all of eternity." Of course, I have no aspirations of burning in hell, but in that fierce moment, I meant it.

I pulled into the Delaney Street Baptist Church parking lot. My kids must have been terrified to see me yelling into a phone. They were crying in the backseat. All of life's reality had placed a terror in us all. Yet, I was the visible monster. Larry met me at the church and took the kids. I didn't hate him yet, and as a result he is alive today and I am not in prison. If the Doughboy Draftsman had crossed my path, he would have had to kill me to stop me from killing him. However, really would I ever want Baby Mama back after all of this? She is married to The Doughboy Draftsman now. Two cheaters that stole from everyone including their own families. Baby Mama is seen as a wicked stepmother by the Doughboy Draftsman's oldest daughter. I am told there is a great amount of disdain towards Baby Mama. That is a crown she can wear for the remainder of her life, and I must admit it makes me chuckle. I was outnumbered by the Baptist and the spouses. Defeat was eminent, too bad I couldn't see then there was nothing worth fighting for outside of my beautiful offspring.

Today, my beautiful offspring are aware of their mother's adultery. They are aware that I had a brief affair with a woman named Amanda. In fact, they have asked me questions for years. I have mostly tried to deflect the attention off that cruel and desperate time. Yet, the

Doughboy Draftsman's ex-wife has made sure the four children know Baby Mama is a villain. My fear is that one day someone will break one of those beautiful offspring's hearts. I suspect the experience will give them a glimpse into their mother's soul. I wonder how the sand will shift in their hearts towards mommy dearest. Cue the Journey song, "I'll be alright without you."

    I went home and did the only thing a self-loathing, self-pitied, and monster of man could do. I got black out drunk for the first time. I liked my bourbon strong and straight up. I was hard up for a hangover. My memory button was on repeat and haunting me. Pain hurts, but 101 proof bourbon can dull that hurt. I took to bourbon because it fights back. The sensation going down is like a bout in a title fight. Eventually someone is getting knocked out. My problems and pain will be there tomorrow, but for now I will go numb. There was no point in going to sleep, because there was nothing left to dream about. I would need to pass out if I expected to escape this reality. I knew I could not run away forever, but what is wrong with trying to get a good head start? The following morning proved more troublesome.

    It wasn't yet 7 AM and there was a banging in my head! Oh wait! Someone is trying to tear my front door down. I tried to ignore the noise, but the banging only got louder. Was my front door about to cave in? I stood to my feet and wobbled across the floor. What big bad wolf was huffing and puffing and trying to blow my door down? It was the police!

    On my front porch stood two policemen. What

the fuck! What were they doing at my home and so early? They started asking me some questions like did I have any weapons in my home, did I own a gun. Why were these police officers trying to piss in my corn flakes so early? I was confused. As I was trying to collect my thoughts, I saw another policeman walk towards me from around the side of the house. I immediately and instinctively knew that these cops thought I might run out of the back door. Why was that a concern? Did he really ask me if I had a gun?

Yeah, I felt some people deserved a bullet, but I never threatened to kill anyone, and I certainly never pulled a trigger. I was still so confused as to why the police would be at my home. Suddenly, there it was! A restraining order to protect Baby Mama and the beautiful offspring. She was being cunning again and wasn't about to let my outburst go to waste. A restraining order implying I was an abusive man was perfect for her story and image. As always, she was several steps ahead of me. They handed me some papers to sign. Explained I was not able to make any contact with her. I could not approach her or call her.

"Am I allowed to send anything in the mail," I asked.

"Absolutely not, you will be taken to jail," an officer barked. I could see it in their eyes that these men thought I was guilty as sin. These cops thought I beat my wife.

"Then that takes care of any child support I was going to send."

I am confident that this only made me look like that much more of a violent and cruel husband. What did I care at this point what these monkeys thought? Could things get any worse? The police left. I shut the door behind them. I sat down and read the paperwork. I tried to read every word, but I was on a subway ride to the pit of hell and Baby Mama was the conductor. In fact, I called her Satan for a long time before I chose Baby Mama because I thought that more endearing. I know, I know what you are thinking! Satan was a very appropriate name for her.

As I sat there in isolation, the hurt felt like open-heart surgery with a chainsaw that went up my ass. I cried so hard that my whole body participated and shook violently. In order to justify her choices and in effort to save her own reputation, she was making horrific claims. She was an actress playing the role of a victim. Who could fault her for leaving me? Who could fault her for finding shelter from my storm with another woman's husband? A man who carries a very real, but slight disreputable odor around with him. I cried. Everything was vivid and surreal. I wanted to be dead and it was in the moment, I knew I didn't have the constitution for suicide.

Leaving her and keeping my reasoning mostly hidden had already caused a heap of judgment to befall me. My Christian friends and church people were vocal and loud about their disapproval of me. I was the bad guy. Meanwhile, so many were reaching out to her, comforting her, and in some cases providing for her. This was simply unbelievable, but it was very real. She was winning. One friend Nathanael and his wife were huge Baby Mama supporters. They never failed to make their judgements known and felt. Even today Nathanael and his wife Anna are the two must judgmental people I know. They were the first to teach me that friends are fleeting.

Another couple, Andrea and Jason sided immediately with my ex-wife. Both Jason and Nathanael taught me a lot about the kind of person I didn't want to be. They taught me that there will be lonely days when you feel you can't find a friend. Once again, I felt the wrath of another Judas' kiss. However, I do feel the judgements we cast on others have a way of finding their way back to us. The Bible does say "by the measure you judge, you will be judged," in, Matthew 7:2.

The plot of my own worst movie was more twisted than Stanley Kubrick's, *A Clockwork Orange*. I trembled on the fault line once again as tremors became more violent. I have always hated men that put their hands on women in any way except a loving fashion. Now, my reputation, my story, and my life was changing because of accusations and falsehoods. I continued to shake and cry for hours. She controlled the narrative. It was the darkest and most alone time of my life up until that point. Baby Mama had not broken just my heart, but my life, my spirit, and my will. I was spread too thin and broken down. She was excelling as the great pretender. Cue the Elton John song, "Rocket Man."

Today I am sober. I feel loved. I have friends, and my life is far from perfect, but I like me, and I like living. I am grateful for a lot. Who knows -- maybe there is another love story in my future? Something real and substantial that will do a heart good. Still, if you told me I would have to experience another day like this, I am not sure if I could handle it. I may have healed a lot since these dark times, but my scars are still tender to the touch.

I tried to pull myself together, but that was impossible. I called friends for refuge, but there was no comfort to be found. All I could see was my God forsaken circumstances. Something in me did die that day, and I am not sure I ever fully recovered from that incident. My wife had become my enemy. She painted the landscape, and I walked perfectly into her claims. Feeling like I was losing my mind, I was proving every claim she made to demonize me. She had walked into a perfect storm and took full advantage. I remember that time and every little detail of those moments as if it happened yesterday. In my mind's eye, I felt sorry for what I saw. I felt sorry for myself, but that was okay because I felt sorry for everyone else too.

The monster of self-destruction had met my need of not feeling anything and self-medicating. The thoughts that embraced me were outrageous. I was ready to fade and waste away. The pain was unbearable. Then the phone rang. It was my mother.

"Marc, I talked to your Aunt Ann. She has a lawyer friend she wants you to go see this afternoon."

I felt it was kind of pointless, but I was a man with nothing to lose. Never underestimate a man with nothing to lose.

Later that day, I went downtown in Orlando. My posture was defeated, and I knew that. I had lost all confidence. My body still shaking like a live wire. I have never been ashamed of who I am or my life, but the image Baby Mama was trying to create was killing me. People tend to believe attractive (Age has not been kind, but she was beautiful when we were together.) actresses.

Today Baby Mama has an older and harder face. I think her actions have caused her a lot of bitterness that wears like a sack cloth. She drinks a lot of wine, and age and the sun have hidden her innocent looking features. She resembles older images of Joan Crawford. If you have seen the film, *Mommy Dearest*, I was certainly feeling the wrath of wire hangers.

His office was above a florist near Lake Eola, a very popular park in downtown central Florida. I walked in the floral shop and in the back of the store was an elevator that led me up to this man.

Walking into his office, I was trembling. My first thought was that the man was huge. He had all the features of an older Greek guy, but hardly the body of Greek mythology. He never rose from his chair, and I reasoned his knees must be bad. I introduced myself as Aunt Ann's nephew. He extended his hand and I jumped into the restraining order. He offered no condolences or assurance that everything would be okay. He just took the papers.

He read and turned the pages slowly. He shook his head as he studied the papers. He seemed frustrated, and this disturbed me. His silence was unnerving, but his focus gave me a tiny hint of hope. He understood the legal language that had gone over my head.

"It doesn't say what you did!" he announced with a perplexed voice.

What does that even mean, I thought. I just allowed him to continue. I felt he was talking out loud to himself more than me. He spoke again, and it was a flash of light and a moment of gold.

Then another pause. He had honed in on something. His focus was hard, and he wasn't flipping pages any longer.

"It's right here. She says you never hit or harmed her or the children, and you never threatened to. For a woman that is trying to make you look like a bad man, she is not very smart." He handed me the paper to see for myself. That is when I realized that her actions were a result of counsel of friends. Most likely, the Doughboy Draftsman and his wife, Ann. His wife was still rooting for Baby Mama, but that would eventually change.

Chills ran up my spine! With my eyes still stinging from all the tears I had cried; it was hard to see the words. I looked at the lawyer through my blood shot vision. Was this real? In her own handwriting, several pages deep in the paperwork it was there. *I had never hurt her or threatened to.* Just like that there was a certain closure. I had proof that I could keep with me and that I could present to my accusers. Those papers stayed in my glove compartment for months.

Now it was time to be a little more calculated myself. The restraining order forbade me from any contact. She needed money, and I knew the Doughboy

Draftsman and her parents were bank rolling her. I was giving her money too. My first order of business was to try and get the court date moved back. This would prolong the time I didn't have to support her, and finally I felt I was able to strike back. If I can't contact her, I can't send a check. This was back in the days, before we could move funds through a series of financial cellphone apps.

Looking back, I was so broken I am not even sure if I was able to postpone the court date or if I even tried. I was breaking down and Baby Mama was trading up! It was so easy for her to walk away and be so cold about it. She didn't even have any regard for the fact she was destroying not one, but two families. I wanted her heart broken; I wanted to see a glimpse of her emotions or her humanity; I wanted to see her world come crashing down. But my hope was in vein. I wasn't even sure she had any humanity left. Baby Mama was not about to die, cry, or hurt over me.

The threesome relationship lasted for a long time, much longer than I expected it could. Eventually, the wife was tossed to the curb. Details have been well hidden, denied and lied about. I suspect Baby Mama was as calculated about the other woman's ejection as she was my own! Ann has spewed a lot of hate concerning Baby Mama over the years. These days, even that doesn't interest me. The Doughboy Draftsman traded in a wife for a better model once; he will most likely certainly do it again. A leopard doesn't change his spots.

On the day we went to court. I had two friends with me - Paul and my friend Faith (One day I plan to write a story about my relationship with Faith.). Baby Mama had her parents there as well. We awaited our turn in the court room before a judge. How could so many bad times be chasing me without relenting or mercy? I would glance over at my ex-wife several times and she never looked at me once.

Larry walked over to me. His face seemed to have compassion. He placed his hands on my shoulders. At least her father, the man of God, still cared. Maybe he had some dreams, visions, or hopes I could borrow? He spoke, and I believed. Once again, I was buying the bullshit as I fought back the tears. I believed in Larry! He was comforting me. I loved him. The pendulum was about to swing to the other side.

He turned his back and began to walk back to Teresa. He paused and made eye contact with a young man, a stranger. Then without turning around, he extended his index finger and pointed at me. I watched everything in slow motion. Just like that, I was served my divorce papers. Larry had pointed me out. Larry was a liar. He didn't care, and all that preaching and sharing over the years about marriage was a lie. The pressure must have been on, and he melted. He conformed to the world he preached against. The future was not what it used to be!

I must hand it to Larry. He did not merely stab me in the back, he made sure the blade went straight into my chest and pierced my heart. It was freakish. The people I could hold onto were dwindling, and nothing but troubled days ahead of me. If I didn't have Paul and Faith there that day I really do not know how I could have survived. I was once sure that Larry was light, but now I knew him differently. His index finger revealed my termination from his family! Darkness cannot drive out darkness - only light. That day I watched the light leave him. Now I wonder did he ever really have it. Larry's Christianity was now just gross. Oh yeah, another great opportunity to call Larry the colostomy bag of Christianity.

After those experiences, I would not date a woman I could catch real feelings for, for years. If we were dating and affections started to creep up on me, I would sabotage the relationship. No woman or family would ever bring me pain again, or so I thought. I had yet to meet Mary from Alaska. She was my greatest love and surpassed Baby Mama in my heart. To be honest, I do not hate Baby Mama these days, but I can't really remember my love for her. All the memories of good were replaced with the memories of who she became. I don't think I could wish her on my worst enemy. Just so happens I was my own worst enemy!

CHAPTER 21

"Just because you got the monkey off your back, doesn't mean the circus has left town." ~ George Carlin

"I have not lost any of my crazy, fearless, raw, soulful, eclectic side and I plan on continuing to tell universal stories in unforgettable ways." ~Janelle Monae

"I don't know how many times I've survived myself, without telling anyone else." ~ Stole this from Pinterest

I'm so sick of black and

white.

Being married left me feeling alone a lot. Teresa, her mother, would hang pictures of her and our daughter, but I was never included. It was a strong statement that I was an outsider. In LaBelle, I was in relationships with people. I had a stronger intimacy with these guys than my marriage was ever able to provide. I felt I belonged to a tribe. I was no longer excluded from family photos like my mother-in-law preferred. The odd truth is that I liked Teresa much more than her own daughter cared for her. I think she is the only one in the family worth celebrating. I do not see eye to eye with her, but I admire that she stands by her convictions. She has her own mind, and that is impressive. Baby Mama changed her beliefs and politics according to the lover she was catering to.

As I wrote before, Larry is a begging evangelist. He was gone most of his children's adolescent years. He abandoned Teresa to play both parental roles. When Larry returned from his many trips, he was only a Disney Dad. This left Teresa as both the disciplinarian and the nurturer. She had all the responsibility while her husband hoarded the weekend joys. Sadly, I miss Teresa the most. She could make these little meatloaves that are simply to die for. She also had a quick wit, and that created a fun dynamic for our relationship.

One of my fondest memories of Teresa was in her living room. She was flipping through some channels. Every time she landed on a film, I blurted out the title.

"How do you know that within seconds? I just don't understand," she proclaimed.

We went on to make a game of this, every time I was in the living room and she landed on a motion picture, she asked, "Okay, what is this?" For once, I was not letting her down.

Sunday, July 16th was National Ice Cream day. I heard about it from the radio that morning. I told Anthony we were having ice cream that day. He just laughed me off, but I went straight to Zach (at this point our head intern) and told him about our eclectic, but sacred holiday. I also complained that it should be an international holiday. This was during breakfast. Every opportunity I had throughout the day, I reminded Zach that we should have ice cream.

Anything to do with food is an honorable mission.

At lunch, a wide-eyed Anthony looked at me, "You might really pull this off; you run this place!" then he started laughing. Anthony has two very distinct styles of laughter. First, his belly laughs where he can't really control himself. Second, he has a more devious laugh that is very deliberate. This laugh usually is a strong indication he is up to mischief. Anthony loved to stir the pot in his early days. Anything he could do to create chaos or conflict was exciting for him. I must admit his antics did add a lot of flavor at times, but anyone can ruin a lasagna with too much garlic.

Zach is Gabe's younger brother (you may remember I referred to Gabe as the Jolly Orange Giant). The two look and act nothing alike. I liked Zach immediately because he had real convictions. One of the very first days in LaBelle, I saw Zach on the third-floor balcony. He was obviously carrying more on his shoulders than he should have been. We were still strangers. He had just made the internship as a peer mentor. He stopped walking near me, almost unaware of me.

"How are you Zach," I asked.

He was puzzled and it was immediately clear he didn't know how to answer.

"Compared to you I am an old man. What's on such a young guy's mind?"

Zach shared that he didn't know how to please God with his new position. He didn't know how to serve God. This was also the moment I knew I loved this man.

"Do you know why you were created Zach?"

He looked at me in awe the same way as Elijah Wood's character Frodo Baggins looks from *The Lord of the Rings* films. An alertness came into his gaze, and he fixed his eyes on me. Then he answered, mumbling and rambling until he stopped and laughed at himself.

"I don't know man", He confessed playfully.

"You were created for fellowship with God. Nothing more or nothing less. Sometimes we try and serve him and that is sweet. In fact, that motivation is noble, but the truth is God has angels to serve him. The secret about angels over humans is that when they serve him, they get it right the first time. My point is, go easy on yourself my friend."

Our eyes locked briefly in a shared understanding. I trusted that what I said was resonating in his soul.

Years later after I left the program and was living in Chicago, Zach told me that he remembered that conversation and that he took a piece of me with him everywhere he went. Funny how God moves. I had been living so reckless and lost, and God was using me. God sure does enjoy using us vagabond humans. In God's currency, there is room at the top when we are at the end of the line.

That night I was invited to ride to Winn Dixie. A couple of the interns pitched in and bought the big buckets of ice cream. Zach made sure we had something to enjoy. Zach is young and was younger back then. He realized that on occasion we needed a victory. This was the most beautiful thing about rehab. You celebrate and rejoice over the simplest things. It puts us in a place where we are not just grateful for our sober days, but, as Greg would say, we're grateful for "The simple things in life."

My immediate family was my mod brothers, but our extended family of men from other mods grew quickly. Zatlokovicz is a muscle-bound Hercules of a man who was in the mod before ours. He tends to have a very disinterested look on his face most of the time. His size indicated he could pop me like a zit if he so desired. He had the outline of an eagle tattooed across his chest. Artwork that was begun, but not yet finished. I liked him right away, but never imagined we would bond so tightly. He is a gentle giant that was raised on Disney animation. Zatlokovicz absolutely loved *The Little Mermaid, Aladdin, The Lion King* and all the classics of the nineties. Our common interest in motion pictures was the seed of our deeper relationship. A game unique to our relationship was born. One of us would name an actor or two and a year. The other had to guess the film. For instance, I might say "A 1990 film starring Eddie Murphy and Nick Nolte." He would of course be thrown off because that is the rarely remembered sequel to their smash hit, *48 Hours*. The answer was *Another 48 Hours*. We were always trying to throw each other off playing this game. It was a challenge because we didn't have access to any cellphones in those early stages.

That fun interaction led to more intimate conversations. Zatlokovicz would on occasion come to my room and we would just talk and share. He was a recovering drug addict and me a recovering alcoholic. Yet, I quickly learned that our paths of destruction made no difference. Our challenges were uniform. Sometimes we shared resentments, at others we untangled memories. More than a few times, we simply played the movie game. Today we live in different states. We don't talk as much; we allow social media to inform us about each other's lives too often. Although on a random occasion, I get a message from him that reads something like this; "1993 romance comedy starring Robert Downey Jr. and Tom Sizemore?"

I reply, "I can't think of the title, but I know it also starred Elizabeth Shue and Charles Grodin".

"Yesssss"!

"A three-word title" I continue.

"Yesssss"!

Only this time I have my phone and Google. The answer is *Heart and Souls*.

In the mod after ours were a lot of great guys. The one who I spent the most time with was named Nick.

Nick is a tall, young, great looking guy who was amazingly sincere. He was full of mistakes and imperfections, but as real of a man as I ever met. He had tried and failed in many programs. However, it was his stint in a Scientology rehab that really captured our imagination and attention. I had all kinds of questions!

I had read Leah Remini's book, Troublemaker: Surviving Hollywood and Scientology, an aggressively honest telling of her life, career, and religion. Nick's accounts of his involvement with the religion were equally captivating. I know very little about L. Ron Hubbard's realm of crazy, but I am certain they freak me out. All my paranoia was only reinforced from watching the film by Paul Thomas Anderson titled *The Master*. A story that resembles the life of L. Ron Hubbard, who lived his later life on ship as a sea captain.

Nick discovered that I had written a story called The Nothing Man. A story still in development. Remember the wise words of Ernest Hemmingway "The first draft of everything is shit!" My story needed a lot of work, but I offered it to Nojo for a review. I knew in his hands I would get a no-holds barred appraisal. I also trusted he could handle the frailty of my ego. When Nick and a few others learned about the story they wanted to know more. For several nights, Nick and some of the guys would come to the room and I would read the story to them. Mostly the audience would vary from evening to evening, but Nick came every night. He has also been one of my biggest advocates of the book you are holding.

"This is going to be epic!" Nick has declared.

One early evening after dinner, Nick and I took a long walk. I was about to graduate the program, meaning Nick wasn't far behind. Saint Matthew's House was my first rehab. He had more experience than me with recovery and institutions, which meant that Nick knew failure more intimately than me.

We are first taught that our addiction is a disease. Then step five demands I take responsibility for being a charming and articulate madman. Most of the time I felt like I had no choice or freewill concerning my drinking. It all feels like a huge contradiction. I am now realizing I must own my behavior. I always knew, but never admitted that most of my life had been governed by fear. I had to admit my anxiety about rejection kept me from real intimacy in relationships. I had been fraught with a fear brought on by shame and trauma. I had to identify so much about my life and only blame me. It all feels a bit like trickery at first.

Thank God for the biblical stories about Jesus' great compassion for the broken and fallen. I had to beg God for help and still fight like hell just to desire sobriety. In step 5 I began to realize that if I do not acknowledge my decisions, I can't change.

Step 5 requires we have admitted to God, to ourselves, and to another human being the exact nature of our wrongs. It is communication with identification and compassion. I was astonished that men could share their hearts, emotions, and epiphanies. We often unloaded and deadened burdens as brothers. This was a new intimacy without fear of rejection and inadequacy. Nothing was ever too terrible or too trivial in these deep conversations.

On this walk, Nick expressed fear about returning to a world that had poisonous influences. He was afraid he might return to his old patterns and life. People make mistakes. It is called the human condition we all live in. However, Nick was no longer bound to live in a punitive version of this world. I reassured Nick he would be fine. He even outpaced me in his growth. I knew Nick had a sincerity about him; I had witnessed a changed man. I had faith in him, and I tried to express the height, width, and depth of that faith.

Currently Nick owns and operates his own moving company. He recently got a real estate license. He also works at a retirement community. Most importantly, he seems to have found the love of his life. Mistakes will happen, but no one is under any obligation to hoard life's errors. Don't allow the past to skew your view of your present.

These relationships and so many more are some of the most special of my life. I have lived mostly in solitude, individualism, isolation, private and lonely. Even before the memory of my childhood begins, my mother always said I had imaginary friends. She also claims I was always one to have just one friend. I never ran in a pack.

Apparently, I was obsessed with the story of *Robin Hood* during my early childhood. I am told I would have my parents read it to me repeatedly. I had it so memorized that I could recite the story word for word. If my parents skipped a sentence or page, I objected. This is of interest to me, because years later when I read stories to my daughter Madison, she could recite the pages as too.

I don't recall, but I had an imaginary friend named Robin. I grew out of having my imaginary friend, but never my imagination. In fact, if I see a counselor, I am charged a group rate. I have all these characters that live inside my head. It stands to reason that I would be a writer.

Too many relationships have combusted. I am afraid of real adults. I am equally afraid of love. Of course, when I hear detailed accounts from the men in rehab about their addictions and moral failures, my heart bleeds love. In rehab, I didn't discover my need for community, but I did begin to accept it. Alone, I am prone to a life that is all about me. In community, I am a different man. I become a guy I like.

In my life, I have had some of the most amazing friends. I have been blessed and often highly favored. However, I think I have always kept parts of myself hidden. Those men once broken in their own addictions helped my heart hatch from the shell, I hid in. I am not sure if it was a matter of sin or a symptom of pride that caused my fear, uncertainty, and isolation. Maybe it was just my genetic makeup that kept me in conflict with intimacy. Yet, with these men my walls were torn down. These days I still build walls; however, I also take a sledgehammer to those walls from time to time. I was giddy about my new relationships, but also longing for many of the people I left behind.

CHAPTER 22

"It's not easy being a mother. If it were, fathers would do it. ~" The Golden Girls

"To describe my mother would be to write about a hurricane in its perfect power." ~ Maya Angelou

My first visit.

My random friends.

On my way to Naples with Michael, we stopped and met, mom and Ed. We had lunch at a Cracker Barrel in Lakeland, and I told them as much about the program as I knew. I could see in her face that this was the answer to her prayers.

It still amazes me the level of selfishness I was capable of. I was not considering how my self-destruction hurt the people around me. That lunch was my declaration of change to my parents. I didn't really have to admit that I was powerless, and my life had become unmanageable as Step 1 requires. I already knew and everyone around me knew. As I said, the first 3 steps were easy for me.

I was slightly uncomfortable sitting with my family. I knew if this didn't work, I was pretty much out of options. I know many guys have tried several programs, but this was my first and only. I needed a miracle. Yet, I wasn't promising anything, because I wasn't sure sobriety would take with me.

Four months later, mother and stepfather were coming to LaBelle.

My father later confessed, he never thought I would stay. When he got my first letter, he simply thought, "Well, he is still there."

I have no idea what my beautiful offspring thought. I called them both and just said told them. That was a pretty epic low point. I wanted to be a hero in their eyes.

If I recall correctly, it was Easter Sunday. On holidays, visitors are usually welcome no matter what stage of the program you are in. At this point I had been in the program four months. This would also mark the first time I had seen anyone from my former world. I know my mother loves me unconditionally, but my anxiety was high.

I was climbing the walls waiting for them to arrive. It was still unbelievable to me that I was in the program. It was even more odd that I was so happy there. I had worried I would be living out the Ken Kesey's novel, One Flew Over the Cuckoo's Nest. Later the book was adapted into a film produced by Michael Douglas, directed by Milos Foreman and starring the magnificent actor, Jack Nicholson (Not the director's first choice. Foreman offered the role to a few other actors including Burt Reynolds.) This motion picture went on to win all five major categories at the Academy Awards.

I was living among men from the streets and from prison. These men had zero pretenses. These guys offered nothing more than vulnerability and their wounds. From a worldly perspective, these guys had nothing to offer. Yet amongst their brokenness, tears, laugher, hurts, scars and in some cases – stupidity, was healing. I wanted my mother to know my friends. I was prouder of these relationships than I ever was my wife.

Cue the Jon Bon Jovi song, "Never Say Die."

I always refered to us as a pack of dogs. Walk into any of our rooms and at any time and we would all be crammed into a lower bunk laying all over each other. It is hard to imagine that when I first met Anthony; I thought he was another species entirely. Now I was among men that taught me my feelings of despair were not unique to me. Slowly our self-pity and self-centeredness was melting away (Not to imply selfishness is not a lifelong battle.) Most of the time we were laughing. At times we were crying, but we were always bonding. It always amazed me that we could share such tiny rooms; three to four men at a time and we had such respect for boundaries. I have had roommates that have no regard for space. Living with some people can be horrific! However, when I lived with The Giles, I always felt a part of a family. Something I have been longing for most of my adult life.

From the dining hall, I could see through the walls of glass into the lobby. The lobby was off limits to residents. I kept a watchful eye on the front door. Most of the men already had family there, and lunch was pretty much over. It was fun to see restoration happening all around me. The faces of family members seeing their loved ones sober and full of hope. It was pure beauty. Broken hearts were mending. Then I saw my family. I could feel my pulse like a runaway horse. I got up from a table and Anthony followed. I am not sure what happened, but before I even got to my mother I started crying. Of course, Anthony laughed with an approving smile. Anthony laughed at everything!

We sat in the lobby and did most of our visiting there. Every resident that walked by me, I tried to make sure I introduced them to my mother and Ed. I admit it; I was showing off these guys. I wanted my mother to know them. My curse had brought me so much blessing in these men. I would share their strengths always with so much adoration and always permission. You would have thought I was introducing my family to their soon to be daughter-in-law.

Understand something - if you do not believe in God, if you doubt that God hears us, if you think He is just a puppet master enjoying our folly for His amusement, get involved with a rehab and see lives transform. Your faith will blossom! I had always said about Rehab, I was there to reconnect with God and faith more than to be sober. I desperately needed a renewed faith in God. I never doubted His existence, but why had he overlooked me?

When I was in my small apartment back in College Park of Orlando, I prayed for God's help, and what I fully expected was God to heal and transform me instantly. I did not want a process, program, or any lengthy involvement. I wanted the quick fix. I read the bible and I was familiar with Jesus healing the leper. When the leper asked to be healed, Jesus touched him. Matthew 8:3 says, "Immediately he was cleansed of his leprosy." There are so many stories in the bible about Jesus healing people. I wanted one of those fast food window drive-up cleansings. I did not understand the community of healing.

After the terrorism of 9/11, the country became mostly united. People from every background and color were brought together. This is the beauty from ashes that tragedy brings. When addicts from every addiction come together and share their sorrows and struggles, they come together in hope. We build a community built on healing and shared experiences. I cannot help but to love people who are intimate with the pain I have known.

I always thought church would provide me with a culture and community that worked much like a hospital. A place where people with broken lives could go and be honest about their sin. In truth, I found people more concerned with buildings, budgets, and appearances. I felt disheartened and that church was broken. When I would share my thoughts, feelings, and ideas with leaders, the most common response I would get was that "I was in rebellion." To that I simply say; I am my father's son after all. God knew these men at Saint Matthew's House would put some feel good back into my soul.

A gentleman named Aylen had just become a case manager. He was mostly working with newer guys. Aylen would be at the program when my nephew, Christian, went in a few years later. As of these days, Aylen has Conner's old job, but his actual title is a mystery to me.I told you, I never really understood anyone's title, I never really cared about titles, not then, not now. When He came out of the office, I was excited to introduce him to my parents. If you were in earshot, you got to meet Bobbi and Ed.

Aylen was rooming with Eric. Eric was head intern for a time. One evening I wrote Eric a letter and slid it under his door. Eric is a great man, but he is a consistent complainer. Grumpiness is the enemy of sobriety. I told Eric about my concern in the letter. Later when I saw Eric, he confronted me. Feelings are very delicate in rehab. What Eric thought was anyone's guess. Failure, envy, and hate can reside in some people even after they complete the program. I cared about Eric or I would not have written him a letter.

"I read your letter to my girlfriend over the phone last night", Eric declared. I raised my eyebrows to suggest I was ready for her reaction. Slowly a Joker style grin came across his face.

"You fucker," he announced, "she agreed with

everything you said."

"Good, because I am right. I care about you Eric." From that day forward, Eric treated me as if I was always looking right through him. I am not that insightful. Eric just wasn't that much of a mystery because he shared his feelings, thoughts, and his many frustrations aloud.

Eric was also the man who would allow me to have private screenings of films occasionally on Thursday nights. As I wrote earlier, the younger men did not share my enthusiasm for cinema. Eric probably saved my life. I write this jokingly, or do I?

During the visit, Anthony whispered in my ear, "Do you think your mom would go get us some dip?" My answer should have been "No!" but I knew mom would in a second.

"You're not going to get in trouble for this are you?" she clarified before heading to the store.

"No, mother", but the truth was I didn't really enjoy being a part of this sneaky behavior. However, I knew the staff all smoked and dipped as well. I reasoned if they are leading by example why should the residents be forced to comply.

Cue the Glenn Frey song, "Smuggler's Blues." Mom carries a purse that is just smaller than a duffle bag. She perches it under her arm like an automatic weapon. She left on a mission and returned with the product. Nojo and Anthony had a good day with new cans of dip. Sometimes breaking the rules is just fun.

It was refreshing for my mother to see me with clear eyes, a clear head, and a healing heart. I think my parents were excited too. Rehab wasn't just helping me, but my family as well. Maybe beauty really is just in the eye of the beholder? On their next visit, they would spend the weekend and bring my beautiful offspring.

My first off-property pass was in July. This was so exciting! Paul and Sheryl were coming to see me. On pass, you must take an accountability buddy. I took Anthony with me. However, the practice of accountability is rather silly.

The idea is to have a guy there helping prevent you from going in a wrong direction or breaking rules. It was a reasonable, but impractical theory. Guys who wanted to break rules always teamed up with guys who wanted to break rules. Often the plan was to meet women and get laid. Glenn was an expert at this breaking or bending rules thing. Glenn worked with me in the kitchen and is an amazing man with a major character flaw. He complains twenty-four hours a day. If Glenn is not bitching, check his pulse. He was also allowed to go on pass with his girlfriend and that bothered me. I wasn't jealous that he could visit with her, because she seemed like a good person. I was upset with him because I knew he was mostly using her. Whenever he went on pass with his girlfriend Glenn made sure his buddy had a girl too. I suppose that was considerate. Glenn would dump that girl well before he left the program. She was older and that didn't appeal to Glenn.

Paul took us out to eat and to see the new

Spiderman: Homecoming motion picture. Of course, coming from rehab we had no money and Paul was kind enough to pay for everything. Freedom for a day was pure magical.

There is a lot of prison mentality in rehab. However, you are forbidden from threatening or touching another person. I heard one man tell another, "I am about to turn that ass into a prison pussy." Talk like that grabs your attention even if not directed towards you.

Men that live together and are going through chemical changes in their bodies as they withdraw from substances are bound to be moody. This is where the rubber meets the road, because at times you just need to beat the shit out of each other. Welcome to thunder dome! Two guys go into a room. Another guy or guys keep watch outside for staff. Then they fight. Thank God I was never invited to Thunder Dome, but it was real. The traditional alibi for a black eye was that they fell off the top bunk. Everyone knew a beat down had just taken place.

I initially thought a few of the guys were stupid. However, I grew to learn that for some, they had brain damage from the consistent use of drugs. In the case of the alcoholics we call this wet brain. The clinical term is Korsakoff Syndrome, a very real condition of permanent damage to parts of the brain associated with memory. I was never afraid of dying, but wet brain scared the hell out of me! God knows I must have gotten close because I was blackout drunk a lot.

The common misconception about being blackout drunk is that a person simply passes out. The truth is that the individual is often conscious and can do a lot: they can eat, drive, have a sexual encounter, to name a few. It is just that the brain fails to move these events into memory.

I know at times I had minor hallucinations, but they were very quick. Those would freak me out. In the blink of an eye, something would startle me. I would be sure I saw something. I do not miss the confusion or paranoia that I would have when I was detoxing from the drinking. It is a painful and frightening time. I would promise myself I would never drink again. The misery was too great a price. Yet time and again, just as a dog returns to his vomit, I went back. It was who I had become, a man that could not go too far.

People will ask, tell you, or even demand you just stop! This is the insanity of the disease. All my anger, shame and insecurities could not stop any of me from going back to the liquor store. Sometimes I would fight so hard, and all I would think is that if I can just get past the 2 o'clock hour, I won't be able to buy anymore alcohol. Then I would lay in bed waiting for 7 o'clock in the morning until I could buy wine from the 7-Eleven. Thank God I was ignorant to some alcoholic tricks like mouthwash.

In rehab, I met a man who drank Listerine. The mouthwash is on average 54 proof and may lessen depending on the minty flavors you choose. Apparently, this is an extremely dangerous way to get drunk, but people do it. People also have their teeth pulled just so they can get high off pain medication. That kind of stuff blows even my mind.

Mouthwash is a great way to relapse or sneak a

drink because you can easily hide the smell of alcohol. It is a surprisingly common means to a buzz or bender. Consider this, the average beer is 5% alcohol, Wine is usually around 12%, malt liquor is about 7% and most distilled spirits are around 40%. Mouthwash is pretty much standard at about 26 or 27%.

Some of the ingredients of mouthwash will cause blindness or a coma to name a (very) few side effects. I am certain that I would have obtained my death wish if I had known about mouthwash.

CHAPTER 23

"Do you not know that a man is not dead while his name is still spoken." ~ Terry Pratchett

"To be absent from the body, is to be present with the Lord." ~ 2 Corinthians 5:8

"The darkest hour has only sixty minutes." ~ Morris Mandel

Time bomb Tom.

Writing this book was interrupted today. Monday, August 20th, 2018, I got word that Time Bomb Tom, died of an overdose. Damn.

Tom was good looking, had a great personality, and was a talented guy. When I first met him, he was only a few months ahead of me in rehab. He worked in the kitchen with Chef Jason and encouraged me to do the same. As you know, me working in the kitchen was not a hard sell.

Tom offered advice. He talked about his struggles, and we laughed a lot. As you may recall, the second floor of our rehab is a hotel to the general public. Tom had met and had a fling with one of the very pretty housekeepers named Christina.

Christina was going through a divorce. She was involved with her church and she seemed to enjoy the attention of our men. She enticed Rob (my mod brother) a lot as well. She was hardly a vulgar woman. However, I wondered why she was so willing to compromise a man's growth and sobriety. When you toy with an addict and his desperate emotions, you are playing with his life.

Once Tom left LaBelle, he would see Christina. I am not sure of the depth of their relationship. However, it did appear that he cared more deeply for her than vice versa. Tom was longing to be loved and to feel like someone. He had a heart cry that was at a frequency that Christina could not hear or understand. I do not fault her for this, because I think women generally cannot hear the masculine cry of a man's heart.

I believe in God; I believe in the bible. In Genesis, Adam and Eve fell into sin. The consequences of that sin according to Genesis 11:7: "Come, let us go down and confuse their language so they will not understand each other." I don't think the Lord just confused our languages among tribes and nations. It is my belief that we misunderstand one and another's words and meaning within the same language. Nowhere does this seem more prevalent than in relationships. In paradise we were a symphony; outside of the Garden of Eden we are The

Gong Show. For my younger readers, The Gong Show was popular in the seventies and eighties. A syndicated Amateur talent contest of mostly awful and sometimes hilarious acts.

I overheard Christina put Tom down when they were dating. She was making fun of Tom behind his back. Tom was looking for a new rhythm in his life. He was learning sobriety and trying to discover the fullness of his masculinity. Christina only offered pressure, false encouragement, and selfish expectations. She did not walk alongside of him with empathy. She was premature to the recovery Tom needed. Sobriety is hardly a smooth transition. I suspect that Christina had her own struggles and was not familiar with addiction. Sadly, none of her relationship with Tom was beneficial. I heard she cried horrifically when he died. It was a hard pill for me to swallow. Why did she not show that compassion when they were together? When he was alive?

The man had everything to offer. In fact, when we first met, he was so friendly and genuine that I could never imagine him having an addiction. That is part of the reality of the disease; it is not selective and will come after anyone.

I will talk more about relapse later, but with Tom's death heavy on my heart I want to point out one thing.

You **don't** get over an addiction by **stopping using**. You recover by creating a **new life** where it is **easier not to** use. If you fail to **create** a new **life**, then all the **factors** that brought you to your **addiction** will catch up to you **again**.

IF ROCK BOTTOM HAD A BASEMENT

Therefore, the prison system fails addicts. People do their time, but they return to an old life with old friends and quickly old habits set in. I have been told that an addict is typically using within 13 hours after being released from jail or prison. That is an incredibly sad reality. Abstinence is not a cure for addiction. In fact, we all can abstain for long periods of time, but triggers lurk inside us all.

I suspect that Tom fell back into his old lifestyle. I also think he wasn't emotionally grounded enough to handle the complexity of romance. God knows I am never ready for love. It is sad he died, but I am encouraged more to share my story. If you are an addict, maybe I can help you see some answer to the prayers you are praying in the dark. If you love an addict, maybe I can help you learn to love, but not enable. Most of the time people stay in their addiction because a well-meaning family member or friend has helped pay a power bill for the seventh time this year.

CHAPTER 24

"I don't like to commit myself about heaven and hell – you see, I have friends in both places." ~ Mark Twain

"Friendship is born at that moment when one person says to another: What! You too? I thought I was the only one." ~ C.S. Lewis

Monstrosity: A species named

Anthony.

Cue the Andy Grammar song, "Good to be Alive (Hallelujah)."

Step 6 of recovery says we were entirely ready

(Entirely willing is more appropriate. Are we ever ready for these steps?) to have God remove all these defects of character. This is one hell of a difficult step to jump into. It requires a willingness to hold nothing back and really take a hard inventory of who you have been and who you are. In my opinion it is also the start of making a new life.

When we defend our addiction, we tend to devote to it. Therefore, owning our shit in Step 5 is so important. Now I find myself stuck between right and wrong, truth and consequences, chance and destiny, light and darkness, a painful past and an uncertain tomorrow, tenacity and terror, who I was and who will I be? I cannot imagine walking through these steps without my friends from the Justin's Place program.

I used to call Anthony Stitch. A character from the 42nd animated feature film of Walt Disney Studios. Stitch was an alien life form that was eccentric, mischievous, chaotic and destruction just seemed to meet him at every turn. Anthony loved anarchy! When I first saw this guy, he was so high he could not hold his head up. His life was going nowhere fast, and I prayed he would leave Justin's Place immediately. Who knew I would form a bond with this kid the way I did? Certainly not me!

It was not uncommon for someone to announce that Anthony was "Stirring the pot again!" It could easily be an unwelcome statement because it most likely was awakening a person's resentments or issues. Some thought Anthony was just a prankster, and at times he was thought to be malicious. I just felt that Anthony was bored and more comfortable in chaos than in peace.

IF ROCK BOTTOM HAD A BASEMENT

You know how some people leave an abusive relationship; however, their next relationship is abusive, and the cycle is relentless. People feel most comfortable in what they know. Anthony knew chaos, and his way of controlling his environment was to be the puppet master. Anthony was definitively everything I hate in a person except for one thing! He is not fake! He never pretended to be anyone but himself, and if his title included asshole, he wore it like a crown. My dumbass found this to be very endearing. I love him as deeply as I have ever loved anyone.

It was within days that people started referring to Anthony as my adopted son. I am unsure if I was able to reason with him or had any influence, but I was able to walk alongside him. As addicts this is what we need, not your pity, praise, or punishments just a connection.

I also found a lot of strength in Anthony. Being in a Christian program was overwhelming to me. I had submitted to a group of people, the likes of which had caused my greatest pains in this life. People who seldom seemed to know their own core beliefs, doctrine or God better than they understood the rules and implementation of religion. There is a huge difference between religion and relationship, but a lot of people in the so-called Christian Ghetto do not see this.

When I first arrived, I was still very raw and said things that I later regretted. I assured one leader that if he hung himself his body weight would snap his neck. It had also become my custom to encourage people to shoot themselves. The very first man I ever said that to was

Larry, my ex-father-in-law. Oddly, the men in the program I encouraged to take a six-foot dirt nap, I now love dearly. As for Larry, not much has changed.

Anthony's obsession with chaos would at times be silly and at other times almost get his ass beat. One day he was provoking Rocky, and I was more than certain Anthony was about to have his clocked cleaned. Just like a schoolyard fight, they headed out to the flagpole after dinner, but a staff member named Isaac knew something was up and confronted the guys. The matter resolved itself within a day or two.

Anthony tried to hide phones but got caught. He tried to make a tattoo gun (which would have been a Hepatitis C nightmare), but they found his stuff. Anthony didn't even smoke or dip when he started the program, but that was the "in" rebellion and he could not be left out! When I first learned he got caught smoking I freaked out. He just walked out into the parking lot and lit up a cigarette while we were still in blackout at the Firehouse. His stupidity was like a tidal wave.

Remember I told you, when we were new to the program, it was Anthony who began sending the homeless people to the store for cigarettes. Again, allow me to point out that Anthony wasn't a smoker. I am sure other men utilized the homeless pony express, but Anthony was perfecting it.

When Anthony was explaining to me that he got caught smoking, I was dumbfounded. I needed the scenario to be explained to me a few times. My outburst went like this:

"You mean to tell me you don't even smoke! Yet, when you decide to light up you go out into the parking lot and do it in front of God and everybody!"

Everyone in the mod found this to be very funny. For the next year of my life, whenever any of us did anything silly, stupid or stubborn it would be pointed out that it was done "**In front of God and everybody!**"

Anthony's mother sent him a camera. Cameras were not a forbidden item until Anthony managed to change the rules for everyone. Who knew a camera could come with Wi-Fi? Certainly not me, but if there was a technology to be found, Anthony got his hands on it. For weeks he was communicating with the outside world. I think a few of us benefited from this camera. I know I used it a few times, but I really didn't have anyone to chat with. I just wanted in on the mischief.

I communicated with a woman I had known from Russia named Svetlana. Svetlana visited me after Kristen's death. She currently lived in Chicago. She was having problems with immigration. One drunk evening we were talking, and I offered to marry her for citizenship. It was a promise I made and we both never forgot. She would call rehab prison, but it was lighthearted. She was a good friend in a lot of ways. However, those damn Russian women may be beautiful, but they never laugh! We continued to talk about our marriage plan. A plan that would eventually help bring me to Chicago.

For weeks, Anthony was getting away with contacting the outside world. It was a freedom we all longed for. However, the idea for most is to keep us away from old influences and bad relationships. Since I was a drinker and I drank alone, I never had to deal with drug dealers or bad influences. My drug dealers were simple stores such as gas stations, Wal-marts and anywhere else bourbon or wine could be found.

Anthony had a good run, but once Glenn (my friend from the kitchen) discovered the camera and the Wi-Fi, things were uncomfortable. Glenn had a pretty faithful girlfriend, but he insisted on talking to any woman that would pay him attention. As I said, this bothered me that he had such devotion and was willing to stand by him in his darkest times and he treated her so badly. In those days I would love to have had a woman that supported me. For me, my houses of love had all been set on fire! There was Glenn with his flame thrower, burning down his own tower of Babel.

The big fall came because Anthony was updating and posting pictures on Facebook. Go figure, the staff was looking for just this kind of thing. The funny thing is that everyone thought he had a phone! They searched his room, his stuff and even his person, but no phone. They knew he was getting online and even threatened to kick him out, but they asked the wrong questions.

Finally, under the interrogation, Anthony confessed to using Wi-Fi from the camera. The staff was dumbfounded. To the rest of us it was all typical Anthony. He was always on the prowl to find a way around, over, or under a rule.

CHAPTER 25

"The pages are still blank, but there is a miraculous feeling of words being there, written in invisible ink and clamoring to become visible." ~ Vladimir Nabokov

"Life is ten percent what happens to us and ninety percent how we respond to it." ~ Charles Swindol

"Every man has his secret sorrows which the world knows not, and oftentimes we call a man cold when he is only sad." ~ Henry Wadsworth Longfellow

Rebellion, but I scare

easily.

The morning, I had an epiphany. The was the moment I realized I was sleeping in a homeless shelter as part of my initiation into the program. I knew I wanted to share this story. I knew I would have a book even though I had no idea how this tale would unfold. Yet, I really didn't have any personal drama. I wasn't creating fun, interesting or suspenseful stories. Anthony was about to walk the plank of eviction from the program every few weeks.

Yes, I had two write-ups! One write-up was for playing gin about two minutes after we were supposed to be in devotion time. It was a write-up that felt more like a peer mentor meeting his quota than truly needed. The second one came for leaving my dorm room light on. The truth is, out of the three of us no one had any idea who left it on. I just accepted the blame. My punishment was that I had to write a paper that was to be turned in the next day. Write a paper? This is a punishment? This guy felt the need to give me a writing assignment as a punishment?! I felt like Brer Rabbit begging not to be thrown into the Briar Patch. For those of you unfamiliar with the Brer Rabbit story, he is a rabbit that survives on his wits as opposed to his strength. It took me about 15 minutes to turn out a hand-written page. It took me longer to find the man and hand him the assignment. Where did this honky-tonk angel from Jackson County go to? My back-sliding ways of failing to have a light turned off needed his attention! I found him walking around aimlessly rather quickly, but I was annoyed nonetheless.

I handed him my paper. He seemed surprised that I had already finished it. He turned to walk away with my work in hand. He was holding a masterpiece of words woven together, by a man that would be famous for words. Yet, my Jackson County peer mentor was clueless. My ego was slightly disgusted.

"Wait a minute! Aren't you going to read it? Aren't we going to discuss it?"

He was puzzled, and his mouth fell open. I already knew I had given my magnificent work to a man that had no intention of reading the work. I was insulted.

"At the very least when will I get the paper back?"

"You want this paper back?" He asked and left his mouth hanging open again. My third-grade teacher, Mrs. Cinnamon, would tell him to shut his mouth, he would catch flies. What was this obsession of being a mouth breather?

"If this is used to correct my behavior then by all means I need feedback. Have a seat." I gestured to my bed and I sat at my desk.

He read, and I watched. He had offended me, and I made sure to use words beyond a 6th grade reading level. My father taught me that it is best to play by other people's rules and then outsmart them. Good advice dad! This was fun. When he finished, I could tell he didn't know what to say or add to my thoughts. That was all the victory I needed. I spoke up and asked questions he could handle. He was a nice enough guy, but he never asked me to write anything for him again.

Step 7 is that we humbly ask our greater power to remove our shortcomings. Dealing with my punisher and my attitude towards him reminded me that I have a lot of shortcomings. Concerning this incident, is it clear that pride is a huge one for me?

Speaking of shortcomings, I can't possibly bore you will all of mine. So, I will offer you my top ten. I know, I know Nick Hornby only ever had a top five list in High Fidelity, but he is a different human. Pride, selfishness, self-centeredness, self-pity, anger, lust, jealousy, envy, indecisiveness, and arrogance are my top ten shortcomings.

Did I mention lust? Oh yeah, number 6, there you are lust. Yes, I craved women like the next guy. However, I lusted for food, alcohol and on occasion material things. Who knew lust covered such a huge area of desires?

Now the real bitch of my shortcomings is anger. Why? I thought you would never ask. You can't just throw shortcomings away. They must be replaced with something else. The only opposite of anger that I know is love. Now, I am left praying that God will help my heart believe that He loves me. His never ending, never failing, all-consuming love will take over me! I need God's love to pour into every dark corner of my being. Of this I am sure, I can only show love when I know how loved I am. I am fairly certain it is the same for all of us.

Again, what is this supposed to look like? The idea is a lot to unpack. I do not wish to be a blah, blah man in my so, so world any longer. Loving people who love me is easy! Loving someone like Larry or even Baby Mama? These are people that leave me confused. What do I do? Where do I go with those people? Baby Mama has aged and looks like she needs the tires balanced and rotated. Let's be honest, we are all aging, but when your ex-wife's forehead is starting to resemble a braille document, that eases some hurt. She is married to a man that traded in his wife for an upgrade. A move that left a lot of resentments with his own children. The grapevine has it, the Doughboy Draftsman will blame anyone, but himself for failures. Cue the Pat Benatar song, "Hell is for Children." (A song about child abuse and the lyrics are fitting concerning divorce.)

In a way, I felt like I must get back into the ring with God! This step requires submission to the man upstairs. I must put my life in the hands of a father that is essentially invisible. The world broke in the Garden of Eden, and I was only broken further. This frustration here for me is that I can hardly collect all my broken pieces to hand over to God. Furthermore, this process doesn't end, I will work step 7 the remainder of my life. Essentially, I will work all the 12 steps in random order for the remainder of my life, but some stand out more than others. Now, tell me it is easy to stop drinking or using? Bullshit if you think it is. Sometimes I think a cat in hell with no claws has a better chance.

The single only way I have found to replace anger towards people is to pray for them. Yes, it is true that when I am sulking over the mess life has made over my best laid plans, it is exceedingly difficult to trust God with the broken pieces. I have prayed very inappropriate prayers towards people on occasion. Don't you dare pretend that shortly after you leave Sunday's pews, you're not cursing people in that same church parking lot. Welcome to the human condition. A life born into sin. My answer to turning anger and releasing shortcomings is to pray blessings over people. Trust me, that is a journey of a thousand miles, but it is all I know to do. Christianity is not for the meek. The bible will kick your ass.

Along the way, I need to unlearn my habit of opinion and expectations I place on people and places. The way things in this world are not obligated to act according to my world view, ideas, or demands. My happiness cannot be determined by the behavior of others. I truly think that if Heather and I didn't have such strong expectations for each other, we would still be together. We needed relationship rehab.

It is not just enough to identify these toxic traits in myself, but I also must replace them, beginning with humility. In other words, acknowledge my own insignificance. This is a far cry from worthlessness because that would only bring me back to self-pity. No, I am valuable and specifically in a group or a part of something. Not in the sense that my ego is overstated. Speaking of self-pity, replace that with concern for others. Trade selfishness for kindness. You get the idea. My writing assignment assured me I had a lot of work ahead of me.

I had already made up my mind to submit to the program. This did not mean I would submit to stupidity. Outside, my will was simply not working. Inside this program meant I had to learn acceptance. The will of God, the actions of others, expectations all had to be curved. I had to learn that no matter how great my ego, I am not in control. This skinny fellow man from Jackson County was helping me learn these lessons. He also reminded me I was a little bored. Breaking the rules is fun! I needed to up my game, but how?

I started to think I needed something outrageous

to happen. I needed stories like Anthony was accumulating. I was boring! Give me death before I become boring! I needed an epic tale to tell. As a result, I would manipulate a situation.

I don't smoke so I wasn't about to be caught for that. Breaking the rules just didn't really appeal to me. What I needed was a solid prank. I wrote a lot of letters. I decided to recruit my sister. She can be an asset to my greatest prankster mind of all time (take that Lex Luther!) My idea was to send my sister my Facebook password, and I would send her my posts in letters. She could then make them for me! Since all she had to do was copy my words from a letter to the screen there would be no doubt that it was me all along. There was a snag, my sister, though lovely, has never had a sense of urgency about getting things done.

Cue the Led Zeppelin song, "Immigrant Song."

My head was spinning with excitement. As a safety measure I told one staff member named Travis, another Jackson county resident. With Travis on my side we could check my Facebook posts from a computer in the kitchen office. Occasionally they were updated, but often it took time, a lot of time. It was just a matter of days before I got called into the office. The interrogation would be spectacular. I saw the whole scenario in my mind's eye. Our head intern at the time was Zach. As I told you Zach is the younger brother of the Jolly Orange Gentle Giant, Gabe. Both men are the same and completely different! Every week I was sending my sister updates. Beth is wonderful, but she has one speed called "in her own damn time." She will act busy but bless her heart she is way too lazy for that. When my sister is motivated, she is a force to be reckoned with. When my sister is not motivated, God help us all! Since my sister is the vagina version of me, I suppose this says a lot about me as well.

Weeks came, and weeks went, but nothing ever happened. No big crash of opposition and anger sprinkled with frustration and riddled with questions. Where was my irate and concerned Zach? Why had Connor not been notified? In fact, my crime should have had the attention of the CEO and President Vann Ellison. My anticipation finally had a breaking point. I went to Zach and demanded to know why I was not in trouble! He just laughed! I was paralyzed as I realized my ruse failed. Zach had outsmarted me! He had not one, but two spies working against me. He was aware of the posts. Yet, never for a second did he think I was doing anything illegal. In fact, he had become Facebook friends with my sister and shared some messages they exchanged. My prank was an epic failure, but with good laughs. To be honest I think Travis sold me out. Travis was the kind to get cold feet. I am sure in his mind; he was protecting me. Our prank died at the hands of Travis! I still love Traffer Haffer as I call him.

After we moved rooms the first time, my second roommates were Anthony and Nojo. Now there is a motley crew if ever there was one. Anthony and I had a lot of fun, while Nojo usually laid in his bed reading his books and making jokes at our expense. The problem is that Nojo is too smart to outwit him. When Nojo cracked a joke there was little chance of a comeback.

IF ROCK BOTTOM HAD A BASEMENT

Here is the thing about me. I like to sleep in the cold. In fact, my thermostat is usually parked between 72 and 68. I slept under Anthony. One night the lights were out, and he was cold. In an uncommon and the sweetest Anthony voice he asks, "Can we turn the temperature up a little just for tonight?" Immediately I thought damn! He was so sweet about it. I laid still and quiet for a minute. An idea came to me.

The temperature reading was digital. It also beeped every time you adjusted the setting. My brilliant idea. I would grab a sock, place the sock over the digital reading. I would hit the setting a few times for some beeps. Anthony would hear the beeping noise. He was then supposed to think, believe, and trust I adjusted the temperature and be none the wiser.

I crawl out of bed and find a sock next to my bed. You see, when I was drinking heavy, I always kept clothes next to my bed in case I started vomiting. Sometimes my body would try and reject the poison, but I always fought it. This man has done more stupid things than most people would dare to.

I grab my sock. With precision and stealth, I make my beeping noises. This is mission difficult, but not mission impossible. This assignment should be a walk in the park. Only one thing, as I begin to cover the digital reading with my sock, Anthony loudly proclaims, "You aren't doing a damn thing!"

He was hanging off the side of the top bunk. His eyes were huge and full of disgust. Nojo burst out laughing! I stood there with a sock in my hand, caught. We

IF ROCK BOTTOM HAD A BASEMENT

all laughed so hard we could hardly breath. I crawled back into my bed, my sides hurting from laughing and Anthony bitching the entire time.

At some point when we were falling asleep, I would wait for Anthony to think I was out like a light. I would sneak out of my bed and climb up the side of the bunk bed really slowly. Trying to appear like that girl from the Naomi Watts motion picture *The Ring*. I would be as scary as possible, and he would scream every time. God knows I miss those times. Anthony called me a lot of unbelievably bad names on those nights.

However, there was another ruse that I unwillingly became a part of. Of course, none other than Anthony orchestrated it.

CHAPTER 26

"Being vulnerable is the only way to allow your heart to feel true pleasure." ~ Bob Marley

"A person is, among all else, a material thing, easily torn and not easily mended." ~ Ian McEwan

Give me ten-steps.

The older you get, some things become noticeably clear. Your first realization is that everyone is full of shit! People think they are self-aware, but they are just buying their own bullshit. I suspect that we need this in order to self-preserve. Is it right? No. Is it bad? I am not so sure. If we were all completely aware of our faults, maybe every nerve and muscle of our being would explode in spontaneous combustion. In fact, I have heard that depression is often just a clearer view of reality. Nowhere is bullshit more prevalent than in rehab.

Everyone in rehab is in a process of discovery. A lot of times we have been victims of our addictions so long we don't know who we are sober. Imagine not knowing who you are without your active addiction beside you; that is uncomfortable and frightening! One day a man is super self-righteous and the next full of rebellion. Justin's Place tries to help the men find an identity by giving them jobs and introducing them to leadership. For example, peer mentors. I talk about these peer mentors a lot, but they are not all bad.

Peer mentors are usually the first line of defense in the program. They are only about 6 months sober, but too often the scene changed, but not the person. The sad reality is that these guys have no leadership training whatsoever. In the truest sense of the word, it is the inmates running the asylum. Most guys are drawn to the position as a way of manipulation.

I will never forget Andy (he was the peer mentor that was sleeping with a woman from the girl's program in one of the vans) taking us to a Friday night A.A. meeting. We were visitors in society. As people shared their stories and struggles, Andy stayed on his phone. He disregarded everyone, and his duty: to chat with women. I had never seen or been so disturbed by behavior from a peer mentor prior. I never understood why Andy could be a peer mentor, but upper management kept him on. I love Eric, but they were buddies and that explained a lot. If Eric liked a guy, he got special treatment. If Eric didn't like a man, then he was lucky to make it to Wolfe. I like and love

Eric, but he was bitter and needed to work on becoming better. Eric too was known to have sex with women in the LaBelle parking lot late, late at night. Sometimes the penis is more important than the program. No man can judge this! Every male human has been guided by his lever, his handle, his pipe, in his life, no exceptions (except Jesus).

One Saturday, Andy took some guys on the weekly Wal-Mart trip. One guy bought a bunch of sleeping pills. It was simply to sneak things past Andy because he didn't care or pay attention. He stayed on his phone! By the way, I still wonder if Andy did the nasty bumpiness with a phone in hand.

This is a guess, but I would suggest that 80% of peer mentors relapse hard, and I am being conservative. I think their recovery just comes to a stop the minute they get their blue and purple shirts. The foundation of leadership is an ability to serve. Some men have it, but too many don't. I was asked to be a peer mentor and I simply said, "No, they are not a group of people I want to be associated with." Too many of them were a stain on the program. However, when Nojo and Tim became peer mentors, they were excellent. Tim had a way of talking to some men that most of us just couldn't reach. Tim always called those conversations "Tim Talks," no doubt a play on Ted Talks.

Now please realize that a lot of the peer mentors were garbage, but a lot were amazing. Remember I told you about Zach buying us ice cream on National Ice Cream Day. That is the action of a beautiful peer mentor. The residents need to feel that they win occasionally. Did

Zach recognize this? Maybe he did or maybe he didn't, but he was clearly open to ideas that were not his own. In my opinion, that is a crucial element of a leader. Zach is just a guy you naturally love and have no idea why. He has an ability to make you want to see him succeed and buy into his vision.

Still, the shit for brains peer mentors did serve a valuable purpose. Life provides us with a lot of challenges. Often, we try and try to be in control, but the truth is we control nothing! I see people who treat fitness as a religion still dropping dead. Hard workers and dedicated employees still lose their jobs. Life happens. One of the values of recovery is learning to accept the things we cannot change. The assholes of the program do teach us acceptance. Later when we leave and enter back into the real world, we will have encounters and dealings with people we cannot stand. There will be people and situations that bring us stress. We need to understand how to deal with these things without reverting to our old addict behaviors. This helps us discover our triggers that make us want to revisit our addictions. I was still very much clueless as to what my triggers would be. In fact, I had no idea what my triggers were because I drank every day. Now back to Anthony's ruse and my involvement.

While we were at the Firehouse, they made Greg Choir Captain. I thought it was a brilliant idea. While Greg was the man, he stood up against all the smokers and tobacco users. He took his role very seriously. I was and am proud of him. Yet, when we were at LaBelle, he went back to smoking and looking for dip every chance he got. For some reason this infuriated our mod brothers. I guess we all hate the hypocrisy in others that we know from our own actions.

Anthony thought it was a good idea to tell Greg I was a snitch. Why was this a good idea? I have no idea, but when Anthony got bored, he came up with wild rides. I had no objection because I really didn't think Greg would believe it. Turns out Greg bought it hook, line, and sinker! (I use fishing lingo because Greg loves to go fishing.) He fell for that bait way too easily. I thought it was hysterical, but Greg was telling everyone that I had it coming. What was it I had coming? I had no idea! Greg believed that I was monitoring and telling on the smokers. Is smoking dumb? Sure, it is, but so is drinking until you black out and a good deal of my relationships. Who am I to judge?

One magical day it was decided for us to go on a scavenger hunt in the woods. Did I say magical? I am so sorry I meant "idea from hell!" I don't do the woods or everglades in Florida, especially in the summer. I told you about this silly excursion earlier in the book. Between Nojo and Rocky, the hunt was over in about 10 minutes. Those two men have tracking in their blood and maybe a bit of Colombo (a detective show from the early seventies). However, we had been dropped off in Mosquitoville and expected to be searching for an hour or more. As a result, we made our way to a picnic area and all sat around under a canopy. That is when Anthony struck out at Greg. Anthony confronted Greg and told him he was a fool to think I was a snitch.

I was relieved that my snitch status was torn away. Anthony had resentments about Greg and his hypocrisy.

As a mod, everyone shared, and it seems like a cruel ritual. No, it was very loving in a twisted kind of way. Harboring resentments is the real act of hate, because nothing gets resolved. When we keep feelings in our heart of resentment, they compound like interest on a bad loan (as if there is a good loan). For those of us at Justin's Place, sharing like this is called a ten-step.

A ten-step is critical and helps save relationships. Look, whenever you have a group of people together, you are going to have a mess. People get hurt, do stupid things, and act according to their own self-interests. In a lot of cases, nobody is deliberately trying to ruin another person's day, life or hurt feelings. However, we all have what I call trip wires inside our brain. It is a passive mechanism that lays doormat close to our wounds, but once disturbed can set off an alarm or an explosion of emotions and memories. Rehab is not unique to these trip wires. If you are alive or dead, you are not a stranger to dark places. No one in this life gets out alive or without bruises and scars. Cue The Lumineers song, "Flowers in Your Hair." Because it is a long way to wisdom and a short way to being ignored.

The ten-step was introduced to us in our first month of blackout. It was mandatory that first month that we had a ten-step once a week. Once we moved to LaBelle, the practice was much encouraged, but not mandatory. My mod continued to have 10-steps weekly, and I believe we were a tighter group of guys because of it.

So once a week and sometimes more often, we would circle our chairs and go around the room. We share, we open up, and we discuss how we hurt or helped one another. It is the highest form of vulnerability there is in the program and requires a bravery seldom seen anywhere in the world. Take me for example; I am not afraid of having a confrontation with a man that may result in physical violence. Dying doesn't always scare me. If you kill me, I go to heaven. However, I am terrified of loving and being rejected. Now I am being asked to reveal my true self. This is asking me to go to hell and try to clean things up a bit. It is alien to most of our John Wayne and Rambo nature, but it is also supernatural and enchanting. Maybe if I knew how to practice these ten-step principles in my marriage, I could have saved it.

Remember I told you about step 7 of the 12 steps. I am humbly asking my higher power to remove my shortcomings. Step 6 is becoming willing to have God remove defects of character. None of these steps are possible without Step 4, make a searching and fearless moral inventory of ourselves. As a result, lists are made, and a lot of self-reflection takes place. However, my examination, investigation and inspection of me, my behavior, consequences and my personality's accessories are evidently subjective. Even with a sponsor, I am primarily governing my own self. The ten-step helps me see deeper into myself.

Now mind you with a group of men like Nojo, Anthony, Greg, Karl, Jacob, Rocky, and Rob, there were always talks among us that were deeper than most in my life. Nojo was great at comforting a broken heart and challenging an ignorant mindset. Yes, I also had great case managers such as Isaac, Conner, and eventually Jim, but much of the work is done on your own. I also had the benefit of working in the kitchen with Chef Jason. As I said we spent many hours in his tiny office. My little orphaned self, idiosyncrasies, and Chef's guidance.

In a strange way we become each other's masters and slaves. Why? Because we hold each other's hearts for one another, and we help each other walk through these trip wires. We begin the program as a group of tender skinned men with chemical imbalances because of drugs and alcohol. We are often scared, and we end the program as a brotherhood with a bond that is unattainable in most relationships. I would compare it to the bond of basic training, combat or survivors of a great tragedy.

The strength isn't just in the sharing. It also requires a great deal of vulnerability in the listening. At one time, Anthony announced in a ten-step that he hated all of us and that we were not allowed to speak to him under any circumstances or for any reason! Only Nojo was allowed or had permission to communicate with Anthony. He was rude and assertive and enraged just about everyone. When he left the room, it was unanimous, we all felt he wore the asshole crown of the week. However, as the wrecking balls were being tossed around in his brain, we had to be ready to love. Anthony was not in too deep; he did not lose any friends. He only really provided us an opportunity to love him more deeply than we had been given or he had known. One-time Anthony told Tim he hated his face. What is the moral of this? Within a week, nobody hated anyone's face any more. **Hurt people, hurt people.**

These are the miracle moments of Justin's Place.

IF ROCK BOTTOM HAD A BASEMENT

Sometimes alone I see these men's faces and the traces they left on who I am becoming. Relationships are not built on good times and blue skies. No, these are merely romantic notions sold to us by such films as *Pretty Woman, Breakfast at Tiffany's* and *While You Were Sleeping*. None of which I downplay, because I happen to be much worse than a hopeless romantic myself, I am a hopeful one. The real glue of a relationship comes from the bad days and hard times. Those were the times that Baby Mama jumped ship and boarded another man's yacht.

Years ago, before Baby Mama had her affair and my marriage went through its battle of Normandy, I was at a park with my ex father in law. I was pulling away from church at that time. We were talking, and I said to him "Church doesn't work." He gave me that look you only get from people whose lives depend on the church to make a living. I was being open and honest, and he saw rebellion. He knew the church's money buttered his bread on both sides.

That is what church people tend to say to a person that questions their effectiveness, their teachings or anything else, "You are in rebellion." However, the truth is that they are full of shit and buying other people's bullshit. The more I drew to God, the more I could see my character defects, flaws and sin. Now I know God forgives, and I believe in mercy, and I have survived on grace, but I don't think that is permission to stay stuck. My righteous work needed to construct my character. I did not want to neglect my redeemer.

I do not mind being a failure or even despised, as

much as I hate being fake! I hate fake in me, and I despise it in others. Now here I am in church, watching people come and go, always trying to look their best. The failure of the church is that it is supposed to be a hospital for the walking wounded and living dead, but instead everyone enters trying to be their best selves. I know, I sometimes repeat myself, but you (my reader) forget things. We all have Facebook - post attention spans these days. There is truly little transparency, and the world has rejected the church's Teflon Christianity (in other words acting like nothing sticks to them). Then I visit rehab and recovery meetings where everyone stands up and confesses their lives are a wreck and often go into great detail about their failures, shortcomings and character defects. Give me the real whores, drug addicts, and drunks any day. I love truth and transparency.

These days I rejoice that Baby Mama married the Doughboy Draftsman; they deserve each other. On occasion, I run into old mutual friends, they always speak of the way her husband talks down and belittles her. Did she trade up? Maybe she traded sideways? Maybe she traded down? Who is to say? Her friends, they say all the time. Yes, there was an answer. That was not a rhetorical question.

Baby Mama grew up in the shadow of her father's ministry. Her mother was the organist of a mega church in central Florida. At Disney, the parking lot is huge and divided in sections with character names such as Goofy or Donald Duck. Trust me this tactic does help you find your car after a long and amazing day at the park. Similarly, the church divided their parking lot in names of the spirit, such as love or faith. That should give you an idea how large this church is. Before we were ever married, I told Baby Mama I had no intention of going to her church. Oddly, I did believe in their senior pastor Jim Henry, but too many of the leaders grossed me out.

Now at Justine's Place I had a group of men confessing their deepest, darkest, and at times disturbing secrets. I had never felt freer in my life. I have heard it said that we only keep secrets with the devil. Our ten-steps provided me evidence that there is truth in that saying. Once a secret is shared, its power mostly diminishes.

I have been arrested and taken to jail 4 times in my life. It seems to happen once every decade. Was arrested at 16 for shoplifting. I was arrested for an unpaid ticket in my early twenties. I was arrested in my thirties for fighting and in my forties for driving on a suspended license, but I have never been to prison.

All the men in our program that had been to prison used to tell me the same thing. They claimed that prison is so much easier than rehab. Apparently in prison, you just do your time and never have to work on your issues. Motion pictures have taught us that bravery is facing dragons, but in rehab you see a bravery of superior depth and strength. That is when you face your own demons and begin to work through issues.

Rehab is not for the weak.

CHAPTER 27

"You ask anyone what their number one fear is, and it's public humiliation." ~ Mel Gibson

"We learn humility through accepting humiliations cheerfully." ~ Mother Teresa

Community.

Recovery demands surrender because what you were doing wasn't working. Your certainty is confused, and you need a new way of life and a new mindset. Your thoughts and whispers in your spirit are lying to you. Religion tries to rope and hog tie you into submission. Now I was needing grace and love as much as anything. My loathing of LaBelle (initially) and the process had to be outweighed by my brokenness. This new life was not only uncomfortable and unfamiliar, but also needed. It took me out of my life, worries, and daily grind. In the months ahead when newcomers would complain, I used to say to them, "Yeah recovery is hard but guess what: we don't have rent to worry about this month." Yes, recovery would make me grateful and not just for sobriety, but also for my hard knocks, because they helped mold me into a guy I like. Cue the Aloe Blacc song, "The Man." I take that back, I don't just like me! I am the man! I will certainly be a king when the kingdom comes.

Regrets outlast the alcohol. However, even a glow stick is broken before it shines. It was the stories of other men's changed minds that filled me with hope and confidence. When I listened to Tommy teach and testimonies of other men in recovery, I would always think to myself, "How could a man like this have an addiction problem?" This is where the magic really began for me. I was beginning to not just hear about lives transformed, but I was watching people change before my eyes. The process of returning to health, joy, and getting better is so beautiful. We live in a world addicted to quick fixes and that is hardly the process I know to become sober. However, when you see lives transform and revolutions of their hearts, it makes it hard not to believe in God. I think it is safe to say **recovery is not for people who need it, but for people who want it.**

When a person says to you they want help, ask them one question. "What are you willing to do to get there?" Usually the answer will be something around, "I am willing to do anything." Put their answer in your pocket because you will need it a lot. Addicts have a million excuses why they can't do something. This practice is not unique to addicts. How many excuses have you made not to work out, to finish your goal, or not spend money you don't really have? We are all living manufacturing plants of excuses. You will often need to remind the addict, "But you said you were willing to do anything!" Their addiction is consistently lying to them and your voice of reason will help more than I can express.

I could not always see these miracles. In fact, I knew that LaBelle had a healthy serving of men who had no regard for recovery. This was another reason I was so reluctant to move from Naples to cow town. However, I shared my concern with a guy named Nick who was hardly old enough to drink. Without hesitation, he agreed that there were bad seeds in the program and then said, "Stick with the winners." His words had a great impact on me.

This really should be our outlook in all of life, stick with the winners. In every group, church, job, or click there are bound to be some people who are no good. You can't stop the direction of a running river, but you can decide where to stand in relation to it. Rehab taught me to simply look for the winners, but it is important to point out, winners are attitudes. If Baby Mama taught me anything, it is that rich people can be just as hazardous as addicts. What I am looking for are the people who don't speak negatively. Get me away from the complainers. We must check ourselves regularly. It is hard to admit, but at times I am the toxic person, and I bet you are too. We make mistakes, but we also freely make bad choices. We are going to hurt people on our journey. Apologizing is important because it helps you as much as anyone else. This is called growth, enlightenment, and improvement.

This is so much better than faking perfection. Never feel the need to rush the process, because it takes time returning to yourself. So, remember this - your circle should want to see you win. Surround yourself with people who clap loudly and cheer you on.

Community was a Wednesday afternoon ritual that truly alarmed me. I am not sure where they came up with this formal procedure, but it was a huge part of the program. This is how it worked. If you got caught with a major offense such as smoking or received up to three write-ups, you were eligible.

Every Wednesday afternoon, a handful of men would be called up in front of the community. This included most of the staff and all the residents. At the front of the room, a few long tables were placed together and about five peer mentors sat facing the crowd. These were essentially the judges. At the end of the line, a fellow oversaw writing down the punishments that the community would select. Basically, it felt like a public lynching to me. I never really saw the biblical basis for such a thing, but we did it. What freaks me out about this ritual is that it is the kind of thing that would make Adam's dick hard!

Now once you were standing in front of the firing committee, three men usually from your group would join you in the front of the room. You faced each other standing tall and ready for their observations of correction. What I witnessed was mostly kind words of edification. The only time I witnessed anyone abuse the platform was Adam, the maintenance man. (Adam is a bully! He is also rumored to hit and abuse women. In a world where bullying is being met with outrage.) He would sometimes stroll in and out just to peacock his influence. When he spoke to the men, it was never uplifting. In fact, he had the simplistic audacity to call other men arrogant. Adam never failed to disgust me, and his words were always out of and demeaning. You know how it is when somebody enters the middle of a film or TV show and they are confused about the plot. That is the single best comparison of Adam's life. Adam's arrogance and ignorance were always racing. He always thought he knew what was going on, he acted as if he knew people's intentions. The man is stupid! (Isn't it ironic how much Adam had a love for nature despite what it did to him.)

Adam walked in one time when Nojo was standing at the front of the room for Community. Adam was always picking on Nojo. In fact, Nojo's intelligence and talents outshined Adam's ignorance on so many levels. As a result, Adam tried to attack Nojo's character. That was how Adam worked. His method was to break you down, put you down, and impress his dominance early in the program so you would always fear him. What a fucking dumbass. There is no barf bag big enough for the shit that man hurled up! It was obvious to everyone that Adam felt inferior to Nojo. It will always be a mystery to me how Adam could feel validated by trying to humiliate others.

Once you go before the Community, your consequences are referred to as being on contract. Everyone carries two sheets of paper with penalties listed. Usually some type of detailed cleaning punishment is given and then some writing assignments. Again, the community raises their hands and two random people pick out your fate. It is not uncommon for these reprimands to be self-serving to whoever suggests them. For instance, if you work in ground maintenance, you might suggest the offended must clean the canoe house. If you work in the dog program, you might try to have doggie shit cans emptied. Anything you can assign to get a monkey off of your own back.

> I never really knew how to feel about this ritual. It still feels a little icky, but in the end the program had a good heart. Yet, I am terrified of the corruption a religious leader could bring. The mind of every Pharisee will cling to rules and power over truth and love, but that does not appear to be the Jesus I know. We are designed to share a depth of love and connection. When rules and religion inevitably become primary in institutions, they will suck the vitality of people's lives out.

CHAPTER 28

> "There is unpanned gold in every soul you run into, no matter what walk of life they are from." ~Robert Downey Junior

> "I've gotten away with a lot in my life. The older you get the more you realize you're not getting away with it, it's taking its toll somewhere." ~ Jon Hamm

The beautiful offspring.

Evidence of alcoholism and addiction is reflected in consequences in all areas of your life. While it is a time of foggy confusion for the drunk or user, the family, friends and loved ones suffer as well. Sobriety is a process that never has a final destination. I know men that have not had a drink for years and still think about it every day. Every day requires some level of navigation and asking for help. You can't wait for life to begin. You must begin living and creating a life. The scars may not matter later, but it will if you don't discover and create a life.

In the program I watched men become comfortable in their own skin. I too was coming in touch with my personality, needs, desires, flaws, and fears. We were at a place we were not trying to improve ourselves for other people. It is a scary cocoon but rewarding, and we desire to share our progress with loved ones. In my case it was my parents and children. Armed with few manuals, fewer tutors, and busloads of critics we embark on sharing our journey although not complete or entirely correct.

We often wonder how a person can commit their lives to drugs or alcohol. I know I have wondered this very question. The simple truth is that it makes no sense to anyone including the addict. However, when you know a person's story you can get a glimpse of understanding. What makes a man or women's soul black and whispery? As I have said, people have all kinds of dreams and aspirations, but I have never met anyone who said their ambition included drugs and alcohol.

One man's story goes like this. Since, this is not my story please forgive any inaccuracies. When he was just a child and too young to really be aware of the dangers this world offers - he met fear. Before he was old enough to start school, have his heart broken by a lover or even get cut from a team he was introduced to his lifelong nightmare. The sun does go down on some of us before others.

IF ROCK BOTTOM HAD A BASEMENT

His father, a Vietnam veteran, came home one-night drunk. He went down to the basement and pulled out his gun. The story goes that the father threatened to shoot his son, but the child was too young to realize the danger of a weapon. His brother only a few years older was aware! The older brother jumped behind the couch. The father turned the gun on himself and pulled the trigger. His father, most likely a hero, became a corpse. Before he knew his ABC's, a little boy heard a bang that would ring in his memory throughout his life. His young eyes glued to pieces of a brain blown into a wall and slowly sliding down to the ground. A desperate boy destined to be a desperate man.

Pink Floyd and the lyrics of Roger Waters suggest there is a pain that you can become comfortably numb with, but this was not it. From that day forward nights were a terror and memories were the monsters under this boy's bed. The brothers would take turns sleeping and watching over each other. When you hear this version of the story told by the survivor, he calls it the good thing. He had his brother and that was a blessing.

One summer the boys went to stay with their grandparents. Every night the grandfather would have a modest drink of Whiskey. This pattern fascinated the boys because the grandfather had no trouble sleeping. Naturally their young minds reasoned that if this strong dirty water helps grandpa sleep maybe we could sleep too? This is how a child becomes an addict before he is in middle school. When you know a person's story, all of a sudden they are more than an annoying soul begging for a handout in the supermarket parking lot.

IF ROCK BOTTOM HAD A BASEMENT

It is quite easy to judge people from a preview of their life or an action, but the picture is much wider than we can see. We never know what lies beneath the surface of a soul. Judging an action is fine because we all need correction and guidance. The bible says in Matthew chapter **7** and verse **1** "Do not judge, or you too will be judged. **2** For in the same way you judge others, you will be judged, and with the measure you use, it will be measured to you.

Consider that verse for a second. For this to be true I think our judgments curse us. Because in order to be judged by the same measure we judge we must fall right into the same lifestyle that we are using to judge a person. Sounds crazy I know, but a few years into this life I have seen this practice repeat repeatedly!

My own trauma (some self-inflicted) took me from everyone. Even my beautiful offspring were left behind. It had been several months that I was absent from a former life. That drive didn't just take me far away in terms of the distance. I was leaving everything I had behind. What I couldn't give away I packed or left. It is a sad man who is tired of his own voice and hates his reflection. Now I had been in LaBelle a few months and would see Madison and Mac for the first time.

When I was with Heather she would laugh when I called my mother Bobbi. In fact, a lot of people find it odd that I often refer to my mother by her name. However, there are mothers all over this world. There are poor mothers and great mothers in all shapes, sizes, colors and temperaments, but there is only one Bobbi! She is the

IF ROCK BOTTOM HAD A BASEMENT

Rambo of mothers. She is a mixed drink of devotion, pride, strength, stubbornness and enabling. I am a grown ass man, but when I need back up, a partner or a ride or die that job belongs to Bobbi. With that said on this day she and Ed (my stepfather) were driving my children down.

As far as moments go this one was monumental. I knew my son was coming with my parents, but Madison was a junior in high school and I really did not expect her. As with every visit the anticipation was thrilling, fantastic and wrecked my nerves. I had no idea what my children thought of their father in rehab. A time of discovery was upon me.

Saturday mornings in rehab were devoted to deep cleaning our rooms. Which wasn't too much of a choir unless Anthony was your roommate, he was a slob back then. He had mostly no interest in cleaning and would prolong the entire process. Then every fourth Friday we deep cleaned and moved rooms. This was when the new guys came from Naples and out of Blackout. If you survived the month-long blackout and made it to the LaBelle phase things were looking good for your recovery. Most often I would play retro Casey Kasem's top 40 rebroadcasts from the eighties.

As was the typical case of visits, I kept looking out the window from the third floor waiting to see my parents Toyota Highlander pull in. When you are waiting with that kind of excitement every minute seems like a miniature lifetime. Rocky was my roommate at that time, and he kept laughing at me. There are approximately five people in this world that I care what they think of me. My Children hold the top three spots!

And finally, I looked from the window, my long-legged daughter was the first to get out the car. Her presence was thrilling to me. Madison is the embodiment of everything that is good in the world. My heart began to beat loud as thunder. My hands shook and eyes filled with water. I have never understood the meaning of hallelujah, but I certainly felt it then. I rushed downstairs with Anthony near behind me. Hugging my beautiful offspring and the joy of seeing them is indescribable.

It is a truly awkward feeling to be the dad and worry about being in trouble with your children. However, I have never been one for fancy potions about how parenting is to be carried out. I suppose my greatest lessons came from my poor example as a broken man. Still seeing my daughter get out of the car was more beautiful of a sight than I have ever seen. If I may be so simple as to quote Melvin from the motion picture, *As Good as It Gets,* "She makes me want to be a better man." I want to be that better guy for my beautiful offspring.

I am not a person who decorates and makes a big deal of holidays. However, every Christmas I watch that James Brooks film and sometimes I watch it repeatedly. Jack Nicholson's performance of Melvin Udall is brilliant and inspiring. Let's be real, all of us wordsmiths are a little odd. I would sit in a chair with a bottle of 80 proof and relive the story and in some strange way it fills me with hope. A hope I cannot identify but was real.

My children make everyone else second rate to

me. Mac is genuine mini me, but only a much better version. God clearly upgraded that guy and to be honest I wish I were more like him. His grandparents are conservative Baptists and I always worried their influence would have a negative impact, but it didn't. He is his own man with his own interests. Even as a little boy he always had a love for nostalgic things. Recently he was given a record player and his love of vinyl makes me a proud old man. He has never failed to win over everyone he met. He greets strangers with his hand outward and ready to embrace each person. He doesn't judge people and that blows me away. His grandmother Teresa judges everyone for every reason. It was strange to me that Mac didn't say his mother sends her love. She must have spent all her love on swinging partners. Did I just write that? Well, thank God you don't have an erase button.

Madison has always been more of a mystery. She is like a smooth whiskey that takes her time. I love that about her. Her mother much more like a Cabernet, a little fruity and leaves you with a headache. Madison knows what she wants and can take the lead or fall back without much effort. She is the real thing, the right words and a perfect rhyme. When she was younger, she was very suspicious of me. However, that is where Mary comes in. When I lived with Mary, Madison just loved her more than anyone I have ever been with. I know that for the brief season that Mary and I were together she validated me to my little girl.

Of course, Hayden is never to be forgotten. He has my temperament. However, his mother has always used him as a tool to hurt and punish me. Oddly, I know she still has a good heart just dumb parents that raised her in their broken way. Now she is remarried to a man that wears his pubic hair around his chin. He only ever wanted me out of the picture. I can't say that I blame him for two reasons. First, Heather is more like June to my Johnny Cash. That is something that the sequel husband could never compete with. Also, he is simply so ugly that I figure his mother must have mated with a critter to make such a horrid child. In simple words, my kids are my heart.

Now my two oldest beautiful offspring were visiting me at rehab. I reasoned they would have questions. So individually I took each one for a walk around the property. Each time I led with the same question "Do you have any questions for me?" My children are no strangers to asking me hard questions and yet they had a grip on my situation.

"You know that letter you wrote me," Madison said.

"Of course, I know," I replied. I had written her a letter while I was in Blackout. In hopes, that I could explain my situation. All throughout my early stages of the program I feared my children would find me as an embarrassment. I thought they might not ever want to hear from me again.

"Well, it was long," She began. No, writer wants to hear we are long winded. I fought back a grimaced feeling and expression.

"I knew I needed to take my time reading it. So, I didn't read it right away. Instead I took it with me to

Axum." Axum is a coffee shop that my daughter adores in downtown Winter Garden. A colorful café that reminds me of Central Perk from the television show, *Friends*. They serve Coffee, tea, paninis and desserts that cater to a yuppie type crowd. However, they give all their profits to charitable causes. I totally love that my daughter loves this place. Although, I prefer a mom and dad type diner with lots of bacon.

Turns out Madison read the letter to her guy friend. At first, when she told me this, I was a little mortified. I was sharing my entry story about rehab with her. Not exactly the kind of vulnerability I want distributed to the general public. "So, I am reading this letter," she continues "And he is crying!" We both start to laugh. Why is this kid crying? "Yeah, he is crying and says that my dad is the most real person he has ever met, and he doesn't even know you! I am thinking to myself that my dad really is real." At which point I am almost crying like her friend, but I hold it back.

I was in rehab. That became a moment frozen in time and burned in my memory. I have felt some pain, I have seen some things. Not everything in my life has been bad or good, but that conversation with my daughter is among my life's best days. I will miss the magic of that conversation until I graduate from this world and life.

My daughter was holding on tight to my heartstrings. She did have questions, but mostly about her mother's affair with her current husband. Madison had made some discoveries and wanted some answers. Divorce orphans a person and leaves their world cold. I knew talking about her mother wasn't the picture I wanted to paint. I had to let go of too much concerning Baby Mama's deceit and betrayal. Madison sharing new insights was only stirring me up. Baby Mama used to say I could never forgive her. However, I will never really know because she was keeping so many secrets and always new lies were being exposed. I wanted to say she should ask her mother this stuff, but that would only make me the jackass. Even Baby Mama's children know she would rather protect her Teflon image than be a real human. Since our divorce I turned into an outspoken drunk and Baby Mama turned into a closeted Wino. We all think we are hiding our drinking problems and we never are.

When Madison was just a little girl, we were play wrestling on my floor. She had me pinned to the floor. As she sat on me holding me down, she shifted gears and asked, "Did mommy really cheat on you?" Like an unexpected head on collision I was blind-sided. I paused, and her innocent brown eyes were locked on me. I had to think fast. My answer could shift the foundation of her childhood. I also knew I wasn't going to lie to protect Baby Mama. That would have been a cold day in hell or Florida and the two can feel equally hot at times. "What happened between me and your mom is a conversation we can have when you are older, but what is important for you to always know is that your mother never cheated on you or your brother." Like a sweet relief she accepted my answer and moved on with our day. However, that question rattled me. What Madison's mother did do was steal a father away from Lauren and Michael's mother. What I didn't realize is that the Doughboy Draftsman's children and ex-wife were revealing a lot of secrets.

IF ROCK BOTTOM HAD A BASEMENT

Now Madison was older and remembered to ask questions. My marriage to her mother was a natural disaster. The Garth Brooks Song She Is Every Woman was her anthem. The perfect song about the contradictions that my ex-wife is. If it wasn't for my beautiful offspring, I am not sure she was worth the storm, but if I believe in God then I must know all things work together for His glory. Which is exactly how I fell so far away from God and being able to trust Him. Where was God's will and why had it forsaken me? Why had he allowed me to marry Baby Mama?

I satisfied Madison's curiosity enough that we could move on to other topics. I talked more about the betrayal of Larry, the colostomy bag of Christianity. The man who introduced me to more of the devil than he ever did Jesus. Larry can lick my sack as far as I am concerned.

Still, my beautiful offspring has always had a way of making me think. She walked along side of me a young lady, but I remember a time I would come home from work, back when she could only crawl across the floor. She would crawl with such purpose. Her mother had fixed her hair in some Pebbles from The Flintstones fashion. I would walk to the stereo and put on some music. Most often I played the Moulin Rouge soundtrack, but some days the music varied. When she heard that music play, she would come my way. Those little girl eyes worked me over as only she could do. She never cried or even begged, but her eyes filled with anticipation. I picked her up and held her close. We would dance around that living room floor and my heart would soar. Even so small she had the vibe. She helped me understand everything love is and everything it is not.

When I walked with Mac, his questions were more basic. Had I seen the new Logan motion picture that was sure to be Hugh Jackman's final performance as Wolverine. I must admit that was a great concern to the both of us because Jackman is Wolverine. We talked about upcoming films. He had questions about the program. Questions about the men, but not a lot of questions about how I ended up at Saint Matthews House. Mac shares my interests, so we always have a lot to talk about. He has a way of loving that I can't describe, but it is true. His demeanor is calming, and his wonder is inspiring.

In the TV room on the first floor we played a lot of card games. One by one, my other friends and mod brothers would come by to meet my family. Of course, Anthony asked if mom would run out to pick up some dip. My mother always willing to be an outlaw agreed. To this day my mother asks about Anthony and Nojo.

On their way into town. Mom had to stop at a local thrift store. Mac found a movie trivia game. Mom also brought some McDonalds back for a few of us to enjoy. Mac picked a couple of motion pictures for us all to watch later. When they returned and a few of us played the movie game, I crushed everyone. We quickly returned to playing card games. That time was magical.

Later Madison took notice of Greyson. Greyson was the kid in the rehab that didn't have an addiction problem. His parents sent him to the program to impress a judge. Little young Greyson was facing some real prison time for calling in a bomb threat at a local high school.

Madison and Greyson talked and hung out a little bit, but they were never out of sight. I think little Greyson was smitten. Which only proved the boy had great taste. I approved of Madison befriending him. Greyson is a good guy.

(Spoiler Alert) That night we rented a motion picture called *La La Land* with Ryan Gosling and Emma Stone. The movie was good, but for a musical the ending was a total Debbie downer. I had no idea he didn't get the girl in the end. Yet, I held onto hope right up until the credits rolled. Mac always recalls how we watched the film with a room full of big tough guys all emotional. It was a splendid evening. Big men from prison sniffling from held back tears.

At the LaBelle property we were not allowed on the second floor. This was where the hotel guests and my parents were staying during the visit. When the film was over and it was time to retire, I walked my children to their room. One of the peer mentors saw me on the second floor. He was a sweet man and tried to correct me for being where I didn't belong.

"My daughter is 16 years old and this is a place filled with recovering addicts. Did you really think I would allow my little girl to walk among these men alone?" I asked boldly and waited for his response. He knew I was right, and he backed down, my friend did the right thing. Truth be told I wouldn't allow my daughter to walk alone at a mall, on a street or even a church isle in those days.

Spending time with my beautiful offspring were equal parts thrilling, fun, terrifying and soul bearing. I recently asked Mac what his best memory of that trip was, and he said all the games we played. It was special to me that my children ask about Anthony and Nojo even now.

It was our tradition to say our gratefuls at meals. At lunch I said "I was grateful for my family and Baby Mama" I thought I would lose my mind, shit, and most of all a flood gate of tears. Baby mama did bake these amazing kids for us!

Note: gratefuls are when everyone in the room shares something, they are grateful for. At the end of that a single person says grace.

The following Sunday proved that I am no good with goodbyes. I make those times move as quickly as possible, if I can't avoid it all together. I do not like goodbyes, and I hate long goodbyes. I was back in my room before they pulled out of the parking lot. I watched the car drive away from a third-floor window. The very same way I watched my family arrive, only this time I cried. I tried to stop the tears, but it wasn't happening. Nojo instinctively knew and came to my room. He hugged me (a very long embrace) and that was it. His comfort can never be explained, and his embrace spoke volumes of love from a brother. We didn't really speak a lot. I just cried, and he simply stood with me. Soon we sat on the edge of the bed and later we played cards. Nojo knew when to speak and how to just be there.

As you can tell it is not just the residents, we become close with. Their families visit. Often these families come from far away and spend a weekend. Sometimes I am invited to go on pass with my friends.

Nojo's mother took us on a day pass to Lego Land with his young son. Afterwards she took us to the Olive Garden. Now to you, Olive Garden may just be a choice between several restaurants, but out on pass from rehab, this is exciting! The day was fantastic. It was also the first time I ever saw Nojo as a father. He is an excellent dad.

David worked with me in the kitchen and the front desk. His parents were from New Port Richie, Florida. They lived in the same county as my family. They took me on a few passes. We went to see the Edgar Wright motion picture *Baby Driver* one time and the Christopher Nolan film *Dunkirk*. I had the opportunity to meet his sister and her husband. Everyone is so kind and encouraging. It took my relationship with David much further. He was just a guy from a loving home. How does one like him get into drugs? You get that sensation from some drugs and you chase it the rest of your life.

Zatlokovicz is the man I always played the movie games with. We always were challenging each other with trivia. His parents came down from Delaware. David and James were mod brothers. They were a month ahead of me. David used to love to pick on James about Delaware.

"What does Delaware even have besides the Delaware river" David shouted one day at lunch. It was in all in good fun. However, for some reason that was so funny to me because all I knew about Delaware was that they have the river. I laughed long and hard at David that day. David has a great sense of humor and quick wit. He could make me laugh at the drop of a hat. Zatlokovicz's mother was extra special.

IF ROCK BOTTOM HAD A BASEMENT

I was working in the kitchen. Zatlokovicz had been going on pass much of the weekend. I would see his family in passing but hadn't really talked to them yet. Every night after dinner a different mod was assigned to clean the dining room and kitchen. On the weekends, whoever was being punished had the kitchen and dining room as punishment. This was easy work, but always there was some person who would skip out on duties and infuriate the others. Since I worked in the kitchen I would hang out and help. Mostly my job was to put away leftovers and such. Who are we kidding, this also meant I could snack!

Zatlokovicz was giving his parents a tour of the kitchen. This is when I met his mother. He had told her about our late-night conversations in my room. He also mentioned our movie trivia, but I think he overlooked that I was the reigning champion. She was so sweet. Surprisingly we talked more about Disney films than we did about her son. Later that night we watched a motion picture with his family downstairs. The same room we watched *La La Land* with my beautiful offspring.

By the way, the night we watched motion pictures with my children, Mac leaned on me with my arm around him for the whole film. Madison and Anthony shared the couch with us. At the end of the night, Anthony leaned over to me and said, "You never hold me like you do Mac". We had a great laugh. I just wish I could convey the mischievous look Anthony gets in his eyes, when he knows he is funny or clever.

I was also invited to go on pass with Nick. His

parents are divorced and both living in the Naples area. We would spend part of the day with one parent and the other part with the other. It was nice because we were able to eat at fun places such as The Cheesecake Factory. We also went to see *War for the Planet of the Apes*. I was shocked that the film was so good. It was wonderful the way our field trips would bond both the residents and families.

In the program I never met anyone's family that wasn't wonderful. My favorite part about weekends was and always will be meeting family members from all walks of life. In my life I have easily spent less than five hours with Zatlokovicz's mom and I still lover her.

My next roommate situation was with Tim. (Remember he was my first friend at the homeless shelter.) It was just the two of us and I loved that because it gave me a lot of time to bond with him. Tim is a deep thinker and an extremely sensitive man. He can have amazing insight at times. The difference between us is that he likes to stay up late and read. In the program I was always exhausted by 9:30. The deal was he would be still and keep the room dark for me to fall asleep. It never took me long to pass out. Rumor has it I snore rather aggressively.

One night I was fast asleep. I hear a howling noise. I am completely freaked out and turn on the light. Tim is in his bed tossing and turning as if he was confined in a straight-jacket trying to break free. I had never seen anyone have a seizure in my life. I ran next door and demanded Rocky come to my room. Even in a deep sleep Rocky jumped to his feet. We both tried to wake Tim and were cautious. This was some real exorcist shit happening.

Finally, I went to Eric and Zach's room and started pounding on their door. It took forever to wake them. Finally, Zach came to the door.

What Tim had tried to hide was that he has epilepsy. He was afraid the program would not accept him if he disclosed his condition. As a result, none of us knew what to do or what was happening. Tim had started spitting and dribbling small amounts of blood. When I arrived with Zach, Tim was wakening up. He was very disoriented, but he seemed to be in a much better place. He was able to communicate with us. My heart rate started to slow down. He had no memory of what had happened, but the blood was clear evidence.

Rocky, Zach and I exchanged looks of concern. Tim managed to convince us that the worst of things were over. He was certain that everything would be fine. Zach and Rocky returned to their rooms. I talked with Tim a little bit. He fell asleep rather fast for him. I laid in my bed for a long time. I couldn't fall asleep in anticipation of more howling.

As soon as I started to sleep again, the howling started. This time the severity was much more intense. I ran and beat on Zach's door and demanded he get an ambulance. Meanwhile, me and Rocky tended to Tim. When the seizure calmed down Tim had no recollection of what had happened again. He was dazed and confused. More blood was drooling from his mouth. I explained we needed to go downstairs that an ambulance was on the way. Tim tried to reject that he needed professional care. Rocky and I insisted he go down to the lobby with us.

IF ROCK BOTTOM HAD A BASEMENT

The paramedics didn't take long to arrive at all. Their timing was very impressive considering we were in the middle of nowhere. In the lobby the paramedics took Tim's vitals. Tim kept saying he didn't need to go the hospital. He was unaware and being unreasonable. I told the paramedics to take him. They informed me that they couldn't take him against his will. He wasn't in his right mind! It took about twenty minutes, but we eventually persuaded Tim to ride with the nice people. These strangers wanted to help. Tim was reluctant, but he got in the ambulance willingly.

I asked Zach why I didn't know he had epilepsy if we were roommates. I felt I needed to be aware and prepared. If I knew what was happening that could have eliminated panic. I was furious. That is when he told me they didn't know. Tim had a secret.

CHAPTER 29

> "So, take seriously the story that God has given you to live. It's time to read your own life, because your story is the one that could set us all ablaze." ~ Dan B. Allender

> "You are so much more than the worst thing you've ever done! God loves you." ~ I stole this straight off Facebook

Santa

and amends.

We went to the Baptist church for classes every morning. Tommy Sloan always taught on Mondays and Tuesdays. Wednesday was more of a free for all. Eventually I was teaching classes on Wednesday mornings myself. Often, we would have special speakers come share.

IF ROCK BOTTOM HAD A BASEMENT

One Wednesday two women came in from a local bank. Both were attractive, both were Hispanic, but only one stood out.

I was close to the back of the room. Which mostly gave me a bird's eye view of the presentation. The men whispered, murmured and looked at the women with googly eyes. I wasn't interested in the women sexually, but I did take notice of the one named Santa. She is stunning in beauty, but she also possessed a sweetness and depth to her. I watched her interact with the men with such ease and grace. She at times looked unsure of herself, but not often. Everyone she spoke with had her full attention. This lady was genuine.

I wasn't in a position to fall in love, but she had me. One look at her and there are poems to write, stories to share, and a soul to bare.

A few weeks later I called the bank and asked to speak with Santa. I was now employed with Saint Matthew's House. Though my income was very modest, I didn't need the money. I needed a bank account.

Still wondering if she really shared a name with Saint Nick. I have never actually met anyone with the name Santa. She agreed to come out to the property and sign me up for direct deposit checking account. We fast became friends and she would often bring me baked goods as well as food from Popeyes. That was a huge treat.

Today Santa is even more beautiful as I know her better. I consider her one of life's greatest friends and wonderful blessings. At times when I have prayed for a wife, I may have mentioned God could use her and Yanet as a blueprint of what I would like.

I had been at Saint Mathew's now for seven months. I had seen a load of compromising, family restoration, people being discharged or leaving, but most of all I had seen loves change lives. My mad season broken down refugee self was starting to feel again.

At this point Jim becomes my case manager. Jim came from the same altar of alcohol that I worshipped at. He was closer to my age and an outwardly and inwardly beautiful man. Jim thought that I was a bit of a diva, but I can't imagine why. With Jim I talked more about my future and less about my past. I was trying to push forward and work towards how I would be. Jim will be apart of my next two steps 8 and 9.

Step 8 is that I make a list of all the persons we had harmed and became willing to make amends to them all. Step 9 is that I make a direct amends to such people whenever possible, except when to do so would injure them or others. Amends means to correct a mistake or wrongdoing. It means that I will change and improve. In my mind, it also means that I have not just decided to correct, rectify, remedy, revise reform, but also that I am teachable. These are difficult decisions and steps to make.

I relied on Jim, Tommy, Chef Jason and Nojo a lot during this time. For most amends, I felt like I was accomplishing that by just being in the program, improving my life, and tackling my resentments.

Sitting down and trying to think of every bad

judgement, mistake and fuck up I have ever committed is maddening. Many people I owe an amends to I haven't seen in years. I decide it is best to attack this process twofold. One, I will stick to my drinking years. Two, I will simply work on what comes to mind and not spend a bunch of time digging up my past. After all let him without sin cast the first stone!

When I think of my family, I am making my amends by fighting to become sober. I have traded a year of my life to save it. Then there are the resentments that I struggle with (even now, my resentments haunt me). That amends will include forgiving people. Was there really any point in my imaginary court of law or judgement seat? The answer is rather simple. Freedom has a price, and it is called forgiveness. I am trying to free myself from my old ways. I know if I stay tied up in anger, I am not creating a new life.

The person I most want to make amends with is Heather, but I feel I can only do that by creating my best life. In my relationship with her, we were both bullies and would not back down. Most of my amends require nothing more than acceptance.

I can't change the past. I cannot really control anything, but I can influence my future with forgiveness. Stop waiting for the apology Larry will never offer.

I would love to be able to simply pay back a financial debt. I would love to write letters and make apologetic calls. However, for me most of my amends were about my attitude and my conduct going forward. I must admit that I am often wrong in my interpretations of people and their actions. If I want a life of purpose and no longer just enduring shit, I need to amend my mental state. Changing my approach to people and expectations. All I now know is that I cannot expect my old self behavior to just go away as quickly as an erection. This will be an everlasting fight that never ends. I think I will call this process "living amends," because I must actively look for opportunities to be more selfless. I am now trying to align myself with a higher power (God) and a new higher version of me.

I am now Neo from *The Matrix* motion picture. Two pills have been offered me. I am trapped in a room with Morpheus. I take the red pill and then I stepped onto Saint Matthew's grounds. The red pill acknowledges all my unpleasant truths. Now I learn who my enemy is, and it is me! The blue pill is sure looking enticing right about now. Maybe I should have swallowed the blue pill because ignorance is bliss.

It is important to realize that we can forgive people and not invite them back into our lives. I think of what my youth pastor Steve Jones said to me when I was still in my late teens.

"Make sure that whoever you run into; it isn't uncomfortable for you because you have unresolved issues."

Bottom line: Love is the answer. There are also more complex things going on in people's lives. The idea that there are two sides to every story is a lie! Every story is much more like an octagon.

I also must realize that people are not required to align themselves to my expectations. I really am not the world's axis. I am hardly worthless, but I am humbly insignificant. These are hard things for a selfish human to accept. I am a selfish human. Jim and Nojo were close to me during this time.

Today I often run into conflicts with people. Promptly I call Nojo. He always reminds me that I am placing my expectations on people again. Just once I want to be smarter than Nojo!

Jim was riding a lonely highway at Saint Mathew's House. Egos and self-importance were always trying to crush him out or at least that is what I saw. In the wonder of this ministry they often take noticeably young men and make idiot leaders out of them. This is both a good and bad tradition. Let's be honest, in life you must work for or with a lot of blazing assholes. The hope is we can all learn to stay sober despite other people. How many times and how many ways have we been taught we cannot control other people? The power, glory and daily grind kept Jim on the outskirts of the ministry. I was never truly sure why Jim was neglected, but my gut tells me he didn't fit a mold or image. This sucked! Because Adam was a poster child of their mold and I think he was the worst leader in the history of the ministry and possibly mankind. I think Jim and I bonded so well because we had this weird habit of always being ourselves. We honored, respected and adored the ministry and still never lost a sense of self.

Now part of the exclusion is that Jim is twice the age of most of the guys. Jim would also do everything to help one of the guys and on that level, I thought he sometimes made bad choices. Yet, he has a much bigger heart than me.

For so long I had been identified as a man who wanted his crowded solitude and whiskey. I knew I was being fixed and yet I would always be broken as well. I was inclined to not revisit the man I had been. However, this journey of change is not for the meek or weak. This is where Jim really shined in my life and growth.

Now I am entering month seven and the kickoff to our new month is my most difficult. For a large part, the program becomes ours and we can make some major choices about what road we will take. Freedom starts to present itself to us. The road we have all shared is about to fork and we start to go in different directions. For me this is a painful time. It feels like another broken family.

Anthony moved to Motrac where he would become the most infamous leader of all time. He did learn that his methods were overbearing, and the guys needed more compassion from him entering the program. Anthony was hated, but he became a better man. He did not immediately see how his new path was another journey. His new position was now teaching him to grow from a kid to a king in leadership.

Rob followed, but he mostly just wanted to get over to Wolfe the sober housing phase. He only lasted in Motrac maybe 4 weeks. Rob was interested in women! Who could blame him? Rob is a young man full of vitality and energy. He loved women. Christina the housekeeper had a heavy flirtation thing going on with Rob. However, unlike her broken down romance with Time Bomb Tom, Rob never took things too far. I suspect Christina was just too old for him.

Rocky went straight to Wolfe. He had a promising life as a fisherman that awaited him. Rocky was a little more levelheaded about women. His great love was the outdoors. He eventually went back to commercial fishing. Just as you are holding this book, chances are that Rocky is holding a fish.

Jacob went to Wolfe as well and got a job right away in a restaurant while completing his time. Jacob always had the heart of Joan of Arc, but also a gigolo and we never knew where he would end up. In fact, we all were worried about how Jacob would make choices. There was still way too much teenage frat boy drive in him. He lived with a massage therapist for a time. I am unsure of his romantic endeavors these days. I am more than sure of his exceptional talent. I suspect Jacob will settle down more into his thirties.

Greg did the unthinkable and stayed to work outside in the heat with Adam. Don't get me wrong! Greg is great with his hands and as a leader in that arena, but I could not understand his adoration for Adam. He would stay in LaBelle for about another year before he headed back to Jackson County.

The problem with Jackson county is that it lends itself to relapse. It is a small-town area with too much corruption, crime, and drugs. Drugs to Jackson County is like baseball to America, a national pastime. You can't stay sober if you return to old surroundings.

IF ROCK BOTTOM HAD A BASEMENT

Nojo joined the peer mentor group and Tim followed his lead. Tim had some issues with epileptic seizures and Nojo was the perfect father figure to step in and help control the episodes. Nojo could be as childishly unreasonable as any of us, but he always managed to maintain the ability to be our caretaker. Even now I can expect regular calls from Nojo checking up on my art of sobriety. Today he still works full time at Saint Matthew's House and is in school full time. He has bought a house with his girlfriend and planning a wedding.

Karl admittedly claimed he was mostly just killing time in the program to appease a judge. Though his initial motivation is true and clear I also know he became a valued part of our group and our hearts. Even now we talk on days that one of us is down. Karl stayed back at LaBelle to be a part of the hotel team. When he left the program, he went back into truck driving and traveling the country.

Then there was me! Yeah, all those months craving the freedom of being out of LaBelle, needing city sounds and smells. I stayed back in the country and worked at the hotel right along Karl. I also wanted to keep Jim as my case manager. Every Monday I would ask Jim if I was teaching the Wednesday morning class and the answer was always "no". Every Tuesday night or sometimes Wednesday mornings Jim would laugh and ask me to teach the class. I always did because I enjoyed it.

There are a lot of rules that are cut lose once you turn this corner. In mod 7 you are allowed a cellphone. Up until this point you could sign up for 15-minute phone calls on Sunday nights.

IF ROCK BOTTOM HAD A BASEMENT

The problem with the phones was that this was way too much freedom for men that still had rules to live by. The number one purpose of the smart phone was pornography and to find women to meet on pass. I felt strongly that phones should be permitted, but flip phones for the first few months. They did implement this rule once I left the program.

It is tradition that on the final night of a group's LaBelle stay, we have a huge dinner. It is a celebration of accomplishments, relationships, and sobriety. It is a splendid way of saying goodbye and looking towards the future. Many of us have never held jobs longer than holding a single dollar. In some lives there were no graduations, promotions, or any significant accomplishments. This night celebrates our faith, fight, and recovery. This is a time that we have dreamt of for so many nights when what we really wanted was to leave. God and confidence are making itself known in lives of broken people. Lives that had rusted had been revved back up and were being used.

The laughter was loud, but the night's meaning had not fallen deaf to me. I knew I was about to be separated from some and participate in the promotion of others. I relived our first days at the homeless shelter. The days when Tim was sure I was gay, and he referred to my backwards ball cap as "Marc's straight hat." I walked over to a round table. I sat alone and involuntarily began to cry. I was alone until Tim found me. Our journey had come full circle in so many ways.

However, not all was perfect in my new world. I

had living arrangements to contend with. My roommate situation would be with Karl and this thrilled me. However, it also meant I would be living with a kid named JoJo (Not to be confused with Nojo). I like JoJo these days, but I absolutely hated living with him. He was a selfish all-consuming brat. He felt he was king of the castle and made sure we all knew it, all the time. I knew JoJo needed back in those days was to be sent out of the LaBelle community and onto Wolfe. However, Jim (our peer mentor) had a huge and unbalanced heart for JoJo. Once any of us come under Jim's wing, he goes to great lengths to care for us. Jim protected him and pampered the kid. Many people hated Jim for this, but we all have our favorites for various reasons. In rehab this can mean that someone's story resembles the story you lived.

One evening I was looking for my headphones. Headphones to me are a very personal item such as a toothbrush. I turned our room upside down, but to no avail. It was dark and raining out and this made it harder to see behind dressers and whatnot. I was turning my small space upside down.

JoJo walked into the room during my search and rescue mission for my headphones. Politely I asked if he had seen them. Jackpot! He had. He took MY headphones to the gym and forgot them. First, I don't want to share earwax with any man. Second, he made no offer to go get them. Something borrowed, something uncared for was his motto. I was livid, and from that minute started counting the days until he was moved on. There were four of us that shared this room at the time. Three out of the four hated living with JoJo. But I was more vocal as I tend to be. Both Karl and Justin weren't looking for confrontation.

JoJo had made a girlfriend that he was visiting when he went on pass. He acted as though she adored him, but the relationship confused me. What does a woman want with a guy whom she met while he was in the middle of an addiction program? The answer is she needs a distraction from her own misery or broken heart. The answer includes that these women are highly imbalanced and whack jobs too. They are the co-dependent women that are very sweet, but very twisted. JoJo was a fun distraction for her, but there was no telling him this. Besides this girlfriend served a purpose for us as well. She was a huge motivator to get JoJo out of LaBelle and she worked for us just perfectly. Sadly, she broke up with him a few short days before he made it back to Naples. At this I really did feel bad. JoJo wasn't a lost cause kid. He was just a boy that needed direction and a strong male lead in his life. The girlfriend wanted a toy as a distraction when she felt lonely. I would sometimes watch him making her crafts and writing her letters and cards. I always felt bad because I knew she would never fully appreciate his efforts.

The morning JoJo left I made no effort to say good-bye, it was just good riddance. However, just like *Jaws*, even after they blew the shark up there was a sequel. Just when you thought it was safe to go back in the water. In my case just when I thought it was safe to move on. In life there is always a sequel. Just ask Heather, she left me for a less appealing guy named – Mark, the pubic faced sequel.

IF ROCK BOTTOM HAD A BASEMENT

JoJo worked at the front desk just before he moved. When he left it was me, Karl, David and Stump. The problem was that two of us four had developed some really bad habits. Soon we would be radically shorthanded.

Jim reached out to JoJo to help at the hotel. We had just lost three front desk guys. All three found a way to relapse while in the program. This left us with a huge void. JoJo thought he was welcomed with open arms. Nope, both Justin and I wanted nothing to do with his upcoming bullshit! Many guys rolled their eyes upon word that JoJo might return.

Now that JoJo was dumped, it fed his ego to feel needed. He came back feeling as though he was the big man on campus. JoJo left Wolfe apartments and returned to LaBelle. He expected to move back into our room. I said "No!" This did not make me popular. My other roommate Justin didn't want him either, but he is a peacekeeper and kept his mouth shut. JoJo had stained his welcome. This left me a lone ranger telling JoJo he wasn't welcome. Now remember Nojo and JoJo are two different people. Jim became frustrated with me very quickly.

JoJo felt he still had claim to the room we once shared. It is like you leave a job and still expect a check for not working. His feelings of entitlement were exactly why we didn't want him back. Still, Justin played the role of Switzerland; he avoided conflict. Between him and Jim I had to hear every day how hurt and upset JoJo was. Back and forth we went on this for a solid week. Justin lost all resolve to fight alongside me. This was beyond frustrating. In fact, once Justin started playing the role of Switzerland,

I became weary. Even Jim was saying to me "Well, JoJo did pick you," when they assigned me a roommate for those in transition. (Transition is when you change mods and move rooms.)

Finally, I relented and allowed JoJo back into the room. But he had to work for it. He thought I hated him. I didn't hate him, and I still don't. He was just a brat and needed to know there were consequences to actions.

When he moved back in, he was very respectful. He was a brand-new man. Justin, JoJo and I would lay in our bunks at night and talk and laugh. We talked about all kinds of things and it was nice. There were boundaries and it was wonderful. I grew to appreciate him again. Today I think very highly of JoJo. I am not sure I would want to risk being his roommate again; however, he is a good guy. Last I saw he was working out a lot, working towards his future and posting pictures without a shirt all over social media. I am most likely just jealous of the latter because my days of looking good naked have long ago passed.

Why did we need JoJo back in the first place? So glad you asked.

CHAPTER 30

"I am not defined by my relapses, but by my decision to remain in recovery despite them." ~ Anonymous

Dave.

There are two suites in LaBelle for the guys that don't move onto Wolfe. I was in one and you already know that story. Two guys living in the other suite. Stump and Dave both started the program together. Now from the first day I met Stump he maintained that he was only doing the program to stay out of jail. His stay in rehab was nothing more than a court ordered mandate. He was looking for a means to an end. Fair enough because I would probably do the same.

Dave came straight from jail. They both had been

in and out of jail and prison. It was sad because they are both very good guys. Stump was annoying all the time, but not a bad guy. Dave is a great looking, funny, fun and talented guy, but he could not get passed the desire or sensation of being high.

It was September and my sister was picking me up for a weekend with the family. My family lived about 3 hours north in a dump of a town called Hudson. It is about 30 to 45 minutes north of Tampa in Pasco County. Pasco County was made famous on an A&E program called LIVEPD. Currently my parents have left Hudson and moved north to Jacksonville.

Dave's family lived in Pasco County as well. About 30 minutes south off Hwy US-19 in New Port Richie Dave's parents owned a beautiful 3 story condominium. It was an ideal situation for us to carpool.

It was my sister's first visit to LaBelle. She had the opportunity to meet Jim. As my case manager, Jim needed to know whom I was with and I had to stay in touch with him while away. After a year living in a rehab, I found it hard to relate to people who lived outside of my bubble. As a result, I wanted to stay in touch with Jim. I needed him to help me balance my feelings, including fear. Inside rehab you may ask a person "How are you?" One of two things is going to happen. One, you will get an overwhelmingly honest answer whether good or bad. The second option is you will get an answer that will require you to call "Bullshit!" Rehab makes you a victim of honesty and being real.

Now I live among people who care more about

their workout outfits than working out. I hate the fakeness that our real world provides. Baby Mama was always prone to be fake; she was certainly a different person in every situation and group. Heather may have been crazy as a sack of cats, but she was thoroughly real. She never tried to be anyone other than who she is. I cherish that about Heather.

Jim remains a sounding board in my life. He also seems to have an eternal alarm when I am in a bad place (more on this later). I enjoy staying in touch with Jim. As of this writing, I have been gone from Saint Matthew's House for over 2 full years. I talk to Jim monthly and at times daily. He is a strong source of encouragement and direction as I navigate these sober waters. Living in the boundaries of rehab, sobriety is a walk in the park. Real life, the real world, and real problems warrant real 101 proof.

My sister, Beth arrived nice and early to pick us up. Dave would ride in the back seat. Dave is a pretty boy, and to look at him he had no demeanor of a man that had been to prison a few times, but he had. This fascinated Beth and she had questions. My sister watches all those jail and prison reality shows. I wasn't sure if I was humiliated by her insistence to know about his jail time. Yet, it didn't matter because Beth can be persistent.

"So, Dave, tell me what was your prison nickname? I know you had one." She asks, and I want to slap her whole face. I was so embarrassed, but that didn't stop us from laughing when he shared the names. Turned out Dave had two prison nicknames: Drosky

(Abbreviation of his last name.) and Little Skyzee. Oddly enough both names seemed very fitting for Dave.

For some time in LaBelle, Dave's behavior was becoming increasingly annoying. Our conversations were becoming shallower and more unimaginative. His fundamental positive traits were slipping away. I had no idea what was going on with him and I kind of just felt that he was living on a crazy train. His roommate Stump was known to be abrasive, rude and all around not fun to deal with. I figured that Dave was just so impressionable and Stump was wearing off on him. Instead of Dave being driven insane by Stump I presumed he was just joining him in his lunacy. Stump was the only man I thought should have been definitively kicked out of the program. Overall, I felt grace should always abound, but Stump did not value the recovery and made it very well known. This upset me deeply because Justin's Place was saving my life. It taught me to stop chasing a moment and to turn my eyes to gratitude and God. Stump was full of empty hallelujahs.

One afternoon I was napping, and Jim came to my room. Two o'clock is my prime-time napping hour. They wanted to move me into the room with Stump and Dave. The program likes to move us around every month. I think Jim knew this transition was not about to go over well with me. Because it was not like Jim to come up to my room with an announcement.

"No, I am not living with them," I declared. This should have been the end of the discussion. I was angrier that I had to be defiant with Jim.

IF ROCK BOTTOM HAD A BASEMENT

Jim's face froze. It was not like me to be defiant, but I also was not one to be silent. Jim said I had to move to their room on the next transition, which was just a few days away. My anger grew. Jim is a lifeline and I would never want to be put in this position, but I was.

"Then move me to Wolfe apartments," I countered. I was past my seven-month mark and qualified to move to the sober apartments. Jim grimaced and nodded no. The decision had been made, and I could see this was not a choice Jim could alter alone. Jim left the room. My face turned cherry tomato red.

"Oh, great! Remarcable (a nickname given to me by Tommy Sloan) is pissed," My roommate Justin announced. "Don't do anything stupid." Some people feel I am very vocal about things I don't agree with. I am not so sure, what do you think?

I went downstairs, and I got on the computer. I was sending a message to my mother. Jim walked over, he was cautious and concerned, but he knew I was beyond upset. "What are you doing?" Jim asked. When Jim is in full confrontational gear, he looks at you and looks around a lot. Jim absorbs every aspect of the environment and situation. His behavior is very endearing.

"My mother will pick me up in the morning around nine," I answered flatly. I did not want to leave the program, but in these tense moments, I knew that they were throwing me to the wolves. I had no idea what Dave and Stump had going on in that room. I simply knew something was radically wrong. Furthermore, Saint Matthew's House is big on proof. I had nothing to offer just a suspicion. I knew I was right, but I had no evidence. When working the overnight front desk shifts, I would see the guys come and go outside in the wee hours of the morning. Something was wrong, but I never expected what the truth would reveal.

Using their cellphones, the two men were having drugs delivered to the rehab facility in the middle of the night. Most of us were sound asleep and I was unsuspecting. I had no idea their behavior was so out of whack because they were high. As a drunk I can spot another drunk easily, but I wasn't so certain about the conduct of drugs back then. None of this had come to light yet, and I was willing to leave the program to protect my sobriety. Irony anyone?

Within minutes I was sitting in front of the computer. All the men that I loved, respected and needed were surrounding me. They stood looking down at me, the men's faces distraught and frustrated. Maybe they thought I could bring some balance to their room, but I wanted nothing to do with the chaos of Dave and Stump. Connor's face was in disbelief; Jim's face was harder to read because I feel most bonded with him. Isaac mostly looked down at the floor with his eyes up at me and the other men. This wasn't me being merely rebellious. I stayed seated and only looked up at each of the men. I made sure I was making direct eye contact. My father taught me to always ask myself one question in a conflict, "is this a hill I am willing to die on?" Just the opposite, I wasn't willing to die anymore.

My explanation was simple, direct and most of all

right. I repeated it several times. "I have no idea what is going on in that room, but I know I want nothing to do with it." They seemed both dumbfounded and at the same time I know they knew I was right. When I looked at each of those men Connor - Jim and Isaac - I saw in their eyes I wasn't merely being a prima donna. They also knew I wasn't about to deliberately allow anything to jeopardize my growth. They relented and allowed me to stay put, but I was a little upset that I had to stand my ground like I did. My victory did not smell sweet. I did not want to disrespect their leadership or rules. I valued the men I had to make a stand against. Also, I felt disappointment when we learned officially that they guys were doing drugs and none of the leaders apologized for doubting me. I was right, but it never felt good! Did I mention that without proof, I was right?

On our drive to the Tampa area, Dave was in the backseat. The plan was to drop Dave off at his mother's place of employment. Everything was simple enough, but we didn't realize that Dave was planning. Dave was on his smart phone putting together a rendezvous with a woman he no doubt met or at least reconnected with over the Internet. Women have always been Dave's downfall. Women are a lot of men's downfall. In fact, a woman is the number one reason that men leave the program. To a degree, my broken heart from women lead me into the program. Often, I met men who entered the program not to get sober, but to salvage a relationship. The wrong reasons for recovery will almost always yield the wrong results.

As soon as we dropped Dave off outside his

mother's work, he had a girl meet him with drugs. His reason was outweighed by want and desire. As an alcoholic, I know that feeling when temptation is so overwhelmingly powerful. He had been having drugs delivered to LaBelle and this only made sense for him. His addiction was fully active. As a result, he was high before he ever saw his mother. Apparently, he figured he'd just go for broke and get high all weekend. None of us were wise to his plan. I felt like it all unfolded underneath my nose, and I never put the puzzle together.

Late Sunday afternoon my sister and I drove to his parent's condo to pick him up. His mother stood in the garage with Dave. Her face was clearly wearing trauma. I know family can induce a lot of stress for an addict, so I didn't initially think too much about their disconnect. We loaded Dave's bags and headed out. Beth and I exchanged uncertain glances. I figured his head was full of heavy thoughts about home. His mother offered no insight into Dave's behavior. In fact, she was caught between denial and uncertainty. She later told me she could not figure out how he was getting high because he was never alone. Rest assured sneaky deeds is what addicts excel in. He was most likely sneaking out in the middle of the night.

In the past I have hidden small bottles of alcohol in the woods, in church bushes, all over my parents' home and garage. I have even hidden bottles so well I forgot where they were for months. I used to buy the quarter pints so that I could tuck them away in all the pockets of my cargo shorts. It is amazing the lengths we will go to nurse our addictions. I have even heard of people drinking rubbing alcohol and mouth wash to get drunk. We are certainly capable of crossing the border of sanity and hide our actions in sneaky behavior.

On the way to Tampa Dave and my sister just chatted away. We were a bunch of homies laughing and enjoying out tiny road trip. On the return trip, Dave was a completely different person. Often not even replying to questions and certainly not participating in the conversation. Little did I know that he was high and had been on a bender all weekend. He was very unresponsive. He was scattered and nothing mattered. I was angry with the way Dave was acting.

Once we pulled off the interstate and were on our final stretch of highway to LaBelle, it was time for a quick off property dinner. We stopped at a Wendy's. My sister and I ate, but Dave disappeared. He headed into the bathroom and we didn't see him again for the remainder of our meal. What the fuck was he doing? I sat in silence listening to what my reason was telling me, but at the same time begging God it wasn't true. I knew Dave was using in the bathroom. Truth lit up my mind like a traffic light at midnight.

I was certain under those cold florescent lights of the restroom he was sitting on a toilet with a needle in his arm. I knew he passed out and I figured we had about 30 minutes before he would emerge. I also knew he was going to be drug tested when we returned to Justin's Place. It was a betrayal that he was putting me in this position, and I was furious. I came very close to leaving him in that bathroom and just driving off. Yet, I was reminded that we all have sinned. I wasn't addicted to drugs, but bourbon had taken me many places and back again.

Driving to the LaBelle property it was past dark. I was angry and most of the final journey was still and quiet. Beth was mostly stone silent as well. At this point she was aware of Dave's condition and the severity of the situation. I asked my sister to pull over and allow me to fill the gas tank so she would not have to do it later alone.

She pulled up to the pump and I went inside to pay. Unexpectedly Dave pops out of the car's backseat and runs up to me. This was the most engaged I had seen him in the last three hours. With his eyes darting all over the place he said he needed a favor.

"I need you to pee in a bottle for me," his face as serious as death. He was pushing my patience and his luck. I looked at him briefly; I had to remind myself repeatedly that I cared for this guy because I was ready to rip his head off. Still, in that moment I kind of did wish I could rescue him from his actions.

"Excuse me?" I needed a second to believe he just asked me to give him my piss.

"I will buy a bottle and you pee in it for me," Dave explained.

"No, I can't do that. I am sorry." I have heard that it is best to always ask a person for something directly. Supposedly it is hard for people to say "No" to our faces. I am not sure of the validity of this claim, but it was hard to say no to Dave. It was awkward and uncomfortable to feel that I could not help him. Dave was asking me to lie for him and risk being discharged myself. Worst of all, he couldn't have pulled off his scheme because he was way too high. Dave had flushed skin and small pupils with watery eyes. Even in his panic, he was still very drowsy. I told him no, but he acted as though he didn't hear me.

We continued inside where I paid for the gas and some snacks. Dave came out of the bathroom with an empty Kool-Aid plastic bottle. I looked and could see blue residue from the flavor of the drink. He hadn't even bothered to rinse it out and I wondered if he even paid for the drink. He was handing it to me as if he did not hear me say I would not pee for him. He looked at me with pathetic desperation that every addict and drunk knows too well. His brown eyes screaming how clueless he was that I would not have his back on this. I hated he made me tell him no once, and now I had to say it again.

All the good intentions I might have had were dry as a bone in this request. My face turned to stone and I looked directly at him again and said, "No, Dave. I just can't break this rule." I found myself among a friend and in need of desperate faith.

His voice of reason had forsaken him. He lost sight of everything reasonable; he was desperate and doomed. Even if I wanted to help Dave, he couldn't fool anyone at Justin's Place. His extreme drowsiness was so telling. He was also unable to focus and very anxious, which was out of character for him. Dave was most often very mild mannered and likable. I thought to myself, maybe this is how people look at me when I am drunk.

Both the road and driveway to The LaBelle Inn

were long. The time passed slowly and quietly as I looked ahead. We passed the small river and I aimlessly looked over the water. I needed the life of the water as I prayed to a supernatural God for Dave. What were the consequences about to be? What was my role? We pulled up to the front doors of the inn. I got out of the car to load our stuff onto a luggage carrier, but Dave was a bat out of hell from the backseat. Recklessly, Dave was looking for urine samples. He asked his roommate Stump, but he would piss dirty too.

Once again, Dave's behavior was proving his guilt. You simply do not avoid coming through the main doors of the facility. In a matter of minutes some of the residents were reporting that Dave was looking for help to pass a piss test. He was caught, and in a few minutes the entire property would be a buzz about Dave.

Meanwhile to celebrate my birthday my roommate Justin, had ordered a few pizzas. However, I needed to talk to Bodey. Bodey was a towering figure with dark features. He is a seasoned martial artist and a soft heart. He was also a mixture of goofy fun and over the top intelligence. I once told him that he spoke over too many people's heads. The men at The Justin's Place may not have emphasized education in their pasts, but they were hardly dumb. The guys were intelligent. Their roads just twisted and bended in mysterious ways. I figured he might as well hear it from me that Dave was coming back wasted. My sadness was crashing against a wall of anger leaving me feeling lost. Now I had to approach Bodey in my darkest and deepest valley of my rehab experience.

IF ROCK BOTTOM HAD A BASEMENT

Surprisingly, when we walked into the dining room where Bodey was going through my bags, he already knew. He was serious and stoic, but never cold. I was saved from having to rat my friend out. I felt good that Bodey is a man of compassion and he too had a love for Dave. The last person I wanted dealing with Dave's condition and situation was anyone that lacked the gift of grace. If Adam was there, he would have thrown Dave under the bus and backed up over his body a few times. I knew that for Bodey, just like me, even if we knew the reasons that Dave relapsed, it would still hurt. Bodey was always a jovial man and on this day he was still. I could read the disbelief on his face.

He went through my bags. This was custom for all of us that went on pass. He handed me a bottle of Lisinopril.

"Why are there two different size pills in here?"

"My blood pressure was high, and the doctor doubled my dose. I had the prescription refilled while I was in Hudson. I just combined the bottles because that is what I always do."

There is a grocery store chain in Florida that offers some prescriptions for free. No doubt this is a way to bring customers into their stores. LaBelle didn't have this shopping chain, but Hudson and most of Florida did.

In LaBelle the program provided medical visits if we required them. I would see the doctor every few months because I have a longtime issue with blood pressure.

IF ROCK BOTTOM HAD A BASEMENT

Bodey gestured that he understood and tossed the bottle back in my bag. I got the feeling this might be Bodey's first time discharging a resident. Not only a resident, but a friend of ours. He walked out of the dining room with his shoulders slumped. I figured he was going to call Jim. Jim was my case manager and Dave and Stump's as well. I had no doubt that Jim would be hurt. He may have been a case manager, but he was a friend too. When you stand close to these men, their failures have an impact. Dave is one of our own. As for me, I kept seeing him laughing at all the things we made fun of. I revisited the times he would sit in my room and we would just shoot the shit.

I was able to go to the kitchen and several Little Caesars pizzas were waiting for my birthday celebration. My roommate, Justin, had really gone out of his way to make my birthday special. The whispers were already starting to circulate. Dave's actions were igniting the rumor fires.

His roommate Stump came into the kitchen. Stump was an opportunist, always looking for ways to take advantage of situations. He always managed to get himself right in the middle of everything. He had sticky fingers and could steal right in front of you. He had a magician's gift of distracting your attention elsewhere. A gifted criminal and back then had no integrity whatsoever. He never walked into a room; it was more of a shuffling of his feet. He had an air about him of self-gratification that was both insulting and gross. He was always testing boundaries. In a way, I faulted Stump that evening because I knew he had to have had a hand in Dave's downfall. Still, we all need to take responsibility for our own actions, this included Dave.

Please understand that I want everyone to get all the help they need, but within reason. If you do not want help for yourself, then you will hardly care about anyone else's sobriety. Stump had no respect for anything. Stump should have been discharged a long time ago.

I was leaning up against a stainless-steel counter when Stump entered the kitchen. Slightly removed for the group with heavy thoughts on my mind, I could see some eyes roll when Stump arrived. The eye roll was common when Stump entered a room. Typical of Stump's style, he helped himself to the pizza. He didn't ask, he simply took food and began to stuff his face. I do not think his demeanor knew any other way than rude.

"Stump, Dave pissed dirty bud," Justin shared. The three had entered the program together. Justin was genuinely saddened to share the news. Stump on the other hand, was alarmed for different reasons.

My eyes were fixed on Stump. Immediately I knew for certain that he would piss dirty as well. He wore the guilt and surprise on his face with horror. I could see the shock and the unimaginable consequences that faced him. Both guys were facing jail or prison time if they failed the program. I felt Stump belonged in prison, and I must admit I wasn't disappointed. I never hated Stump but hated his behavior. He could truly be fun.

It was just a matter of time now before Bodey would ask Stump for a piss test. Turns out that Bodey was just minutes away from the request. In the program, if anyone in your room failed a drug test or got busted some way, everyone had to be tested.

When Bodey came into the kitchen to get Stump, I casually followed them to the lobby. Stump was explaining to Bodey that he just used the bathroom and couldn't pee right away. Bodey was a patient and genuine man. He just explained that he could sit down drink water and wait for the urge to come again. I listened to Stump with little effort because he was loud. He could be heard all over the property. His voice always yards ahead of his arrival. If you met him believe me, he was a presence you could never overlook.

I watched Stump walk up and down the hallway. His behavior was a dead giveaway. He was about to fail this test and what he was doing was planning his escape. Stump would never go to jail freely or easily.

Now all the pieces were coming together for me. It was obvious these two were getting high together. In their room there was one other guy named Jayce (that is what we will call him). Jayce was very much to himself. He would spend all his time in the room whenever possible, but he wasn't getting high. Jayce had replaced his addiction with pornography. Jayce was also very disconnected to everyone in the program. Again, we could share our concerns, but without proof nobody did anything about Jayce's mysterious ways. Jayce graduated from the program and died from an overdose a year later. He was a perfect lodger but had his own agenda. A 12-step program only works if you work the program. When someone from rehab dies, it never matters how close I was to them. I always just thought that could have easily been me.

Meanwhile another peer mentor was up in Dave's room helping him pack. Jim, our case manager, had come back to the property. His coming so late on a Sunday night was highly unusual. Jim had been a participant in the program and graduated. Now a case manager, he had his position for several months. Yet, Jim had not yet become numb to seeing relapses. Numb may seem like a cruel word, but I can't imagine how you could watch men you fall in love with so dearly fall off the wagon so often. Please never lose sight of the fact that you cannot relapse if you are not trying to get sober. So, I never fault anyone who has an episode, but it is also never easy to see or even be aware of. The look on Jim's face that night is etched in my memory. His expression was telling a story filled with hurt and sorrow. I wondered if he felt responsible in some way. If he did that would be foolish because we can never control the actions of other people. You can only control how you react to other people's actions. Yeah, that is another Facebook meme stolen for my book.

The most stressful part of watching a brother from the program leave is wondering where they will go and what will happen. My heart was really pumping as he came down the elevator with his bags. The surreal experience of the night was closing. It occurred to me that if he was discharged with Stump, it would only lead to more drugs and God only knew what else.

They took him to the Labelle Motel off Highway 80 right in the middle of town. The place is an absolute dump. You rent a room from a woman through a tiny window. Looking at her through bars. The window is much smaller than that of a drive through establishment. In fact, there was a sign that warns you to stand back. Prostitutes hung out around the hotel as well, but trust me these were not high-class call girls. These are the kind of women that should come with a penicillin shot. Women from broken homes most likely sexually assaulted. Now they were getting paid for it. It was a heartbreaking sight for a man who has a daughter. I am sure they wanted to turn tricks for heroin, but late at night they might settle for sharing a room. Jim didn't speak to anyone that wasn't directly involved with Dave's situation. Jim stood with the distinction of Lord Grantham from the British television show *Downton Abbey*. The good news was that Dave left without Stump.

Stump could stall no longer and failed his piss test as expected. Stump would no doubt run to get high and hide. Which is exactly what he did.

Connor did not call his probation officer until the following Monday morning. Soon Stump was picked up and put in jail, but his stay was very limited. The judge let Stump off the hook because he was only days away from completing his court ordered time. Cue the Charlie Daniels song, "Simple Man". The lyrics talk about things that make him madder than hell, like some panty waist judge. In this case, I think the judge was weak, but I also feel that jail and prison do nothing to help an addict recover. Most addicts are using within 12 hours of leaving any kind of incarceration. The hard truth is that forced sober time does not equate sobriety.

IF ROCK BOTTOM HAD A BASEMENT

When Stump left, I deleted him from Facebook and blocked him a few days later. He realized this quickly and shared his anger publicly, but I simply explained that if he wanted to self-destruct, I don't have to watch it.

Jim was going to bat for Dave. I knew he would because Jim always had the back of the men who he managed. However, the program's policy was to kick you out for a minimum of 30 days as the result of a relapse. The bigger issue with Dave was that another resident was involved. It is a very escalated matter when you are pulling others down with you. However, everyone including myself saw this more of Stump's brainchild. In truth, I gave Stump too much credit. Dave was every bit as guilty and probably a more levelheaded mastermind. Stump isn't tree stump stupid, but he wasn't the sharpest pencil in a box either. Still, the devised a plan to have their drugs delivered like a pizza at two in the morning.

The next day they were going to pick up Dave and take him to the David Lawrence Center in Naples. The center is a mental health facility with several programs and branches. Dave was going to Crossroads where they help with addictions. Crossroads was able to give 24-hour medical monitoring while Dave detoxed from his substance abuse. Saint Matthew's House is not a medical facility and therefore not a good fit for his recovery at this point. Detoxing can be very deadly. This stay would be brief but allow the leaders of our program to decide what was next for Dave. However, those choices were quickly taken away from our rehab. Dave had violated his probation.

IF ROCK BOTTOM HAD A BASEMENT

Dave also failed to get permission from his probation officer to go to Pasco County. He never consulted anyone. This landed him in jail for a short vacation from freedom. When the jail time was served, Saint Matthew's allowed him back to the program, but they put him back to the first month motrac phase.

The morning they were to transport Dave from the motel to Naples. I asked Jim if I could go and ride with Dave to Crossroads. Jim felt that was fine and I was glad about that. I wanted to reassure Dave that I still loved him and that we all did. Never kick an addict when they are down. It only makes things worse. He was quiet again, but this time he felt defeated and wasn't high. I am not sure traveling with him helped, but I knew he would know I loved and supported him. Sometimes a little is a lot during a downward spiral.

When we got to the motel. I was disturbed at how nasty the establishment was. I am talking third world kind of accommodations. I walked into his bathroom and the area was being remodeled. However, it looked like a project that was begun, but would never be finished. Everything was dirty, and the linens were frayed. The curtains looked as if they had been hanging since the seventies. They were heavy, sullied and kept the room a very dungeon-like dark. Even the odors were offensive.

A few months later, Stump came back to LaBelle one time while I was working the front desk. I was dumbfounded when I saw him. He looked like hell walking. I was speechless. He had sores all over the exposed parts of his body. I got the impression he was living in the woods. Maybe he had not had a bath in days. He wanted a hug and it was all I could do to touch him. He was softer and gentler than I had ever seen him. I looked at him and thought now he is ready. Over the next several months there were always rumors of him returning to the program, but nothing ever came together.

After I graduated the program, Stump did find his way back to Saint Matthew's House. Sadly, only lasting a few days. Stump was just never ready to give up his will to be in control and his own boss. A lot of people are like this and I get it. We want to be free. We want freedom to make our own choices. We want to be in control. The sad truth is we are never in control, and life proves it daily. Our addiction is always lying to us. Our minds need to be rewired and this is the longest part.

CHAPTER 31

"Life is a business of making choices, history will define us the way we intend to author it." ~ Njau kihia

"I've been accused of vulgarity, I say Bullshit." ~ Mel Brooks

Itching Powder.

In rehab there is a lot of accountability. For people from the prison system, all they understand is a snitch mentality. Snitches get stiches is their motto. In jail, I must say this makes sense, but in rehab snitching is an important thing. Every time a person brings drugs into or around the facility, they are putting dozens of others at risk.

My brother has been an addict his whole life. One

of the greatest and most talented people living, but also enslaved. He tried rehab for about 4 days and left because he said there are snitches and he doesn't go for that. "I am a convict," he claims and therefore lives by another code of conduct. What he fails to realize is that his code of conduct has literally left him with nothing! A lot of dead ends when we close our minds to new possibilities. Cue the John Mellencamp song, "The Authority Song."

Just two short weeks later, another one of the guys would fail their drug test returning from a weekend pass. This time it was a mod brother and my roommate Karl. Losing a guy from the program feels a lot like a divorce. No matter how much it may be needed it never feels good. I was still a little down over Dave leaving. However, they allowed him back into the program after he got out of jail.

Karl's story was that he met with a girl in the middle of the night. She had drugs and of course it had been awhile since he had been with a woman. He was excited and leaving his experience in rehab behind. More than blood runs through your veins when you are a horny man. He was offered drugs and he did them to soothe his nerves. This was purely a lust driven decision and Karl is a young man, so I get it! Life is certainly no beautiful experience all the time. This was Karl's story and I am sticking to it.

It was a Sunday night, and I was waiting for Karl to return. I had no idea I was going to have to say hello to another good-bye. He was a few hours late and that made me nervous, but when I saw him, he looked great and in good spirits. Remember Karl was always hard to read. I had no idea he had been high that weekend. The significant difference appeared to be he just used once as opposed to all weekend like Dave had done. He simply did not look high. However, like they say, you only need to have sex once to get someone pregnant.

The bullet in the gun was this strange woman in the middle of the night. Now my curiosity has always wondered, if a woman who barely knows you is willing to meet you in the middle of nowhere with drugs, how many other men has she done this with? I don't know about you, but I don't usually carry Penicillin with me on dates! STDs freak me out, but I am sure that is because I lived through the AIDS crisis of the eighties. When we knew almost nothing about the disease. I have also known several people to die from AIDS and it is a heartbreaking demise.

Now that Karl was back, I headed to the barn. The Barn is exactly that - a spider infested barn. It also houses all our donated gym equipment. Gym equipment often turns into nothing more than clutter and a place to hang clothes in people's homes. So, you see treadmills, and home gyms in the thrifts shops and donation bins a lot. Everything we had in our gym felt as if it was falling apart and older than me. However, I would occasionally go down to the place.

I couldn't work out during our peak times because so much of the music the younger men listened to was simply gross. In fact, if I listened to their music I would have to continue to drink because it is so awful! In fact, one time I was working out and a guy changed the radio station with no consideration of others. I volunteered to finance his relapse whenever he wanted. Grossly, I never felt bad about that and maybe I still don't! Probably something that should have been addressed while working on my steps 8 and 9.

That night as I was headed down to the barn. Jose' stopped me. A Puerto Rican American from New York, Jose' was a graduate from the program that stayed on to work. He knew his job inside out. He had a meek look on his face as he waived me over. His head tilted down, and he looked over the rim of his glasses. I figured this was a gossip call. My thought was who got caught smoking or with a can of dip. However, what Jose' said next blew a fuse in me!

"Karl failed his drug test," Jose said softly.

Just another broken skyline. What would lay ahead I had no way of knowing. I just let the news sink in and thought about my relationship with Karl.

In mod four, Karl was my roommate. He had a fondness for NPR (National Public Radio). He would lie in bed and just listen to stories and news for hours. Sometimes the programs were amazing like an interview with the rock/punk group Blondie. NPR introduced us to Lindsey Buckingham Christine McVie's new album. I learned that ABC cancelled the popular Tim Allen show *Last Man Standing*. My sister really turned me onto that show, and I was not disappointed. I learned that Bill Paxton and Sam Sheppard died that year from NPR. However, the story that remained with me the longest from NPR was learning that a Chicken lived 18 months without a head. The chicken belonged to Lloyd Olsen in the forties. Olsen had a small and struggling farm. One night he was chopping heads off chickens and then his wife would clean them. Well, one chicken survived. In fact, he would go on to live another 18 months. His name was Miracle Mike the Headless Chicken. Life magazine did a story on Mike and he even went on a U.S. tour before he died in 1947. Today in Fruita, Colorado where Miracle Mike was from, they have a statue devoted to this chicken. That story both freaked me out and fascinated me.

Sometimes Karl and I would lay in bed and talk for hours. Other times we would just read our books. It was during those nights I really learned just how deep Karl's waters really ran. He was always learning, and I considered him a modern-day Socrates. Our last month in the LaBelle program, we would be roommates again and that last time Jacob joined us.

Karl was very forthcoming with what happened and how he got high. I think the leadership felt he had more of a knee-jerk reaction to temptation. They moved Karl out of our room and placed him with a lower mod. He lost his job at the front desk and all his privileges. The good news is that he wasn't kicked out and though he was sent backwards, he was still able to graduate with us. Now it was time for me to focus on another crucial mission.

With Karl gone from the front desk this left an opening. At first, Hatley gave the position a shot and I had a lot of fun with him. The issue was that Hatley is not a customer service kind of human. I think we all readily knew that Hatley would end up pulling some Hulk kick ass on someone eventually. This is when Hatley headed over to Motrac in Naples. I never could get him to walk over to the Wal-Mart.

Keith came next and was excellent. Keith was about three months behind me, and I had never had a chance to know him well. He was the perfect image of a perfect hardened convict. I wasn't sure I wanted to know him too well.

Once Keith was at the front desk, he became another brother. We played gin for hours at times. Other times, I sang songs to him from *The Greatest Showman*. That film really ministered to me because it was about discarded misfits that came together and found meaning in one another.

Vivian was an older Indian lady that had been at The LaBelle Inn long before it became a rehab facility. She knew the hotel from back in its high class, high baller country club days. Vivian was set in her ways! Then there was me. Vivian was famous for complaining about me weekly and in turn I was infamous for not giving a rat's ass. (That is something my mom would say.)

Vivian liked to steamroll the guys at the front desk. No matter, what we did we were wrong. Everyone behind the desk or at the front office thought I was funny because I blew her off. I didn't take shit from an ex-wife; I wasn't starting with her. I was a shock to everyone's system regarding Vivian. Jim Particularly would laugh at the way I handled Vivian. I don't think I was ever mean, but I sure as hell stood my ground.

Eric got his brother into the program. When his

brother entered Eric was already head intern. It never served family members well when they had bonds with people in authority. Eric's brother received a lot of favoritism and special treatment. We will just call this man Jack. Eric moved to Wolfe, but we were stuck with an entitled Jack.

Jack had sold Jose' down the river over dip. Yes, I think Jose' did buy dip for Jack and Jack got caught. The man was an egomaniac. Jack freely admitted and told on Jose'. Why did this upset me? Because everyone was bending rules for Jack. Jack had an affinity for sneakers. This movement that Nike created where men collect shoes is something I never understood. Jack had shoes all over his room. He also stored shoes in the laundry room. This made sense because Jack worked in the laundry. Jose' told me about the incident and that Jack was a snake. I had an idea.

"What are you doing," Jose asked me. We were both working a shift together at the front desk.

"I suppose you could say sneaky behavior," I replied.

I had learned from a resident that once we were in the older mods, the staff stopped confiscating our mail, especially packages. I was a little over Jack and his arrogance.

"You know all those shoes Jack keeps in the laundry room?"

Jose' nodded yes.

"Maybe I am ordering itching powder for some of those shoes. This stuff is surprisingly expensive." I figured by the time Jack discovered my trick or fell victim to it, I would be long gone. I would not be able to see the fruits of my labor. It was still worth it because we were all sick of Jack!

"Who knew this stuff is primarily made of fiber glass?"

"Remind me never to piss you off," Jose said.

CHAPTER 32

"To be human is to feel inferior." ~ Alfred Adler

"It's only after we've lost everything that we're free to do anything." ~ Tyler Durden, Fight Club

"The Negative screams at you, but the positive only whispers." ~ Barbara Fredrickson

Not splendor in the grass.

It was years before I entered the program. It was years of having my ass kicked by Bourbon.

I was laying down. My consciousness was slowly returning to me. I felt hot. Through my eyelids it was so bright. I just laid still. My body ached and I didn't welcome being awake. Something began tickling my face ever so gently. I reasoned something was flying around. Why was it so hot? I carefully opened my eyes to realize the sweltering heat was from the sun. I was lying about 6 feet away from US-192 in Kissimmee.

IF ROCK BOTTOM HAD A BASEMENT

I had reasoned the grass was just tall enough to conceal me from the heavy traffic of the congested highway. This is a prime tourist road. Was I addicted to chaos or alcohol, I wasn't sure, but I did not immediately get up. Instead I called Heather. She answered right away, which was unusual. Now, that Hayden was born she often didn't answer calls.

"Hello," she said in her voice. Now, you are thinking of course she answered in her voice. What you don't realize is that Heather's voice is magical. It could relax me, soothe me and encourage me. I was lying next to a highway, and I needed to hear her. I missed her. She was hell on wheels and hard to hold, but I loved her. I would refer to Heather as the perfect storm. I knew how to make her laugh or mad at me. The problem with us is that the highs were too far and in between to match our lows. She was sunshine when she wanted to be, but her mood swings were the worst hurricane.

"Where are you?" she asked. She could hear the passing cars. I told her and she laughed because she couldn't believe it. It wasn't a cruel laugh, but a laugh of disbelief. Just talking to her for a few minutes gave me the resolve to get back on my feet. The liquor store was close and that was also calling out to me. I remember thinking I should feel stupid and I didn't. I wasn't bleeding blood, but I was bleeding brokenness.

Now, ten months of my life had passed since I gave up my life. I was in a program and starting on my tenth step. In step 10 we continued to take personal inventory and when we were wrong promptly admitted it.

This is what I refer to as a life support step. Religion had taught me to have a great deal of resistance to conformity. I had a lot of internal work to do in order to not be so obstinate. I had determined that my life won't be about pursuing escapism, pleasure or mere satisfaction.

This step is about preserving the progress I have made in recovery. I stopped drinking, but life didn't stop hitting me hard. This step is geared towards is cognizance. Counselors had praised me for years about my self-awareness. Now I needed to monitor myself, my feelings and emotions. I am looking for those moments that turn me from Dr. Jekyll to Mr. Hide, when I transform from Bruce Banner to The Hulk. You see once the cerebrum part of my brain fills with information; I haven't always reacted logically.

People have suspected that I may be bipolar, and I can see why. My checkered past has been full of acting without thought, thinking too much and being impulsive. My mind can resemble the destruction of a Quintin Tarintino film or *The Towering Inferno*. My old thoughts aren't just done with. My manifesto needs a new author, the sober and more rational me. This means being honest, but hardly stupid. At Saint Matthew's House I have the support of community. In fact, Nojo notices shifts in my behavior before I recognize anything.

Conflict can be abrupt or sneaky with equal parts disruptive, or destructive. When conflict arises, I feel discontent. When I feel discontent, I become agitated and angry. More importantly, I am afraid. If I exercise this step correctly, I will deal with my wounds, humiliation, shame and embarrassment so much better. If not, then things like this next story happen. I fail epically.

One night I was on the computer while working the front desk. I came across an email. My son was using The Doughboy Draftsman's last name. I was paralyzed in disbelief. Time seemed to expand and contract as it tends to do in shock. Heat fell over my body. I felt emotionally waterboarded.

Please understand my son is one of the three greatest human beings to ever live. He is the man I aspire to be when I grow up. He is talented, nonjudgmental, he is a miracle, wonderful and most of all he has a virtue I lack. He is a reasonable person. He is calm and levelheaded. I never mastered those gifts. Even with the help of the twelve steps of recovery, I am still a beginner. Still learning to navigate my stimulus, fluctuations and learning to deal with emotion. Most specifically I didn't know how to handle hurt. How do my beautiful offspring manage to master life so well when their parents are both so flawed? However, the last name incident carried deeper memories and revisited

This is one event I would rather bury in unconsciousness, but that only means disconnection. When Baby Mama told me she was pregnant with Mac, I was excited and thrilled. However, pain and suffering are no respecter of people. Quickly my mind filled with doubt. She had begun her affair on a Thanksgiving weekend. Back then she had somewhat of a moral fiber. She called and confessed to me while I was lying in bed. That was the day she admitted her affair with the Doughboy Draftsman.

I was scared to death that my son might belong to another man. I lived with the torment every day. Yet, here is where it gets sketchy! I was partially to blame for all this chaos. Our first year of marriage we discovered talking in bed. We would pretend to meet at a bar, maybe I was her teacher and her in a catholic schoolgirl outfit. It was thrilling and my wife's whisper in the dark could make my dick hard enough to cut diamonds (a Richard Pryor joke). Sharing fantasies and scenarios that turned us both on. Eventually, the tales and our imaginations grew to include other people. We were both careful to insist we knew these were only fantasies never to be acted on, but she went ahead and onto the other side.

In her defense, how long can we smell a feast and be tantalized by it before we eat? Now I was left wondering if the preacher's daughter baptized in dirty water was carrying another man's child. Where would this leave me? Could I love him? What would he look like? Would everyone always say the boy didn't look like me? I tried hard not to think about these things, but my mind was underneath a sea of torment.

Eventually, I made up my mind that I would love this child no matter what transpired. Every child born looks like a prune. I knew it would be years before I would know for sure. Today I am as certain that Mac is my son, as I am the sky is blue and water is wet.

Now he was using the name of my greatest fear. Larry had already evicted, vacated, expelled, and uprooted me from the family. He paved the way for the Doughboy Draftsman to be my successor. All Baby Mama needed to do was wait for her to destroy his marriage as well. Baby Mama is an ambush predator. She was able to lay in wait a long time before she struck.

Mac using his stepfather's name should not have affected me the way it did. Suffice it to say I did exactly what my Grandma Tew always warned against. She would tell me, "Quit acting the fool," in other words acting like a deranged psychopath. Sadly, my greatest strength is acting like I have lost my mind or at least my common sense. A switch was flipped, and my monster growled, barked, panicked and had a fit.

My hurt feelings turned me into the Pharisee that I so loath. Something was radically wrong with the way I handled the situation. At Saint Matthew's House, I had learned that Jesus had this totally intense thing for people like me. The drunk, the liar, the fake, the mess that I was and will always be. I withheld grace from my own son. I had fights with both of my beautiful offspring.

When I talked to my friends in the program and said my son wasn't using my last name, they were always speechless. Maybe this is a matter of pride for all men. Had Mac just gotten tired of me?

The intensity was so great I did not even bother to invite my children to my graduation ceremony from the program. A graduation that was more important to me than anything else I had accomplished in my life. Cue the Rich Mullins song, "We are not as strong as we think we are". I was clearly chocking on the fumes of my selfish rage. At some point I demanded they not speak to me if they are using another man's name. My huffing and puffing and emptiness were not serving me well at all. I felt an overwhelming sense of guilt. I had become a weapon to my own beautiful offspring. We didn't speak for what felt like months, but maybe only several weeks. With my own son I was twisting grace with my loyal bondage and small mindedness.

Then one day I get a random email from Madison that simply reads "I am pregnant". I paused for a moment. I knew her mother would be too self-absorbed with her image to handle the situation well. I simply wrote back "We will get through this." Although, I had no idea what that looked like.

I must admit there was a small part of me that found humor in my daughter being pregnant. Baby Mama frequently takes advantage of every opportunity to paint me as the villain. Often exaggerating my failures, faults and frustrations, she never missed an opportunity for a tailspin to make herself look like a victim, heroin or avoid responsibility and accountability for her own actions. She deflected using me.

When the beautiful offspring had cavities during their elementary school years, it was entirely my fault. I had my children every other weekend and on Wednesday nights, 8 nights a month versus her 24 nights a month. Do the math. The cavities weren't my fault. If Baby Mama were Delilah, she would have cut off all my hair. Funny how she could put me down for drinking the devil's whiskey while she gets drunk on the savior's wine.

Turns out my daughter was not at all pregnant. She just wanted to get my attention. I must say her methods worked. More importantly, I didn't fail her like I had my son. The name thing was still a very touchy subject for me.

"Madison why did you tell me you were pregnant?"

"How else was I supposed to get your attention dad. By the way, thanks for how you would have handled it."

Names have been an issue for me. When Heather was pregnant with Hayden, I was certain we would bond beautifully over our unborn son. Cue the Ozzy Osbourne song, "Crazy Train" or "Let's Go Crazy" by Prince. She remained confrontational, and she certainly made sure our train got off the rails. I had ideas with his name, but she flat out refused to consider me at all. Further proof that allowing her to get away was wise on my part. With Heather it is her way, or she complains all the way! I loved her, but also could not stand to be around her. She complains for 32 hours out of a 24-hour day.

Surprisingly when she is kind, she has an ability to speak life into a person that is astounding, but she seldom did with me. Years later after she married the pubic faced sequel, she sent me a message apologizing for being so complicated and hard to get along with. She shared with me that The Sequel had all the same concerns and complaints as I did. I knew I put us both through hell too. Don't feel bad Heather, I got tired of me too. I am not saying she wasn't a problem too. It was unnerving how easily she trusted someone else. Now we were friends again.

We talked every day for about three months. She was a wonderful friend but married to a new man now. A man that hated me. Of course, it did not help matters that I said he was too damn ugly to raise a son as beautiful as mine. We also share a same first name, but different spellings. I may have also said she had to marry him because she was never going to stop saying my name. I may have been right.

My anger with Mac using The Doughboy Draftsman's name did not easily subside. After leaving the program Mac was in a show. He was born to two creative parents. My children were in student films both before they started school. Mac made his film debut before he was a year old. His love for performing was natural. Madison is talented, but far less passionate about theater and film. It baffles me that my daughter has the talent but no need to be the center of attention.

I was invited to see the show and was excited to watch my son perform. Mac was in Pinocchio at The Orlando Reparatory Theater. This wasn't a simple school play; my guy was big time. One day before the show he messaged me. He wanted to inform me that his stage name and name printed in the program was not von Wellsheim. I don't think I replied, but I knew then I wasn't able to attend the stage play. Baby Mama and The Doughboy Draftsman would certainly be there. They would be the victors and I knew Baby Mama would love the rub that he was choosing their name over mine. Make no mistake, Baby Mama keeps score.

It was a conversation with Madison that corrected

me.

"Dad, Mac is too young to know what he is doing! You can't pull away from him". She may have even said he needed me. Which was always hard to imagine that anyone really needed me.

I invited my dear friend Rayna and she went to the show with me. I have always felt uncomfortable at my beautiful offspring's events that included my ex and her new family. The exiled leaper who sits alone and watches. Wondering what defaming whispers were being uttered. I knew Baby Mama, and she would never allow a chance to slander me slip through her fingers. I am no better. We walked up to our seat passing Baby Mama and her family. Larry should praise my resistance from all the things I wish to say to the man, I see as Satan's errand boy. She once asked me if I had told someone that she was a homewrecker and swinger. Cue the song, "Don't Let Me Get Me" by Pink.

"No! I didn't tell anyone that! I tell everyone you are a homewrecking swinger!" I am a hazard to myself, but I can't allow these clever rebuttals and lines just go to waste. I am gangsta with the insults. My son reminded me of that conversation years later and he still laughs. Incidentally, I went and saw Mac's play twice. The second time it was just me. That is the day I met my son's friend Grady - what a great friend Mac has.

Now for my greatest shame.

CHAPTER 33

"If we can share our story with someone who responds with empathy and understanding, shame can't survive." ~ Brene' Brown

"I am a Christian, not because someone explained to me the nuts and bolts of Christianity, but because there were people willing to be the nuts and bolts." ~ Rich Mullins

"Without suffering grace is hard to see." ~ Mercy Me

The great wall of guilt.

This story most likely kept me drunk more often and longer than any regret. I can't be sure, but it always required a drink to talk about.

The tragedy of sin is not moral failure. The

misfortune is that gnawing sense of shame that leads us to believe grace cannot reach us. We think we do not qualify for the forgiveness that God is eager to offer. We are never discarded from God's love or even God's application. Read Psalm 51 and feel King David's pain sometime. This is one of those moments for me. A time and event that made me feel separated from God. A time that Heather and her family will never forgive and have never allowed me to forget.

Something I have seldom spoken about but carried with me for years like a weight. My greatest inadequacy and deepest depth of shame comes in this moment. Heather would not include me in naming our son, she would not give him my last name. In this way she was insanely cruel. She also had a history of extreme promiscuity. However, isn't everyone a whore currently. Virtue is lost. I started to strongly suspect Hayden might not be my son. What kind of mother would treat a father with such disregard? The answer is Heather.

Almost every conversation was filled with pressure and unmistakable tension. Her eyes and tone were always ablaze with accusations and fire. However, what I said next is almost incomprehensible. The scope of what transpired was unbelievable. I doubted my own actions.

In a fit of drunken rage, I texted to her the worst words I have ever written, "I hope the kid dies." I was desperate to hurt her. I wanted her to experience my pain. After I sent the message or series of messages. I sat on the edge of my bed. I was stunned at my own hate. I sat still and my room was quiet as a tomb. For those words, I do not blame Heather or her family for never forgiving me. To be sure, they never did. Suffice it to say being human is not easy.

Her family has used that ammunition against me every day since. They will use that information for the remainder of my living days. Who can blame them? In their eyes I traded in my complex kindness, inner struggles, sadness, and humanity and became a monster. I am my own worst enemy. Heather even complained in bed. The way she excluded me made me wonder if Hayden is my son. She could ruin a moment faster than anyone I have ever known. I suspect she even annoyed herself.

Now you know. You might give into alcohol as well in a situation like mine.

Two incidents with my sons are the lowest moments of my life. More destructive than any of my drinking could have ever been. In fact, a change came to me that I never saw coming. I stood outside myself as an observer taking mental notes over those events many, many nights. I had to drink. That is something in the soul that must be medicated and dulled. My only prayer is that God makes my beautiful offspring better men than I am or have managed to be (Mac already achieved this). Still, the relationship with Mac and Madison was stressed when it came time for our graduation.

Graduation is a huge deal with Saint Matthews House, and it should be. They have speakers, testimonies, music and of course a huge and grand dinner for both graduates and donors. This is not only a celebration of the men and women who completed the program. It is also a chance for donors to see the beautiful changes in lives that they invested in.

The ceremony takes place at Moorings Presbyterian Church in Naples. The sanctuary is a magnificent combination of modern and traditional architecture. A huge stage with lots of stained-glass surround worshippers. The pews easily accommodate around 500 guests. The Justin's Place graduation will fill almost every seat.

My parents were invited and certainly came. However, without my beautiful offspring I needed another ally. Cue the Clarence Clemons & Jackson Brown song, "You're a Friend of Mine." At least once a month I try and either send my friend Tiffany a card or message and remind her that I love her. I bonded with her and others very tightly when Kristen died. Remember Tiffany came over and sat in my lap during our gathering at the bar Cheers. That somber evening, she never left my side. Which was a miracle because I didn't realize people knew that I had such an affinity for Kristen. Just goes to prove that we think we have secrets, but people always know. The truth always surfaces. With every doubt and sorrow that blanketed me, she was there. I sat in a corner of shadows in hopes to be hidden. It was going to take some time to clear all the mess in my head.

During one of our casual conversations I was hesitant to ask Tiffany if she would be interested in attending the graduation. Without hesitation and with much enthusiasm. Her voice was animated. I was already living with The Giles in Orlando. I remember a few of my brothers from the program were afraid I might not return, but I rode down with Tiffany.

She had an amazing road trip play list. Cue the song, "Walking in Memphis" by Marc Cohn because we almost always play and sing this song when we are in a car together.

At any rate, there was still the matter of moving into a new life with Svetlana. She and a friend came down to Florida to scope the area. She was looking for a home and a job. We were speaking or texting daily about our marriage plans. However, when she went back to Chicago, she had a new idea.

CHAPTER 34

"I'm very good at understanding the past -- it's the present I can't understand." ~ Rob Gordon, High Fidelity

"I've thrown away the blues." ~ Lionel Ritchie, Sail On

"A saint is not someone who is good, but who experiences the goodness of God." ~ Brennan Manning

I treasure love, but

still don't understand it.

My final days at Saint Matthews House in Labelle were sad. I really had fallen in love with that cast of characters and oddballs. I had been praying for weeks what my next move was to be. What would be my great awakening? Every day I would talk to my brothers such as Nojo. I sought a lot of counsel. I suppose I was hoping for a paint by numbers exit strategy. I had lived a wonderful life almost in solitude. I was safe, sober and satisfied. I had earned some respect among leaders such as Connor and Jim. I had security. People knew I would not cheat the program and I don't think I ever did.

So, I prayed and I prayed. God what will you have me do? I thought and I fasted for about two weeks. Eventually, I passed out one day when I stood up. How Jesus fasted for forty days and nights is nothing I can comprehend. I fell on a concrete floor and it was amazing I didn't bash my head in because the conditions were ideal. I presume I was only out for mere seconds, but maybe a minute. I opened my eyes to see several people standing over me. All with freaked out expressions. Rodney and Rich were the first two faces I saw. Collectively the few faces looked at each other with that, "What do we do?" look.

"I will be fine," I answered as they helped me up.

Rodney insisted that I go to my room and rest. Which was a good idea because I collapsed in my room and fell into the steel frame of the bunk beds. That hurt! My forty day fast lasted only two weeks.

I was double minded about my future. I knew life would be easier if I transitioned into the sober living apartment community known as Wolfe. However, I also knew it was time to move on. I just kept feeling like God was pushing me to live the life I had hidden from for so many years. The life that my egotistical demands forbid me from enjoying. I was no longer stuck in negative and unhelpful mind sets.

The changes were too radical to take a giant leap. Everything was about to change, but I had no idea how. I wanted to be prepared, but I had not been sober for years. I had no clue what my new life would look like. My new leap of life needed to be handled in installments. I did not want to overwhelm myself. Moving in with The Giles had been understood from the first day I went to rehab. When Paul and Cheryl came to visit me in Labelle, they emphasized that I could live with them when I was finished.

My next order of business was that I needed a job. I did not want to move back to Orlando to idle hands. Returning to my old job at Rainforest Café felt like a bad idea. I did not want to work with the ghost of Kristen. I would rather live with the memory of her.

A long-time friend named Lori was following my progression on social media. We worked for the same company (Landry's) for years, but never together. I had met her in 2009 at a Halloween party. I don't usually go to parties, but I was pursuing a woman named Giovanni. I was there dressed as a pinhead manager that I was impersonating. I walked around all-night writing people up and telling everyone how great I was. I was the best thing that ever happened to the restaurant. My character portrayal was spot on and everyone was on the floor laughing. Of course, entertaining drunks has never been difficult. Lori thought I was hysterical. What can I say? She was right. To this day she brings up that party and my performance (or Halloween costume).

Lori had a heart for me and my rehab posts. As a result, she suggested that I go to work with her at her new restaurant. An authentic tex-mex establishment known as Chuy's. I prayed and I felt like I was safe with Lori. She knew my style of working, my commitment and most importantly that I am an alcoholic.

Training at the new job was intense. My primary trainer was a guy named Jason whom I hated (I eventually came to love the guy). However, he talked too fast and taught in a way completly opposite of my learning style. On more than one occasion I had to demand he slow the fuck down. He had an intensity that was very hard for a laid-back guy like me to keep up with.

Working with Lori was the best thing for me. She naturally understands me and more importantly my idiosyncrasies. I was only there a few weeks before she shouted at me across the kitchen one night, "Who do you think you are, a manager? I don't need to handle anything when you are here," then she burst into laughter. As an employee, I would follow her to the ends of the earth. Lori is excellent. In Labelle my mind was made up. I would work with Lori at Chuy's. She was an important part in my rebirth. Installment one had been decided. Installment two was my living situation. Of course, the hardest installment was leaving the program and closing a book.

Heather has this thing, where she likes to troll my social media friends. She then sends them messages about the kind of scum bag pig I am. I absolutely never get mad at Heather for doing this because it works out great for me. My friends usually reassure me that I am a loved asshole. This was the case with Lori one afternoon.

"You know I will never stop thinking you're amazing right? I already know you are a bitch," Lori said to me. "As for Heather, I realize there are two sides to every story, but I know you! So, bye Felicia!"

"Just never forget she is a better person than me," I reply.

"Shut up!" Lori's shut up is always drawn out.

Old and true friends such as Annette, Paul, Art and even Lori used to ask me what my triggers were. What caused the knee-jerk reaction that frequently resulted in drinking? The simple truth was I wanted to drink every day that ended in a "Y." This would later be problematic for me because I didn't know what encounters or situations would make me want to numb myself with alcohol. Let me assure you that there are events that can bring this man to his knees. There are hurts that bring me back to a desire for muddy water.

Anyone who has ever worked a recovery program will explain to you about higher power coincidences. Paul and his wife presented the notion of a rehab. An idea I flatly refused for about twenty minutes. However, in this vast world of addiction, broken and shattered people, God placed me in the perfect combination of men. Greg, Anthony, Rocky, Rob, Sean, Cory, Nojo, Karl, Jacob, and Tim were my brothers. They were the men I entered the program with, and they all left an impression on my soul. I really didn't want to leave these guys.

Not to forget the many other individuals that all helped me thrive. Remember that we get into the depth of addiction primarily from our actions. A self-perpetuating dogma accompanied by fear and an unfavorable regard for ourselves. There is no way after all those bad choices we can recover on our own. It doesn't' matter what your addiction is: dysfunctional relationships, junk food, pornography, cell phones, spending or anything else we take to extremes. Our judgment lies in us. Our misery, medicating and mental process cannot be trusted.

As step three from the twelve steps says, you must decide to turn your life over to God as you understand him. The bonds I made at Saint Matthew's House were of compassion, change and connection. Many outside relationships are a twisted sincerity because others didn't understand me. Hell, I didn't understand myself (most likely I still don't). Tackling my despair was intelligently dependent on every man and path I crossed in the Justin's Place program. Now, it was time for another chapter. I had learned and healed a great deal, but there was still one punch that I was not expecting. However, I would not be brought to my knees until I went to Chicago.

Nojo and Chef Jason had become guiding lights in my life. Two men that really seemed to understand me. Although the Chef and many of the other leaders were fond of telling me I was like no other man they had ever met. Connor often laughed and assured me I was one of a kind. I may be an acquired taste, but the men understood me. I knew The Giles home would be a safe place. I longed to live with Paul and his family again. That has always felt as close to family as I may ever know. The decision was made that it was time to leave. Cue the Lindsey Buckingham song, "Holiday Road."

The day my parents came to pick me up. I had orchestrated everything to happen when I wouldn't be able to say good-bye to many people. Almost everyone was at the Baptist church in class. Greg, my mod brother was the last guy I saw. As he helped me load my parent's car with mostly books and few clothes, I cried. Greg didn't say much to me. Words weren't really needed to convey the feelings. It hurt tremendously to say farewell. The send-off was mostly uneventful. Plus, I knew I would return in a few weeks for the graduation ceremony.

The future was feeling brighter and better than a handful of stars. I wasn't living with the past anymore. Fear had given way to hope and I liked that. Life felt like something to pursue rather than something to endure. I was aware as opposed to unconscious. My next great adventure, my most significant lesson, and another top five heartbreak awaited me. In other words, I had learned a lot in rehab and was thankful for every lesson. Yet, rehab shuts out the realities of real-life living. At Justin's Place I didn't have to be entangled or enslaved in the common obligations of everyday life. Rent and transportation were not rituals I had to consider. A person has proven they can ride a bike, but the training wheels haven't come off yet. So, I set out and hit the big city of Chicago and it hit right back!

When I lost my friend Kristen, it was a very

different kind of broken for me. I was imprisoned with that grief. Now I had spent a year recovering from the situation. Oddly enough, my beauty for ashes is that I became insomniac friends with her mother. A relationship that I cherish for two reasons. First, being that Andrea is a wonderful woman and a kindred spirit. As I mentioned we both struggle to sleep. Second, is that my relationship with Kristen's mother keeps her very much alive in my life.

Back in 2017 after Kristen passed away, I fell further into a hole of despair. I had one friend from Russia named Svetlana. We had met years earlier on a dating app. She is one tall blonde drink of water. When she was in Russia, I had a definitive crush on her, but that faded quickly. However, we remained friends. She worked in a bar and would be getting home around three in the morning my time. We often spoke. One night talking about Kristen, she agreed I shouldn't be alone. She flew down to spend a few days with me. I enjoyed her company, but no romantic flame was ever ignited again.

Svetlana is a genuine woman. I wouldn't call her wholesome, but we shared a very gritty attitude about the world. I still believe in throat punching a person, she thought that was cool. She was definitively bossy. As roommates I had to remind her we weren't fucking. If you are going to be that bossy with me, I expect you to surrender the pink. She is a very serious person, while I am much more lackadaisical kind of dude. A little bit of a wino, but I can see that as attractive as well. My past has a history of enjoying the company of toxic relationships. This woman was different. She rarely had an expression no matter the content of our conversation. I have found

IF ROCK BOTTOM HAD A BASEMENT

Russian women to be without much of a sense of humor until they are three sheets to the wind. Maybe that is why the Russians love their vodka so much.

Paul took me to the airport to pick up Svetlana. He then bought us a late-night breakfast after midnight at the local IHOP. In a booth Paul sat across from us. Paul has been a part of my story for years. He was bewildered by the entire event. He repeatedly asked how I knew this girl. I figured trying to explain I met her on the internet might be too much for him to swallow. Although, I suspect Paul was accustomed to my unpredictability.

I was once told I didn't live a unconventional life. That is because conventional wouldn't have me.

However, at the restaurant Paul asked us both how we met. Svetlana curiously looked at me.

"Do you remember?" She asked without expression.

"We met on a dating app while she lived in Russia," I answered.

"I was wondering if you would remember. Or how many women you confuse me with." She did not hesitate or break eye contact. I wasn't sure if that was a question or accusation. It is true I prefer the company of women over men, but I am hardly the whore people suspect of me. I was once asked what I love about women so much. I was raised by a woman and made love to by women. What isn't to love? When they say behind every good man is a great woman, I must confess I think there is a lot of truth there.

Paul's jaw dropped, then he half smiled and insisted we were lying. This made us laugh.

"So, you have never met each other before?"

"No," I explained "but we have been talking for years and became buddies."

In truth, I think I bored Svetlana to a large degree. She was much like Baby Mama always wanting to be doing something. I am content to hide from the world in my home. I like adventure, but not in a crowd. My mother always said growing up, I always preferred just one friend.

It was a lot of fun to see the disbelief in Paul's face. Even Svetlana was chuckling at him. You see, truth really is stranger than fiction.

She stayed with me in my most awesome studio apartment. The one true residence that always felt like home. We shared my bed, but again nothing happened. In fact, when Michael visited, he always slept next to me as well. It was just something that worked and never felt weird. Trust me I don't share my bed with just anyone.

The next morning Paul came over and brought us breakfast. We told him we were planning on getting married. Paul didn't accept our story at all. When he left, we laughed. He had no idea I had really proposed marriage to Svetlana, but of the green card variety. This was not a "marry me because I would like to date you" moment from the motion picture, *The Proposal*.

IF ROCK BOTTOM HAD A BASEMENT

She was living in Chicago now as an illegal alien. One day we were walking through my neighborhood. We had dinner at Christo's in College Park area of Orlando. Stopped at a Publix and headed to my place with a few bottles of wine. She shared with me her situation. I must admit I never wanted her to return to her country. I wanted her to stay where she had found her joy.

"Then Marry me," I said without a single second thought.

Still, no expression. She looked at me with those stern and stoic blue eyes.

"I am for real," I continued.

Nope! No, expression. Not a smile, smirk or grimace!

This was in no way a declaration of love. In fact, it may have just been my simplemindedness at full speed.

"Look," I explained, "I have no intention of ever marrying again. Why not use my holy matrimony for a good cause. Too much spilled blood on this broken heart to ever love that much again."

She was thinking and I could tell, but she thought without expression.

"Plus, you think I am a good writer. I could use a woman like you in my corner. I think you would bring out the best in me." The only muse I had in my life was a woman named Giovanni and she was now married with children. That can really fuck up a relationship.

Now, I had some expression. Her eyebrows raised. She kept implausibly artistic eyebrows. I could see just a hint of life around her eyes.

"We could get caught," she offered.

I shook my head no.

"We will be roommates. Fuck and date whomever you wish. Move to Florida," I offered. "However, first I am doing this rehab thing".

We were holding hands now like school children.

"You would do this?" her accent was thickening.

"I have been married twice. Both times to women I loved, but for selfish reasons. It might be nice to marry a woman and only have her best interest at heart for once and not my selfishness."

"What about your kids?" she asked.

I hate when people call my beautiful offspring kids. Young goats are known as kids. I politely correct that my children are known to the world as my beautiful offspring.

She laughs ever so slightly. Any chance to break her stone expression is a minor victory.

"Trust me, my beautiful offspring have come to know their father as a rather different man. Someone not too wrapped up in tradition or expectations for that matter. They will love you. I think they will love anyone who they think makes me happy."

"What do they think of you?"

"Wouldn't I love to know that too."

We walked in silence for a bit. It all felt very abstract, but I was sincere.

Later that night we sat on my bed YouTubing motion clips. This was my element. She enjoyed the same type of films as I do. Her favorite Motion Picture is Quintin Tarantino's *Pulp Fiction*. Which also happens to be my beautiful offspring Mac's favorite film.

Her silly/happy buzz kicked in way before mine, but I liked that. With a 7.5% alcohol beverage in her, she becomes much more fun and sweeter. One minute she starts to laugh at her own stories. In another moment she is asking questions of depth and sentiment.

"Marc," she asked in her thick Russian accent. She spoke slower and louder. She was rolling many of the alphabet sounds, but she never slurred. She then paused. She raised her eyebrows, and this was always a sign she was becoming more earnest.

"What makes you happy? Your children I know, but what else?"

That certainly was not a question I expected. Laying next to her I felt like Luke Jackson from the 1967 Paul Newman motion picture *Cool Hand Luke*. I just don't conform to the idea of being happy. I paused and her eyes locked on me. Svetlana is not the type of person who will allow anyone to change the subject.

I looked at her for a moment and thought. If she had a blue bandana tied up in that blonde hair, she would resemble what my mother looked like when I was a child. However, the thought was too sappy to share. I thought of Jack Nicholson, he once said in an interview that I read "I can't explain why I need this pain." Maybe it was time for me to turn into Jack. Over the years I had perfected an impersonation. In fact, in some relationships I remained Jack throughout, never allowing a few people to ever met me.

"I don't tend to chase happiness," I eventually answered.

Her inquisitive eyes seemed to change. I got the feeling she felt sorry for me.

"Happiness is like chasing an erection you know. It never really lasts long. What is the point?"

She took my phone and wanted to show me some Russian film clips. She narrated each one. This was as intimate as we ever became, and it was more meaningful than most relationships I have known. I think we earned a lot of trust with each other that night, but we never spoke about it again.

And just like that the wheels were set in motion. She would move to Florida and we would marry. We planned to live near the ocean. I would write and dream about motion pictures that would never be made of me. She would get her citizenship and eventually I would do what I knew best. Just be alone. Spending most of my nights with books and a computer screen. However, until the bird on the wire brought me back to her, I still had a stint in Naples.

The days were long, but the weeks were fast. I thought about my promise often. Never did I feel like my plan with Svetlana was a bad idea. However, I also never told a single person about our situation. We told Paul and he didn't believe us for a second. Finishing with Saint Matthew's House a whole new life awaited me. I spent my first few days out with my parents.

Soon I was living back with the Giles and slept in the corner of their living room area that opened into the kitchen. I had slept in that corner of the world before and it is my favorite spot. I never once felt like a stranger. Sleeping beside the kitchen always meant I had an early morning wake up call. Sheryll always walked in quiet and methodical. Often, I was already awake. They have two cats, Casey and Tommy. Casey would follow Sheryll meowing for her breakfast. Casey would not eat day old food. She expected fresh Tender Vittles every new dawn. As for Tommy, it was anyone's guess if he was inside or out, but not mine. Most nights Tommy meowed for me to let him out or let him in. That cat had me trained. Casey is a timid cat, but Tommy is a street fighter. You could say he is the Marlon Brando from *On the Waterfront* of cats. Yet, Tommy would never throw a fight like in the 1954 motion picture. If Tommy wasn't a cat, I could see him in the thick smoke of a bar.

Sheryll prepared the girls lunches and shortly after

started to wake up the middle daughter. Then she made her way to awaken the youngest. Seldom did mom have to wake up the oldest daughter. Three young girls were up early for school. McKenzie always the first. Kiley always dragged herself out of bed. She is the least enthusiastic to greet the morning. She grapples snoozily with the morning and inquiries about her lunch box. Inevitably one of the three girls will give their lunch an eyeroll of discontent. This is the highlight of the morning. Sitting in a corner at the desk in my space. Listening to the banter of teenagers and their mother. I am a spectator enjoying the view of a family so alive. A life that I envy but am grateful that this family accepts me as one of their own. Depending on the previous night's ball games determines when Paul will stroll out of his room. He will say good morning and make inquiries of his own about the girls' schedule. Most likely there will be a volleyball or soccer game or practice that evening. Then Paul routinely checks his e-mails in his office which is next to my sleeping area. You forget he is in there until he overhears a conversation and then shouts out his thoughts. It is not uncommon for Sheryll and I to laugh quietly with each other. Somehow Paul could always sense it.

"Hey, what are you guys laughing at? I want to know," he shouts from the other room.

Naturally, we play dumb. Of course, I wonder how he knows we are laughing.

Hannah was perfectly on time. She was never late, but certainly never early. I had better pee before the youngest got in the bathroom. Otherwise, I would be peeing in the yard. Which I only had to do about twice.

Soon Paul will emerge from his office. About four days a week we go to the gym. Where there happens to be just the right amount of people and at least two women that I love to see every morning. These women don't know my name, but they occasionally say good morning and inspire me.

I will finish my workout routinely ten minutes before Paul. Walk over to Publix the next-door grocery store and buy me breakfast. Whatever my choices Paul will ridicule for being unhealthy. I just gave up bourbon. I will work on other sacrifices much later. Still, sleeping on his floor almost in their kitchen, I was content.

Paul and Sheryll had college friends that chastised them for allowing a Hobo (McKenzie's nickname for me) to stay in their home. People such as a Sonia, a self-righteous woman they had known for years. In all reality, I get it. To someone like Sonia I am just a vagabond man sleeping on Paul's floor. Did I have other options? Absolutely! I thrive around that family. Who made her the impassive and intense centurion of Paul's tiny kingdom?

This is the thing about Sonia. I had spent a year working on my resentments and Satan brings her judgments. She certainly had me revisiting a few of the 12 steps.

Steps eight and nine were difficult for me. Mostly the amends I needed to make were from things I have said and ways I have acted. However, I meant the things I said and my mind hasn't changed. I still think Larry in the colostomy bag of Christianity. I have come to realize that I will never get amends from him and I no longer hate the guy. I still wouldn't piss on him if he was on fire, but I wouldn't be the guy to douse him in gasoline. Suffice it to say, I am a work in progress.

I no longer desired to harm myself or anyone else. Hard drinking required hard recovery! Hard recovery demands a line from the Cameron Crow motion picture *Jerry Maguire* when Tom Cruise's character says, "I had lost the ability to bullshit." I had to lose my ability to bullshit with myself, which wasn't too terribly difficult. I have always been praised by counselors as being extremely self-aware compared to most people. At Saint Matthew's House, I was released from my epic, grandiose, selfish and all-consuming desire to self-destruct.

This is not to imply that all my behavior was universally bad. Yes, I was prone to emotional outbursts and erratic crashes. I carry a tremendous amount of tenderness, compassion and even honesty. I could be known for my nurturing, kindness and generosity. Sometimes my actions, good or bad, were calculated and other times unconscious.

Amends for me did not equate to good intentions and doe-eyed repentance. I did not reach out to too many people. Mostly I would confess my concerns and regrets to Tommy Sloan from the program. I had to mostly live out my amends, which meant to me it was more dependent on changing behavior. My amends began when I entered rehab. In many cases it was too long of time for amends to be appropriate. Many women were now married or moved on and most likely preferred to be left alone. At least that is the impression being blocked on Facebook has given me. My beautiful offspring made it so easy; I was confused. When I would ask if they wanted to share anything or speak to me, their only words were "You're my dad and I love you." Heather and her family only saw me unfavorably and their regards are understandable.

Today I look for opportunities and divine appointments to help others when I feel it is timely and right. When I am in alignment with a person's needs, I offer help or guidance, but I never try to force myself on anyone. I am hardly perfect, but I know love is always the answer. Sadly, I still love to be a smart ass. Most of my insidious thoughts don't weigh me down anymore, but as I would learn in Chicago, living selflessly and in self-realization would not always come easy.

I was at the gym on the elliptical machine when Svetlana sent me a text. She was suggesting that I move to Chicago. My first impulse was no, but within minutes I started to consider her idea. I hated the heat of Florida. In fact, I always loathed Central Florida and all its man-made amusement parks. There is no natural beauty to the area. In fact, I only ever lived there to be with my children. I had wanted to move for years. I had also been to Chicago several times and I love the city. Unlike most metropolitan areas, the people there are much kinder.

Unlike leaving Saint Matthew's House, her idea didn't involve so much wrestling with the perfect plan. If it didn't work, she agreed we could move back to Florida. Just so happened that there was another huge reason to move to Chicago, and he has a name - Hayden.

I believe that parents are the image of God in a child's heart and eyes. I also think that when two parents divorce, we unintentionally teach that child that there is something you can do to make you less lovable. I have known people from divorced families and they always seem much more insecure and uncertain than others. This is a fact not lost on me as well. Heather left me before Hayden was ever born. She was always so incorrectly sure that I was cheating on her. As a result, instead of investing in us she spent her time on dating sites until she met the sequel. The man with the pubic hair goatee (I just love saying that truth). Heather's strategy has always been to get over one man she needed to get under another one. I am not judging her. After all, when she left me, I drank to deal with our love lost and failure. As a result, our love story was untold because there were too many of her family members in our union. Her family fired me.

It is also important to point out that I also drank to be married to her.

I talked to both of my beautiful offspring. Madison said "Dad, Hayden needs you." Mac felt the same way. Once I was settled, I would go and visit them frequently. With their approval and support that was really all the affirmation I needed.

I flew to Chicago to spend some time researching the city, jobs and living arrangements. Svetlana had found us the perfect 2-bedroom apartment in the Wicker Park area. I loved it. I went to the management company and immediately filled out the application. They approved me relatively quickly. I bought an air mattress and slept in our new apartment a few nights before returning to Orlando. We had a perfect apartment with the only downside being that we were on the third floor with no elevator. Stairs. I hate stairs like Indiana Jones hates snakes.

Chicago was a go!

CHAPTER 35

"Great men are not born great, they grow great." ~ Mario Puzo from The Godfather

Chicago and the great fall.

I did not move to Chicago with the mentality of conquering a new city. No, I moved there with the mindset of an explorer and I loved it. I love the energy of a huge city. It was terrifying to always feel so lost, but surpassingly exciting at the same time. An exceedingly prosperous place. I even grew to love the noise. In fact, our apartment was next to a fire house. Every night I would hear sirens and I found the sound comforting.

Chicago was bliss. My son Mac collects vinyl and there was a record store on every corner. Across the street from my apartment was a place called the Dusty Groove. I felt like I was living the life of John Cusack from the motion picture *High Fidelity*.

Everywhere I went I took the time to talk with people including some of the homeless residents. Homeless people are everywhere in the windy city, with over 80,000. Panhandling, the practice of street people requesting immediate donations, is legal. At the intersection of the Wicker Park neighborhood I lived in, I became familiar with the same faces I would see almost every day. One man would ask for money and when you denied him, he would shout profanities at you. At the risk of offending Joe Pesci, (a *Goodfellas* reference) he amused me. There was one guy whom we will call Reggie (because I think that was his name, but not certain) that begged for money. He was in a wheelchair. One day as I walked by him, he came rushing over on his motorized vehicle that he was bound to. I was about to walk into the grocery store Jewel Osco. He asked me for money and I simply didn't have any. Once inside I had a revelation.

Back outside the motorized wheelchair was hot and speeding away. I ran to catch Reggie at the edge of the parking lot. Let's be clear, I don't run for anyone or anything. Shouting at him, he eventually stopped.

"Look, I got to thinking. I don't have any money, but I have a card. Would you like me to get you something to eat?"

Reggie lit up with a smile that revealed several missing teeth. He was so happy and that in turn made me smile.

IF ROCK BOTTOM HAD A BASEMENT

"A Home Run Pizza," he said with no hesitation. I got the impression he had been craving this for some time.

"Where would I find that?" I had never heard of a Home Run Pizza.

He explained to me that it would be with the frozen pizzas. Which made me foolish for asking.

"Ok, do I need to figure out a way to heat it up for you? More importantly what kind of pizza do you want?" I was as excited as he appeared to be.

"Nope, I will be fine." He was so grateful, and I had a good feeling. As for the toppings, he wanted meat lovers and I knew we were kindred spirits.

Soon I returned with the pizza. We exchanged introductions and he was off. This began my first ritual of Chicago; I would seek Reggie out every time I headed to Jewel Osco and I visited the grocery store every day.

One day I was waiting for a bus a few blocks north of my apartment. Being bored I was looking around taking in the city sights. I never got tired of seeing the skyline. Unexpectedly I see the motorized wheelchair speeding around a corner. From across the street, I watched Reggie ride into a tiny liquor store. In truth, Chicago has a liquor store on every corner. Unlike the south you can also buy liquor in Target, Walmart, Walgreens and CVS. The grocery stores such as Jewel Osco even had a bar inside their supermarket. In the south you can only buy beer and wine at a supermarket. Hard liquor is sold by state agencies known as ABC stores.

Reggie rode in and in the blink of an eye he came back out with his brown bag. Best I could tell was that he simply treated himself to a pint, but of what, who knows? He was on a mission and he never noticed me. Again, me and the old guy had a kinship. I have a history with my own dirty water.

I would always stop and speak to him when our paths directly crossed. He never asked me for anything ever again, but on occasion I would offer. One evening just as the sun was going down, I saw Reggie heading north in his wheelchair. The thought crossed my mind, where does he go when it gets dark? So just like one of those detectives shows from the seventies and eighties (Think *Magnum P.I., The Equalizer, The Rockford Files*) I followed Reggie. I wasn't sure why I wanted to know his story, and a part of me was simply bored. I was lucky because he didn't have his wheelchair at full throttle, and I was able to keep up with him.

He weaved in and out of side streets. I started to wonder if I would get lost returning home. It was not uncommon for me to get lost in that great big city. Svetlana always warned me to stay away from the south side and I would be fine. She is not the kind of woman that extends much compassion or understanding. She is the Yoda of Russia and her motto is much like his, "Do or do not, there is no try!"

Eventually he went up to the gate of a building. I am guessing it was about ten stories tall. A man opened the chained link fence for him, and he scooted in. I watched from the corner of the street. Once he went inside, I quickly lost sight of Reggie. Casually I walked to the front of the building. Outside of the fence I am guessing was about 20 yards from the front door.

Another man who was walking aimlessly around the grounds noticed me. He clearly gave the impression he was mentally challenged on some deeper level. There was no sign to indicate what type of building Reggie had just entered. No, indication it was a mental facility or homeless shelter. Maybe it was subsidized housing. My curiosity grew, but now the wandering man had clearly locked his sights on me. He was even speaking to me in some indiscernible language. He didn't appear dangerous or threatening, but I was uncomfortable. I acted as if I didn't hear or notice him and went on my way. My adventure was over, and I was none the wiser. Reggie would remain a mystery. More importantly he was my first friend in Chicago.

One fine day a friend from Raleigh suggested I meet a buddy of hers that lived in Chicago. Stephanie and her husband James have been a part of my life for years. The city I mostly grew up in after my parents divorced and mom remarried was Raleigh, North Carolina. I wasn't interested in church as a teenager. However, as I got older, I developed an interest in God. I had seen how some of my friend's lives had changed and this intrigued me. Once I became involved with church, youth group, and eventually I was a youth pastor. Stephanie and James were involved in the church circles that I ran in. I had even worked alongside of them in youth groups. I knew if Stephanie suggested a friend, I could trust that. Most church folk to me are beneath dirty politicians. Maybe even that is too generous of me.

Dave is a pastor. Now understand I feel about people in full time ministry much like I do a hot stove top. They can be useful, but they can and will burn the shit out of a person. I connected with Dave through Facebook. He was nice. I might even go so far as to say cheery. He suggested we meet in Albany Park at a Persian restaurant that he frequented called Kabobi.

I knew immediately that going to another unfamiliar area meant I would get lost. I knew how to use google maps when driving, but I had no idea how to apply that to subway and walking traveling. Yes, I got lost and at one point found myself looking up at Wrigley Field. Several texts back and forth to Dave and he helped me find my way.

Turns out that Dave wasn't the pretentious ass whip of a pastor that I feared. He was a humble and kind man. We even shared a love for John Lynch, the author of a book called *The Cure* and co-author of another book, *TrueFaced*. Both books were part of my faith's foundation. They helped undo the damage that religion had caused in my life. I learned that Jesus was for sinners, not just high achievers. I was shown a new way of seeing Christians after Larry had poisoned the Holy water. Rest assured the devil didn't just go down to Georgia (reference to a Charlie Daniels song), I had seen his face and ate at his table in Florida.

What impressed me most about Dave was that he felt a little unsure about his calling to the ministry. We must have talked for about 2 or 3 hours. I knew this man had the correct heart to work for my God. Usually I am quick to tell men in ministry that they belong selling insurance because they suck at their job. My blunt honesty always really upset Baby Mama. Posers are her people.

I paused and looked directly into Dave's eyes.

"I know you just met me, but you must know I speak my mind and tell people things the way I see them."

Dave Laughed, "I have only known you a few hours and I am sure of that about you."

"You fucking belong in ministry! You have the heart and the temperament for it. So, stop doubting yourself because I rarely get to encourage a man in such a way. I despise most men who call themselves pastors." I looked as deeply into Dave's eyes as I was able.

It was rewarding to meet such a cool man. It was encouraging to believe in a man's heart that wanted to serve our God. I left blessed that day and maybe he did too.

Living with Svetlana was very pleasant. She would often come sit at the edge of my bed or lay next to me and we would talk. She always drank about two bottles of wine a night. Once the first bottle kicked in, she was laid back. The eyebrows relaxed. Her stoic expression gave way to more emotion, smiles and laughter. She became a kinder version of herself. One night she said to me the most surprising thing.

IF ROCK BOTTOM HAD A BASEMENT

"Once I get American citizenship, we can stay married if you want. I am never going to marry anyone else."

That was almost romantic in a twisted kind of way. Nevertheless, it was certainly endearing. I also had no plan to ever marry again. Baby Mama and Heather had taught me that nobody means those wedding vows anymore. Baby Mama traded up and Heather traded me for the sequel. I thought silently for a moment.

"That would be nice. I think we make a good team. And you do bring out the best in me."

She would soon return to her wine. There I was sitting and lying next to a beautiful woman. I should have wanted to kiss her, touch her or at least lust for her. In truth, I was hankering for the wine. I could smell it on her breath and my it made my dick harder than Chinese algebra.

Outside our back door a little convenience store opened. It was open late and literally only about 15 yards from our building. One-night Svetlana had a craving for chips. No shit, I thought, she had been eating mine. I didn't mind her eating my BBQ Kettle chips, but when we went grocery shopping, she was clearly acting as the grocery gestapo. Isn't it funny how health food nuts always steal our so-called junk food? She was gone much longer than the trip normally took. I soon learned why.

She came in giddy like a schoolgirl. Crawled next to me in bed. Her face was glowing with excitement.

IF ROCK BOTTOM HAD A BASEMENT

"You will never guess what happened," she said through her biggest smile.

The truth was I could smell the answer. She wore her tequila fragrance well. Not my drink of choice, but it certainly was the beginning of a stirring in me.

"I went down to the store to get the chips."

Thank you Captain Obvious, that much I already knew.

"The guy behind the counter offers me tequila. I had a few drinks with him," she started laughing. Wine makes you friendly and liquor makes you giddy I thought.

"These kinds of things always happen to me," she announced.

Of course, they do. You are a blonde haired blue eyed Russian built goddess with an ass made of steel and pillars for legs. Cue the Marvin Gay song, "Let's Get It On." Men want to get lucky, get it on, get busy and do some humping. She was a big girl, and I didn't have to explain that to her.

From that moment forward my envy for her two or three bottles of wine a night grew. Such a strange thing to be jealous of a beverage. Little did I know that something was lurking in my mailbox that would bring me to my knees. A death blow punch that resembled any of the most violent from *Game of Thrones*. A double edge sword that was crueler than anything ever done to me. As you get older it is hard to tell who the least likable person in your life has been thus far. The Doughboy Draftsman is certainly evil. Baby Mama held the top spot for years, but anger gave way to pity. She isn't even a shell of the person that once held good inside of her. Now Mark the sequel was influencing Heather.

It was Father's Day morning. I was up early as I usually am. I was about to walk to the Jewel Osco a local grocery store. This was my daily ritual. In Chicago, a car is more of an expensive nuisance than luxury. As a result, instead of carrying several bags of groceries I would just make frequent trips. This also gave me an opportunity to check in with Reggie, my wheelchair bound friend. However, this morning I made a mailbox detour.

It was a perfect and bright summer day. The sun was shining, and the wind wasn't too strong. What you hear about Chicago being the windy city is no joke. I grabbed my mail and noticed an odd letter from an attorney. It was a lawyer's office in McHenry, Illinois. Where the hell is that? I wondered.

I opened the letter and fell back into the wall. Amber alert, the sequel wants to steal my son away completely. The breath had been knocked out of me. A sobering dose of reality served in an unprecedented way. I felt abandoned and jilted all over again. I walked back upstairs to my apartment. Went in my room and sat on the floor. My emotions had captured me.

Heather and her husband were seeking to terminate my parental rights. We had given each other a lot of grief after our breakup, but this was a new level of horrible and horrifying. Even typing this now I feel numb so many years later. I wonder who is out there reading this. Almost wishing this were a blog and I could read your comments. Baby Mama had done some wicked shit and she always managed to sideline me when she could.

"Mayday! Mayday! What the fuck just hit me?"

I am a lot of bad things, but I think I am a good dad. Even if I am not the best role model, I love my children. It was the absence of my beautiful offspring that caused me to drink in the first place. Not that this is valid reasoning for my behavior, but it was the springboard. (Note: Usually I can type a few pages at a time, but reliving this moment took me several days. This and the loss of Kristen have been hardest to revisit.)

When I first saw Heather, she was a dream come true. I loved her in an instant. Our first conversation made me wish I had never known a life without her. She taught me that living with expectations has its consequences. In truth reality failed to live up to my delusions. I don't put all the blame on me for our failure. I think we were both too stubborn, prideful, self-protective, and selfish. Now we were in this new world order and the hate was overwhelming. Although, I know her Father Don and the sequel Mark had more to do with influencing her. Heather is miserable, but she doesn't delight in causing misery.

After Heather's daughter was born, she sent me a message one day on Facebook. She was depressed, discouraged, and seemingly suicidal. I reached out to her as soon as I got the message. I was shaken at how sad she was. She expressed she would like to talk, and I gave her my phone number. It was hours later before she called. I parked in the Florida mall parking lot. We must have talked for an hour. It was a wonderful reunion. We laughed, shared, and even praised each other. Things seemed as though they had changed. She was married, but I didn't care. As the call concluded I asked how she felt about me talking to Hayden. Excitedly, almost giddy she agreed. We had a clean slate; clear heart and it was a new time for us. She was a part of me once even if she wasn't now. I was reminded it was hurt and not hate that drove us.

The following day I called her. She was just as excited to chat as the day before. Now, she was laughing. She had been reading my Facebook posts and just thought I was hysterical (For once, the girl wasn't wrong). I was hesitant to ask about Hayden and I was also a little nervous. He was four currently. Eventually she tells me he is there and asks if I would like to talk. Of course, I wanted to chat with him. He wasn't shy about talking on the phone.

"Hey Hayden, this is your dad."

He was silent for a minute before he returned a hello. The next words out of his mouth were years beyond his age in depth.

"Have you been mean to my mom?" His boy voice with grown man words.

"Yes," I answered. "We have been mean to each other, but I promise you those days are over."

We talked a little more before he returned me to

his mom.

Heather was just as surprised as I was with Hayden's straight forward question.

"Marc, I have no idea why he asked you that! I promise I don't speak bad of you to him."

"Children aren't stupid. Plus, they overhear things. In my mind I think there are not secrets in the spirit realm. He knew. People generally know."

I was impressed with Hayden. He clearly got his straightforward nature from his parents.

Cue the Michael Jackson Song, "Speechless." That was the first song we ever danced to. Now that I had spoken to both Hayden and Heather, we started talking every day. Often, we would talk several times throughout the day. She would call me on her lunch break, if her husband (the sequel) went to the store and at night when he was working second shift. We would send videos back and forth. Mostly they were for Hayden and of him. Heather never realized that she was super model alluring, dazzling, enthralling, mesmerizing. What Heather lacked (and I would learn this slowly over time) was empathy.

When Heather left me, it was very abrupt. Just one day she stormed in and said she was leaving. She had already packed the car. We could not cohabitate. I had framed pictures of my children that had been with me for years. One day I came home from work. She had taken my children's pictures out of the frames and replaced them with pictures of her family and her dog. I was livid! I also had several back issues of GQ, Vanity Fair, Rolling Stone, Esquire and other magazines because I never had a television. I would come home from work, open a bottle of bourbon sit in the tub and read (I wasn't always a sloppy drunk). Heather told her mother I had a huge collection of porn. I didn't even know how to defend that. I soon learned that there were absolutely no boundaries. Heather told her family everything. I don't mind being transparent, but if we are fucking please draw some lines!

I did not want our relationship to end, but I needed a rest. I had felt that maybe we needed to stay closer to her family before we moved to Florida. I wish I had trusted that instinct because I feel that would have been our fighting chance.

It also didn't help that I was drinking every night. In fact, we had been given a lot of money from her family and friends. I spent a great deal of those funds on Wild Turkey 101. On my way home from work, I had three liquor stores that were frequented. We fought so much and so intensely, the drinking helped slow the force in which my world felt it was spinning on its axis. Back then I would always self-destruct by my own hand.

One morning I arrived at work and a co-worker (Tracy) pulled me aside. I get anxious when people need to talk with me. My paranoid insecurities kick in. I didn't know Tracy well and we had never socialized outside of the restaurant, but she was a person I would call a friend. She was speaking low and making sure no one could overhear. I thought the precautions were comical until she spoke.

"I got a Facebook message from some chick named Heather."

My face hardened. There was no way the remainder of this conversation was going to be comfortable.

"She told me that she was with you. She demanded I never message or talk to you. I just felt you should know." Tracy was to the point. My heart raced in humiliation. The worst part was that this would not be my only conversation with women such as this. Even after Heather was married, she would message girls I was talking to. She was telling them to leave me alone. She was married!

I am a drunk! My hobby is self-deprecating humiliation. Heather always managed to embarrass me just a little bit more.

She would even call me mad as hell that I was dating anyone. Again, Heather was married. Eventually, this all started to make sense. Heather is much more stuck than she is in love. As with all rebound romances, things were complicated in her castle of bliss. The realization came front and center the day Heather said to me.

"I wish you never let me leave you that day in Florida."

"I am sorry Heather. Hog tying people making them stay is frowned upon."

The sequel and Heather were always fighting.

Hayden wasn't happy with him as a stepfather. Heather said that her new husband always wanted to spank our son. So far, she had prevented it. The sequel admitted that he wasn't used to children and was struggling. Ladies, men have a saying "win the baby, win the lady." That was how the sequel won Heather. He thinks he is the alpha male when really, he is the runt of the litter. Heather's story and version of this man changes like the direction of the wind. I think of the motion picture *American Beauty* (a 1999 film directed by Sam Mendes) and the plastic bag scene .In one call she is for the man (I honestly believe because she feels stuck) and later he is a villain. I know this, on her darkest days she didn't turn to him.

Now I was headed to court to defend my parental rights.

CHAPTER 36

"Beauty is not who you are on the outside, it is the wisdom and time you gave away to save another struggling soul like you." ~ Shannon L. Adler

Not humble and kind.

      One day after court over Hayden and my parental rights, I was walking out of the courthouse. I ran into Heather and her husband in the parking deck. They were in Heather's Nissan. I was walking through. The sequel stopped their car. He was making a mean face at me, but in truth he looked more like a constipated vampire bat. I looked in at them through their windshield and smiled. Giving that little fucker my best "You want a shot at the title?" look. Heather grabbed the sequel's arm. He was huffing and puffing, I was smiling (my instrument might have got a little hard too), she was panicked. She had seen me in confrontations before. She witnessed the take down of more than one man in the early morning hours while I was more than slightly drunk. Heather knew that I could and would end the pubic faced sequel. He pumped the brakes on his foolishness. She gave him an out; he could pretend she talked him out of his death wish. No, he knew better.

I am much more a fool than a tough guy but given the right amount of anger we all turn into a junk yard dogs. I long ago lost track of my bad decisions, and that day I had another one in me. Truth be told, the only thing that guy ever beat was his own pecker. Holy shitake mushrooms, he drove off. Later, upon reflection, I felt grateful she saved his life or at least his privilege to walk. Orange may be the new black for some, but prison colors never really suited me. I have thrown a punch or two and I have never been one to back down. Every Superman has his kryptonite and mine is bourbon, Jack Daniels, Jim Beam or a flock of Wild Turkeys might kick my ass, but not the constipated vampire bat (I just really love insulting this guy). In the end, yeah, I could have punched the dude, but it is better to just allow life and living with Heather to bend him over. Heather was not a warm and bubbly person to live with. In fact, she was negative, nasty and narrow all too often, and that is life bending you over.

Even while I was in rehab, when Heather had no means of contacting me, she would call my mother. Telling Bobbi how unhappy she was. Telling my mother that Hayden did not get along with the sequel. Hayden was in special counseling at six years old. I mentioned that Heather was stuck. She always told me that she couldn't leave the sequel because it would upset her parents.

Please know I tried to be respectful of the sequel. He drew first blood. In relationships I allow other people to set the bar. I simply rise to the occasion. He wanted to be an asshole; I am so much better at it than him. I learned to be an asshole both from genetics and practice.

One of the more upsetting aspects of my breakup with Heather was her family. After Baby Mama's family I wanted to be in with a people that were good. Not the fake Baptist Stage performers Larry breed. I immediately liked and loved everyone. However, I quickly learned that my southern ass, with a Yankee twist, didn't speak their Midwest language. They didn't understand my wit and sense of humor. Every word I spoke they took at face value. Anyone who really knows me realizes I talk shit! I am well suited for it. This helped me understand why I always had to explain my jokes to Heather. Heather is hardly stupid, but she doesn't follow analogies, symbolism or sarcasm well. A trait no doubt in her genetics passed down from her father, Don.

Don is a simple man. He loves God, his wife, children, and dog (Sadly, Nindo has since passed on). Don is a PE teacher in a small community suburb an hour outside of Chicago. A quiet place where conservative religious values still prevail. I liked the man tremendously. However, once the milk went sour in my relationship with his daughter, it went bad with us even faster. Now, I rarely regret things in life. However, sometimes the valleys are deeper and the mountains higher than I ever expected. My bag of regrets, I should have done and not yet, may be small. Still, it is heavy. Even my mistakes have helped shaped me into a man that I like. I am further from perfect than the galaxy that is far far away. However, with the help of my friends at Saint Matthew's House Justine's Place program, those men helped me like me. They taught me almost as much about love as my beautiful offspring.

I had expectations of Don. Again, I think, feel and am certain that expectations were the overwhelming death of my relationships with Heather and her family. Of course, I live too loud and I talk too much, I often speak my mind when I am feeling most incomplete. Why is my first reaction to give my own flawed opinion? Once I became combative with Don, I said some things I may regret. Don's brother had died of cancer. When I was looking to Don for help with Heather, he naturally did not know what to do. I saw this reminiscent of my other dreaded father in law, Larry the barbarian back stabber. I got mad at Don. The infamous fight or flight struggle kicked in and kicked my ass. I chose to fight.

"Don, the wrong brother died. You are worthless, you should have died not your brother." Yeah, that really came out of my mouth. My intention was to say something so provocative that his behavior would change. You know how people say that you lure more flies with honey than vinegar? Even Proverbs 15 verses 1 & 2 says, "A soft answer turns away wrath, but harsh words stir up anger. The tongue of the wise commends knowledge, but the mouth of the fool gushes folly." This isn't about beating myself down, but I do wish I practiced humility just a little bit better. I wasn't terribly much better with Heather's mother.

IF ROCK BOTTOM HAD A BASEMENT

Dawn may just be the sweetest lady on the planet. At least, my encounters with her found this to be true. She carries a smile on her face all the time. At the time the family had a cocker spaniel. He was extremely territorial and protective of the family. This dog would bite and attack any stranger. Dawn was warning me.

"I promise you Nindo won't bite me if you listen to me" I offered.

Dawn's perfect smile fell from her face, her look of concern and uncertainty was not wasted. I loved her caring and treating me instantly like I belonged. Heather's family was very welcoming. Her sister Courtney, who I thought was awesome really didn't seem that interested in me. However, I went through her DVD collection and I judge people based on the films they enjoy. When I saw she had *Benny & June* a 1993 motion picture starring Johnny Depp, Mary Stuart Masterson (whom I love from *Some Kind of Wonderful* from 1987 and my favorite of the John Hughes films) and directed by Jeremiah S. Chechik. What Dawn didn't know is that I learned my most valuable dog lesson from a man named Andrew Kvarda. "Dogs are pack animals" he once told me.

We arrived at their townhome.

"Go get Nindo on his leash and bring him outside," I said.

Dawn's eyes were still so uncertain. She went in and brought the dog outside. Upon seeing me, he pitched his K9 fit. Barking loud enough to raise the dead.

IF ROCK BOTTOM HAD A BASEMENT

"Now walk with me."

We started walking with Nindo in the lead, but he stopped barking. About five minutes later I asked for his leash. Dawn was scared to death. I had the reigns and there was no turning back. We walked for about five more minutes.

"Now, you go inside and wait for me inside the door. I will be there in five minutes."

Dawn's smile returned. I was smiling too.

Dawn walked away and Nindo noticed. He looked back at me and we continued to walk. I was introducing myself to the pack, his pack. Would my idea work? I really had no idea, but suffice it to say, do not try this at home. Everything was fine and we walked without incident.

We returned to the home and I knocked at the door. She opened the door with Heather beside her. Their faces delighted and surprised.

"Now, allow Nindo in first to establish this is his home. Then I will come in as his guest."

Once inside I went upstairs and sat in a chair. Nindo jumped in my lap. He loved to sit with me, and I enjoyed him.

They were amazed. I have always missed those days of being their friend and ally. The man who really did love their daughter, I just didn't know how to conquer her negativity. However, back in my Wicker Park apartment I was realizing that in some people's story I will be the villain. Even harder to accept was that in many respects I was just as vile as The Joker from *The Dark Knight*, Le Chiffre the villain from the James Bond Film *Casino Royale* or maybe more appropriately Darth Vader, "Hayden, I am your father!"

I wanted to fight until the death like they do in *Game of Thrones* (have you guessed that I really enjoyed that show?). Yet, once again I became a house divided against itself.

Remember when I talked to Hayden that first time? He asked me if I was mean to his mom. I promised him I would not be mean to her ever again. It is funny how we think God has called us to love and be with someone. We make vows, promises, commitments and moves, but later when life is hard, we feel it is time to jump ship. As if we think God has ever said "It's ok to hate him or her now."

"In sickness and in health, for better or worse," are the odds stacked against us now. Since our song that we danced to was always Michael Jackson's "Speechless." It is fitting that we Cue the Michael Jackson song "She is out of my life."

I never hated Heather. In fact, I always had faith in her even after all that had happened. This just hurt so much more than anything I had known. Maybe I would be better served to say it was a different kind of pain all together. I called work immediately and explained that I was ill. I stayed in bed the next several days. My eyes felt welded shut from the hours of crying, shaking and disbelieving. I simply did not want to move. There were

IF ROCK BOTTOM HAD A BASEMENT

even worse factors to all of this.

Once I left Saint Matthew's House, my Uncle Matthew and Aunt Cheryl had paid for me to go to a writing conference. They had even paid for my airfare. A lot of people have praised my writing, but never in my life has anyone put their money where their praise is. I was so excited about this conference. I could not even get out of bed to take the trip. I had lost something inside of me. Something was missing and I could not identify it. Baby Mama had done so many cruel things that I never thought she could be trumped. But my sad reality was Heather with the help of her family and the pubic faced sequel had found a way. Oddly I didn't drink right away, but even that was about to change lanes. This was not my meant to be.

I have heard of good things going wrong, but now even the bad things were going wrong. I felt defeated when Baby Mama left me for the Doughboy Draftsman. Not so much because I lost a wife, but not living with my beautiful offspring was the worst condition of my life. Now, I was told I wasn't even worth visitation, phone calls or any type of place in his world. This was a new low in the stratosphere of life. Now, I had also disappointed the two people that invested in me. Could this life be any more of a bitch?

I tried to talk with Svetlana when she would come check on me in my room, but she didn't understand. She was much like Heather in that she lacks empathy. I don't think it is a choice to not be empathetic, I suspect some people are just not capable.

In the meantime, Madison my beautiful eldest

offspring was planning to come visit soon. For the first time in my life even that did not excite me. She was coming to celebrate July fourth with her old man. I was broken and borderline despondent. She would surprise me with Mac. I would introduce them to the worst version of myself.

IF ROCK BOTTOM HAD A BASEMENT

CHAPTER 37

"It's never too late to become who you want to be. I hope you live a life that you are proud of, and if you find that you are not. I hope you have the strength to start over." ~ F. Scott Fitzgerald

"Hearts will never be practical until they can be made unbreakable." ~ L. Frank Baum

"The best way to break old habits is to make new ones." ~ Craig (played by Morgan Freeman) from the film Clean and Sober

Objects in the rear view

mirror.

Cue the Bruce Springsteen song, "Working on a Dream."

IF ROCK BOTTOM HAD A BASEMENT

"Oh my God," Baby Mama was fond of saying.

"What do you want custody of Him too?" I would answer.

Now in honor of one of the greatest motion pictures of all time, *High Fidelity* (From the book written by the amazing Nick Hornby. The Hulu show starring with Zoe Kravitz is great too.) here are my top five greatest regrets. For the record, narrowing it down to a top five feels criminal -- just so you know!

1.) Saying I wished Hayden would die.

I explained this earlier and do not want to revisit this all-time low.

2.) My anger towards Mac over him not using our last name.
3.) Being drunk when my children visited Chicago.
4.) My inability to be the man to slay Heather's dragons.
5.) ?

I figure I am young enough. I better save space for another epic fuck up. Just Sayin'. There is one honorable mention that comes to mind that did not make my top five regrets. It is a memory that I don't suspect Madison remembers, but when I revisit this in my mind's eye my eyes water and stomach hurts. Baby Mama had left me for another new and improved life with revamped dreams. I was living in a constant state of downhearted, discouraged, depressed, and dejected (all those words are synonyms, but I still felt like none of them were strong enough on their own).

IF ROCK BOTTOM HAD A BASEMENT

I was living with a friend who also happened to be going through a divorce. Baby Mama had her own rented house. On Wednesdays I would go to her place and spend the evening with the incredibly beautiful young offspring. It was uncomfortable being in her home because she went to great lengths to exclude me. I didn't snoop much, but it doesn't take much. One night I found a small collection of vibrators. That was unsettling enough to mind my own business.

Later that evening I was giving Madison a bath. She had long and beautiful hair even as a preschooler. She was playing in the tub as I was washing her hair. As I remember it, she turned her head and I pulled her hair. This was not my intention. It was more of a knee jerk reaction on my part. I hadn't even realized I pulled her hair. She stopped and looked dead at me with her big brown eyes.

"Why did you pull my hair?" her voice so small and delicate.

"Baby, I am so sorry. I didn't mean to do that," I answered.

Her face burst into tears. My heart sank and I wanted to cry as well, but she was more important. I apologized repeatedly. Told her I loved her, and it was an accident. Please know it was a very subtle pull of her hair. I was just repositioning her for whatever reason. I knew I hurt her feelings and for some reason that just crushed me. I rinsed her hair dried her off and hugged her repeatedly. I don't remember much more about that incident, but I know I didn't share that story with dry eyes in this house.

IF ROCK BOTTOM HAD A BASEMENT

Being the father of a daughter changed me. In a sense it is the biggest cock-block of my life. Now, when I am with a woman. If I am kissing her, wooing her, trying to make her laugh. If the female is a lover, love interest or friend, at some point I will look at that woman and think she has a dad who loves her. I never made it to Frank Gallagher from the Showtime series *Shameless* status, but damn close.

I don't have a DeLorean so I can't go back in time, but I can assure you these are the moments that when I relive, I reach a little harder for dirty water. When this tape of failures plays in my head, I want to numb myself. I wish I could say I am a better person. Maybe God has used this to make me love a little harder, reach a little further, be more authentic, work for less regrets in the end, stand a little taller, dig deeper and write this tale. Hoping that there is just enough magic to touch a few of the broken hearted and misguided that lived like me.

A few days before my beautiful offspring were to arrive, my broken bitch version of myself was miserable. I came home on a Sunday morning and Svetlana and her best friend were drinking mimosas. The difference is that they can drink responsibly. They were kind and offered me a mimosa of my own. I declined their generous offer. Not everyone understands that one drink is too many and a thousand is never enough.

I visited the two ladies for a few minutes. Their fun, easy going buzz was just beginning. As I said, alcohol always brings expression to Svetlana's face. I envied them and their freedom.

IF ROCK BOTTOM HAD A BASEMENT

I retreated to my room with the intention of working on this book. Yes, the pages you now hold in your hands. However, at my desk, my addiction started to bend my ear. As an alcoholic, your addiction talks to you. This inner voice is an expert at lying and creating confusion for the individual. I was hearing that I was strong enough to be just like them. The conversation is full of rational thoughts for an irrational person. Hell, if you tell yourself the same lie enough times eventually it will feel like truth. About 15 minutes later I was back on the street. I went to a CVS just 2 blocks down the street. I bought a fifth of bourbon and a bottle of Gatorade. I wasn't accustomed to needing a chaser, but it had been over a year since I had a drink. When I returned home. I don't think the women even noticed what I had done, but honestly, I don't recall.

The first shot is poured into a glass and is the equivalent of about four to five shots. It takes about ten minutes for the sensation to kick in, but when it does my mind changes. A new determination is born in me and that is to sustain this feeling. The rush is going to keep me longer than I want to stay; it is going to take me further than I really want to go, and it is going to cost me more than I wish to pay. Yet, in this moment it owns me.

Now most people can drink and be normal. I get that because there was a time I could too. Yet, those days are gone forever. There is no rebirth for an alcoholic. That person can never return to social or casual drinking. When Alcohol hits me I evolve (maybe the exact opposite of this word is more appropriate). Robert Downey Jr. said it well, "I have an allergy to alcohol; I break out in handcuffs."

Immediately there is a payoff! In fact, frequently the payoff is huge. In my case, I relax, I can be funny, I feel accepted and my problems do wash away. Cue the Brantley Gilbert song, "Just as I am." None-the-less, it is a trap. I was fully trapped the day my beautiful offspring arrived at O'Hare International Airport.

When I went to meet Madison, I half expected to see Mac, but it was clearly communicated that he wasn't making the trip. Earlier that year we were having struggles concerning his last name (See top five mistakes number 2). However, Mac came too and even in my heavy haze, I was happy to see him.

My beautiful offspring knew I had a fever for the flavor of dirty water. What they had never witnessed was a drunk dad. One holiday week in Chicago changed all that. The phenomenon of an alcoholic and his first drink cannot be explained to sober people. Only one alcoholic to another speak each other's language. This is exactly why programs such as Alcoholics Anonymous work.

Seeing my daughter is always awe inspiring. Mac snuck up behind me. They later confessed they immediately knew something was off. I had never felt so defeated that I didn't try to hide my addiction from them. I was sorry, but they knew. I had open and empty bottles all over my room.

Growing up, my son's favorite actor was Matthew Broderick and one of our favorite films is *Ferris Bueller's Day Off*. We should have toured Wrigley Field, Art Institute of Chicago, Lake Shore Drive and Willis Tower. We should have recreated scenes from the motion picture and sang Twist and Shout like Ferris did on the float. None of those things happened. I stayed in bed drunk for their entire visit. I was under the impression I had reached my all-time low. Now my good intentions had gone dry as a bone.

This is where Svetlana rose to the occasion. She spent quality time with my beautiful offspring. She took them places, including to free movies in Millennium Park. The motion picture they watched that time was *High Fidelity*.

Talking about films, directors, and tv series are a huge part of my bonding with my beautiful offspring. It has always brought me a tremendous amount of joy turning my children onto things that meant so much to me growing up. For instance, when my daughter was all about Disney's *High School Musical* (directed by the all too talented Kenny Ortega), I introduced her to *Grease*. To this day John Travolta is my favorite actor. When Mac was little, I introduced him to Underdog. I was even able to find him an action figure that included a real size power pellet ring.

One late night I was passed out in my bedroom. Svetlana came in screaming at me, a growling utterance that mimicked sounds from an exorcism. She was furious over my neglect. She started hitting me and cursing. She was right! I took every blow she gave me.

"You have great kids," she snarled as she hit me.

When she stormed out, I waited a few minutes. The warpath had calmed. Madison and Mac were laughing on the mattress we had laid out for them in the living room.

    We visited and talked a bit. Svetlana would look in on us from time to time. She wore her disgust as if it were a cardigan sweater. Incidentally that was the last and final time she ever spoke to me. I did see her once when I left my room wandering to the bathroom. She was entering her bedroom. We stopped and looked at each other. Her disgust had grown substantially. It crossed my mind to say something, anything, but I felt it best to stay shut up. I had no worthy excuse or explanation. We just stood still, and I thought to myself "Svetlana I am sick of me too." I suppose falling short was always in the cards. I had hoped I would be a better man in Chicago and this new lease on life. I managed to define loser.

    The children left the following morning. When we said goodbye, I walked straight to the CVS and got more Bourbon. I remained drunk for the rest of my time in Chicago. It is a shitty feeling to hate yourself. I had disappointed my Uncle and Aunt by missing the writing conference, I disgusted Svetlana, I felt I let down all the men from Saint Matthew's House. I failed to fulfill all expectations my friends may have had. Worst of all, I never expected my children could forgive me.

    I went radio silent on social media because of my bender. It is funny that I was hiding my behavior, but everyone knew. Friends like David (a friend since high school), Kara (a friend who has been in my life since I was a youth), Jim Frick (my last and longest case manager while I was in the program), Art VanZanten (the program director), Nojo and Anthony all began to reach out. Jim and Art claimed they just knew something was wrong. I was stuck and drunk, but unlike my past, I didn't want to go out like that! The significant difference is that before rehab I had a death wish. During the Chicago relapse I never wanted to be a drunk, I just didn't want to feel.

Most people I can ignore when they offer advice. You know the old saying "Never give advice. The wise do not need it and the ignorant won't heed it." However, there is a handful of people (I didn't name them all) that know the dark corners of my soul. They can communicate with me in a manner that I hear.

"Marc, you need to get out of Chicago! You need to go back to Naples." Kara sent in a text. I was humiliated. Saint Matthew's House was the very last place on earth I wanted to bring my failures. I have known Kara for easily over thirty years. One of the same things I love about her, I also hate! The woman has never been wrong in dealing with me and my irresponsible ways.

On a Friday morning I was lying in bed. I could hear the rustling about on the other side of my bedroom door. I knew that Svetlana had packed her shit and was moving out. From the sound of things, it sounded like she had three other sets of feet walking in and out of the apartment. I felt alone and knew at this point the only friend I had was me.

I got on the Priceline website and booked a flight to Naples. I was so hung over that I thought I was booking the flight for Sunday morning. What I had done was book the flight for Saturday. Nojo called and in talking to him I realized I had the dates wrong. I panicked. I called the travel site and explained my situation and they fixed everything for me. It was amazing. Otherwise, I would have been stuck in Chicago.

When I finally ventured out of my room. The place was completely empty. I walked into Svetlana's room and there was no evidence she ever was in that room. She left nothing behind. Svetlana was a task master, but she also brought a lot of life to our little home. I missed her immediately and I suspect in a small way I always will.

"Marc! Why aren't you writing? You have a talent! I have not seen you write anything while you are here," her voice just below a shout.

"I write every day," I fired back.

She paused. This was a good sign or so I incorrectly thought.

"What? What have you written?" Her voice crawling closer to a shout.

I paused. "Facebook posts."

She didn't say anything, but she stared at me hard. Her eyes were not blinking. How could she be doing that? Svetlana, you are supposed to blink 15 to 20 times a minute, in the arena of 1,200 an hour and as much as 28,800 times a day! It was creepy that she could just stop, but those Russian women excel at being stoic.

The night before I was to leave was agonizing. My body violently shook. Packing what little I was taking with me took all the strength I had. I would try and stand only to fall over. I would shake violently, and my pours rained sweat. At one point I just laid on the kitchen floor begging God and crying for strength. My worries just raced around my mind. I left the following morning.

At the airport everything hurt. My body, my head and most of all my ego. I had failed or so I thought. On the plane my mouth was dry, and I needed water. Lots of water, but the damn stewardesses were slow that flight. Hangovers require a lot of hydration! I need these flight attendants to rescue me. I hadn't had a drink in a few days, but I suspected I reeked of bourbon. The hangover was hanging on much too tightly.

Anthony met me at the airport.

"You look like shit!" he said laughing.

In Chicago I had lost more weight than I had ever in my life. All my clothes were too big for me. My skin was blotchy and everything in me just hurt. As for my ego, that felt destroyed.

Anthony was right and I didn't care; it was amazing to see the guy. I pointed to the exact spot I needed to wait for him to bring the car around. I stayed with his girlfriend for about two weeks. In fact, it was her idea that I lodged at her place, but I could tell she was becoming uncomfortable with the idea quickly. I had expected Anthony would be with us, but no he went home and only visited randomly. We were essentially two strangers in her home. I suppose I could have felt more out of place, but I am not sure what that would entail. She had a lady from church discipling her and my presence was a sin. Another woman of God more concerned about appearances than truth. Never are we more righteous than when we are wrong.

One day sitting at her table writing out thoughts and trying to begin this story, I got a text. It was from Madison. My daughter texting me? I was certain that she would never speak to me again. Maybe I am the only von Wellsheim that can hold a grudge with G.I. Joe kung-Fu grip.

"Are you in Florida?" is all it said.

I am no coward, but I am also not that brave. I was scared to reply. I knew she must have spoken with Svetlana. I did not expect my daughter to want to speak to me for years.

"Yes, I am looking at going back to Saint Matthew's."

We didn't speak or share very long. She did confirm my suspicion that she had spoken to Svetlana. In fact, I could not get any idea of her feelings towards me. I opted to just say "Touchdown Jesus." She reached out and that was more than I could hope for or deserve.

While I was in Naples, I made an appointment to visit Tommy Sloan. Tommy had been my hero when I first went to Naples. The first Christian male that had walked a mile in my moccasins and loved God. He wasn't afraid to tell people they were full of shit or to fuck off. We met at a Starbucks inside of a Target.

IF ROCK BOTTOM HAD A BASEMENT

"Kemosabe" was always his term of endearment. We shook hands, hugged and took a seat. I shared the debauchery of Chicago. Tommy listened intently, he laughed some and looked at me with those purest of blue eyes.

"I am thinking of doing the program again," I offered.

"You don't need the program brother; you need to learn to walk what you already learned out. That is the hardest part."

I was surprised at his response and he could see it on my face. He repositioned himself in his chair.

"Marc, most of these guys are scared to death. They don't know what to do and don't want to leave. You moved to Chicago by yourself. You screwed up and got out of there. You are already making right choices. You are a smart guy." He paused. "I have to be honest; I doubt this will be your only fall. You have a few more in you."

That declaration felt like emotional bullet holes. Up until then I thought those wounds were reserved for Heather.

"I am so scared that I won't be able to put myself back together if I relapse again," I inserted.

I was scared and I knew I think too much.

Tommy continued, "You are a strategic man. You will always figure out how to get back on your feet."

IF ROCK BOTTOM HAD A BASEMENT

While staying with Anthony's girlfriend I was further away from my Saint Matthew's tribe than I desired. A few people came to see me or get me. Chef Jason and I had dinner one night. It was fabulous to visit with him.

Art came to visit me one afternoon. We sat at the kitchen table talking. Then Art said something that really made me uncomfortable.

"Your friend David from Raleigh called me."

David is a friend from many years in my life. We were in each other's weddings and we bonded again during our divorces. Both events happened within 6 months of each other. However, David never mentioned calling my rehab program on my behalf or to be inquisitive. Upon learning of this I played it cool with Art, but there was a stirring in me.

Because living with David was such a good move while Baby Mama was sleeping with The Doughboy Draftsman and having threesomes including his wife, we made a good pair. I was thinking that maybe I needed to move back to Raleigh, North Carolina and be his roommate again. David's phone call behind my back squelched those plans. I decided to stay with some other friends in North Carolina. I wasn't mad at David but was uncomfortable he felt so at ease crossing boundaries. I told myself he was most likely worried about my drinking in Chicago. Maybe he was uncomfortable with me and the relapse. Whatever the case, it caused a disconnect with him for me.

Once I built a bridge from Naples to Raleigh, I

was ready to go. I called a few friends making my intentions known. One call was to Paul. He wanted me to stop and spend a few days with him and his wife. The three girls were off to camp in North Carolina of all places. This excited me because I love being around The Giles family.

On my last day in Naples, Nojo came to pick me up and treated me to lunch. Nojo is indescribable in his wisdom and discernment.

"You've easily lost 25 pounds man," he observed.

I knew because all my clothes were falling off. We spent a little time together and he sat with me at the bus station until I left for Tampa. Paul would pick me up there and we would go to his mother's house for dinner and board games.

These days I continue to work the twelve steps often. I feel they can be applied to any situation, conflict or struggle. Step 11 says "We sought though prayer to improve our conscious contact with God as we understood Him, praying only for knowledge of His will for us and the power to carry that out." This is an important step and I suspect the one I struggle with the most. Yes, step 11 is where I am in most need of improvement.

I am familiar with irony, isolation, distance, and relapses. Whenever my eyes divert from God to me, my needs, my feelings -- I am much more prone to have a drink. I think we all know one negative thought can be followed by more. I am, but flesh and blood. Patience, tolerance and even kindness do not always come easily to me. My ingrained, unproductive, and painful patterns are always just beneath my surface. It is easy for me to discover new rock bottoms. Anxiety, blurred boundaries, varying degrees of crisis, inadequacy and personal myths all work in favor of this chronic drinker's need to guzzle.

Ego so easily become the vine that seduces me and chokes at the same time. My fragile and flimsy balance between admiral intentions and a lust for glory often create a jungle of conflict. Note how familiar I am to these character defects, but still wrestle with obsession and compulsion.

From step 11 I know that when I begin to guzzle, beat my dick, spend, eat, obsess or use any of the other dozens of outlets, I have lost that connection with God. Staying sober for me entails gardening my spiritual condition. I know my spirit craves connection with my higher power. I desire a different kind of inner life. I need a more fulfilling relationship with God! If I can turn within and find solitude with God, my core fears that want to dominate me and assert anxiety come up void. Sometimes I can pray and practice enough self-compassion that the outside world does not immerse me. Sometimes I need a friend to help realign me. We all live in our minds and if I do not invite real friends in, I will fail. We cannot survive if we try and work the program alone. There is no sole survivor of addiction, we need each other. However, don't take my word for it.

Proverbs 27: 17, "As iron sharpens iron, so does one man sharpen another."

IF ROCK BOTTOM HAD A BASEMENT

1 Thessalonians 5:11, "Therefore encourage one another and build one another up."

Galatians 6:2, "Bear one another's burdens, and so fulfill the law of Christ."

Don't shout me down when I am preaching good!

I know because of Saint Matthew's House and the 12 steps that ego will always lead me to suffering. Ego cost me so much already. I could have saved my relationship with Heather if my ego didn't dominate me.

Those mental attacks are as sure as the sun rising, water is wet, and the sky is blue. If I can begin each day in gratitude, if I stay connected to prayer when I am humbled unwillingly, I will not succumb to the demands of my ego.

I have accepted that I am an imperfect human. I too often feel inferior and frequently fail. Some days old patterns regain traction. However, I do have higher intentions among my continuing complexity.

Step 12, "Having had a spiritual awakening as a result of these steps, we tried to carry this message to addicts, and practice these principals in all our affairs." The long and the short of it, you holding this book is my working step 12.

I know my default emotion is self-centeredness. I know how quickly I can become selfish and lack empathy. Yet, my life lived differently and with different perspectives is my goal. Life to me is not simply an impending funeral.

Today I allow my pain to remind me of my most subtle foe - ego. Happiness is no longer minor distractions from my pain. I keep my cards on the table as opposed to held close to my chest. I am having some success. I have some failures too. My mind is consistently changing, and I think it is time to Cue the Keith Urban song, "Somebody Like You." There is nothing as powerful as a changed mind. I changed my mind about wanting to be a drunk.

We spend so much of our childhood wishing we were grown. Looking forward to the day that we won't be told what to do. Life isn't like that. We still answer to a boss, a spouse, the law, God or many other areas of life. The 12 steps remind me of that.

Paul's mother is one of the most generous women ever to live. She is also thoroughly blunt and to the point. She had remarried a man named Jim after Paul's father passed away. While we were at the table relaxing, she had questions.

"So, you moved to Chicago and lived with a Russian woman?" her southern accent was thick. She cocked her head like a confused cocker spaniel. I was never sure if she would rebuke or praise.

My first visit to her home was an experience. She had prepared a small feast for us. In the middle of the meal, she stopped eating and looked at me with disdain.

"You aren't one of them are you?" She asked, but it sounded more like a declaration. I froze. One of who?

IF ROCK BOTTOM HAD A BASEMENT

Did she suspect I was a member of the communist party? All eyes at the table made their way to her inquiry.

She pursed her lips and titled her head down and stared at me. Still unsure of what she wanted to know, she waited for answer to her question. Importantly, she was my landlord that evening and I best keep the peace.

"You eat one thing at a time? You don't take a bite of everything and work your way around your plate?"

Despicable me, I have had my fair share of criticisms and misguided notions in life. However, I felt a little caught in the headlights of sincere judgement. Sheepishly, I nodded yes.

"Why?" She was quick with the question.

I simply had no confession, rhyme, or reason for my dining etiquette.

"I tend to compartmentalize. Never was great at multi-tasking, so maybe this is just my way."

She returned to her food and I returned to mine. I looked at Sheryll and her eyes were as big as saucers.

Now, I was back at Paul's mother's and she had another question.

"Marc, what will you do now that things didn't work out in Chicago with your Russian girl?"

"The only thing I can do. I am going to move to Wisconsin and meet a German girl." The room erupted

IF ROCK BOTTOM HAD A BASEMENT

with laugher. Bam! I made Paul's mom laugh. I am good at this funny shit! Now, I just need to eat my super correctly.

IF ROCK BOTTOM HAD A BASEMENT

CHAPTER 38

"Define yourself radically as one beloved by God. This is the true self. Every other identity is an illusion." ~ Brennan Manning

"All you have to do is write one true sentence. Write the truest sentence that you know." ~ Ernest Hemmingway

Mona Lisas and mad hatters.

At this point I am sure you realize this book was not intended for the spiritually masculine. This was not a tale told for those living on their mountain tops. It was not written for the theologians, academics, the religious, legalists, judges and certainly not the smug (Although, I am certain I have been smug to all those groups at some point.)

IF ROCK BOTTOM HAD A BASEMENT

I wrote this for my brother and sister misfits. I shared my story for the inconsistent, uncertain, insecure, poor, weak and those with hereditary frailty and failure. Those of us with sin at our door. If grace has ever been twisted into some form of perversion in your life - I hope these words written to you comforted and included you and maybe you laughed. If you laughed, we call that a touchdown!

Of course, I wrote this for my children. Madison, my first uncompromised love story. My son Mac, I hope his old man has shown him an authentic self. My beautiful offspring embody the man I aspire to be when I grow up. I have written this for Hayden as an introduction to a man he does not know - YET! They could steal my name from you, but not the blood in your veins.

On occasion, Heather or I will reach out and talk like civilized people. It is always rewarding when she laughs. I am not sure why our paths crossed, but I do know that God handpicked her to be Hayden's mother. We now know that Hayden has a very functional type of Autism. In some ways he is not as advanced as other children such as social ques. Oh, but in so many ways he is so very advanced.

As for Mac, he just got his first car. It is an odd feeling to be driven around by a son I still see as a child. Madison continues to blow my mind as she enters adulthood. Those two are everything I am not but aspire to be. People will take different things from my musing. My prayer is that my children understand me more and know me deeper. As I grow older and maybe not so much up, I still hope to be like my beautiful offspring when I become an adult.

It is true I still see Baby Mama as a bottle blonde blue-eyed devil, but I really do not hate her. In fact, after completing this book, I can occasionally find a good memory of her that was buried for so long. My biggest hurt regarding her is that she was once an amazing person. A person I wanted to marry and give my every tomorrow to, but she changed. Evolution is inevitable as we grow and maybe mature. Still, I have told my beautiful offspring more than once I wish they knew the version of their mother I first met. The version that made me want to be the new sheriff in town. I know there is a difference between wicked and weak, but I cannot judge where she falls.

Now I have forgiven myself, my past and steadily work on forgiving others. I cannot account for those four AM wake up calls that replay my hurts. I still think dreams unexpected in the dead of night can be cruel and unrelenting. However, I don't hate. I may not respect, but I no longer hate. Would it really have made a difference if Larry had stabbed me in the front as opposed to my back? I am still that same insecure and vulnerable boy, but my past no longer dictates who I will be. I am no longer daunted by my yesterday.

I am certainly no angel as I am sure these pages have demonstrated. I continue to clean up my act just a little at a time. I still have no accurate count of the people I have let down or the hearts I have hurt. No, I am still just a man that most likely has a few more dances with the

IF ROCK BOTTOM HAD A BASEMENT

devil. In fact, I might need you to help me overcome some of these uphill climbs and battles. I have a long way to go, but I recognize I have come a long way. Most importantly I do not hate the man in the mirror. After I wrote my final sentiments of this story, I walked into my roommate Robby's room.

"I am going to need a hobby. I am done with the book."

"Then start working on the screenplay," was his reply.

I don't want to be perceived as a false prophet (or false profit which ever your definition). I have struggled and had a few minor benders that I am not proud of. Cue the Macklemore song, "Starting Over." Still, my drinking days are radically fewer and further apart. I still stand up and do what must be done without retreat or surrender. Some days I am the inspiration and other days I need to be inspired. I remain one thing – an imperfect man! Sexy as hell, but imperfect too! Bam! Take that critics.

Cue the Rob Thomas song, "One Last Day (Dying Young).

The sun doesn't shine every day, but I live a silver lining.

I am not better every day, but I am better most days.

I am not sure when God is going to pull the plug

IF ROCK BOTTOM HAD A BASEMENT

on this life and though this book is finished my story is far from over.

I still have the same heart and some of the same scares.

I have had a few minor hiccups since Chicago, but when you try and walk on water, you will get tripped up on some waves.

Until then I will wait for The Giles family to buy a bigger property and put a tiny house somewhere for me to reside.

I am getting closer and closer (wink).

Stay tuned.

And I have realized that there will always be a part of me that will wonder how you are, where you are.

"The world breaks everyone, and afterward, many are strong at the broken places." ~ Ernest Hemingway

ABOUT THE AUTHOR

Alfred Marc von Wellsheim resides in Raleigh, N.C. He has a master's degree in communication and script writing. He is the father of three beautiful offspring, Madison, Mac, and Hayden. This is his first published work

Made in the USA
Columbia, SC
15 March 2022